YOTSUBA&!

4

KIYOHIKO AZUMA

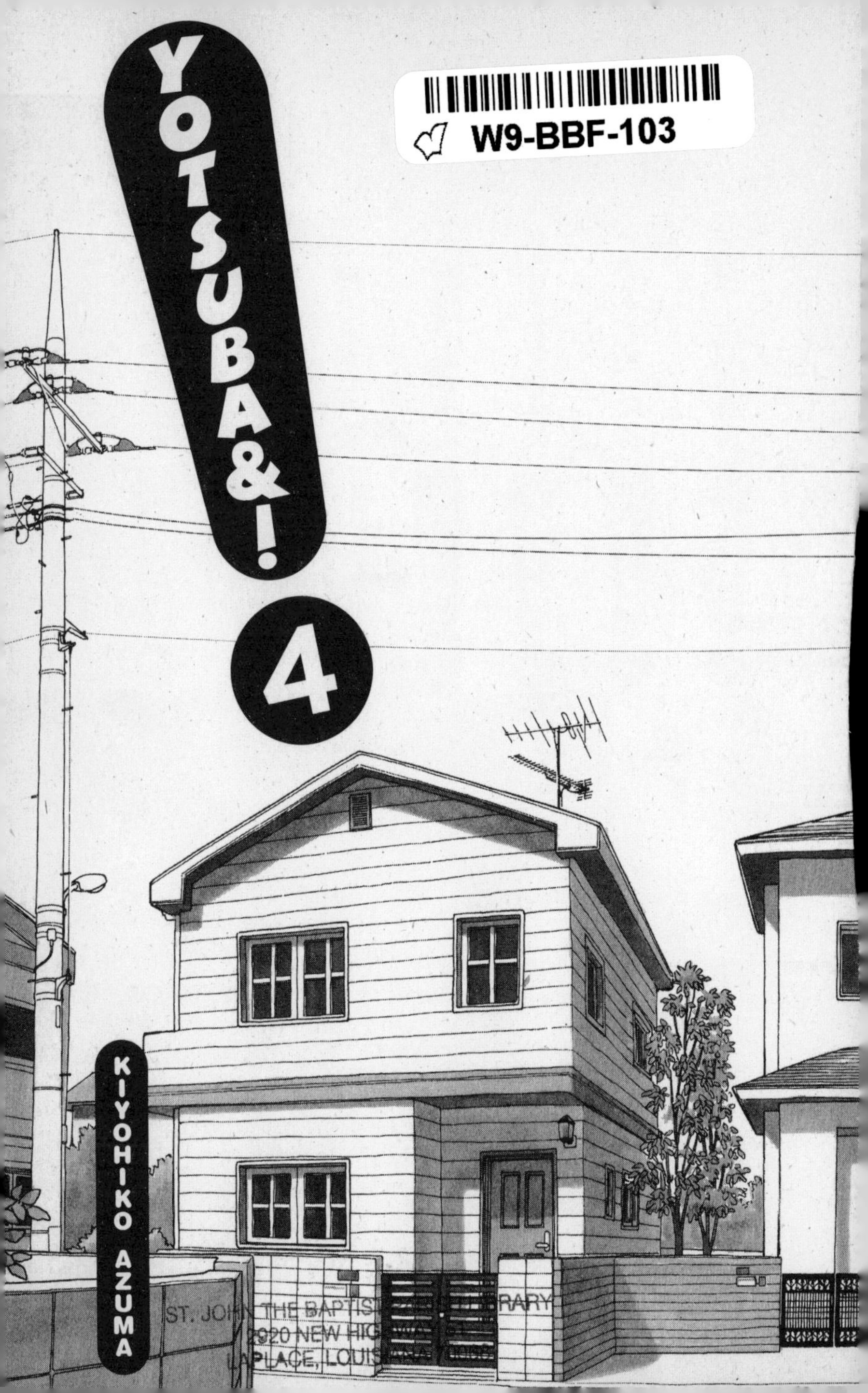

CONTENTS

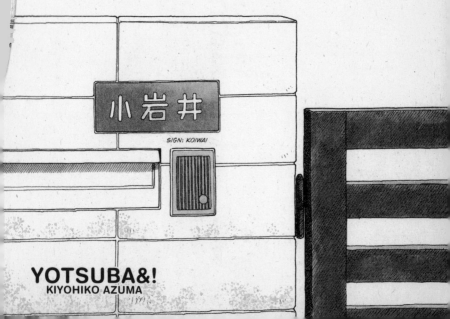

SIGN: KOIWAI

YOTSUBA&!
KIYOHIKO AZUMA

YOTSUBA&

COMPETITIONS!

#22

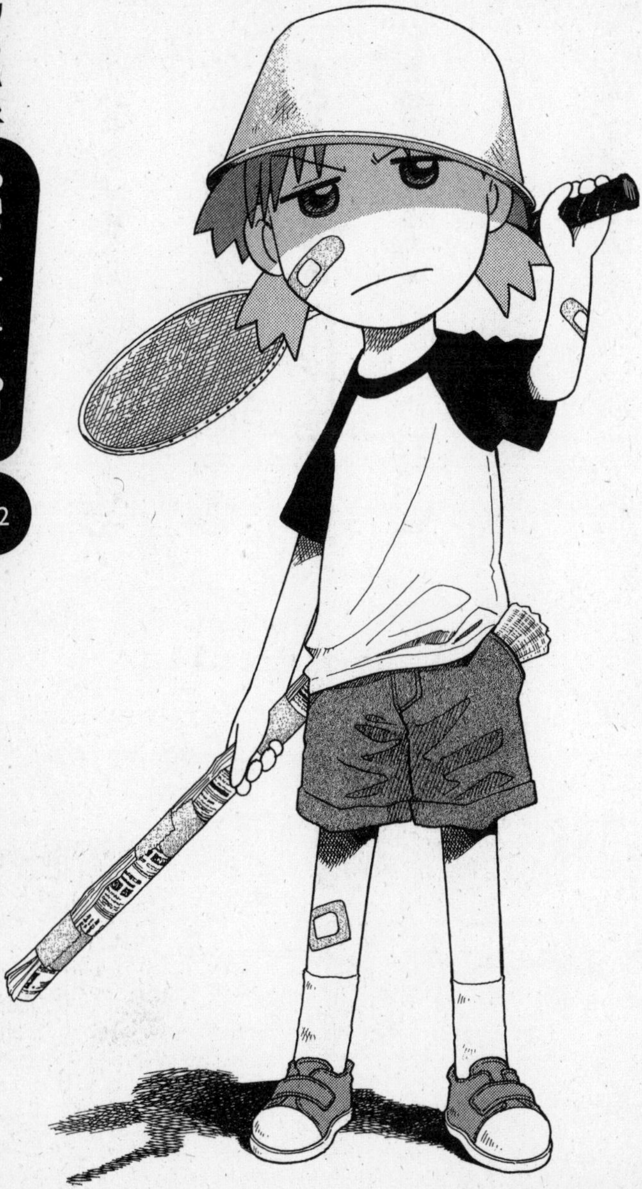

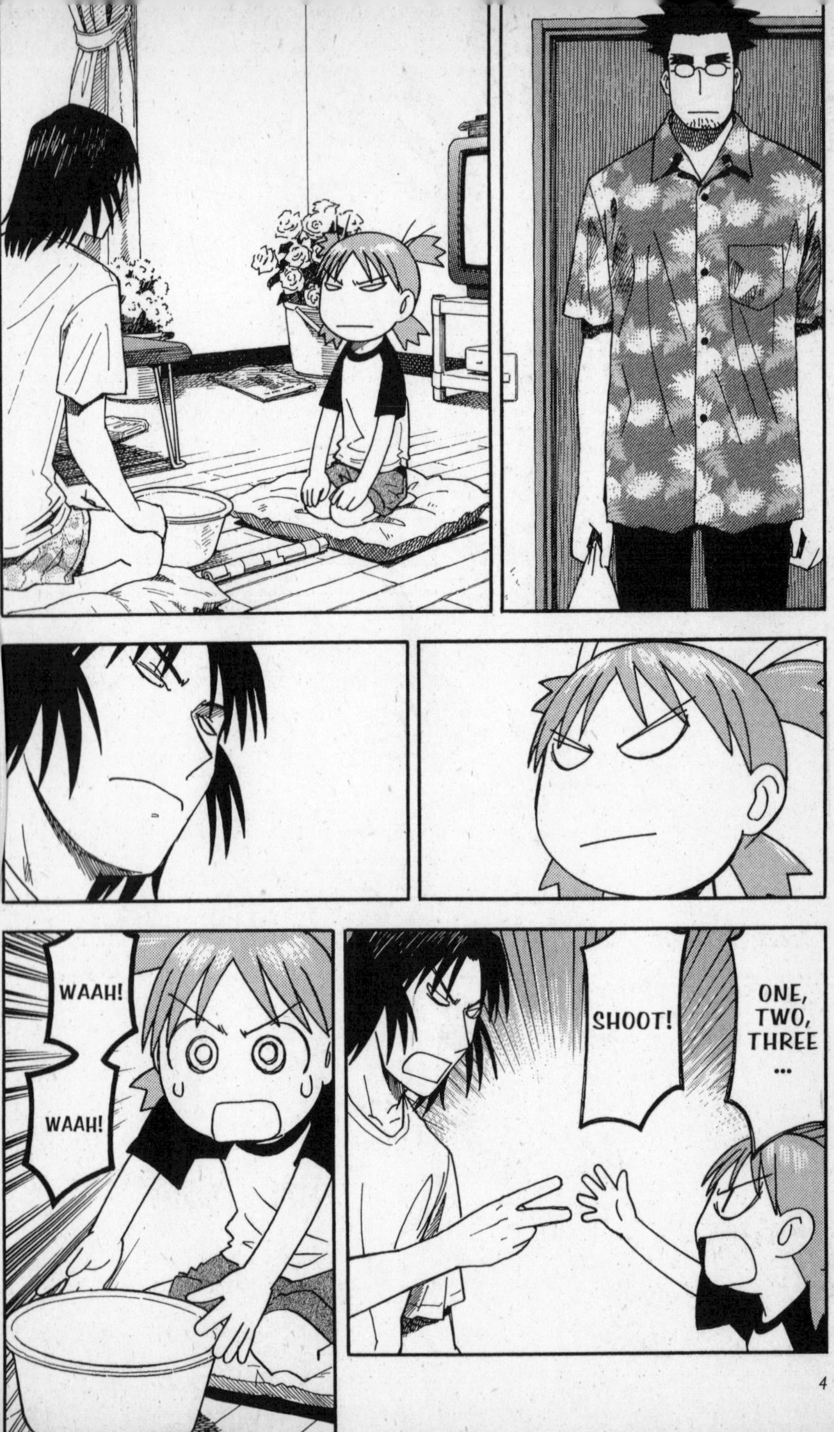

ONE, TWO, THREE ...
SHOOT!
WAAH!
WAAH!

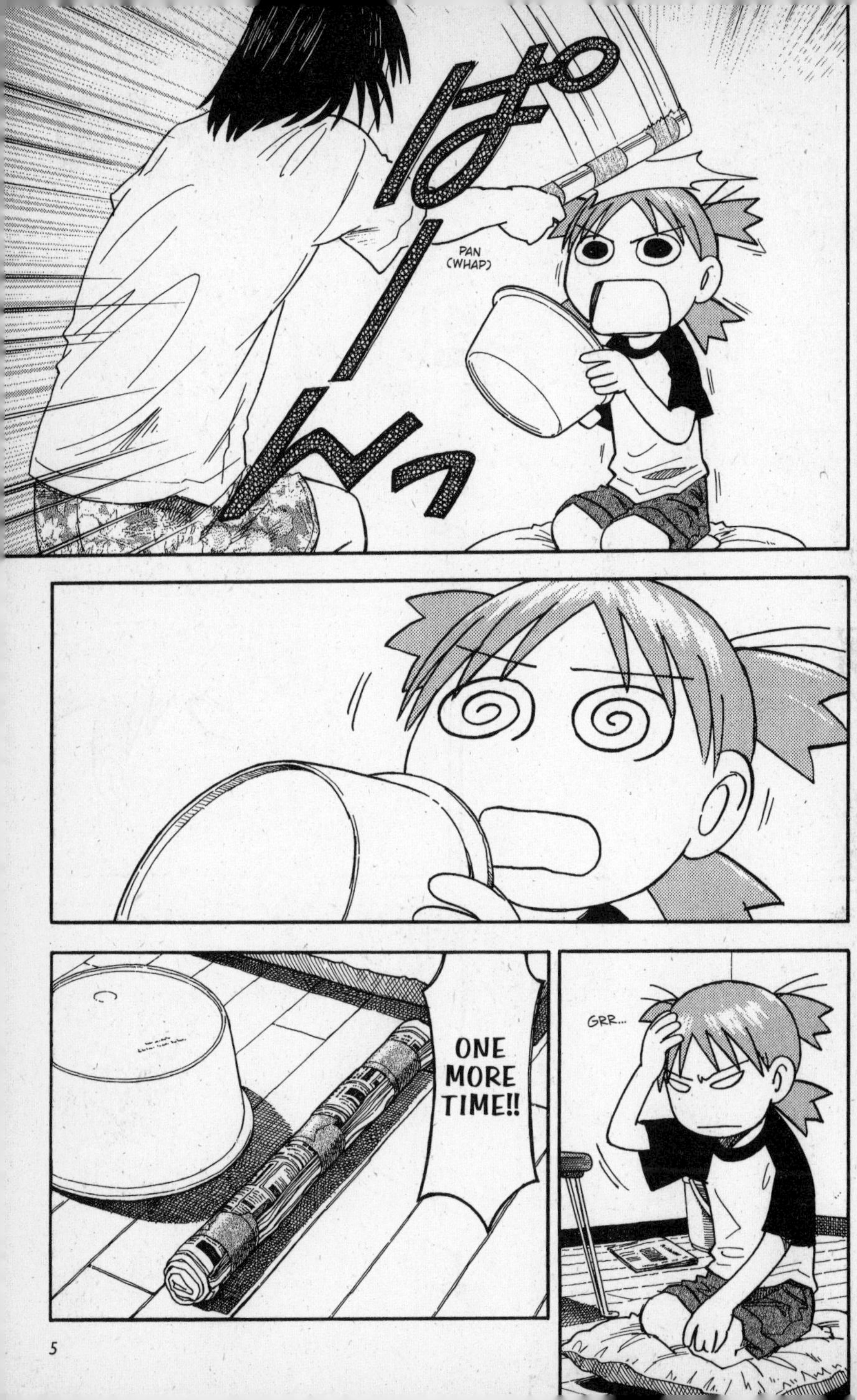
ぱーんっ
PAN (WHAP)
GRR...
ONE MORE TIME!!

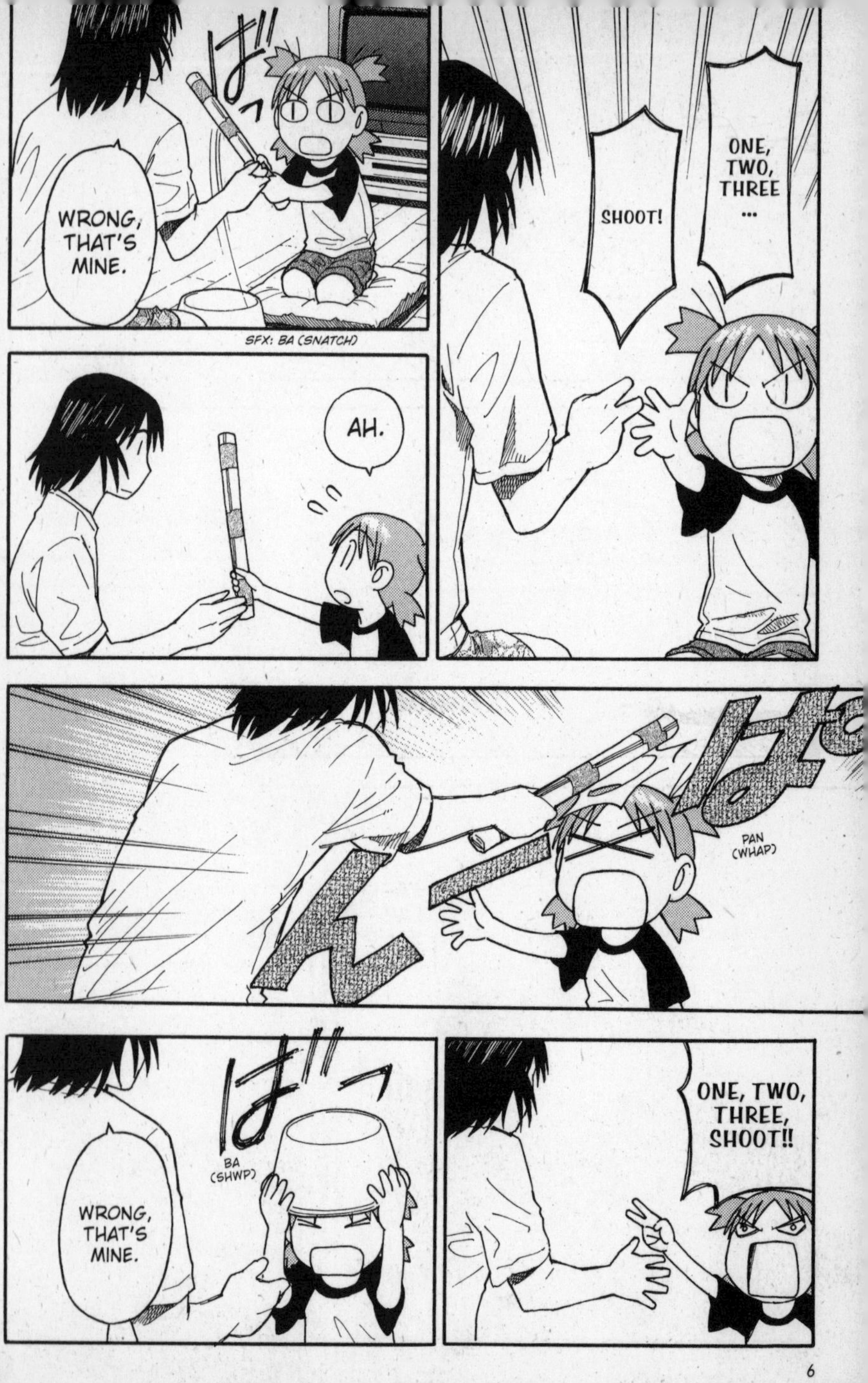
ONE, TWO, THREE ...
SHOOT!
WRONG, THAT'S MINE.
SFX: BA (SNATCH)
AH.
PAN (WHAP)
ONE, TWO, THREE, SHOOT!!
BA (SHWP)
WRONG, THAT'S MINE.

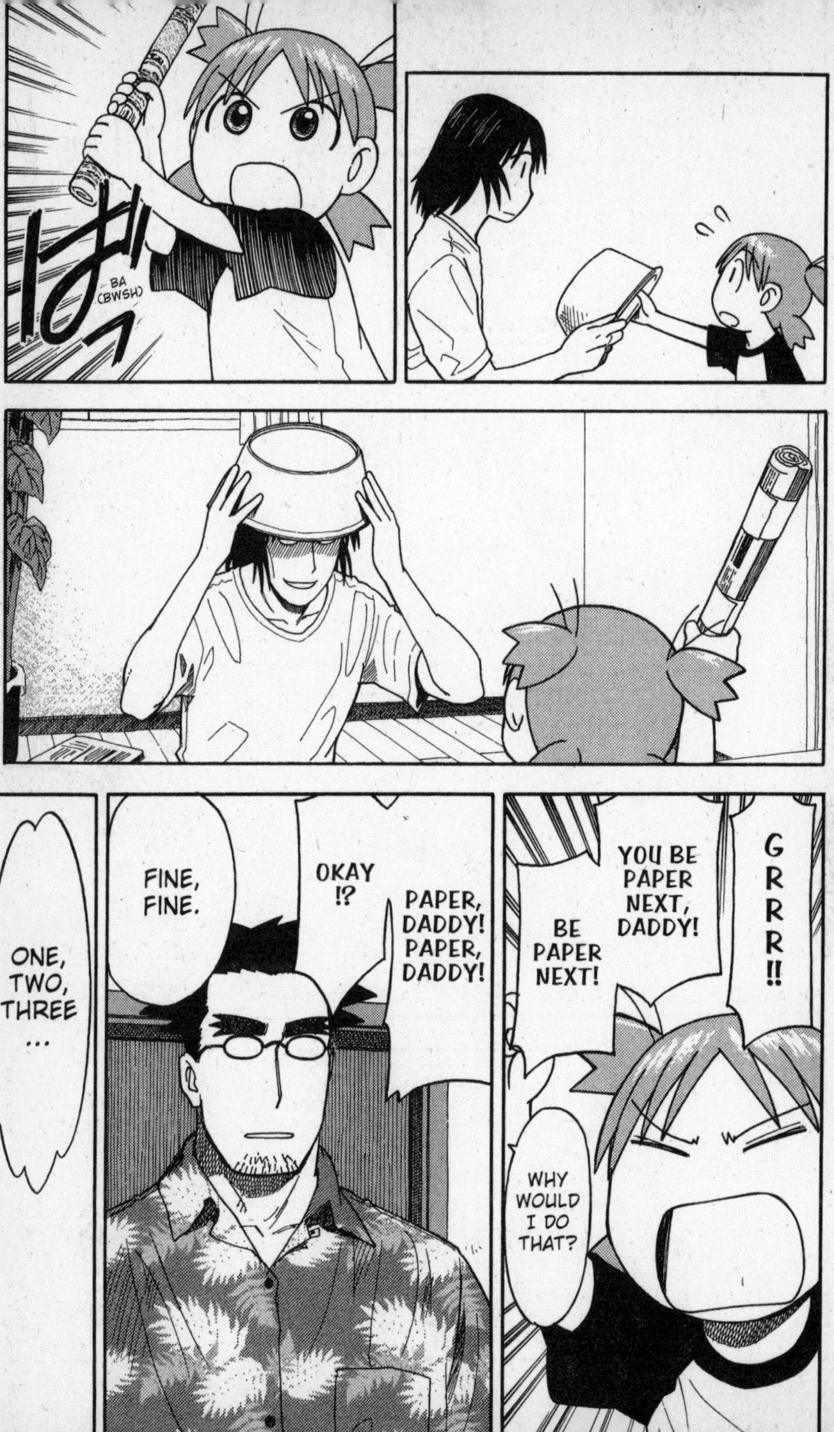
BA (BWSH)
GRRR!!
YOU BE PAPER NEXT, DADDY!
BE PAPER NEXT!
WHY WOULD I DO THAT?
PAPER, DADDY! PAPER, DADDY!
OKAY !?
FINE, FINE.
ONE, TWO, THREE ...

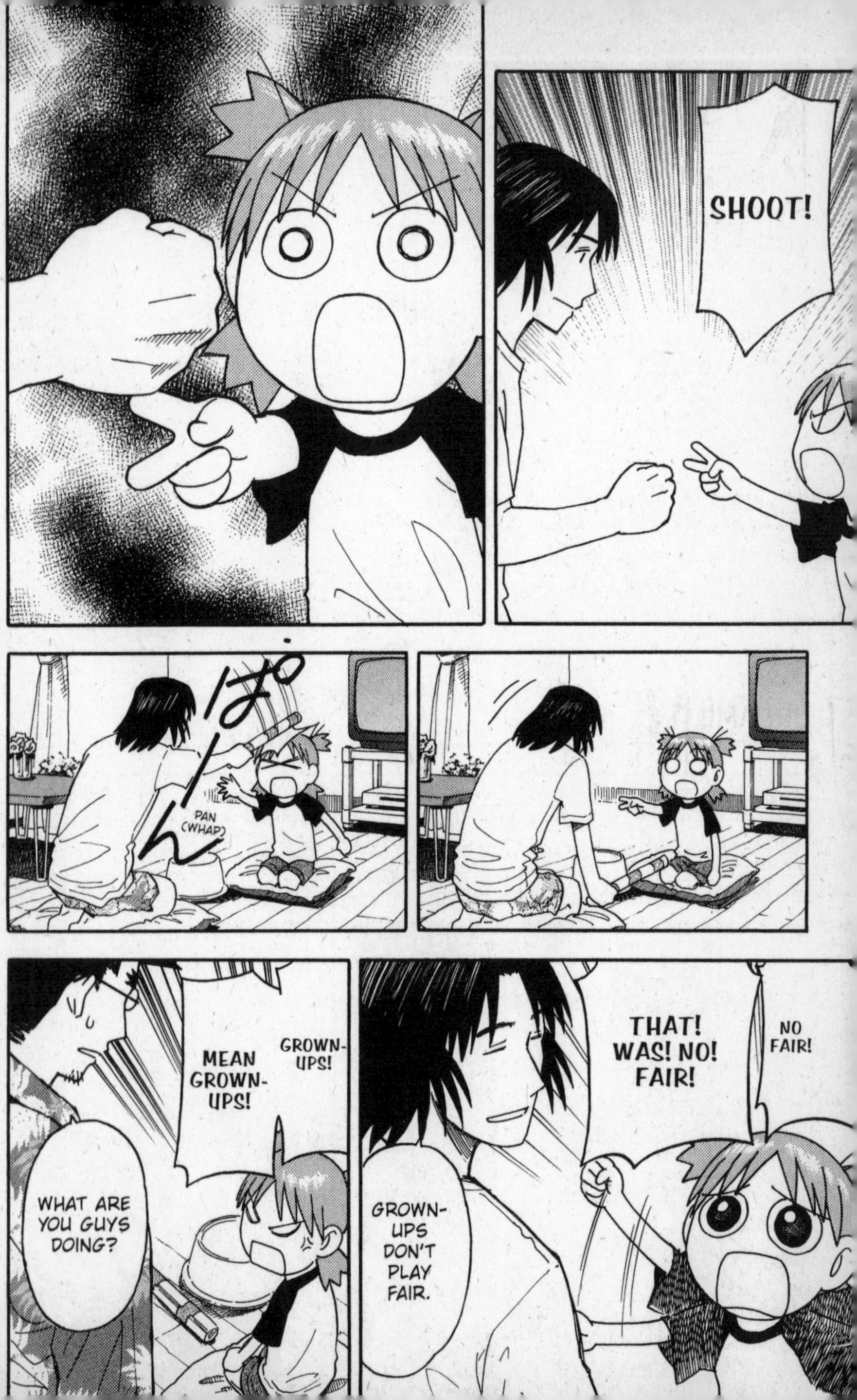
SHOOT!
ぱーん
PAN (WHAP)
NO FAIR!
THAT! WAS! NO! FAIR!
GROWN-UPS DON'T PLAY FAIR.
GROWN-UPS!
MEAN GROWN-UPS!
WHAT ARE YOU GUYS DOING?

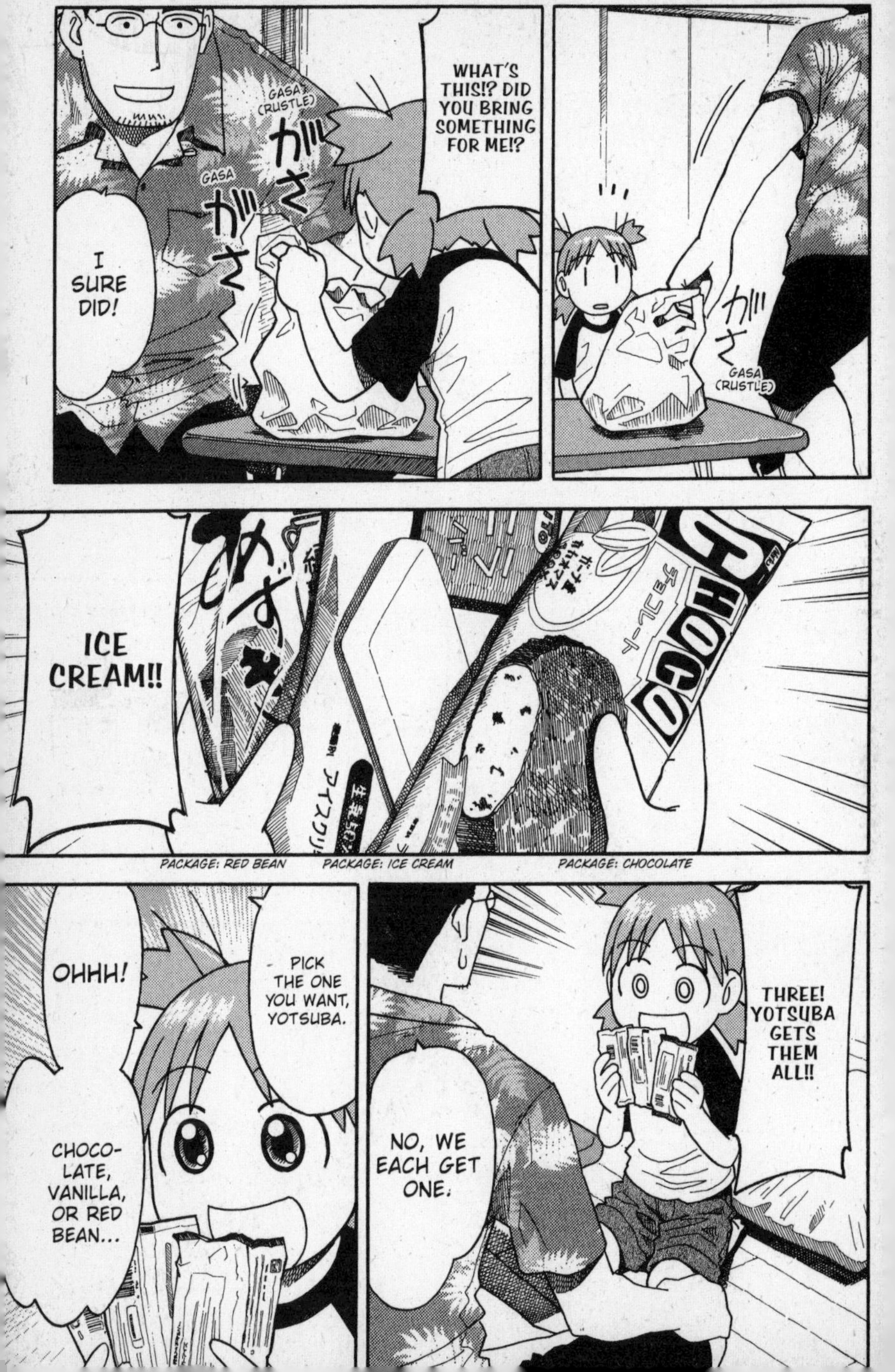
GASA (RUSTLE)
WHAT'S THIS!? DID YOU BRING SOMETHING FOR ME!?
GASA (RUSTLE)
GASA
I SURE DID!
CHOCO
ICE CREAM!!
PACKAGE: RED BEAN
PACKAGE: ICE CREAM
PACKAGE: CHOCOLATE
THREE! YOTSUBA GETS THEM ALL!!
NO, WE EACH GET ONE.
PICK THE ONE YOU WANT, YOTSUBA.
OHHH!
CHOCO-LATE, VANILLA, OR RED BEAN...

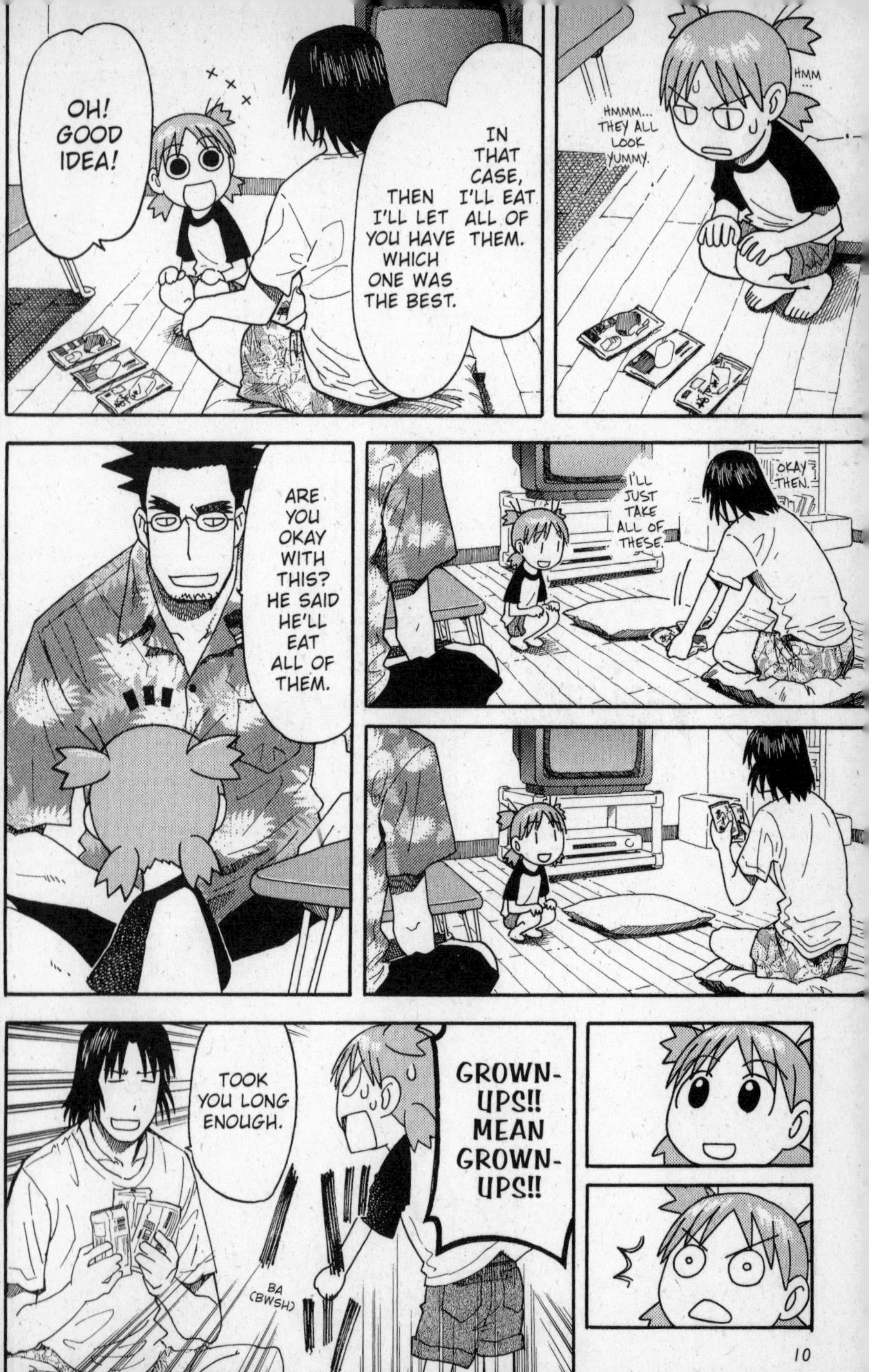
HMMM... THEY ALL LOOK YUMMY.
HMM...
IN THAT CASE, I'LL EAT ALL OF THEM.
THEN I'LL LET YOU HAVE WHICH ONE WAS THE BEST.
OH! GOOD IDEA!
OKAY THEN.
I'LL JUST TAKE ALL OF THESE.
ARE YOU OKAY WITH THIS? HE SAID HE'LL EAT ALL OF THEM.
GROWN-UPS!! MEAN GROWN-UPS!!
BA (BWSH)
TOOK YOU LONG ENOUGH.

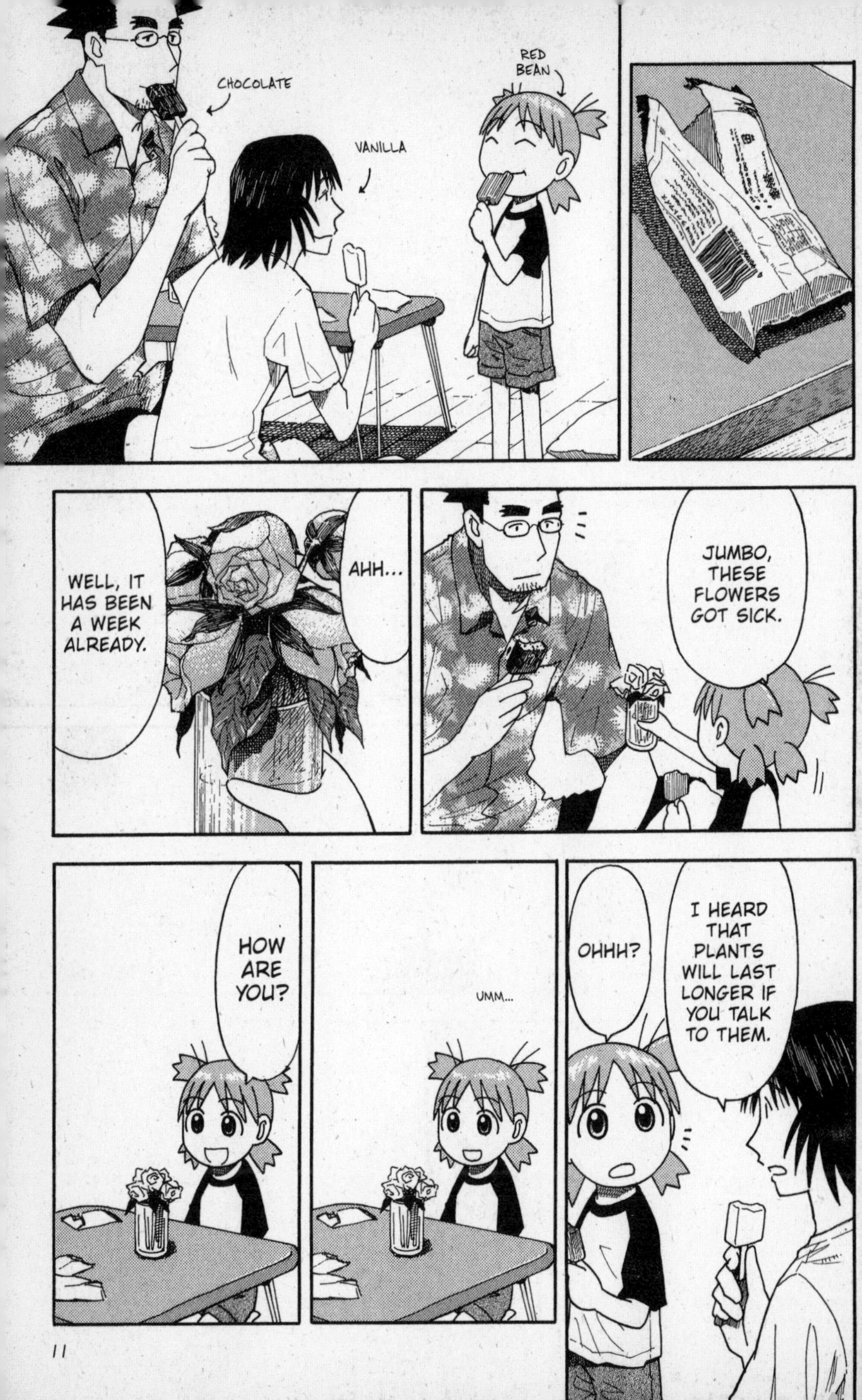
RED BEAN
VANILLA
CHOCOLATE
JUMBO, THESE FLOWERS GOT SICK.
AHH...
WELL, IT HAS BEEN A WEEK ALREADY.
I HEARD THAT PLANTS WILL LAST LONGER IF YOU TALK TO THEM.
OHHH?
UMM...
HOW ARE YOU?

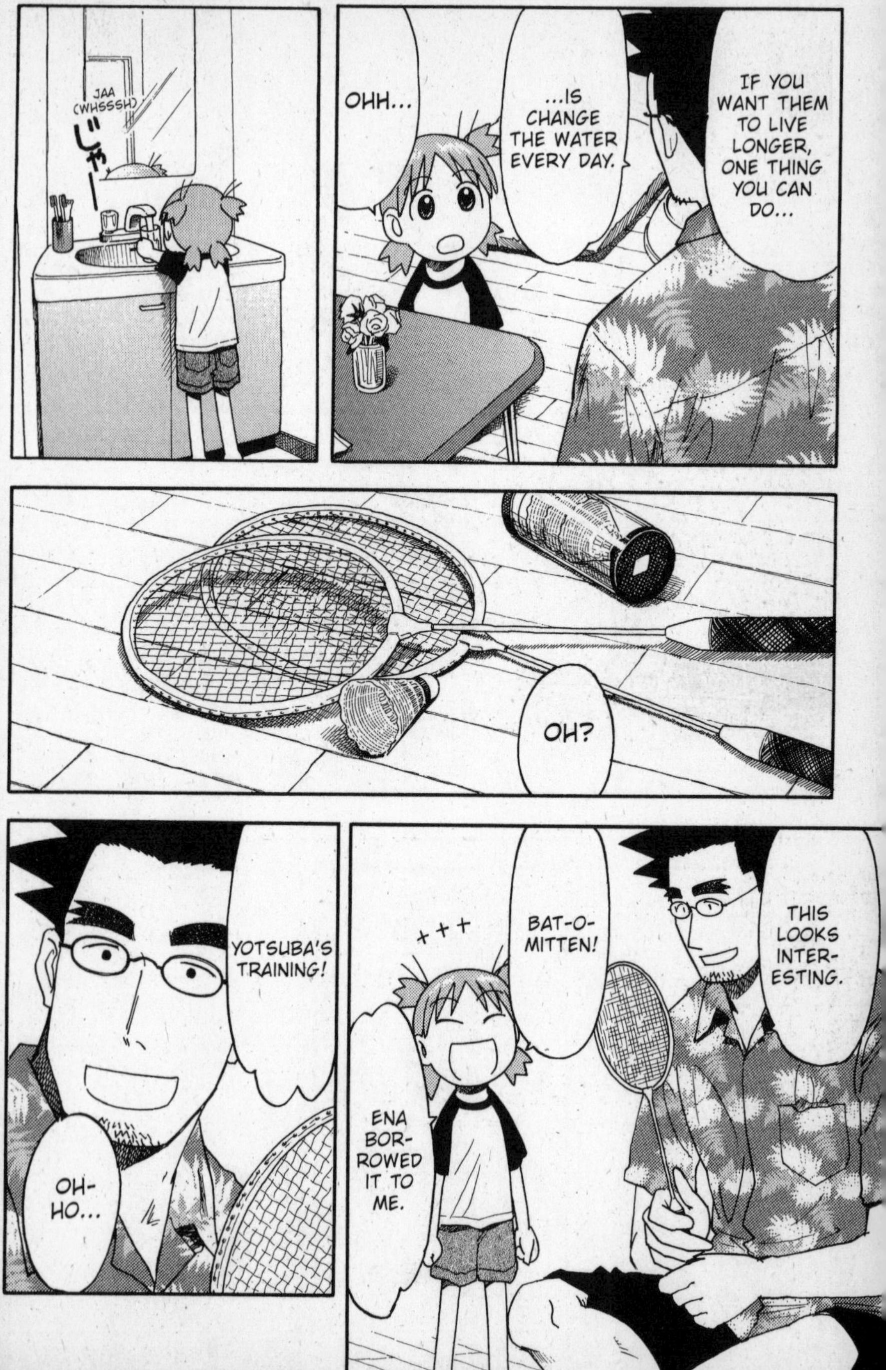
IF YOU WANT THEM TO LIVE LONGER, ONE THING YOU CAN DO...
...IS CHANGE THE WATER EVERY DAY.
OHH...
JAA (WHSSSH)
じゃー
OH?
THIS LOOKS INTER-ESTING.
BAT-O-MITTEN!
ENA BOR-ROWED IT TO ME.
YOTSUBA'S TRAINING!
OH-HO...

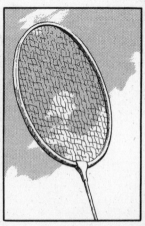

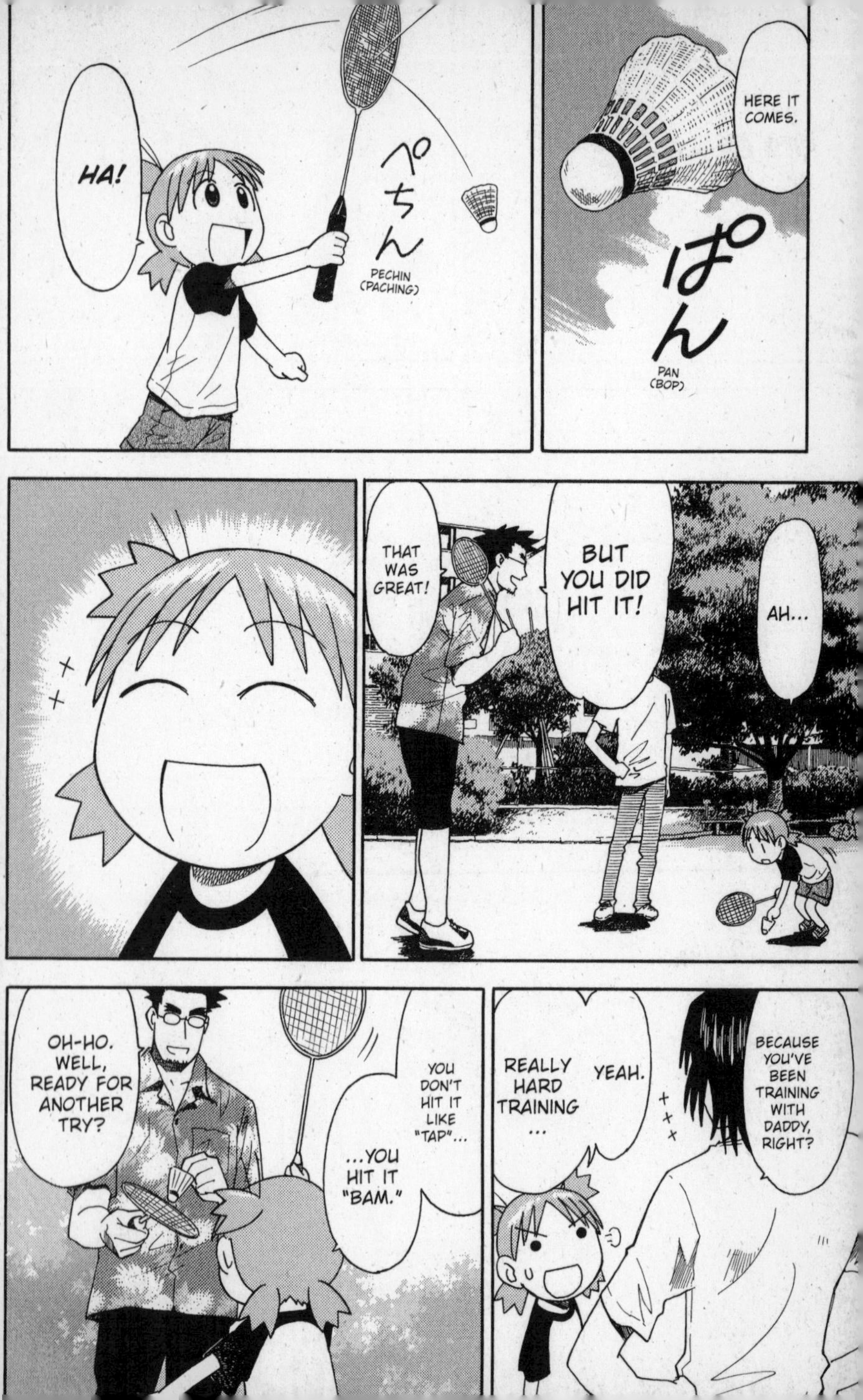
HERE IT COMES.
ぱん
PAN (BOP)
HA!
ぺちん
PECHIN (PACHING)
AH...
BUT YOU DID HIT IT!
THAT WAS GREAT!
BECAUSE YOU'VE BEEN TRAINING WITH DADDY, RIGHT?
YEAH.
REALLY HARD TRAINING...
YOU DON'T HIT IT LIKE "TAP"...
...YOU HIT IT "BAM."
OH-HO. WELL, READY FOR ANOTHER TRY?

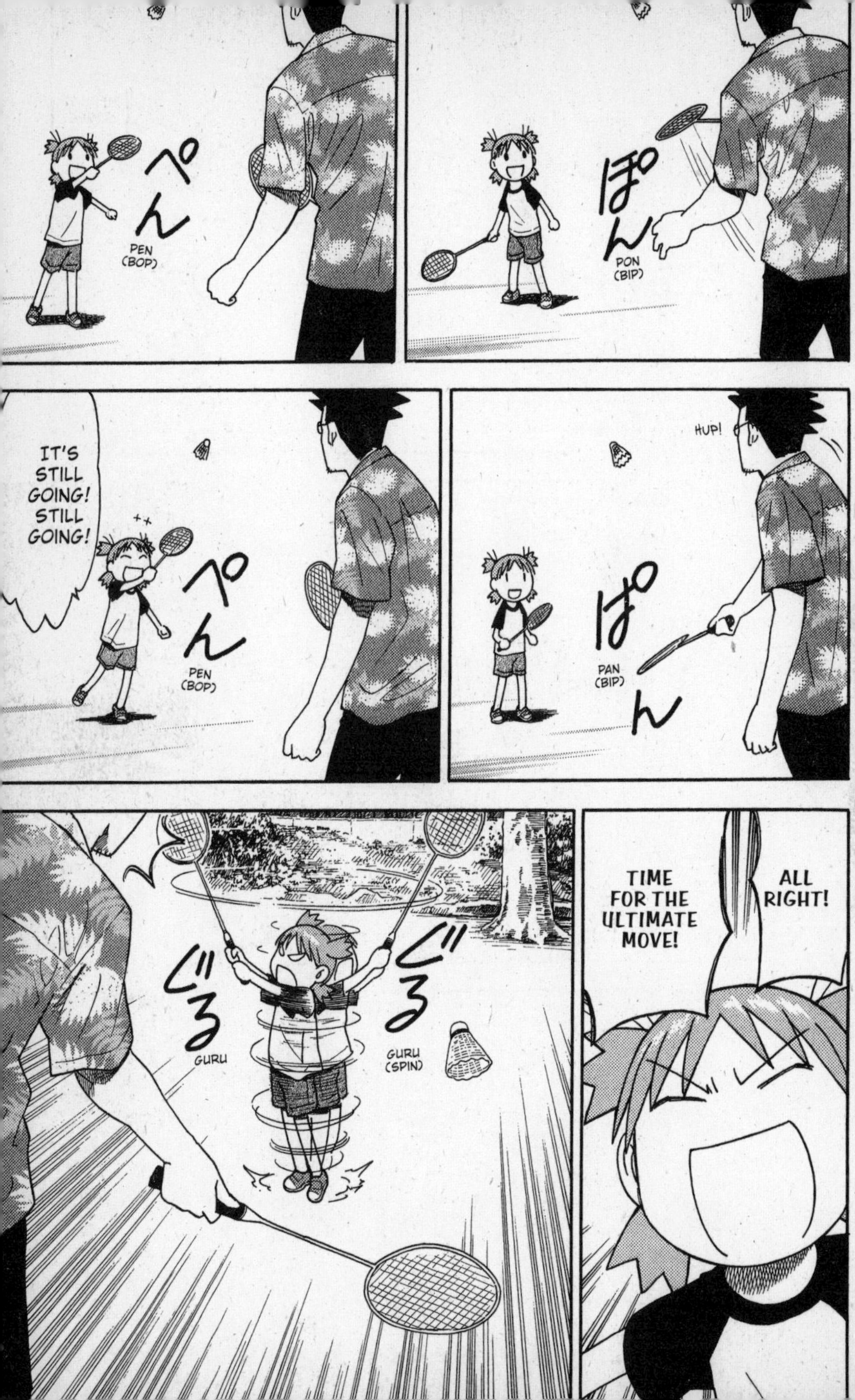
ぽん
PON
(BIP)
ぺん
PEN
(BOP)
HUP!
ぱん
PAN
(BIP)
IT'S STILL GOING! STILL GOING!
ぺん
PEN
(BOP)
ALL RIGHT!
TIME FOR THE ULTIMATE MOVE!
ぐる
GURU
(SPIN)
ぐる
GURU

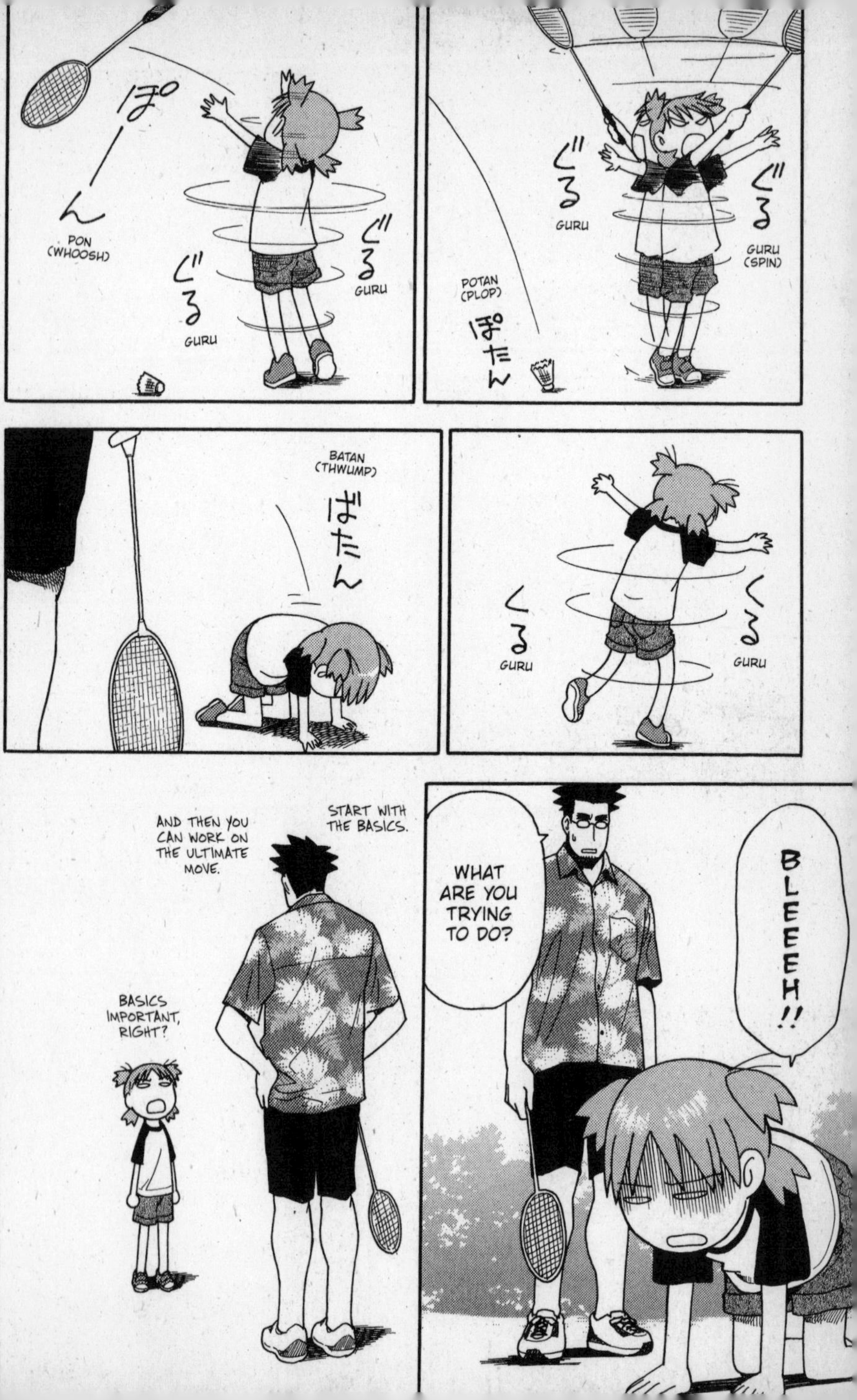
ぐる
GURU (SPIN)
ぐる
GURU
ぽたん
POTAN (PLOP)
ぐる
GURU
ぐる
GURU
ぽーん
PON (WHOOSH)
くる
GURU
くる
GURU
ばたん
BATAN (THWUMP)
BLEEEH!!
WHAT ARE YOU TRYING TO DO?
START WITH THE BASICS.
AND THEN YOU CAN WORK ON THE ULTIMATE MOVE.
BASICS IMPORTANT, RIGHT?

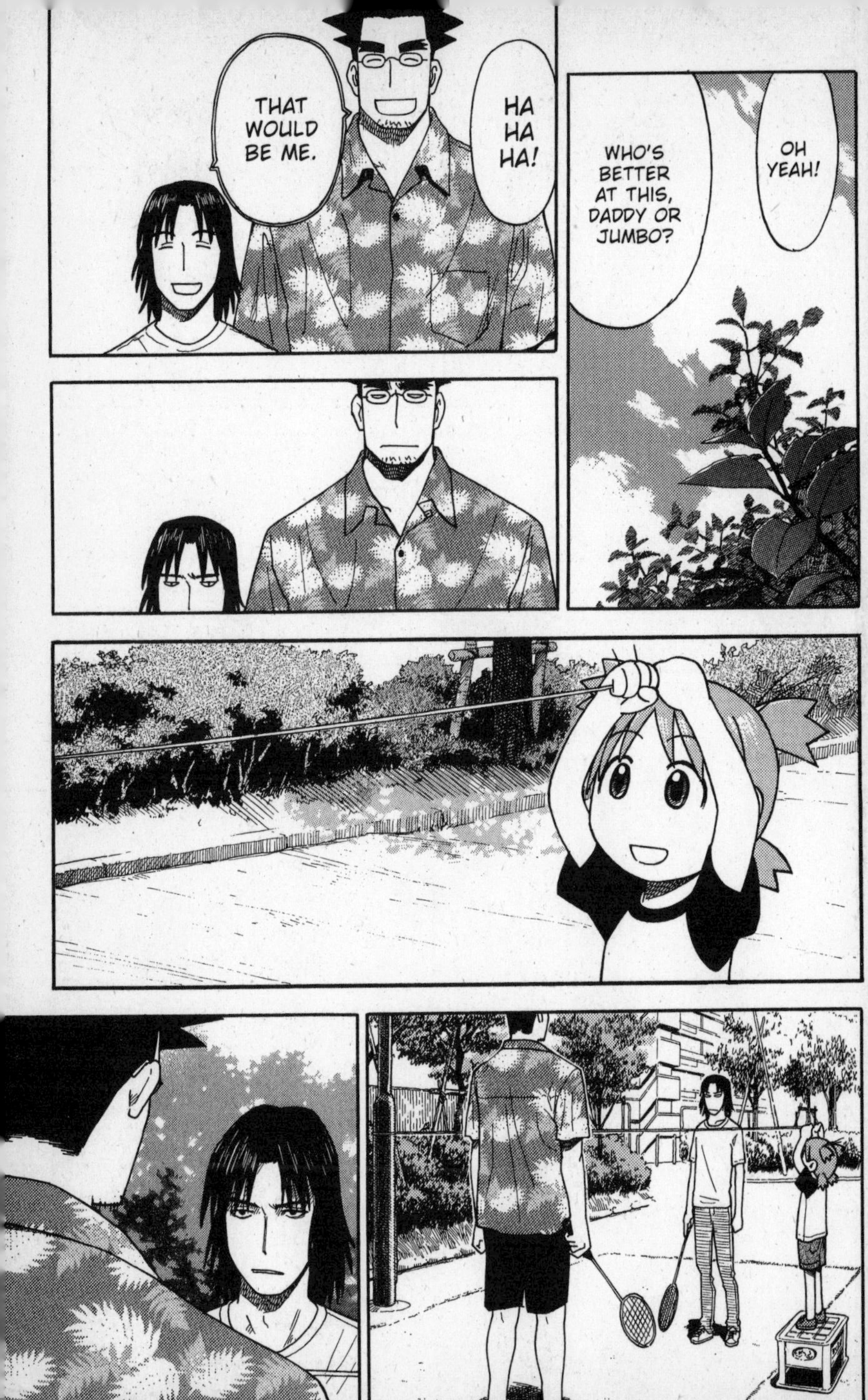
OH YEAH!
WHO'S BETTER AT THIS, DADDY OR JUMBO?
HA HA HA!
THAT WOULD BE ME.

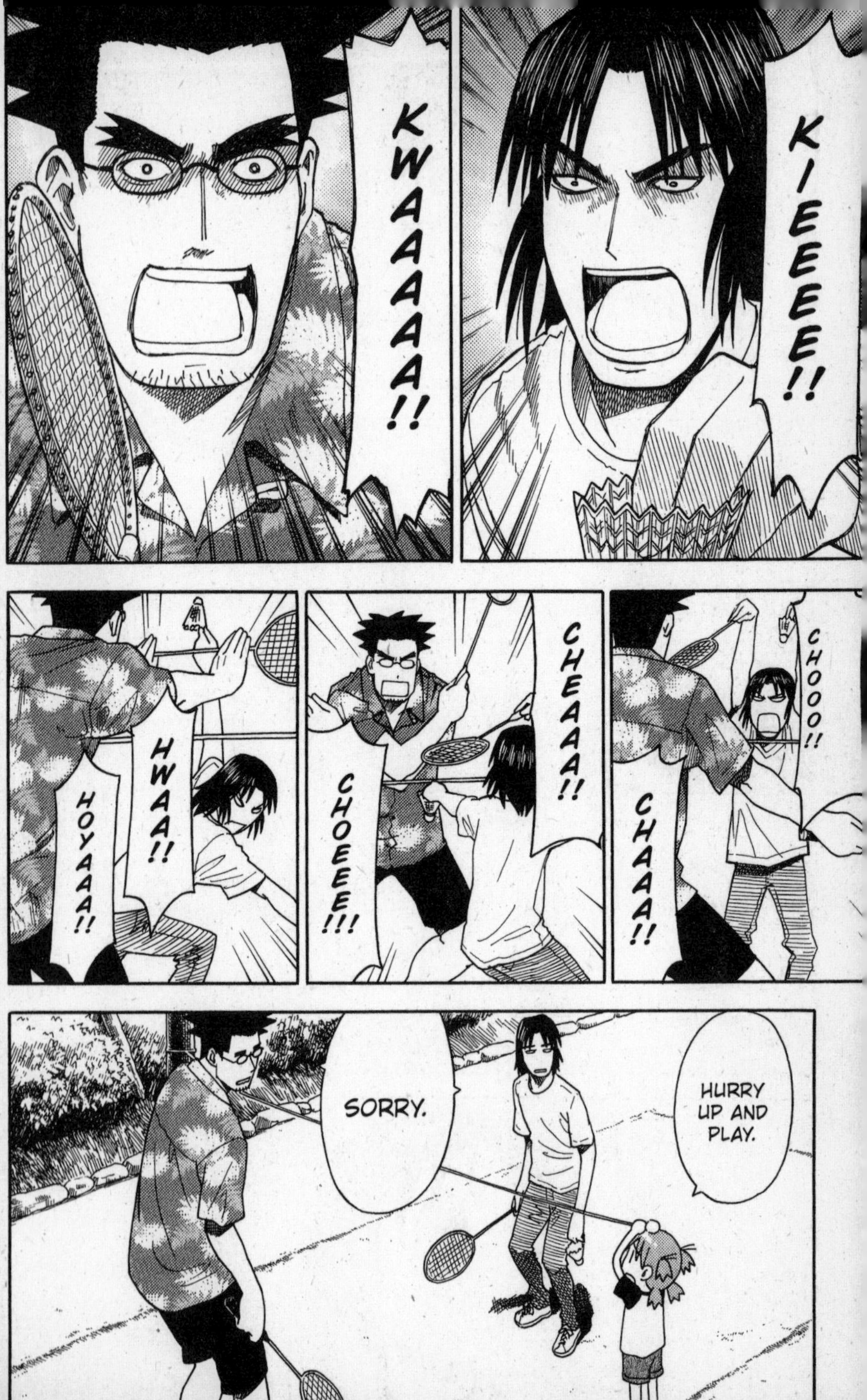
KIEEEEE!!
KWAAAAAAA!!
CHOOOO!!
CHAAAA!!
CHEAAAA!!
CHOEEEE!!!
HWAA!!
HOYAAAA!!
HURRY UP AND PLAY.
SORRY.

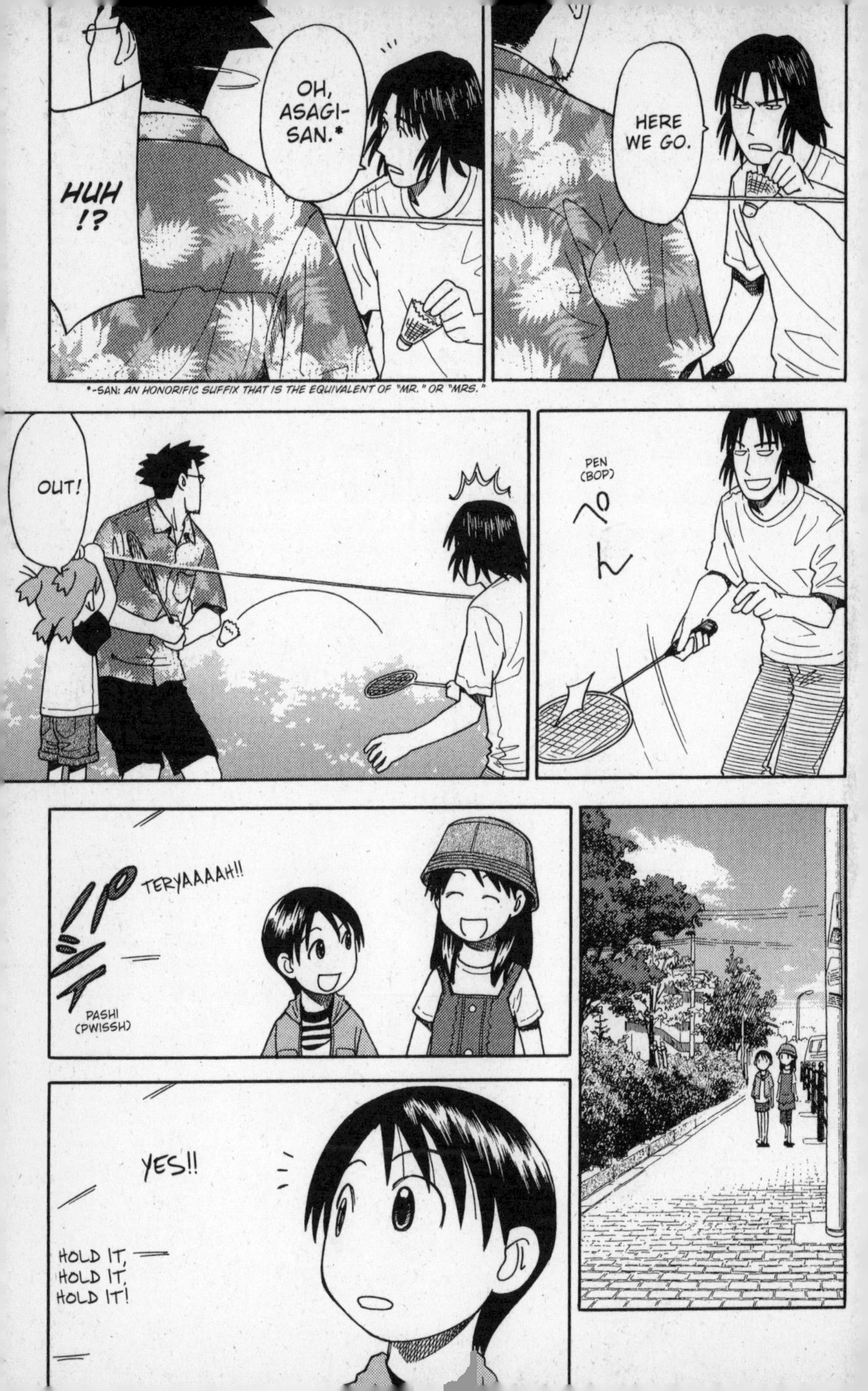
HERE WE GO.
OH, ASAGI-SAN.*
HUH!?
PEN (BOP)
ぺん
OUT!
TERYAAAAH!!
PASHI (PWISSH)
YES!!
HOLD IT, HOLD IT, HOLD IT!

*-SAN: AN HONORIFIC SUFFIX THAT IS THE EQUIVALENT OF "MR." OR "MRS."

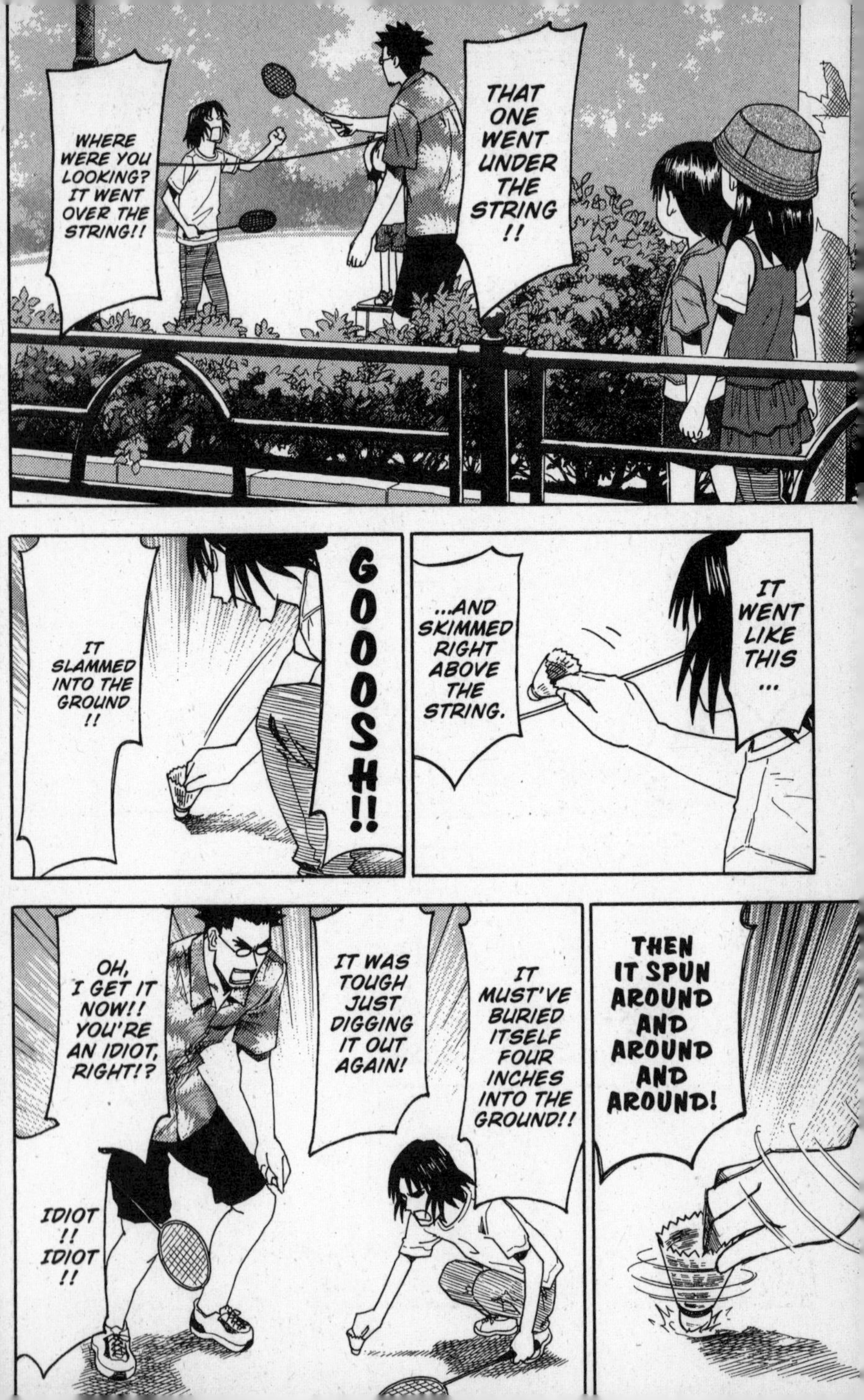
THAT ONE WENT UNDER THE STRING!!
WHERE WERE YOU LOOKING? IT WENT OVER THE STRING!!
IT WENT LIKE THIS...
...AND SKIMMED RIGHT ABOVE THE STRING.
GOOOOSH!!
IT SLAMMED INTO THE GROUND!!
THEN IT SPUN AROUND AND AROUND AND AROUND!
IT MUST'VE BURIED ITSELF FOUR INCHES INTO THE GROUND!!
IT WAS TOUGH JUST DIGGING IT OUT AGAIN!
OH, I GET IT NOW!! YOU'RE AN IDIOT, RIGHT!?
IDIOT!! IDIOT!!

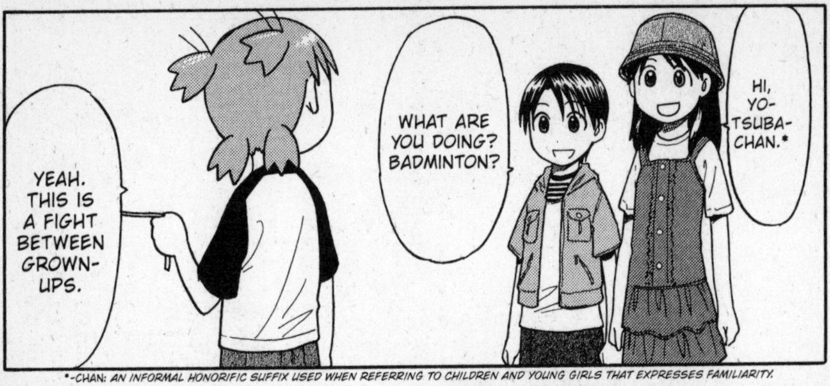
HI, YO-TSUBA-CHAN.*
WHAT ARE YOU DOING? BADMINTON?
YEAH. THIS IS A FIGHT BETWEEN GROWN-UPS.

*-CHAN: AN INFORMAL HONORIFIC SUFFIX USED WHEN REFERRING TO CHILDREN AND YOUNG GIRLS THAT EXPRESSES FAMILIARITY.

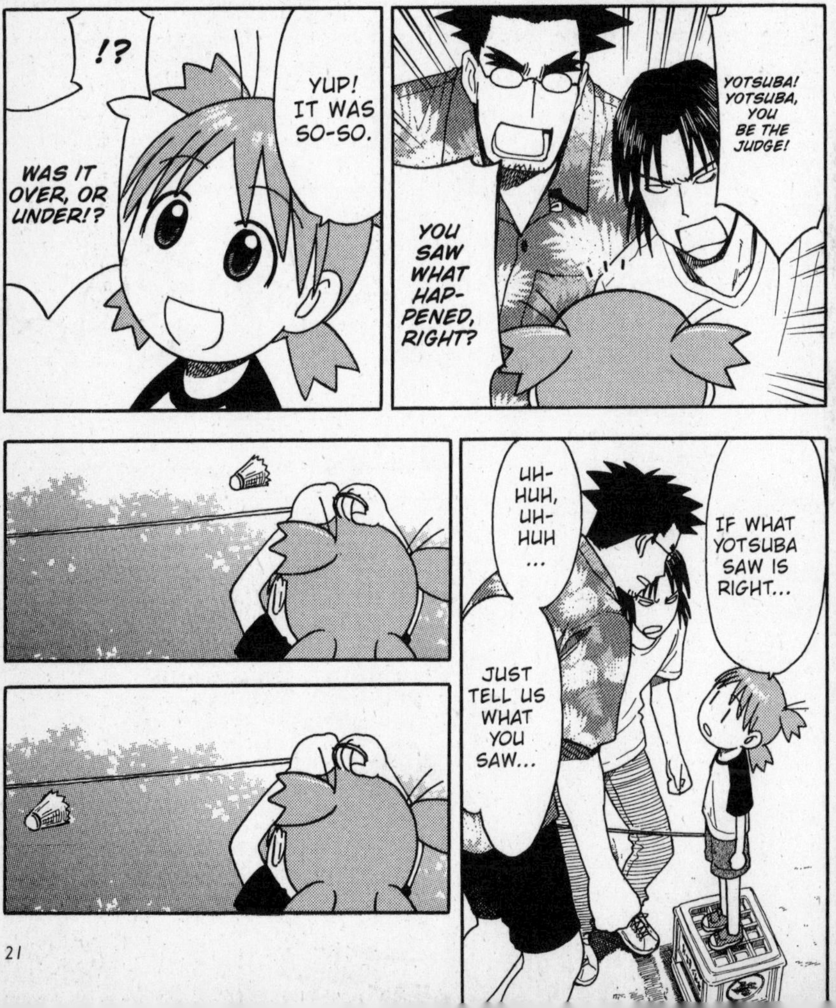
YOTSUBA! YOTSUBA, YOU BE THE JUDGE!
YOU SAW WHAT HAP-PENED, RIGHT?
YUP! IT WAS SO-SO.
!?
WAS IT OVER, OR UNDER!?
IF WHAT YOTSUBA SAW IS RIGHT...
UH-HUH, UH-HUH ...
JUST TELL US WHAT YOU SAW...

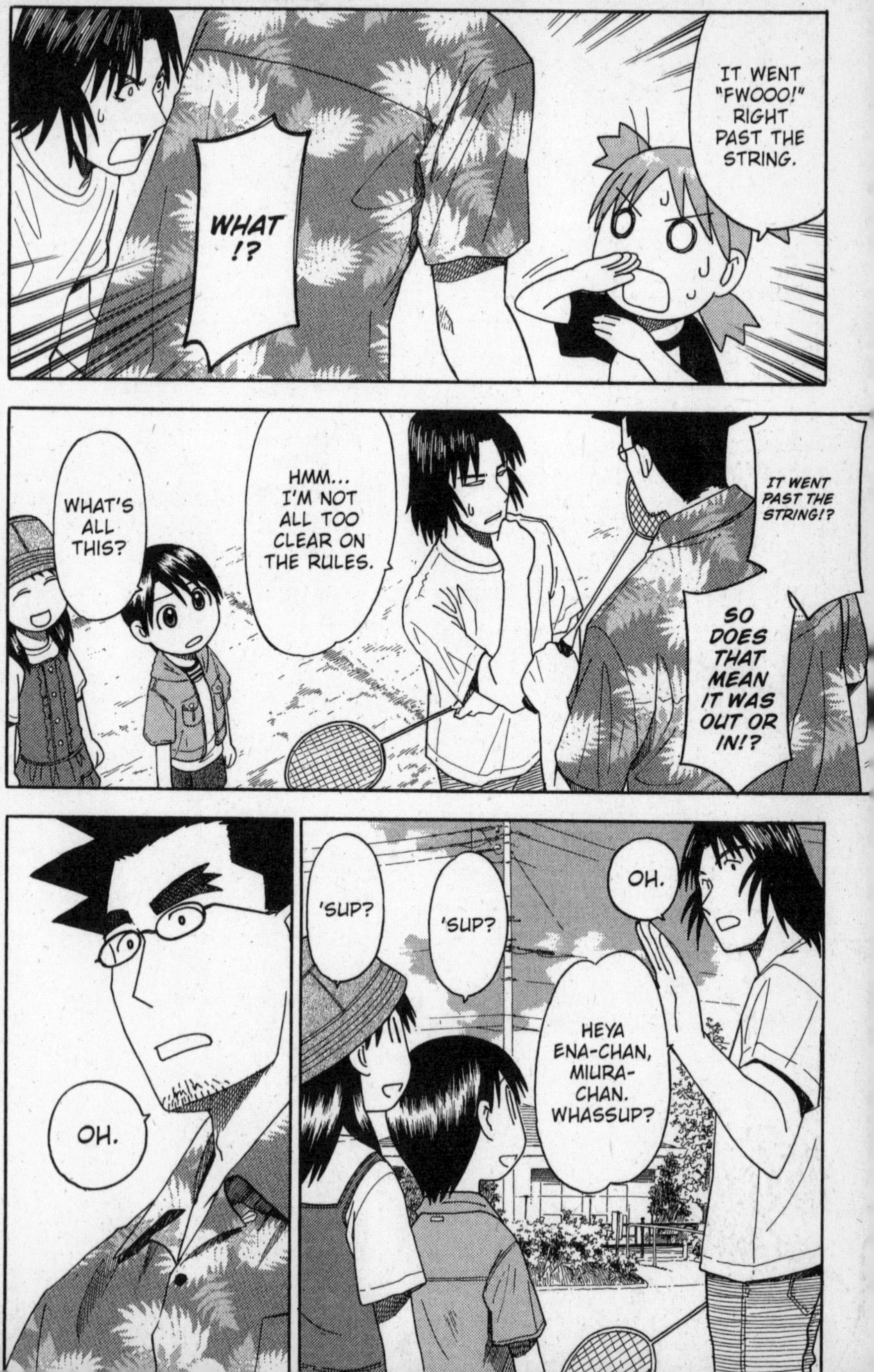
IT WENT "FWOOO!" RIGHT PAST THE STRING.
WHAT !?
IT WENT PAST THE STRING!?
SO DOES THAT MEAN IT WAS OUT OR IN!?
HMM... I'M NOT ALL TOO CLEAR ON THE RULES.
WHAT'S ALL THIS?
OH.
HEYA ENA-CHAN, MIURA-CHAN. WHASSUP?
'SUP?
'SUP?
OH.

A SNAIL?

THAT'S RIGHT. SHE'S NOT A SNAIL.

I'M ALWAYS A GIRL.

LOOKS LIKE "LAMBORGHINI MIURA" DECIDED TO BE A GIRL TODAY.

WHOA...

SNAILS DON'T HAVE "MALE" OR "FEMALE."

YARGH! JUST SHUT UP, WILL YA!!

I'M SORRY, DID I WOUND YOUR GIRLISH HEART?

WHO ASKED YOU?

AND I TOLD YOU, I'VE ALWAYS BEEN A GIRL.

...THAT'S WHY YOU DECIDED TO DRESS LIKE A GIRL TODAY, RIGHT?

JUMBO-SAN CALLED YOU A BOY YESTER-DAY...

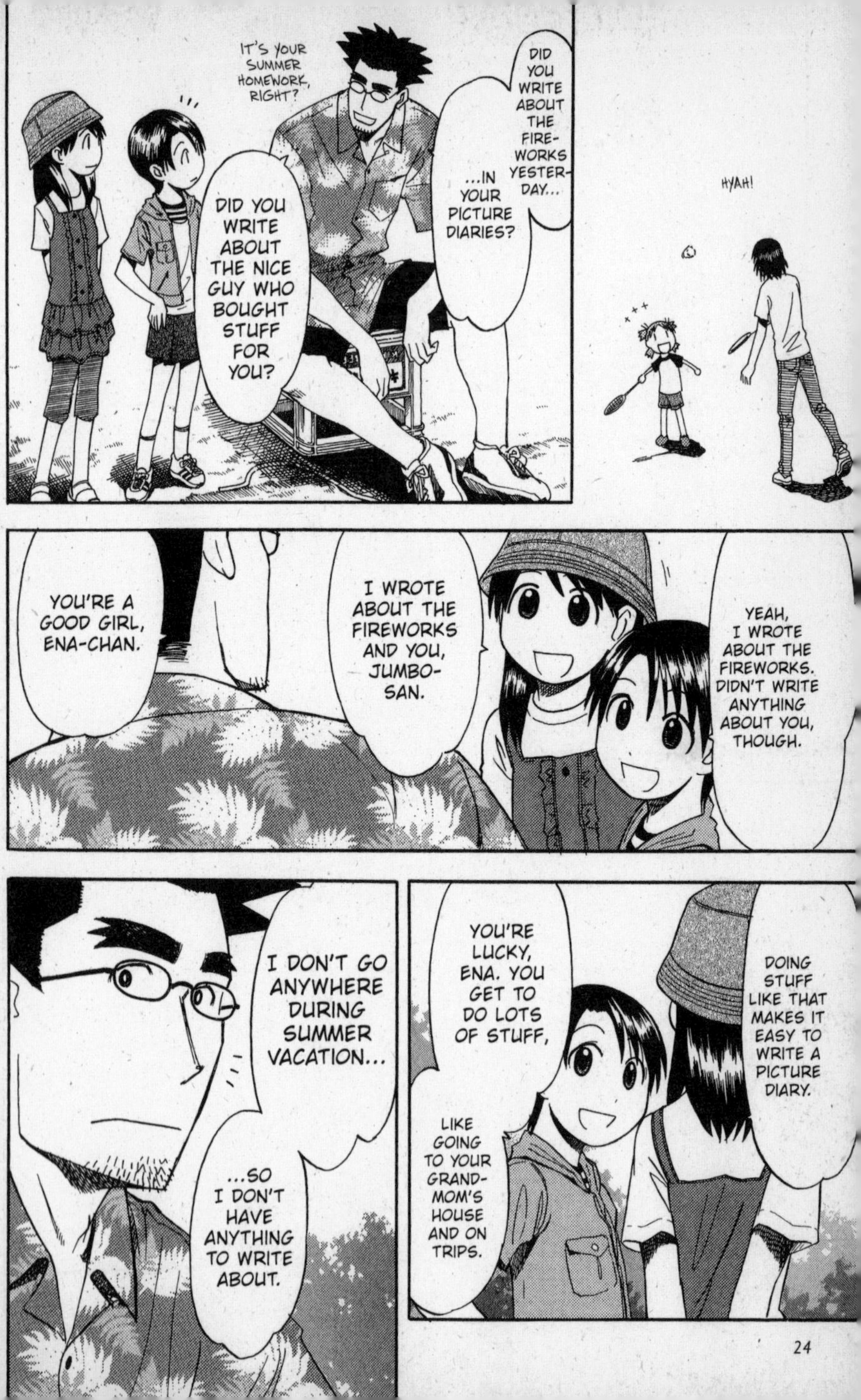

HYAH!
DID YOU WRITE ABOUT THE FIRE-WORKS YESTER-DAY...
...IN YOUR PICTURE DIARIES?
IT'S YOUR SUMMER HOMEWORK, RIGHT?
DID YOU WRITE ABOUT THE NICE GUY WHO BOUGHT STUFF FOR YOU?
YEAH, I WROTE ABOUT THE FIREWORKS. DIDN'T WRITE ANYTHING ABOUT YOU, THOUGH.
I WROTE ABOUT THE FIREWORKS AND YOU, JUMBO-SAN.
YOU'RE A GOOD GIRL, ENA-CHAN.
DOING STUFF LIKE THAT MAKES IT EASY TO WRITE A PICTURE DIARY.
YOU'RE LUCKY, ENA. YOU GET TO DO LOTS OF STUFF,
LIKE GOING TO YOUR GRAND-MOM'S HOUSE AND ON TRIPS.
I DON'T GO ANYWHERE DURING SUMMER VACATION...
...SO I DON'T HAVE ANYTHING TO WRITE ABOUT.

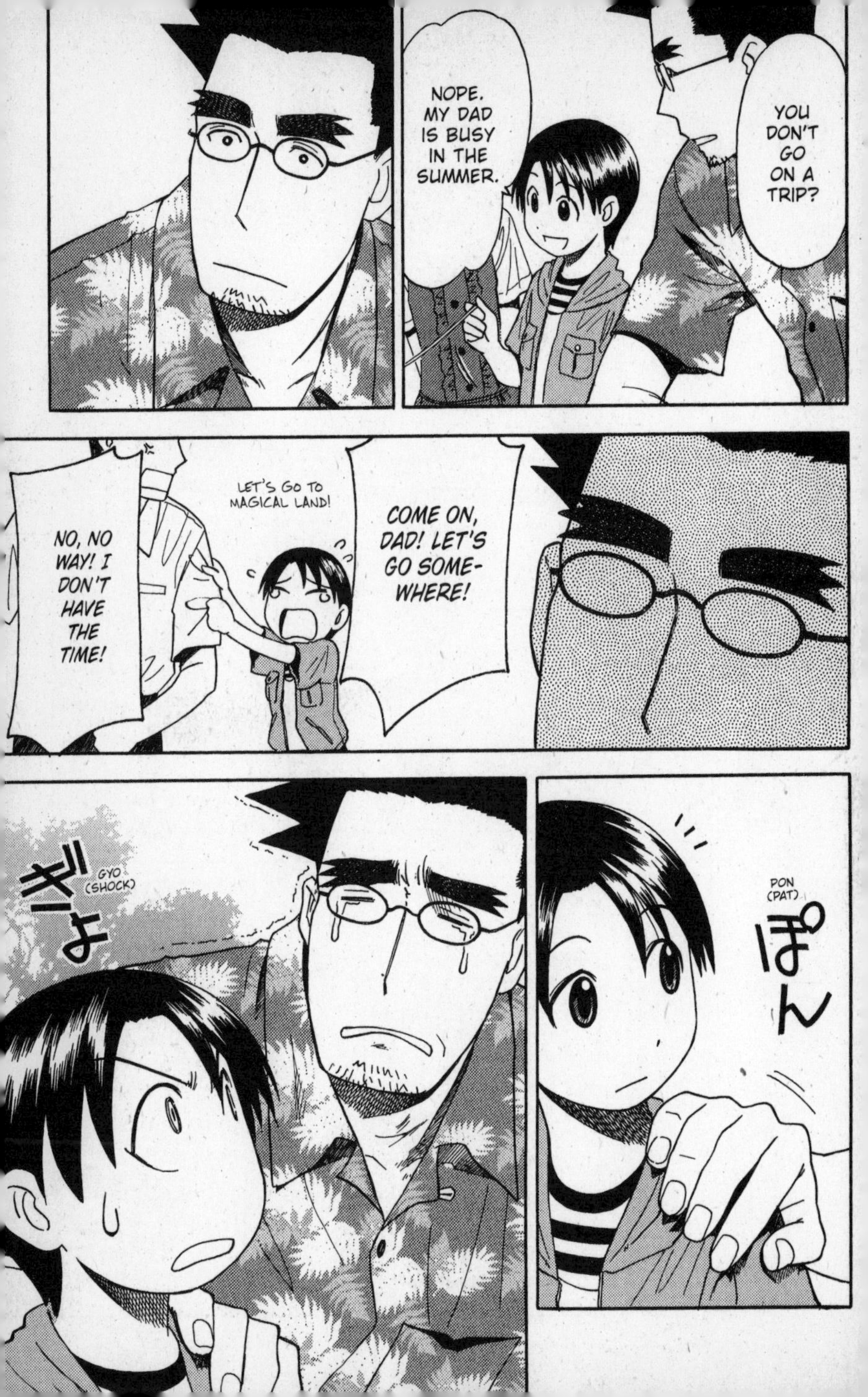
YOU DON'T GO ON A TRIP?
NOPE. MY DAD IS BUSY IN THE SUMMER.
COME ON, DAD! LET'S GO SOME-WHERE!
LET'S GO TO MAGICAL LAND!
NO, NO WAY! I DON'T HAVE THE TIME!
ぽん
PON (PAT)
ぎょ
GYO (SHOCK)

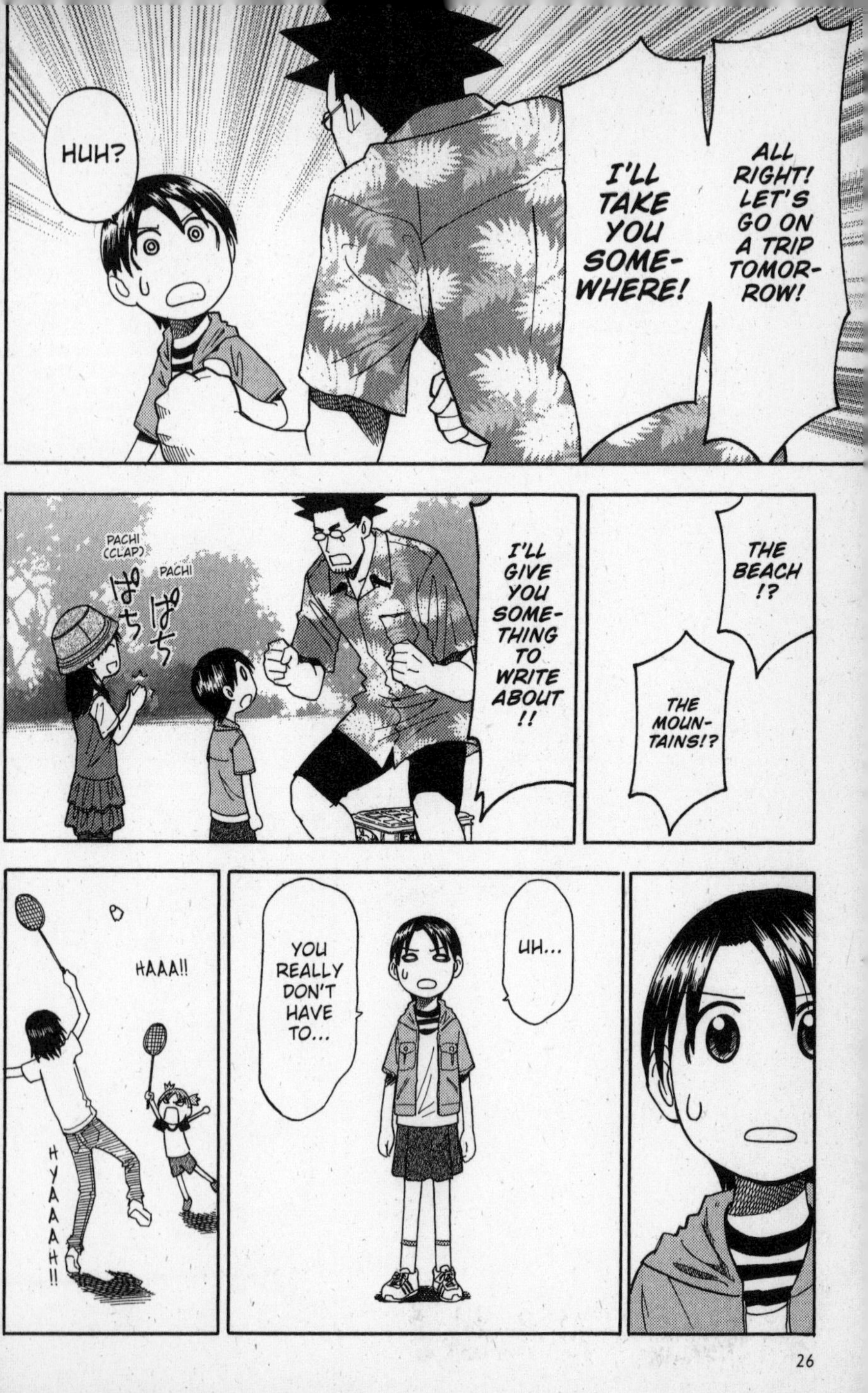
ALL RIGHT! LET'S GO ON A TRIP TOMORROW!
I'LL TAKE YOU SOMEWHERE!
HUH?
THE BEACH!?
THE MOUNTAINS!?
I'LL GIVE YOU SOMETHING TO WRITE ABOUT!!
ぱち
PACHI
ぱち
PACHI (CLAP)
UH...
YOU REALLY DON'T HAVE TO...
HAAA!!
HYAAAAH!!

YOTSUBA&!

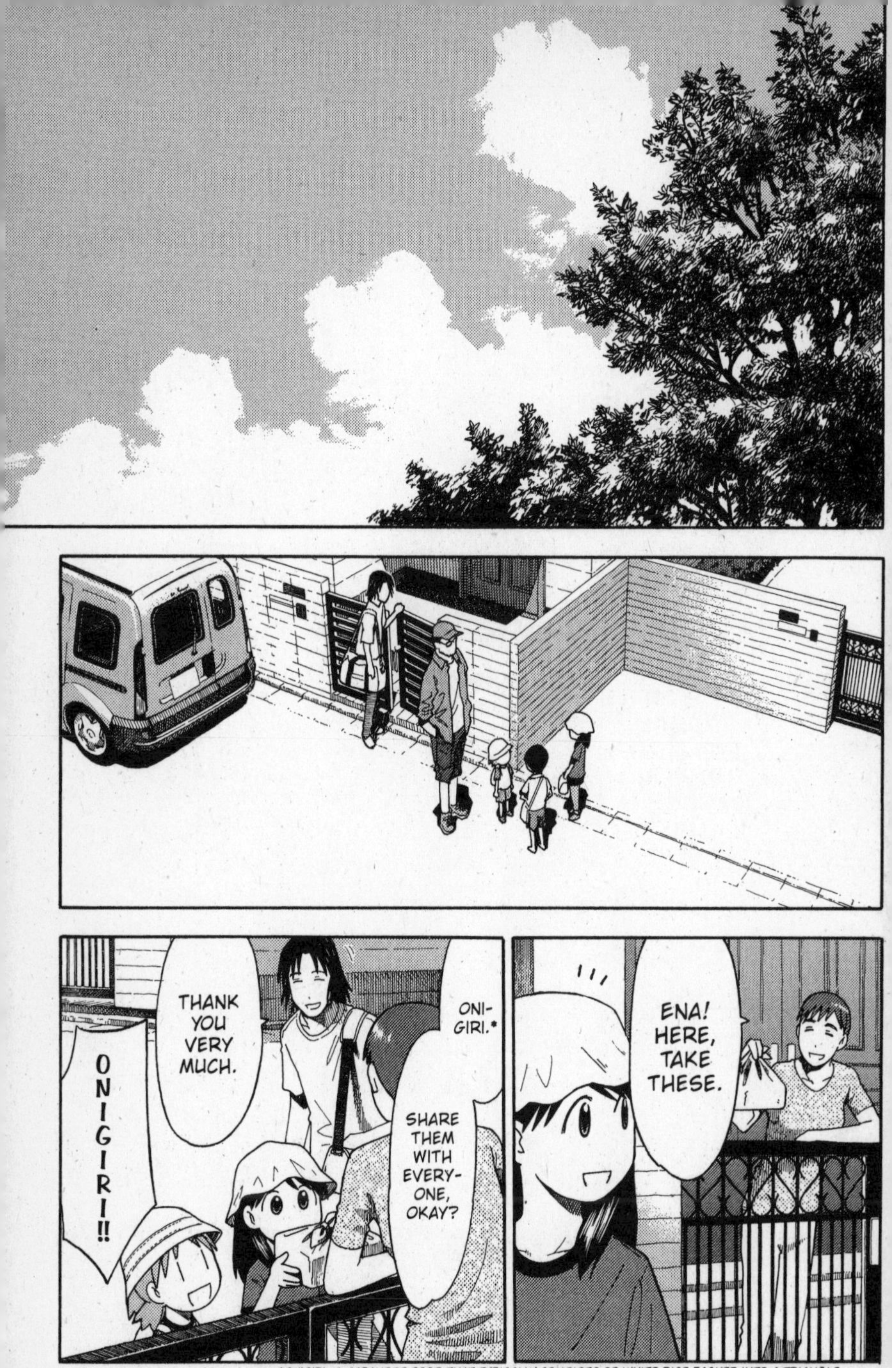
ENA! HERE, TAKE THESE.
ONI-GIRI.*
SHARE THEM WITH EVERY-ONE, OKAY?
THANK YOU VERY MUCH.
ONIGIRI!!

*ONIGIRI: A JAPANESE FOOD THAT TYPICALLY CONSISTS OF WHITE RICE PACKED INTO A TRIANGLE SHAPE AND WRAPPED IN SEAWEED WITH A SAVORY FILLING, LIKE SALTED FISH OR PICKLED PLUM.

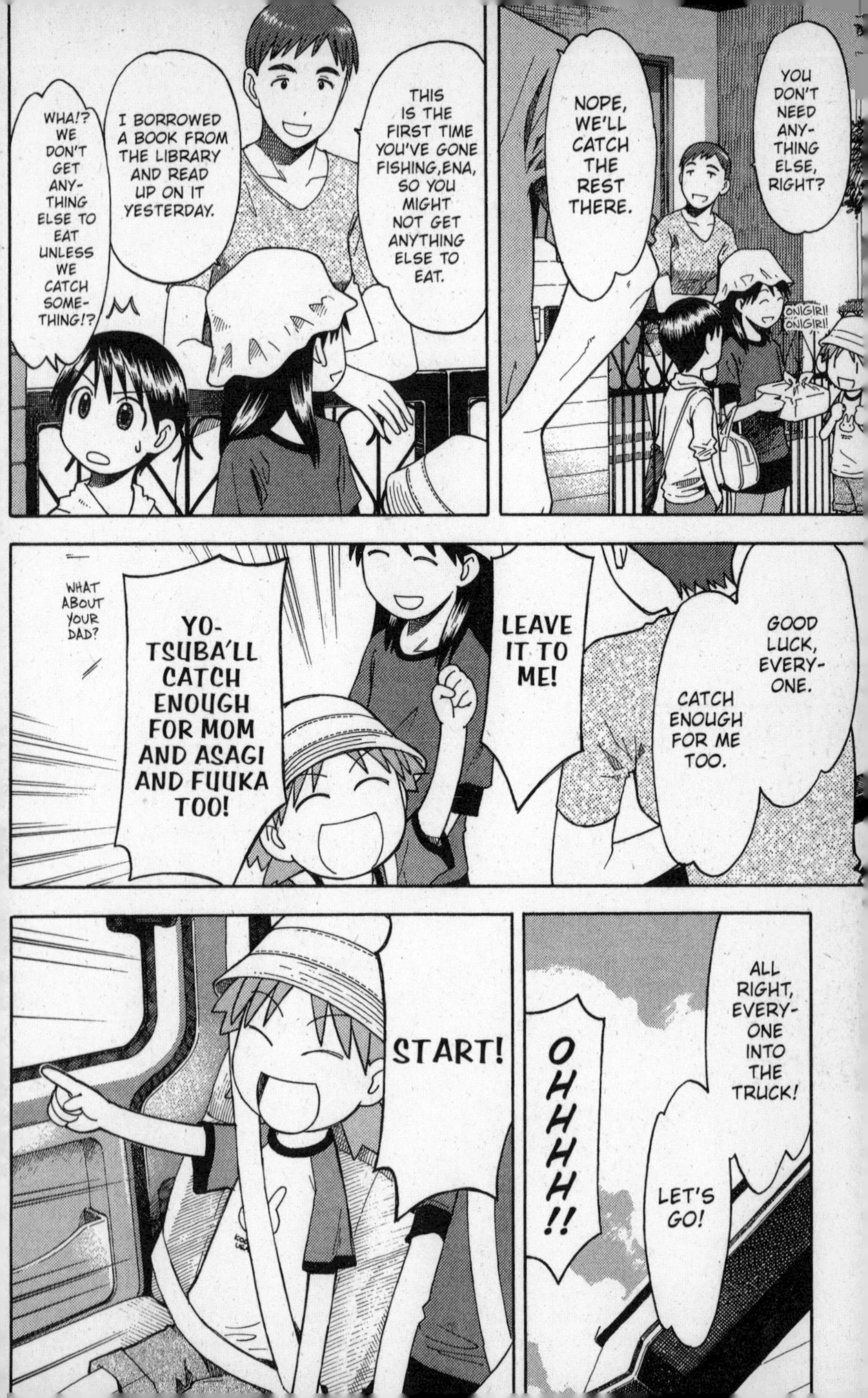
YOU DON'T NEED ANY-THING ELSE, RIGHT?
NOPE, WE'LL CATCH THE REST THERE.
ONIGIRI! ONIGIRI!
THIS IS THE FIRST TIME YOU'VE GONE FISHING, ENA, SO YOU MIGHT NOT GET ANYTHING ELSE TO EAT.
I BORROWED A BOOK FROM THE LIBRARY AND READ UP ON IT YESTERDAY.
WHA!? WE DON'T GET ANY-THING ELSE TO EAT UNLESS WE CATCH SOME-THING!?
GOOD LUCK, EVERY-ONE.
CATCH ENOUGH FOR ME TOO.
LEAVE IT TO ME!
YO-TSUBA'LL CATCH ENOUGH FOR MOM AND ASAGI AND FUUKA TOO!
WHAT ABOUT YOUR DAD?
ALL RIGHT, EVERY-ONE INTO THE TRUCK!
LET'S GO!
OHHHHH!!
START!

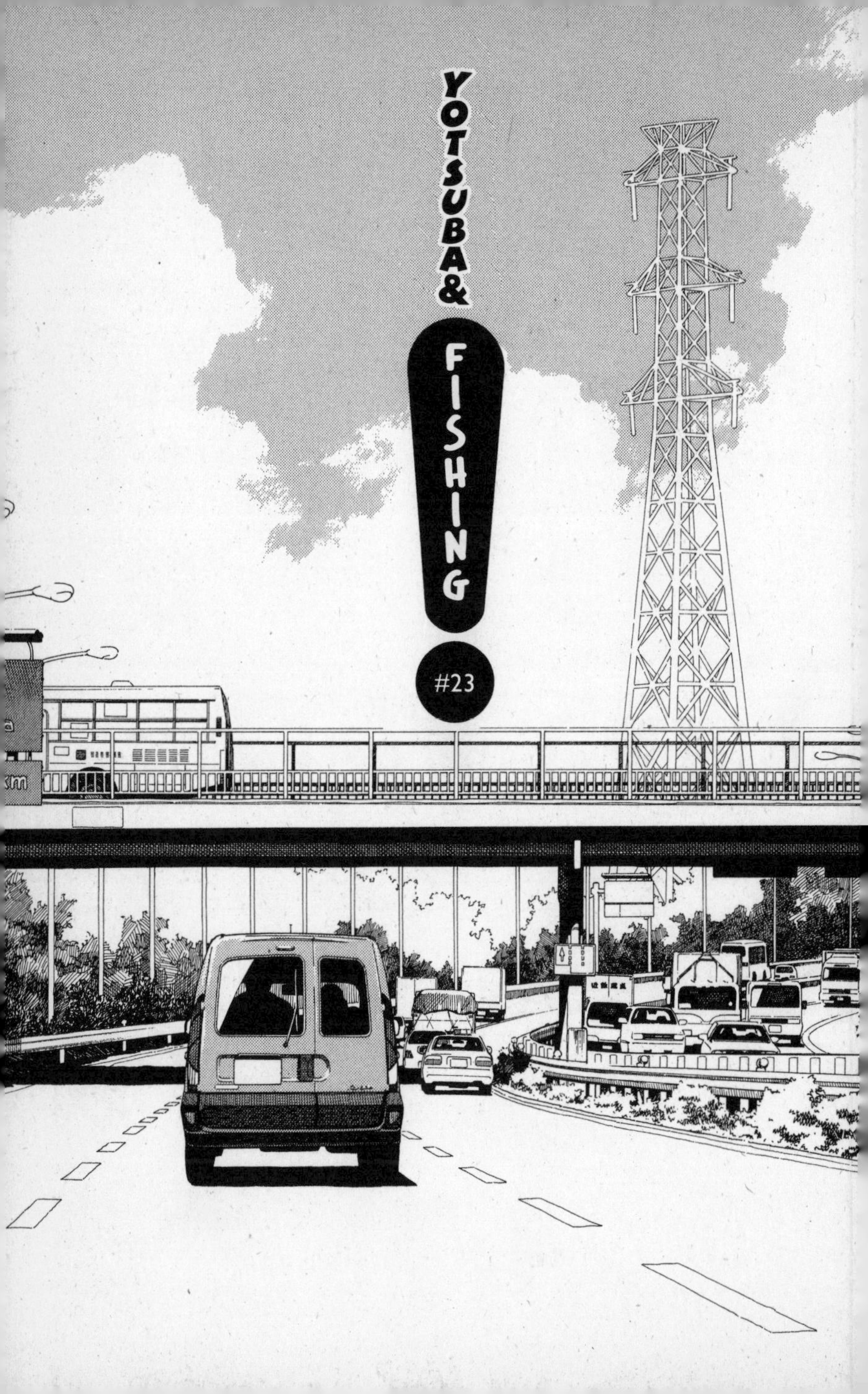
YOTSUBA&
FISHING!
#23

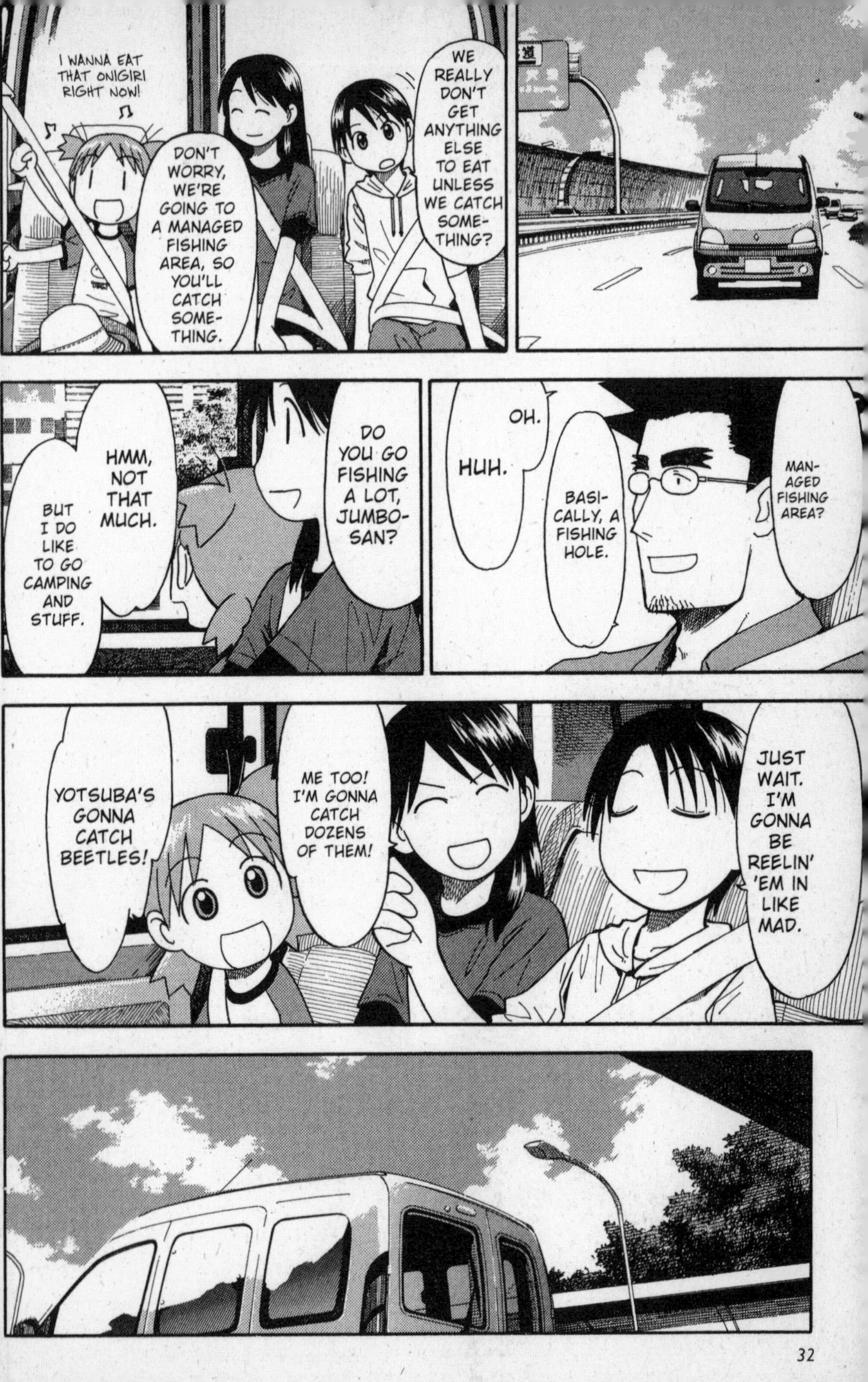
WE REALLY DON'T GET ANYTHING ELSE TO EAT UNLESS WE CATCH SOMETHING?
DON'T WORRY, WE'RE GOING TO A MANAGED FISHING AREA, SO YOU'LL CATCH SOMETHING.
I WANNA EAT THAT ONIGIRI RIGHT NOW!
MANAGED FISHING AREA?
OH.
BASICALLY, A FISHING HOLE.
HUH.
DO YOU GO FISHING A LOT, JUMBO-SAN?
HMM, NOT THAT MUCH.
BUT I DO LIKE TO GO CAMPING AND STUFF.
JUST WAIT. I'M GONNA BE REELIN' 'EM IN LIKE MAD.
ME TOO! I'M GONNA CATCH DOZENS OF THEM!
YOTSUBA'S GONNA CATCH BEETLES!

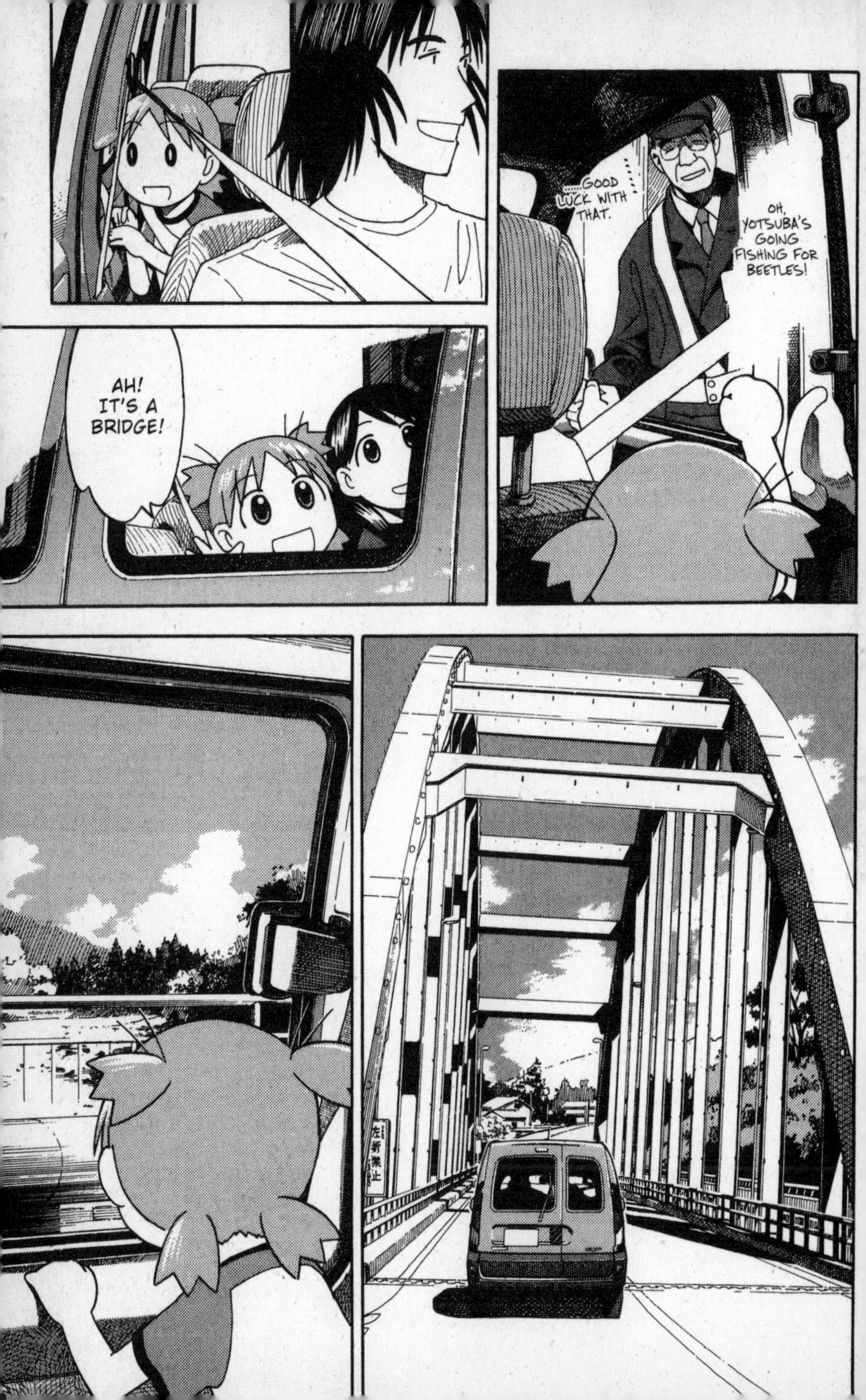
OH, YOTSUBA'S GOING FISHING FOR BEETLES!
......GOOD LUCK WITH THAT.
AH! IT'S A BRIDGE!
左折禁止

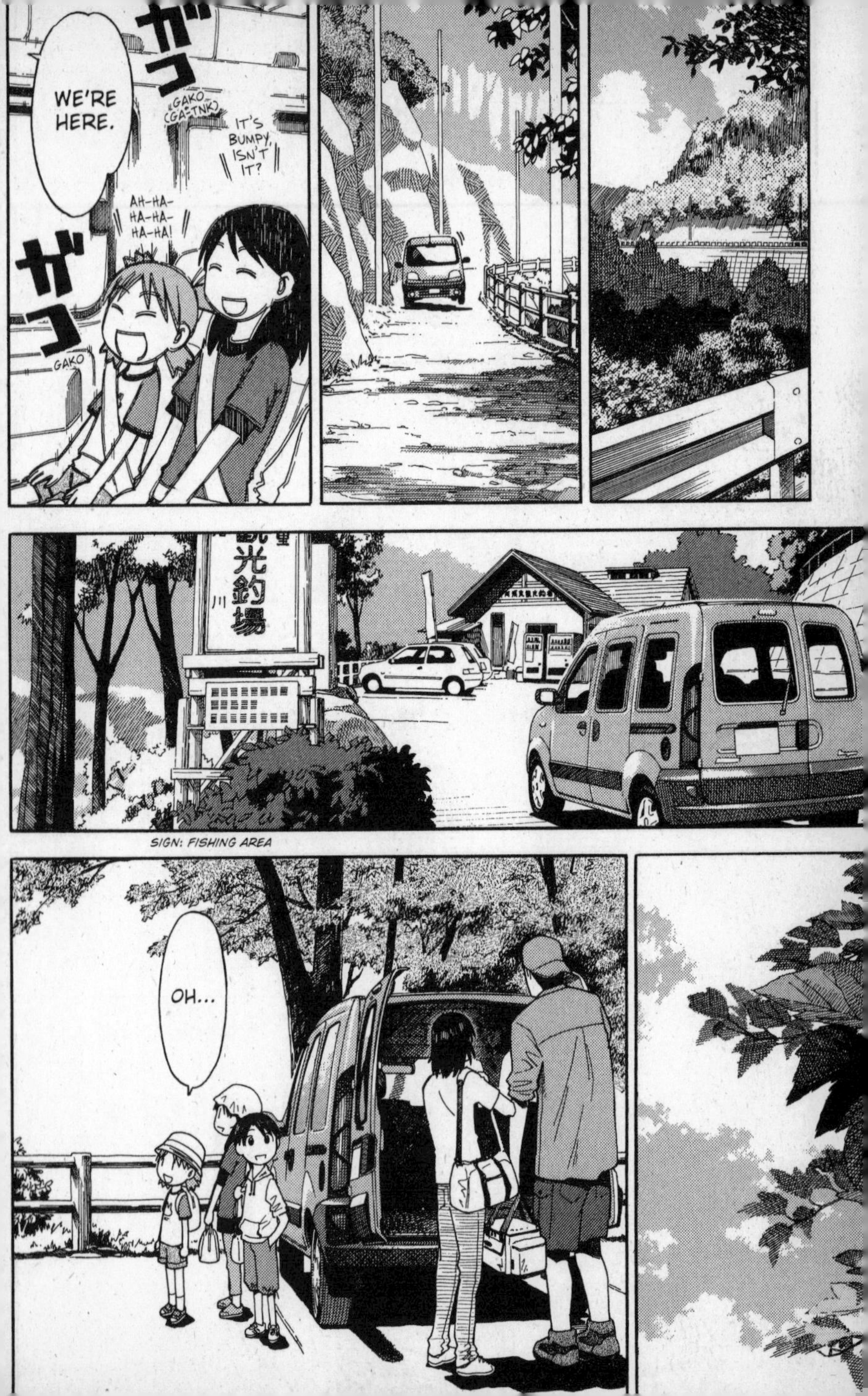
ガコ
GAKO (GA-TNK)
IT'S BUMPY, ISN'T IT?
WE'RE HERE.
AH-HA-HA-HA-HA-HA!
ガコ
GAKO
観光釣場
SIGN: FISHING AREA
OH...

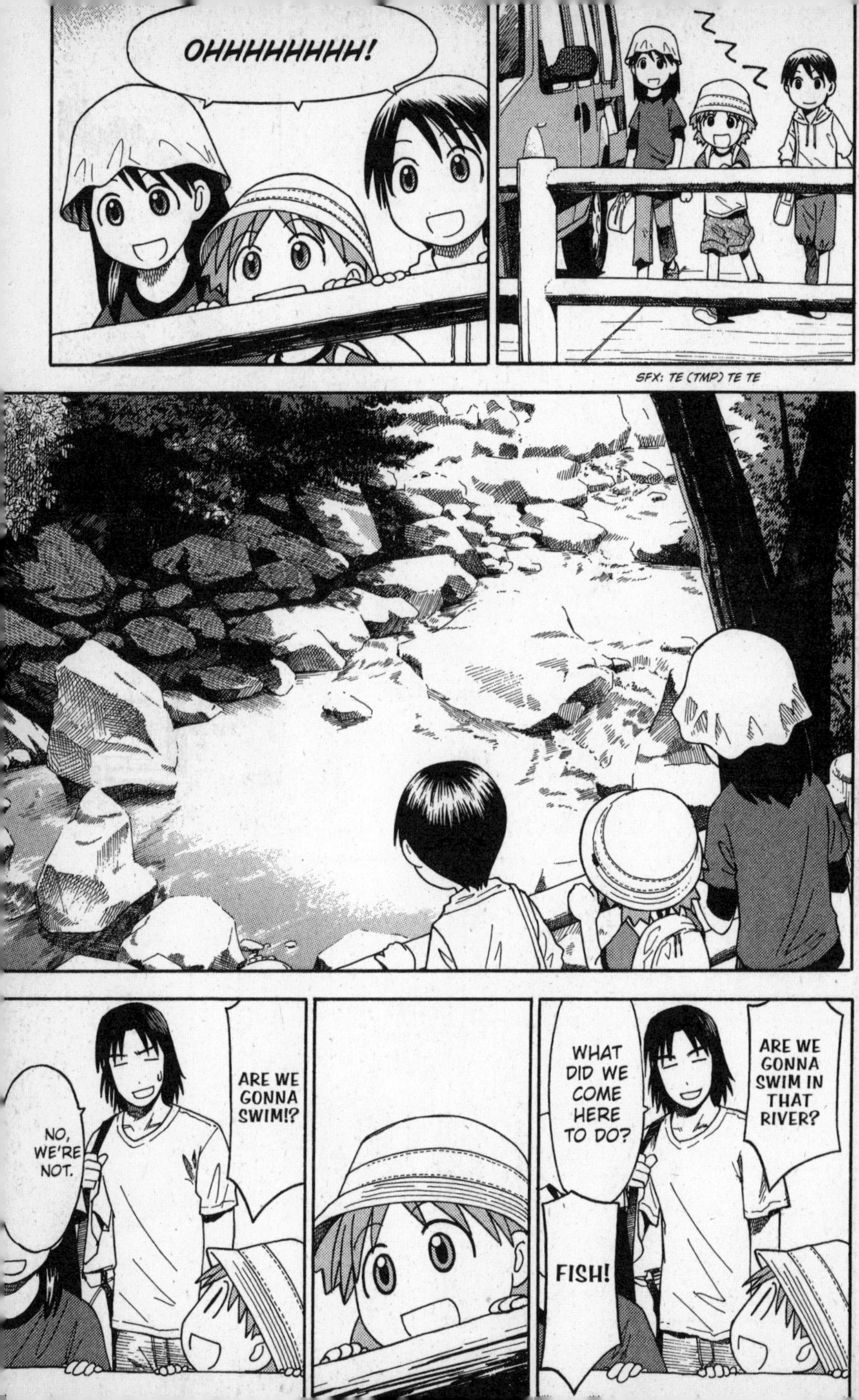
SFX: TE (TMP) TE TE
OHHHHHHHH!
ARE WE GONNA SWIM IN THAT RIVER?
WHAT DID WE COME HERE TO DO?
FISH!
ARE WE GONNA SWIM!?
NO, WE'RE NOT.

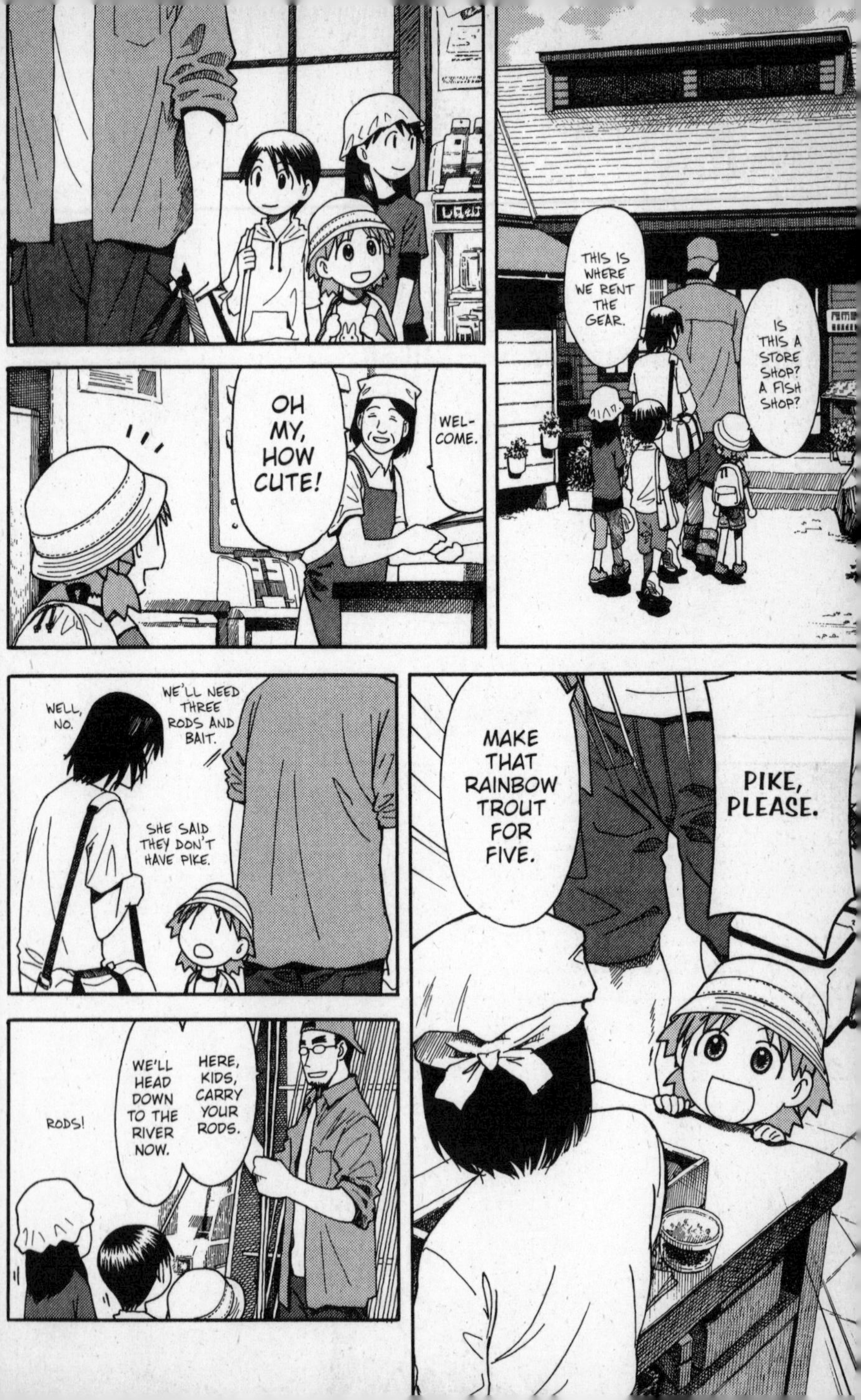
THIS IS WHERE WE RENT THE GEAR.
IS THIS A STORE SHOP? A FISH SHOP?
WEL-COME.
OH MY, HOW CUTE!
PIKE, PLEASE.
MAKE THAT RAINBOW TROUT FOR FIVE.
WE'LL NEED THREE RODS AND BAIT.
WELL, NO.
SHE SAID THEY DON'T HAVE PIKE.
HERE, KIDS, CARRY YOUR RODS.
WE'LL HEAD DOWN TO THE RIVER NOW.
RODS!

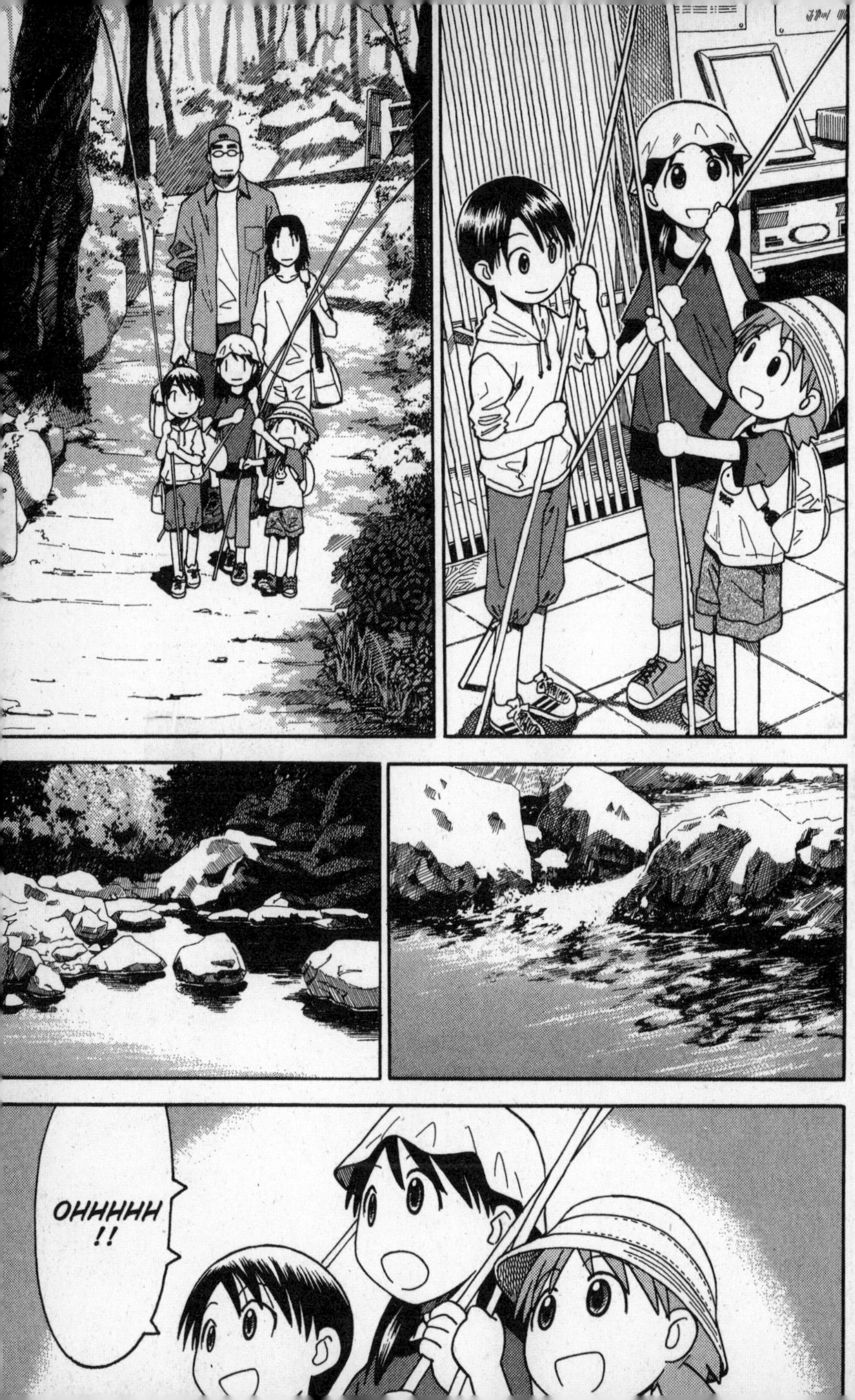
OHHHHH
!!

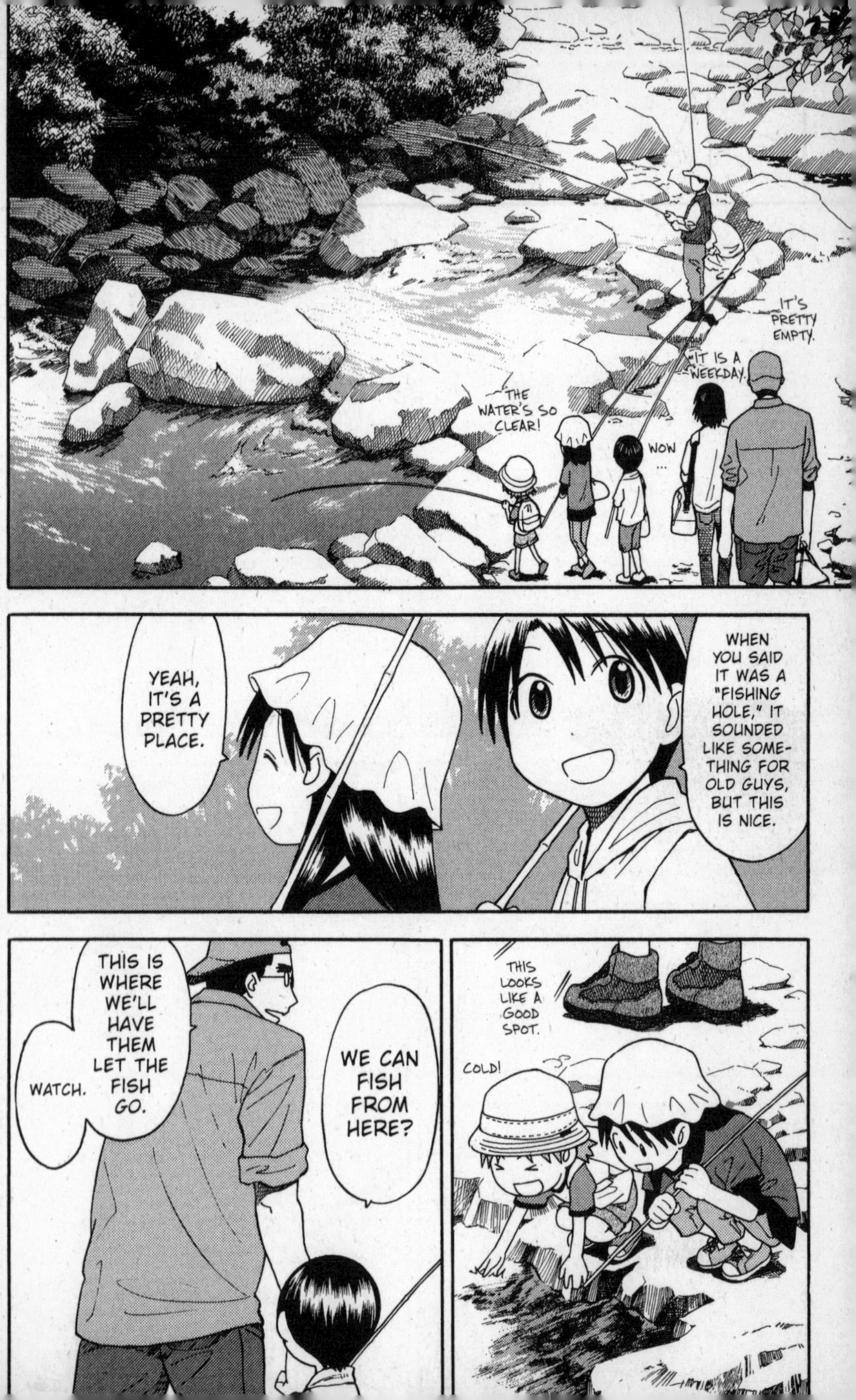
IT'S PRETTY EMPTY.
IT IS A WEEKDAY.
WOW ...
THE WATER'S SO CLEAR!
WHEN YOU SAID IT WAS A "FISHING HOLE," IT SOUNDED LIKE SOME-THING FOR OLD GUYS, BUT THIS IS NICE.
YEAH, IT'S A PRETTY PLACE.
THIS LOOKS LIKE A GOOD SPOT.
COLD!
WE CAN FISH FROM HERE?
THIS IS WHERE WE'LL HAVE THEM LET THE FISH GO.
WATCH.

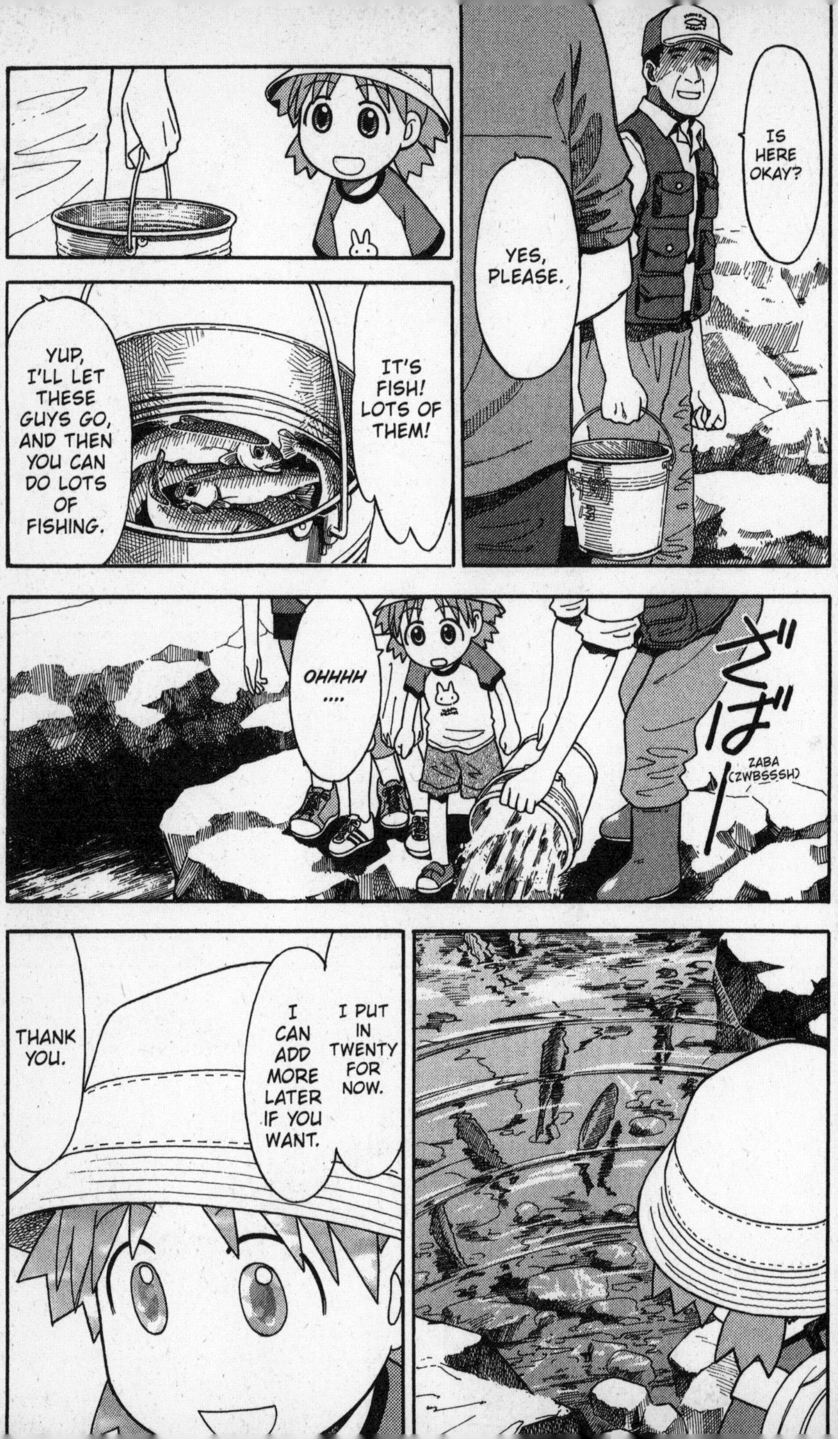
IS HERE OKAY?
YES, PLEASE.
IT'S FISH! LOTS OF THEM!
YUP, I'LL LET THESE GUYS GO, AND THEN YOU CAN DO LOTS OF FISHING.
ざばー
ZABA (ZWBSSSH)
OHHHH ....
I PUT IN TWENTY FOR NOW.
I CAN ADD MORE LATER IF YOU WANT.
THANK YOU.

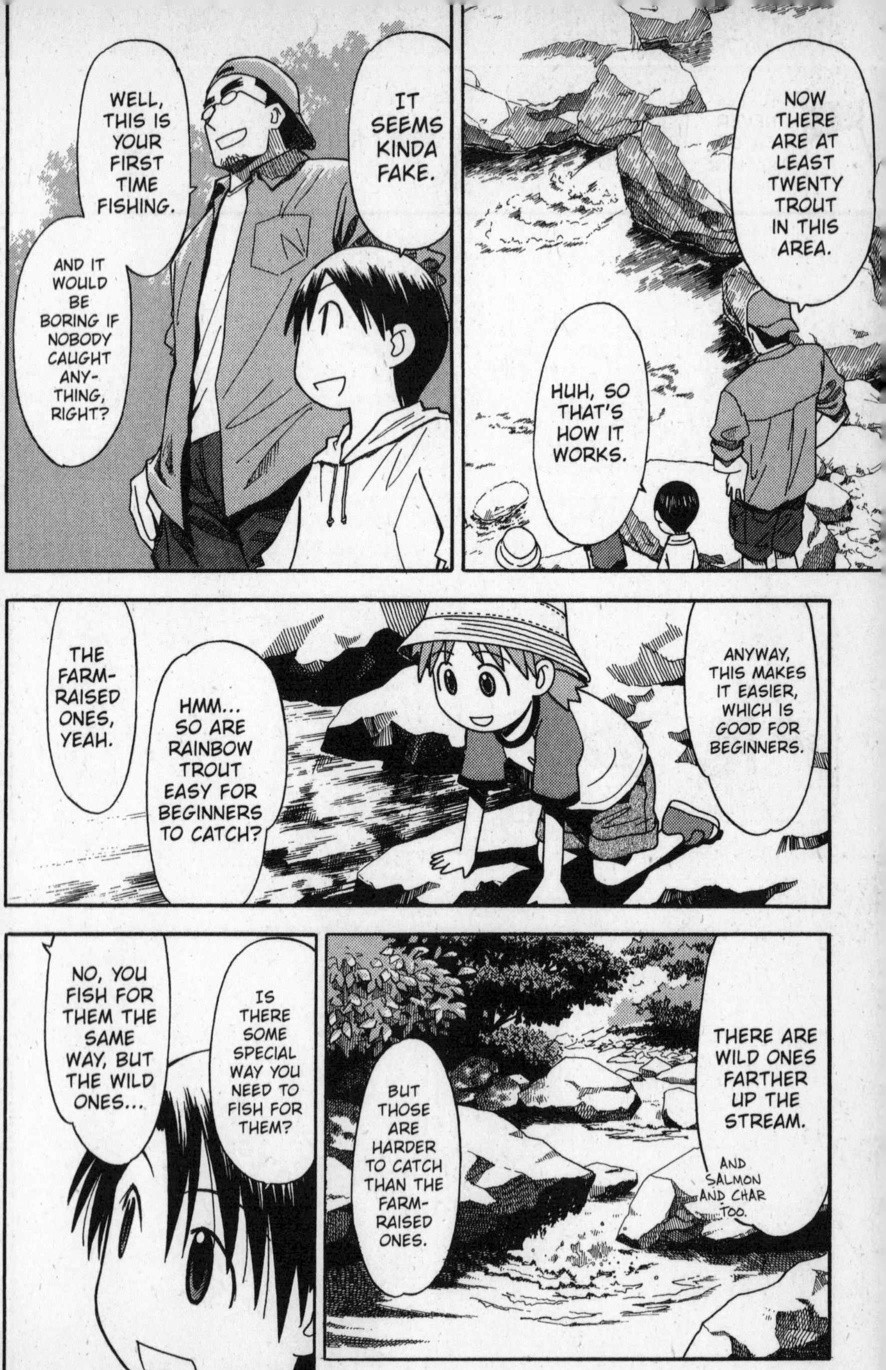
NOW THERE ARE AT LEAST TWENTY TROUT IN THIS AREA.
HUH, SO THAT'S HOW IT WORKS.
IT SEEMS KINDA FAKE.
WELL, THIS IS YOUR FIRST TIME FISHING.
AND IT WOULD BE BORING IF NOBODY CAUGHT ANY-THING, RIGHT?
ANYWAY, THIS MAKES IT EASIER, WHICH IS GOOD FOR BEGINNERS.
HMM... SO ARE RAINBOW TROUT EASY FOR BEGINNERS TO CATCH?
THE FARM-RAISED ONES, YEAH.
THERE ARE WILD ONES FARTHER UP THE STREAM.
AND SALMON AND CHAR TOO.
BUT THOSE ARE HARDER TO CATCH THAN THE FARM-RAISED ONES.
IS THERE SOME SPECIAL WAY YOU NEED TO FISH FOR THEM?
NO, YOU FISH FOR THEM THE SAME WAY, BUT THE WILD ONES...

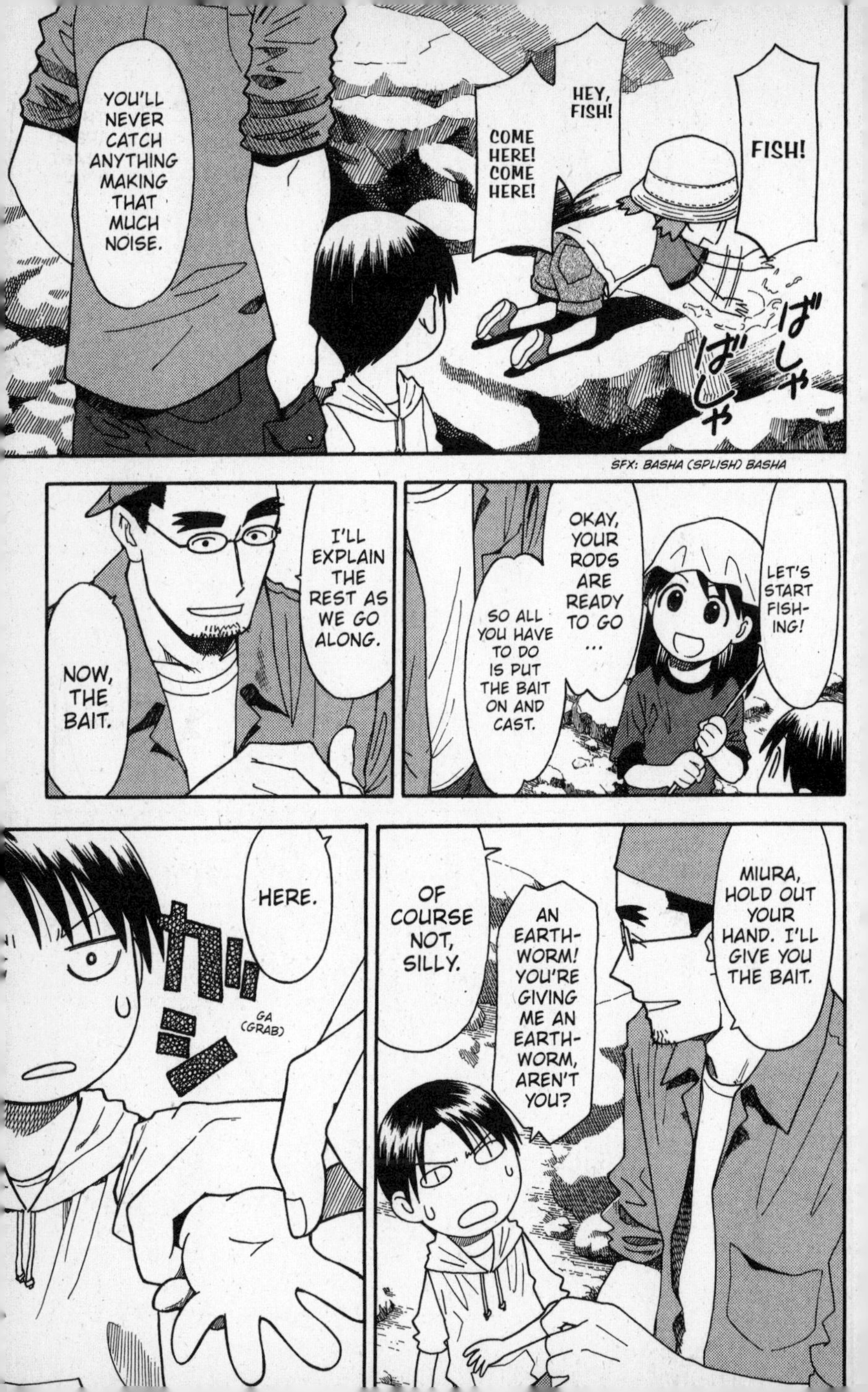
FISH!
HEY, FISH!
COME HERE! COME HERE!
YOU'LL NEVER CATCH ANYTHING MAKING THAT MUCH NOISE.
ばしゃばしゃ
SFX: BASHA (SPLISH) BASHA
LET'S START FISHING!
OKAY, YOUR RODS ARE READY TO GO ...
SO ALL YOU HAVE TO DO IS PUT THE BAIT ON AND CAST.
I'LL EXPLAIN THE REST AS WE GO ALONG.
NOW, THE BAIT.
MIURA, HOLD OUT YOUR HAND. I'LL GIVE YOU THE BAIT.
AN EARTHWORM! YOU'RE GIVING ME AN EARTHWORM, AREN'T YOU?
OF COURSE NOT, SILLY.
HERE.
GA (GRAB)

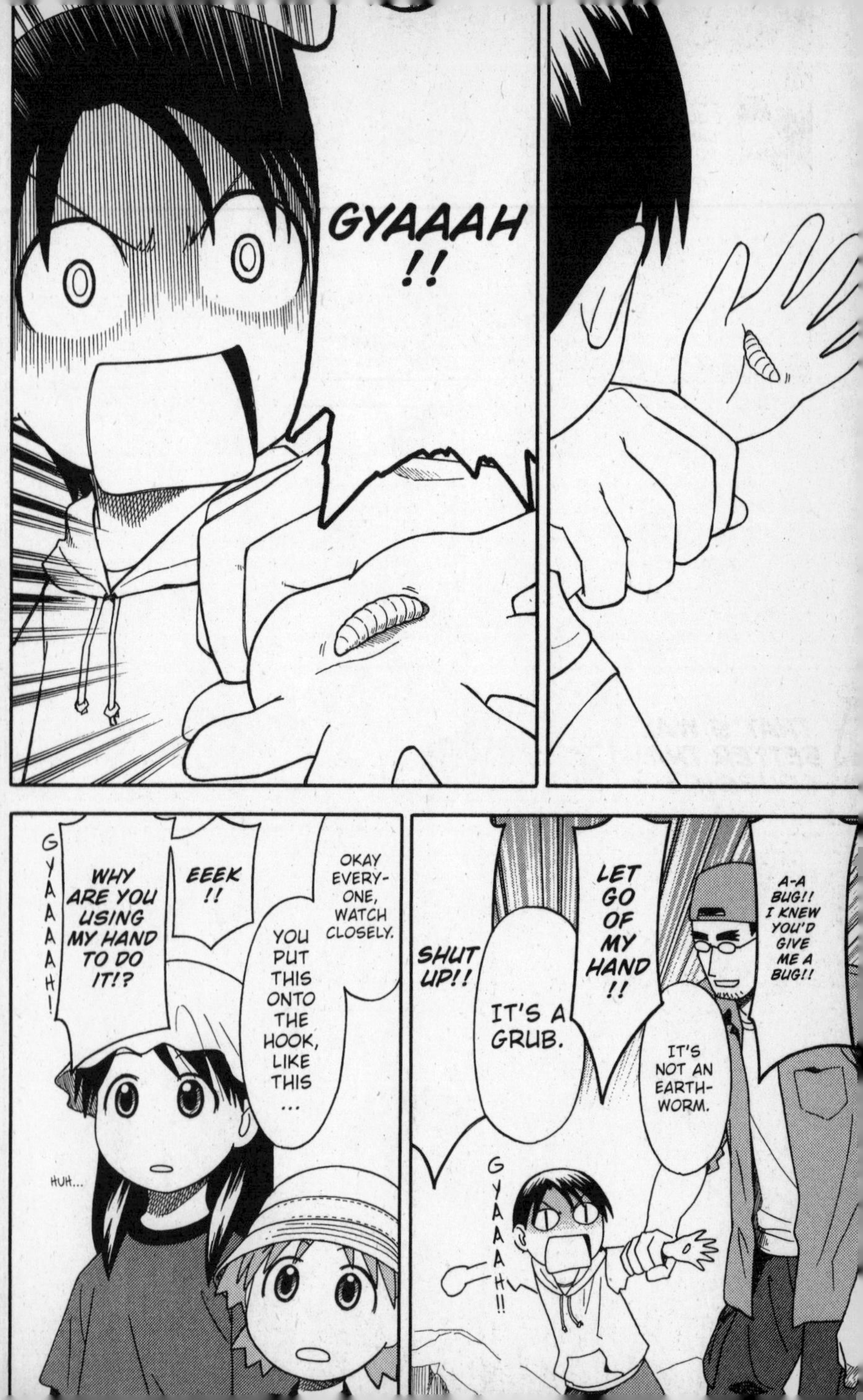
GYAAAH !!
A-A BUG!! I KNEW YOU'D GIVE ME A BUG!!
IT'S NOT AN EARTH-WORM.
LET GO OF MY HAND!!
IT'S A GRUB.
SHUT UP!!
GYAAAAH!!
OKAY EVERY-ONE, WATCH CLOSELY.
YOU PUT THIS ONTO THE HOOK, LIKE THIS...
EEEK!!
WHY ARE YOU USING MY HAND TO DO IT!?
GYAAAAAH!
HUH...

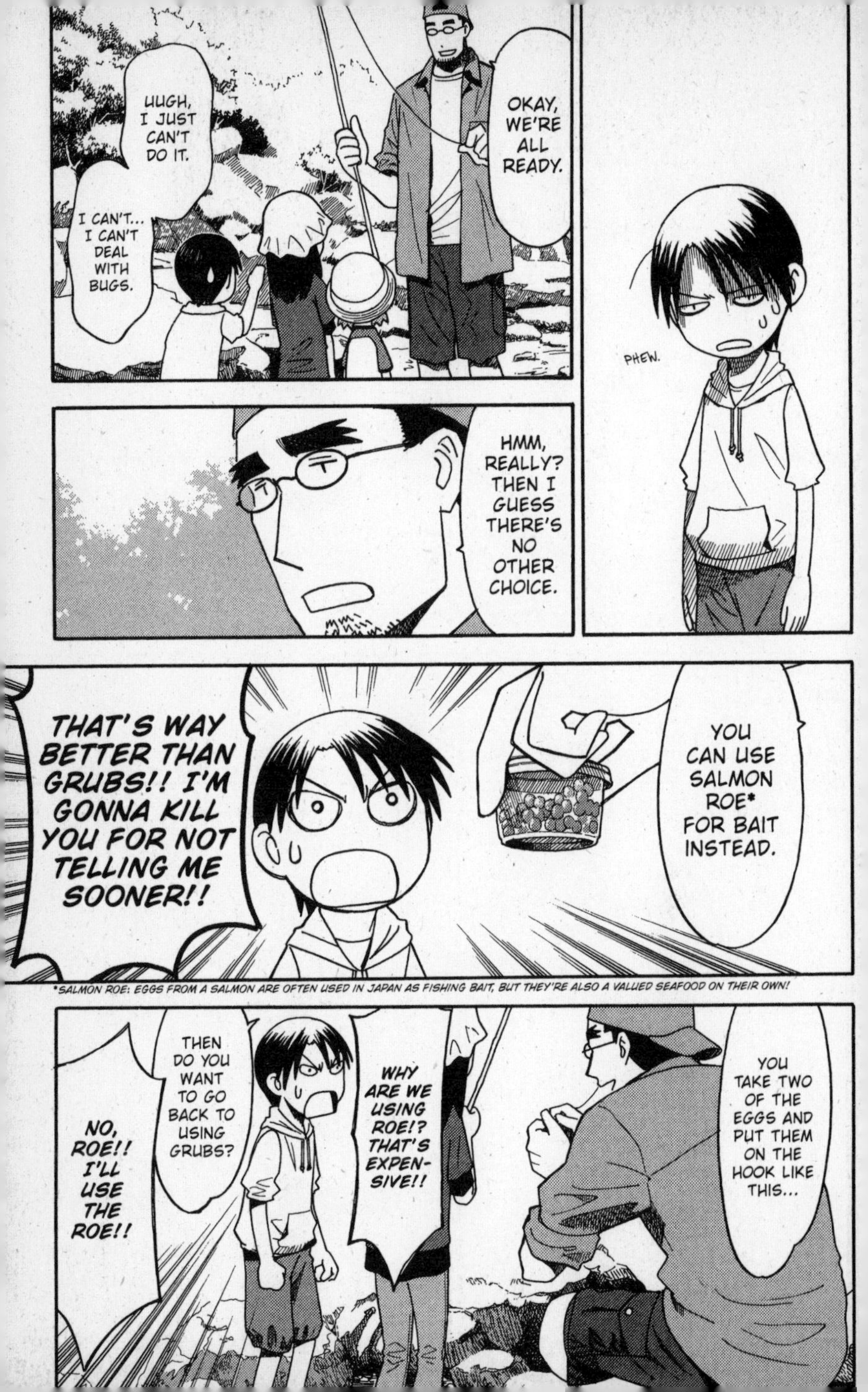
PHEW.
OKAY, WE'RE ALL READY.
UUGH, I JUST CAN'T DO IT.
I CAN'T... I CAN'T DEAL WITH BUGS.
HMM, REALLY? THEN I GUESS THERE'S NO OTHER CHOICE.
YOU CAN USE SALMON ROE* FOR BAIT INSTEAD.
THAT'S WAY BETTER THAN GRUBS!! I'M GONNA KILL YOU FOR NOT TELLING ME SOONER!!
YOU TAKE TWO OF THE EGGS AND PUT THEM ON THE HOOK LIKE THIS...
WHY ARE WE USING ROE!? THAT'S EXPEN-SIVE!!
THEN DO YOU WANT TO GO BACK TO USING GRUBS?
NO, ROE!! I'LL USE THE ROE!!

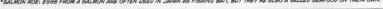

*SALMON ROE: EGGS FROM A SALMON ARE OFTEN USED IN JAPAN AS FISHING BAIT, BUT THEY'RE ALSO A VALUED SEAFOOD ON THEIR OWN!

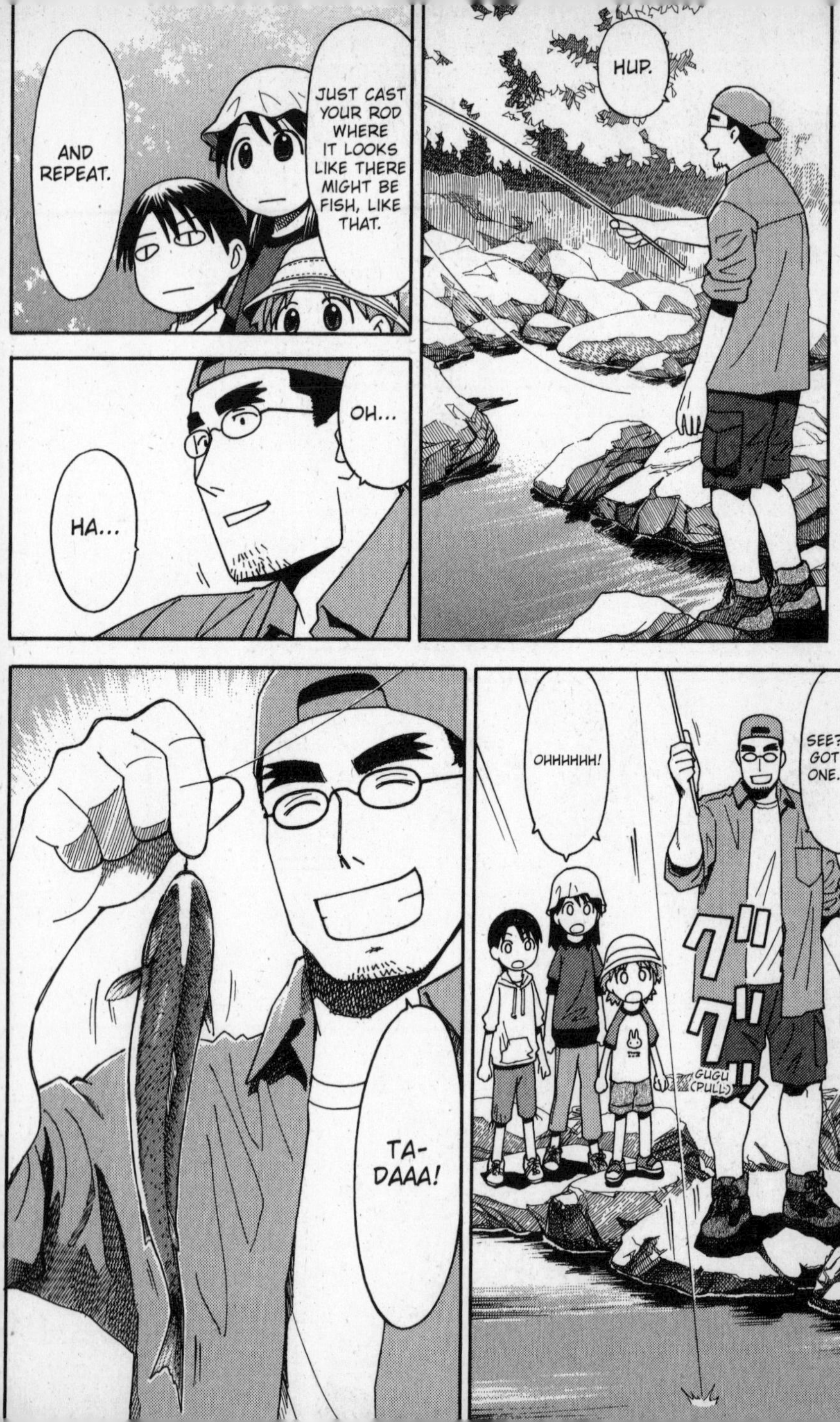
HUP.
JUST CAST YOUR ROD WHERE IT LOOKS LIKE THERE MIGHT BE FISH, LIKE THAT.
AND REPEAT.
OH...
HA...
SEE? GOT ONE.
OHHHHHH!
GUGU (PULL)
TA-DAAA!

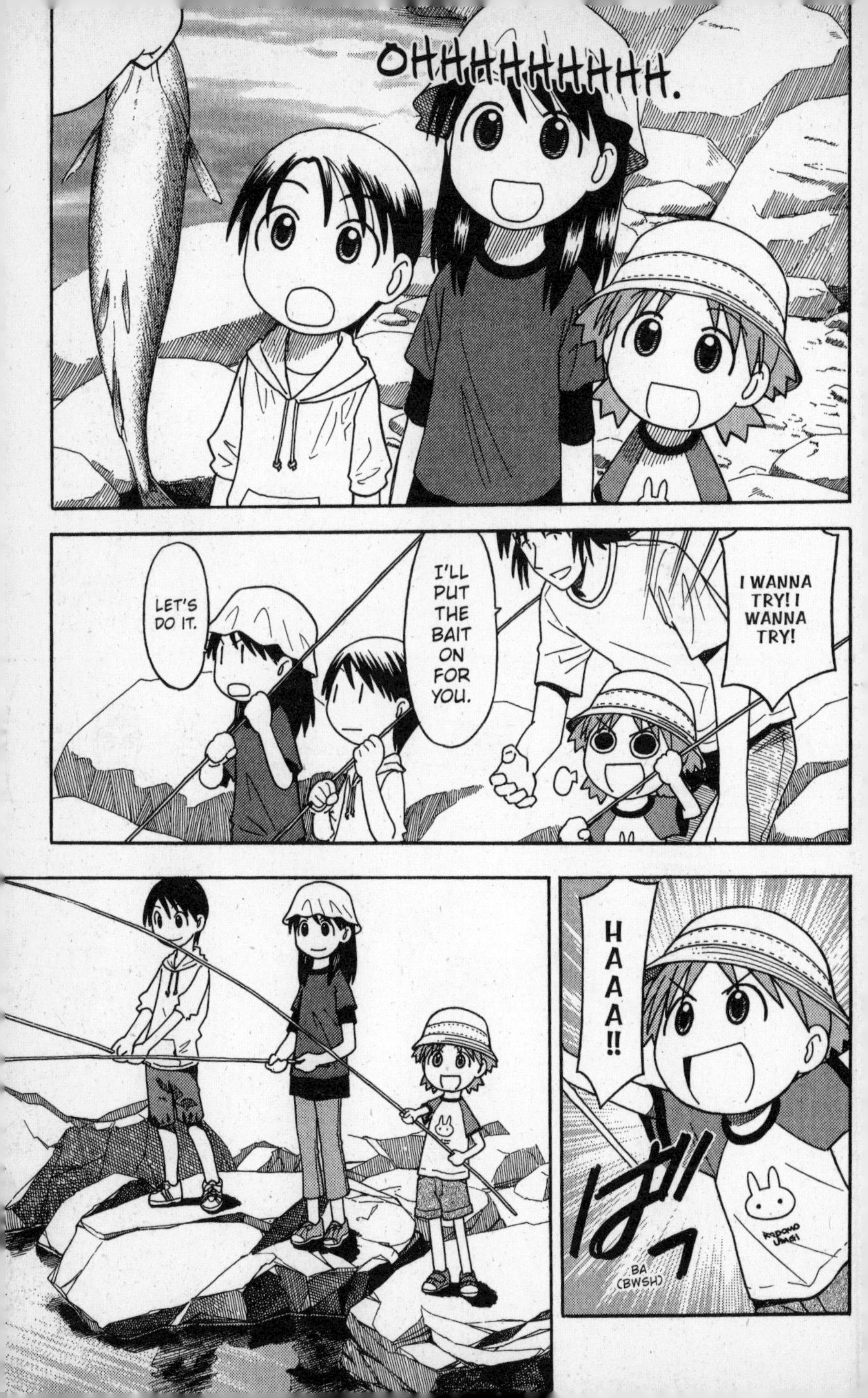
OHHHHHHHHH.
I WANNA TRY!! I WANNA TRY!
I'LL PUT THE BAIT ON FOR YOU.
LET'S DO IT.
HAAAA!!
ばっ
BA (BWSH)

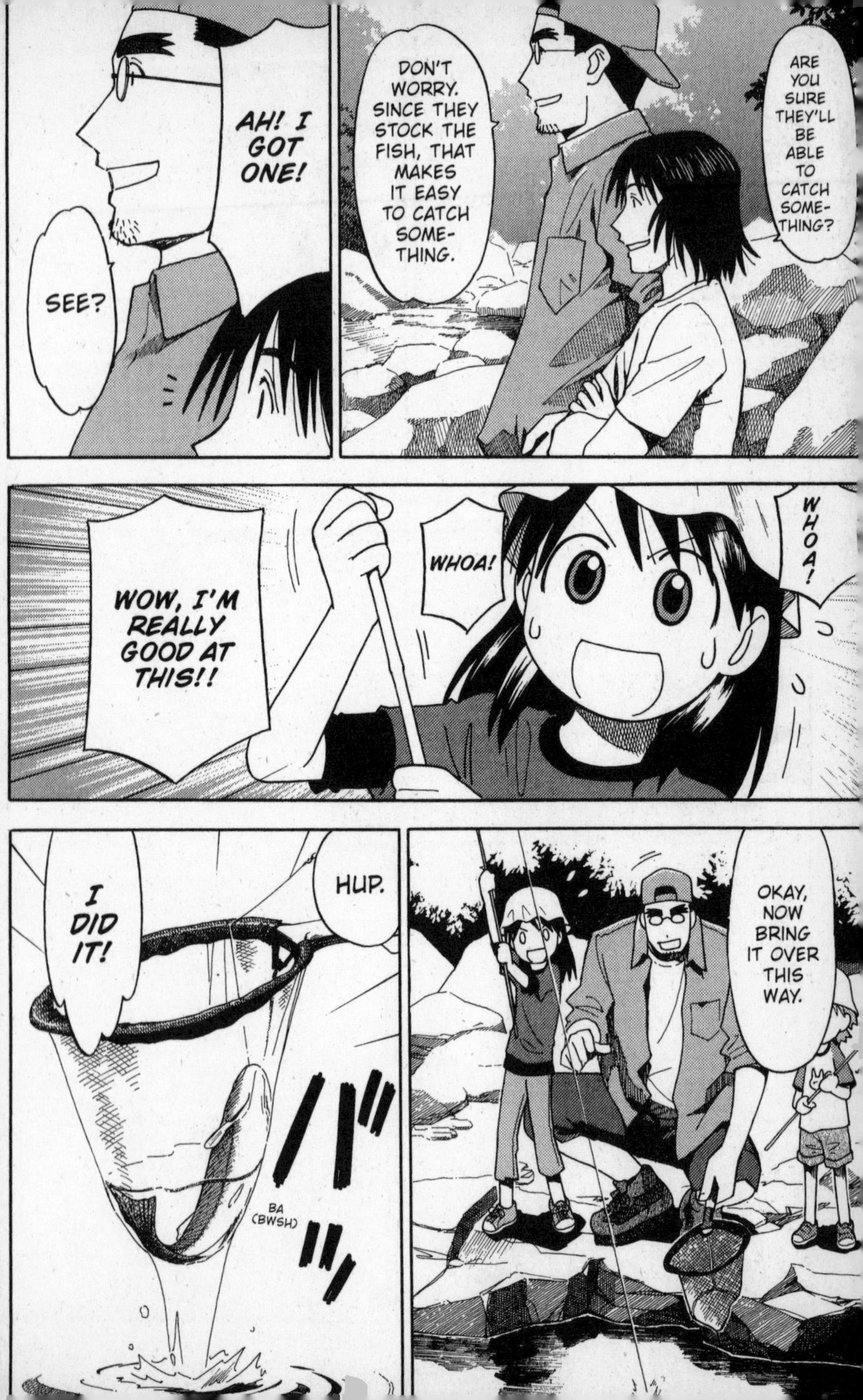
ARE YOU SURE THEY'LL BE ABLE TO CATCH SOME-THING?
DON'T WORRY. SINCE THEY STOCK THE FISH, THAT MAKES IT EASY TO CATCH SOME-THING.
AH! I GOT ONE!
SEE?
WHOA!
WHOA!
WOW, I'M REALLY GOOD AT THIS!!
OKAY, NOW BRING IT OVER THIS WAY.
HUP.
I DID IT!
BA (BWSH)

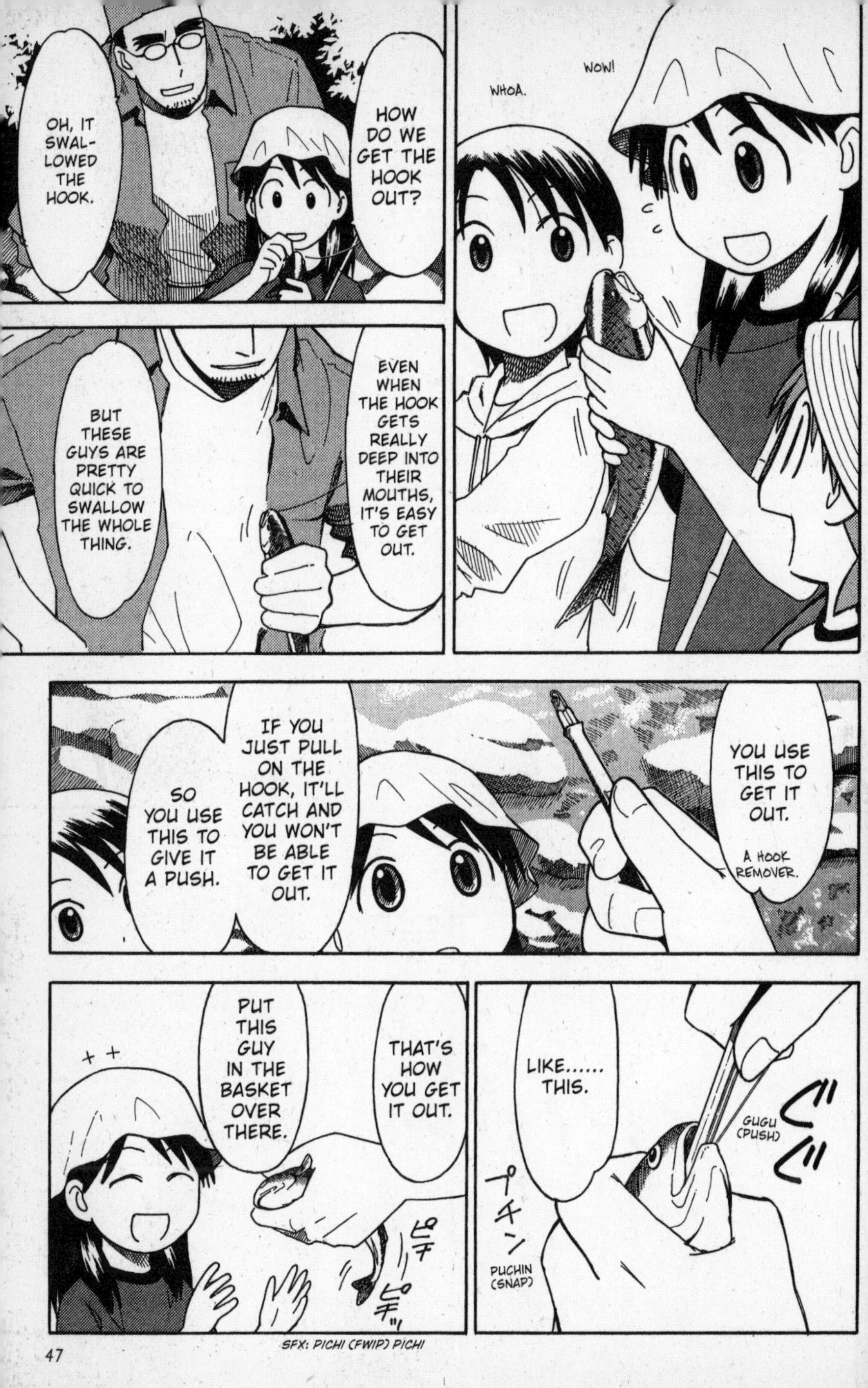
WOW!
WHOA.
HOW DO WE GET THE HOOK OUT?
OH, IT SWAL- LOWED THE HOOK.
EVEN WHEN THE HOOK GETS REALLY DEEP INTO THEIR MOUTHS, IT'S EASY TO GET OUT.
BUT THESE GUYS ARE PRETTY QUICK TO SWALLOW THE WHOLE THING.
YOU USE THIS TO GET IT OUT.
A HOOK REMOVER.
IF YOU JUST PULL ON THE HOOK, IT'LL CATCH AND YOU WON'T BE ABLE TO GET IT OUT.
SO YOU USE THIS TO GIVE IT A PUSH.
LIKE...... THIS.
GUGU (PUSH)
PUCHIN (SNAP)
THAT'S HOW YOU GET IT OUT.
PUT THIS GUY IN THE BASKET OVER THERE.

SFX: PICHI (FWIP) PICHI

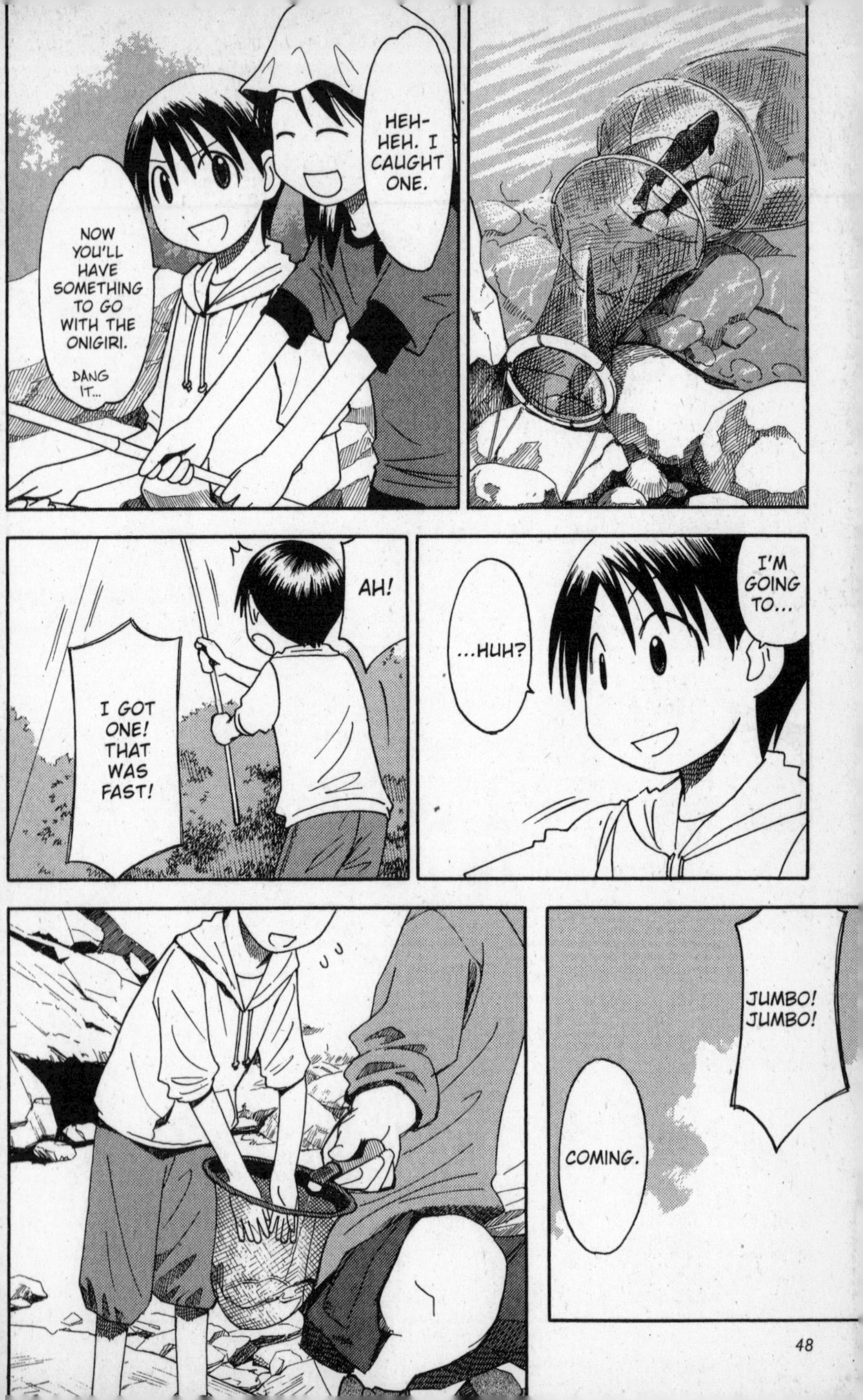
HEH-HEH. I CAUGHT ONE.
NOW YOU'LL HAVE SOMETHING TO GO WITH THE ONIGIRI.
DANG IT...
I'M GOING TO...
...HUH?
AH!
I GOT ONE! THAT WAS FAST!
JUMBO! JUMBO!
COMING.

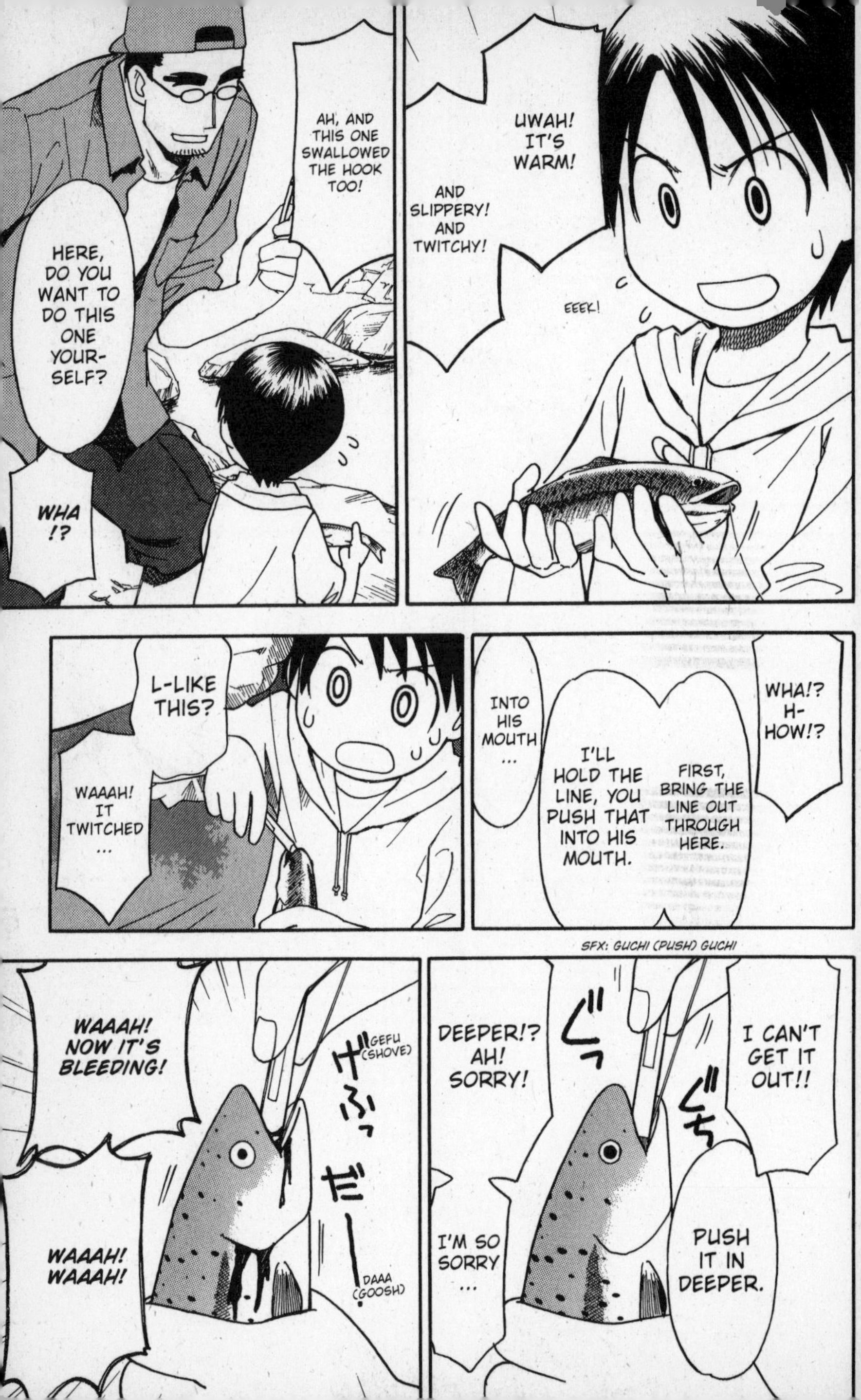
UWAH! IT'S WARM!
AND SLIPPERY! AND TWITCHY!
EEEK!
AH, AND THIS ONE SWALLOWED THE HOOK TOO!
HERE, DO YOU WANT TO DO THIS ONE YOURSELF?
WHA!?
WHA!? H-HOW!?
FIRST, BRING THE LINE OUT THROUGH HERE.
I'LL HOLD THE LINE, YOU PUSH THAT INTO HIS MOUTH.
INTO HIS MOUTH ...
L-LIKE THIS?
WAAAH! IT TWITCHED ...
SFX: GUCHI (PUSH) GUCHI
I CAN'T GET IT OUT!!
ぐっ
ぐち
PUSH IT IN DEEPER.
DEEPER!? AH! SORRY!
I'M SO SORRY ...
げふっ
GEFU (SHOVE)
WAAAH! NOW IT'S BLEEDING!
だー
DAAA (GOOSH)
WAAAH! WAAAH!

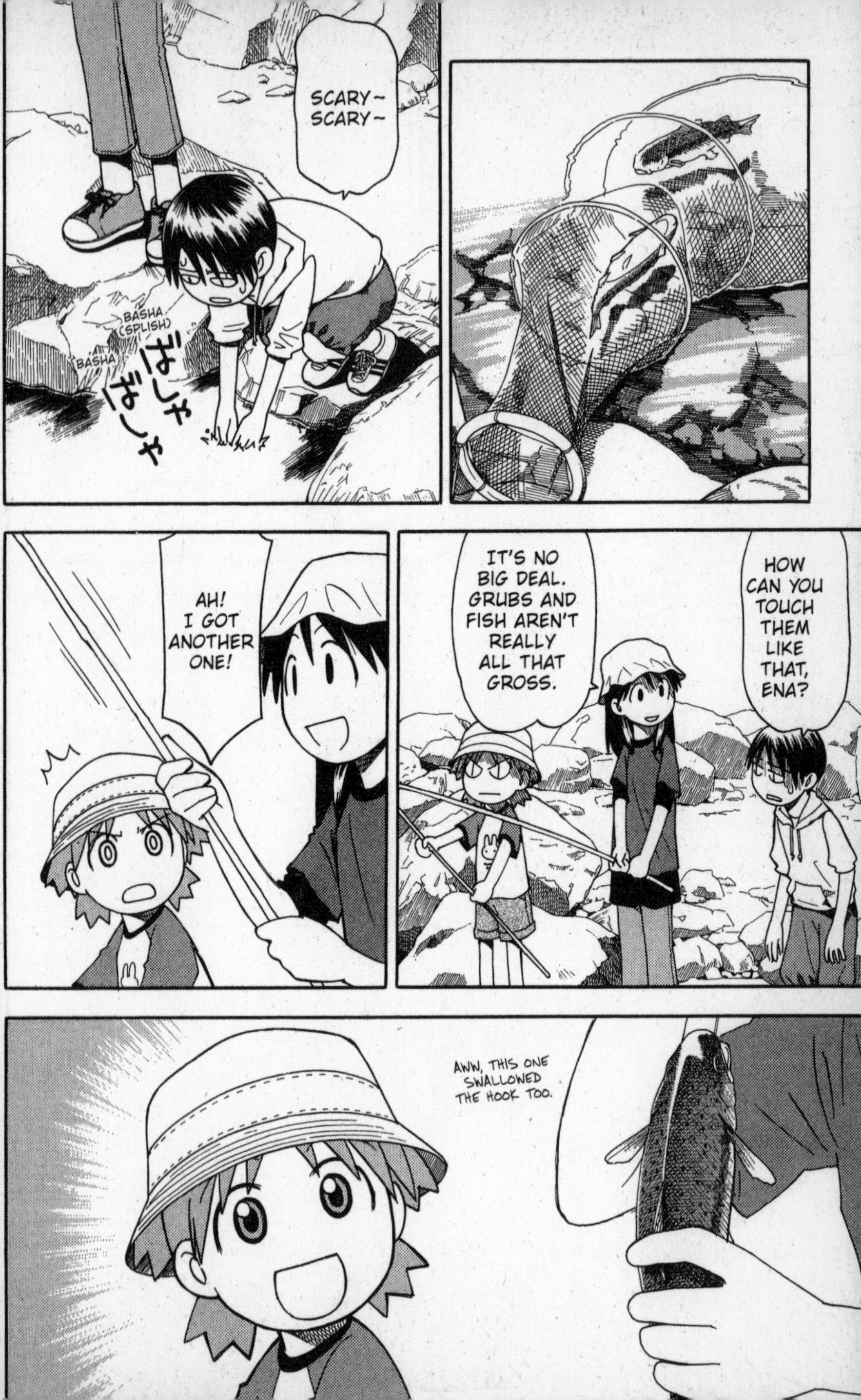
SCARY~ SCARY~
BASHA (SPLISH)
BASHA
ばしゃ ばしゃ
HOW CAN YOU TOUCH THEM LIKE THAT, ENA?
IT'S NO BIG DEAL. GRUBS AND FISH AREN'T REALLY ALL THAT GROSS.
AH! I GOT ANOTHER ONE!
AWW, THIS ONE SWALLOWED THE HOOK TOO.

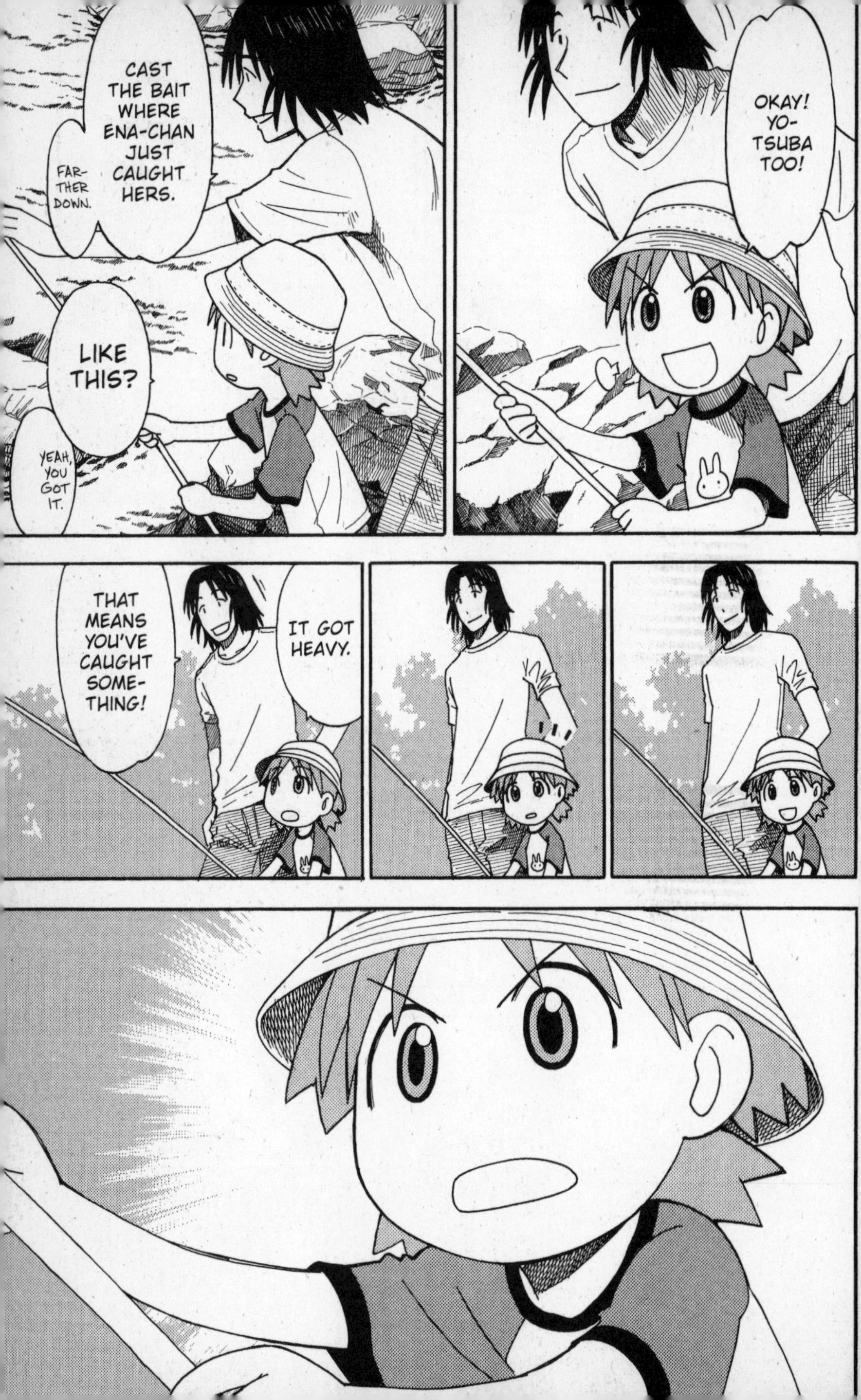
OKAY! YO-TSUBA TOO!
CAST THE BAIT WHERE ENA-CHAN JUST CAUGHT HERS.
FAR-THER DOWN.
LIKE THIS?
YEAH, YOU GOT IT.
IT GOT HEAVY.
THAT MEANS YOU'VE CAUGHT SOME-THING!

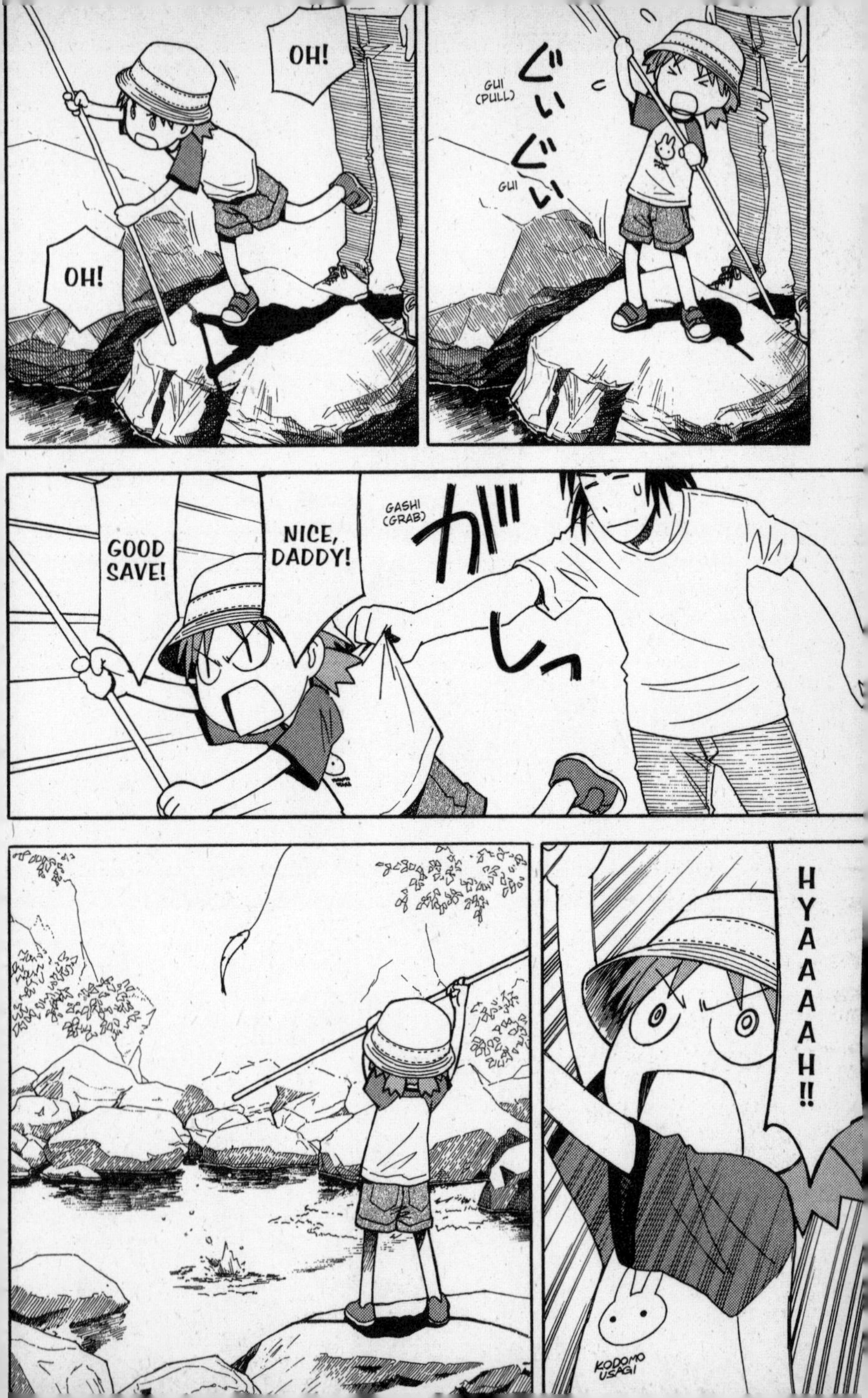
GUI (PULL)
ぐい
GUI
ぐい
OH!
OH!
GASHI (GRAB)
ガ
しっ
NICE, DADDY!
GOOD SAVE!
HYAAAAAH!!
KODOMO USAGI

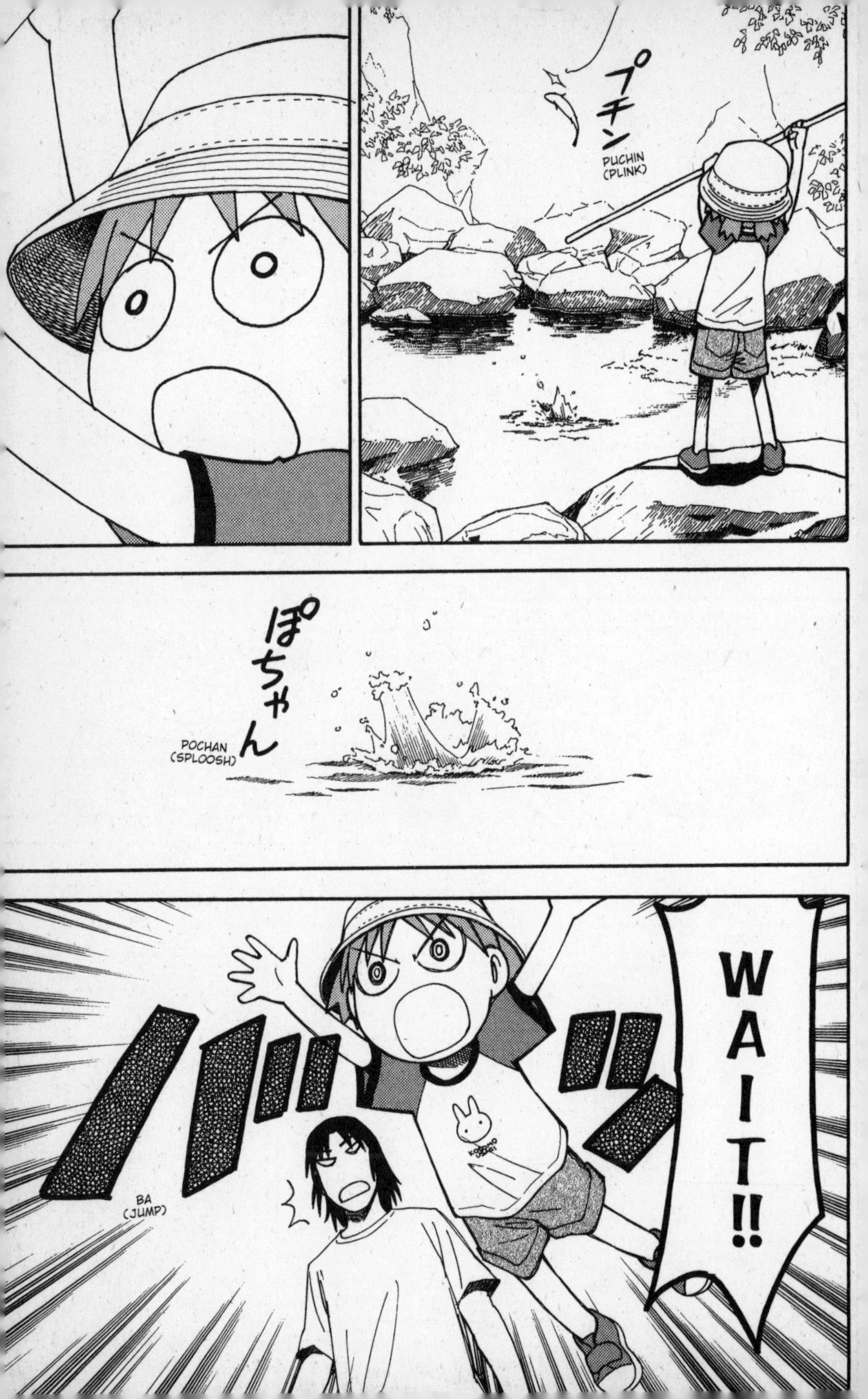
プチン
PUCHIN (PLINK)
ぽちゃん
POCHAN (SPLOOSH)
WAIT!!
BA (JUMP)

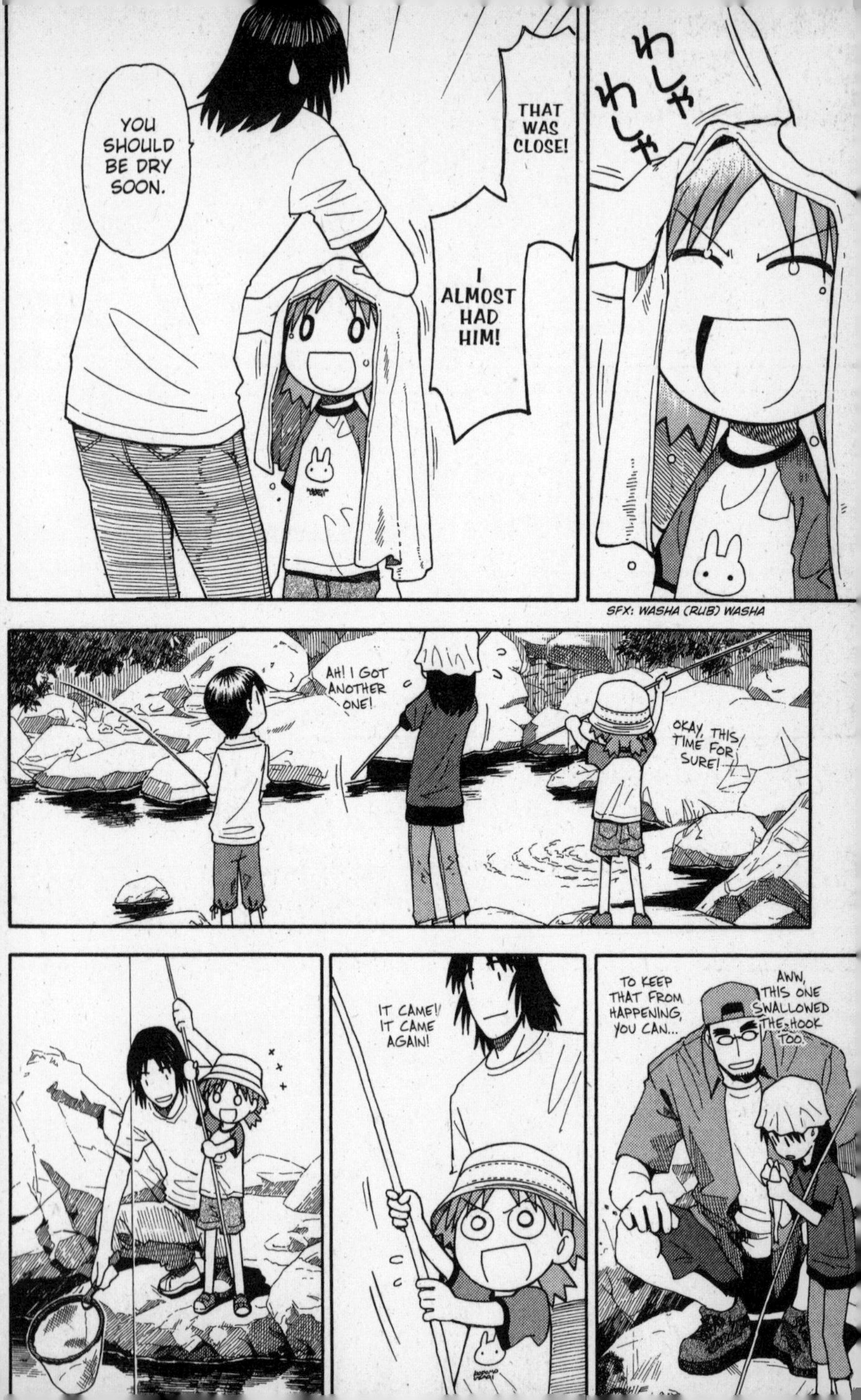
わしゃわしゃ
SFX: WASHA (RUB) WASHA
THAT WAS CLOSE!
I ALMOST HAD HIM!
YOU SHOULD BE DRY SOON.
OKAY, THIS TIME FOR SURE!
AH! I GOT ANOTHER ONE!
AWW, THIS ONE SWALLOWED THE HOOK TOO.
TO KEEP THAT FROM HAPPENING, YOU CAN...
IT CAME! IT CAME AGAIN!

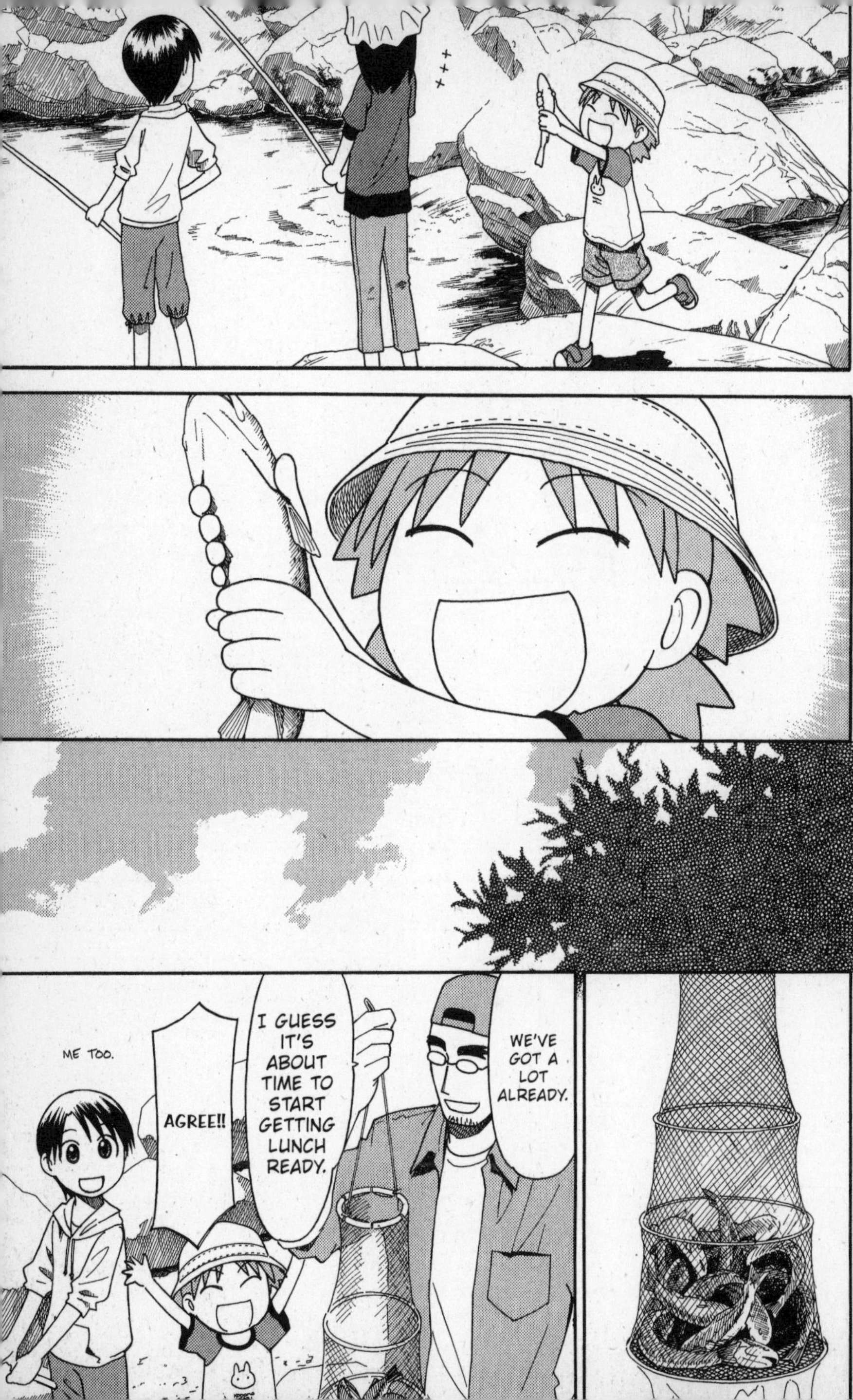
WE'VE GOT A LOT ALREADY.
I GUESS IT'S ABOUT TIME TO START GETTING LUNCH READY.
AGREE!!
ME TOO.

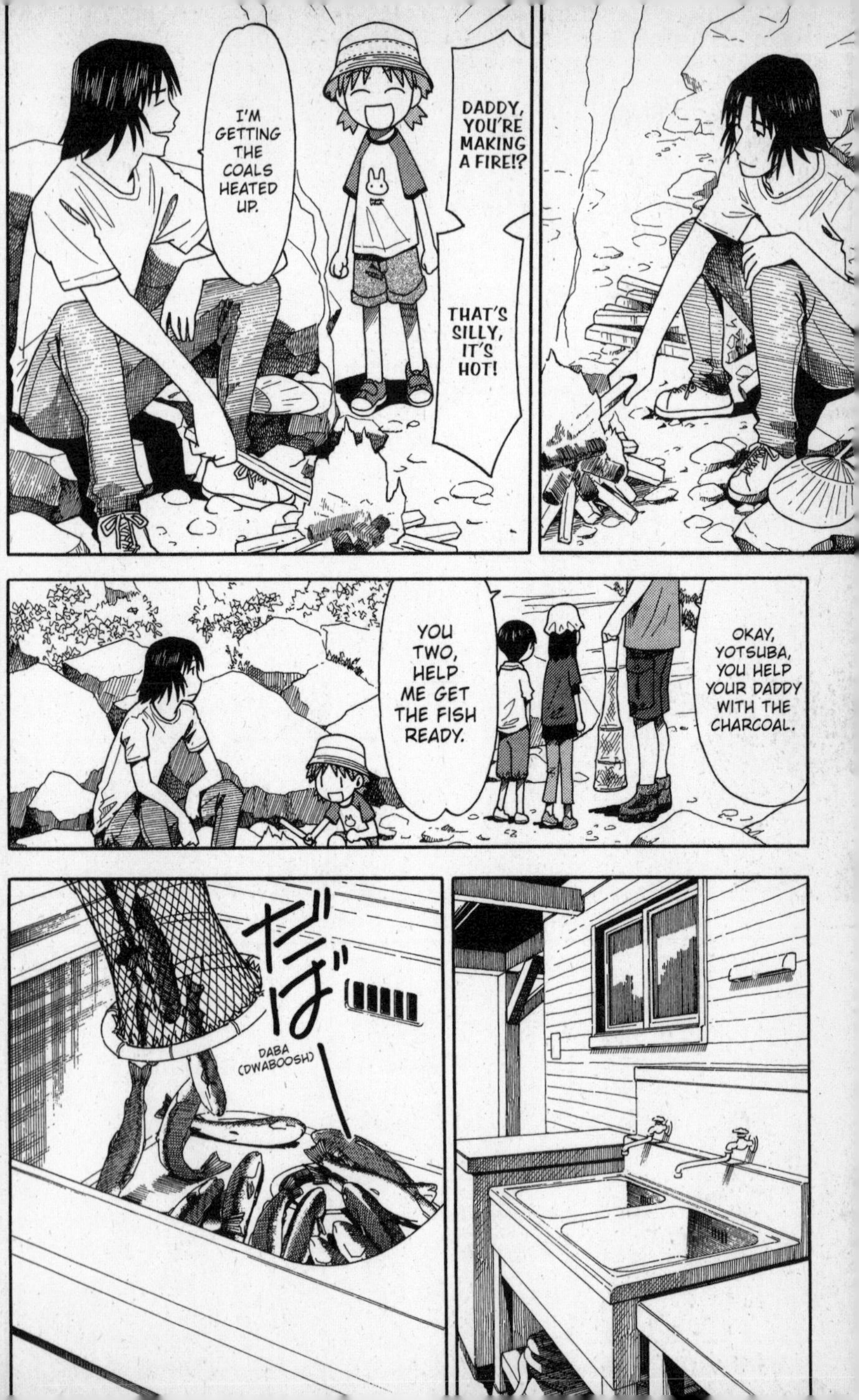
DADDY, YOU'RE MAKING A FIRE!?
THAT'S SILLY, IT'S HOT!
I'M GETTING THE COALS HEATED UP.
OKAY, YOTSUBA, YOU HELP YOUR DADDY WITH THE CHARCOAL.
YOU TWO, HELP ME GET THE FISH READY.
だば
DABA (DWABOOSH)

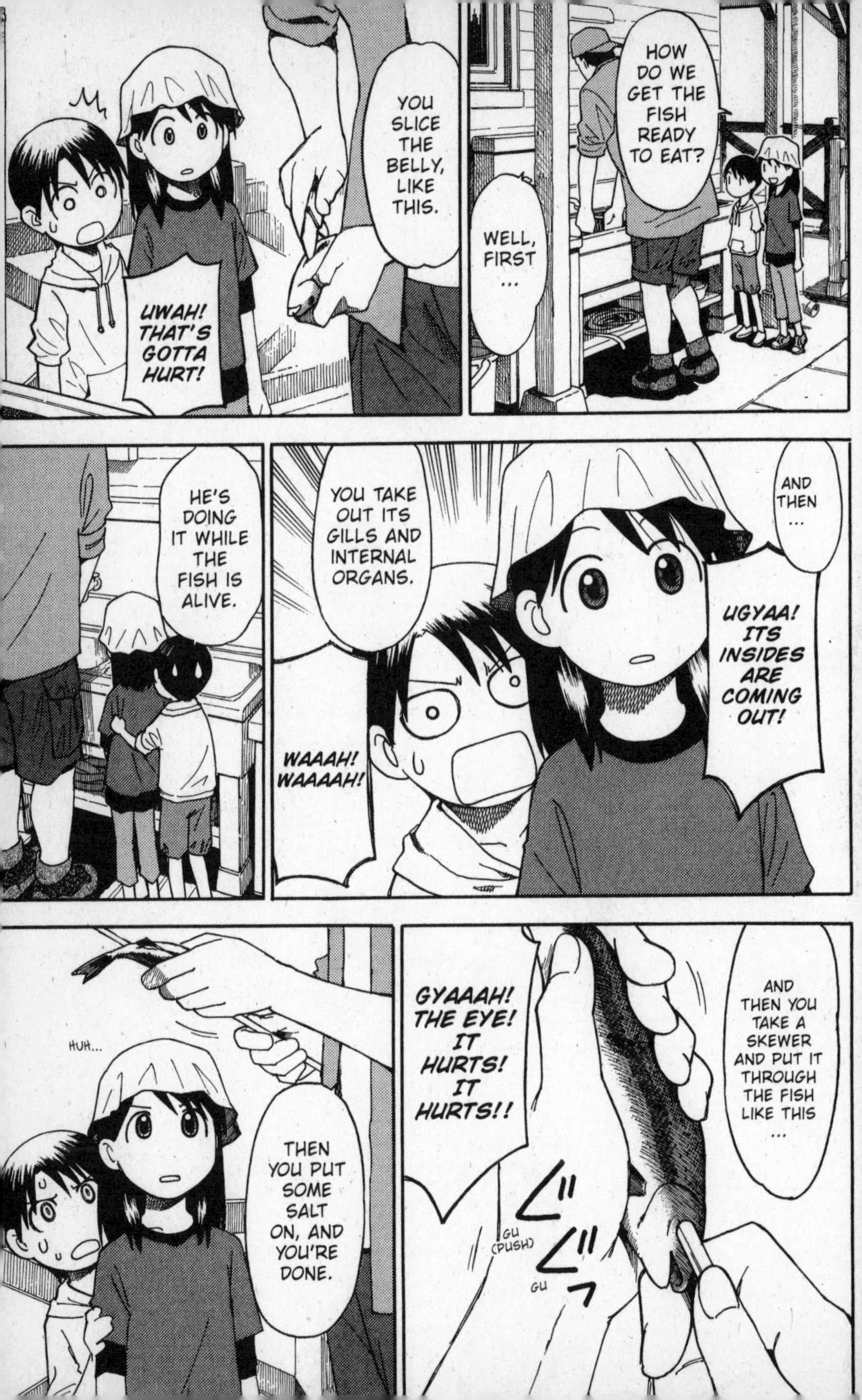
HOW DO WE GET THE FISH READY TO EAT?
WELL, FIRST ...
YOU SLICE THE BELLY, LIKE THIS.
UWAH! THAT'S GOTTA HURT!
AND THEN ...
UGYAA! ITS INSIDES ARE COMING OUT!
YOU TAKE OUT ITS GILLS AND INTERNAL ORGANS.
WAAAH! WAAAAH!
HE'S DOING IT WHILE THE FISH IS ALIVE.
AND THEN YOU TAKE A SKEWER AND PUT IT THROUGH THE FISH LIKE THIS ...
GYAAAH! THE EYE! IT HURTS! IT HURTS!!
GU (PUSH)
GU
THEN YOU PUT SOME SALT ON, AND YOU'RE DONE.
HUH...

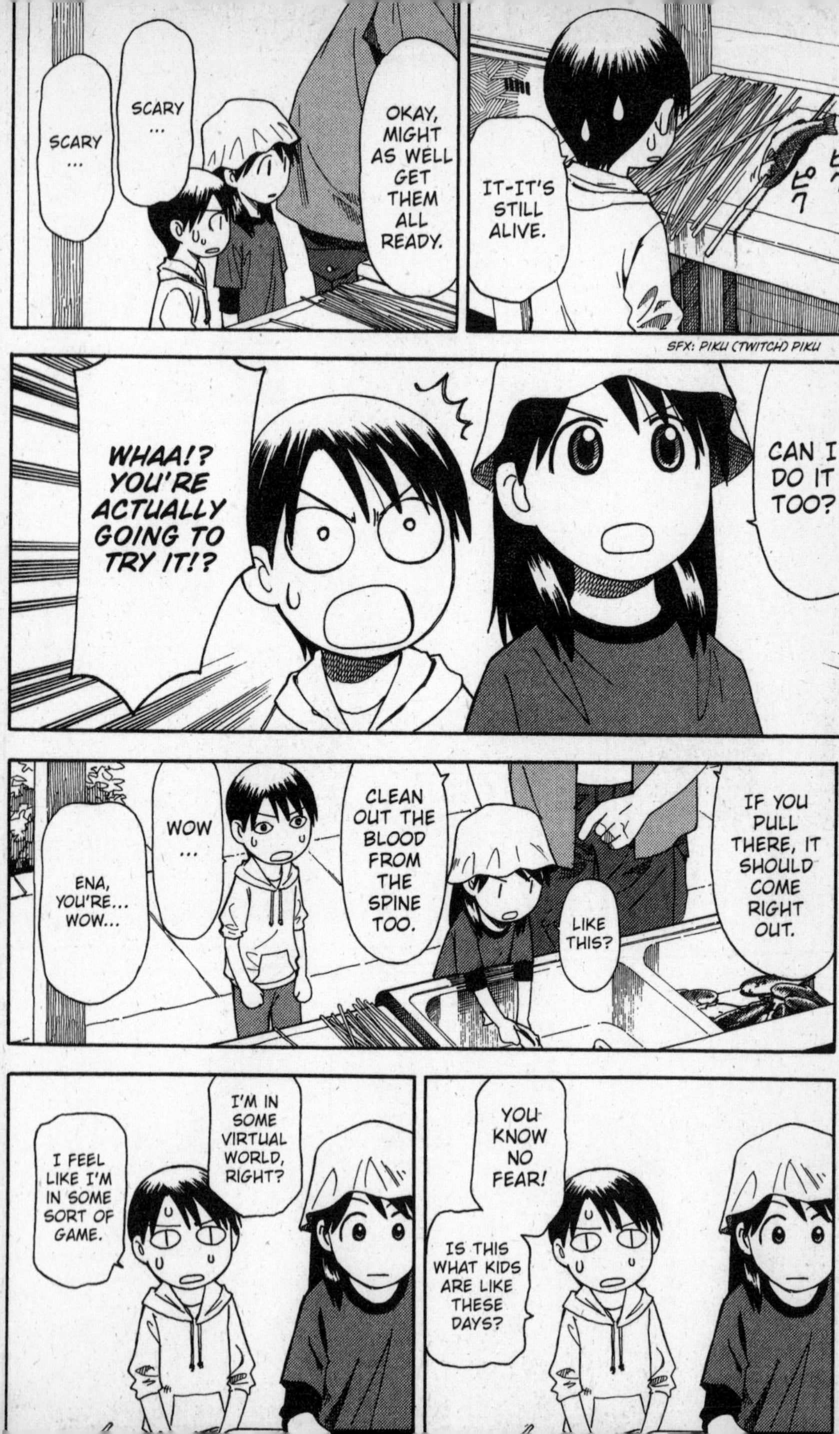
IT-IT'S STILL ALIVE.
ピクピク
SFX: PIKU (TWITCH) PIKU
OKAY, MIGHT AS WELL GET THEM ALL READY.
SCARY ...
SCARY ...
CAN I DO IT TOO?
WHAA!? YOU'RE ACTUALLY GOING TO TRY IT!?
IF YOU PULL THERE, IT SHOULD COME RIGHT OUT.
LIKE THIS?
CLEAN OUT THE BLOOD FROM THE SPINE TOO.
WOW ...
ENA, YOU'RE... WOW...
YOU KNOW NO FEAR!
IS THIS WHAT KIDS ARE LIKE THESE DAYS?
I'M IN SOME VIRTUAL WORLD, RIGHT?
I FEEL LIKE I'M IN SOME SORT OF GAME.

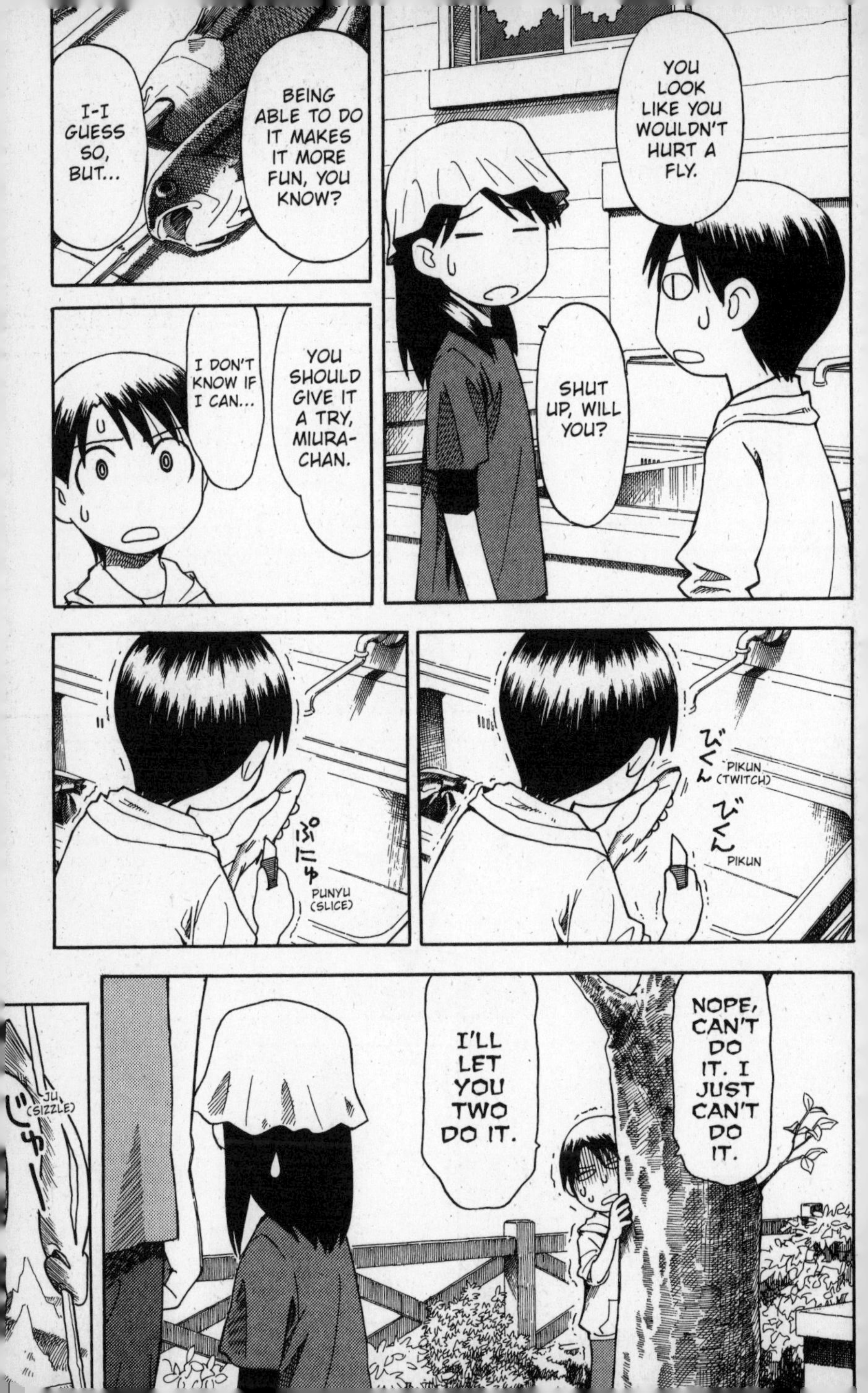
YOU LOOK LIKE YOU WOULDN'T HURT A FLY.
SHUT UP, WILL YOU?
BEING ABLE TO DO IT MAKES IT MORE FUN, YOU KNOW?
I-I GUESS SO, BUT...
YOU SHOULD GIVE IT A TRY, MIURA-CHAN.
I DON'T KNOW IF I CAN...
ぴくん
PIKUN (TWITCH)
ぴくん
PIKUN
ぷにゅ
PUNYU (SLICE)
NOPE, CAN'T DO IT. I JUST CAN'T DO IT.
I'LL LET YOU TWO DO IT.
じゅー
JU (SIZZLE)

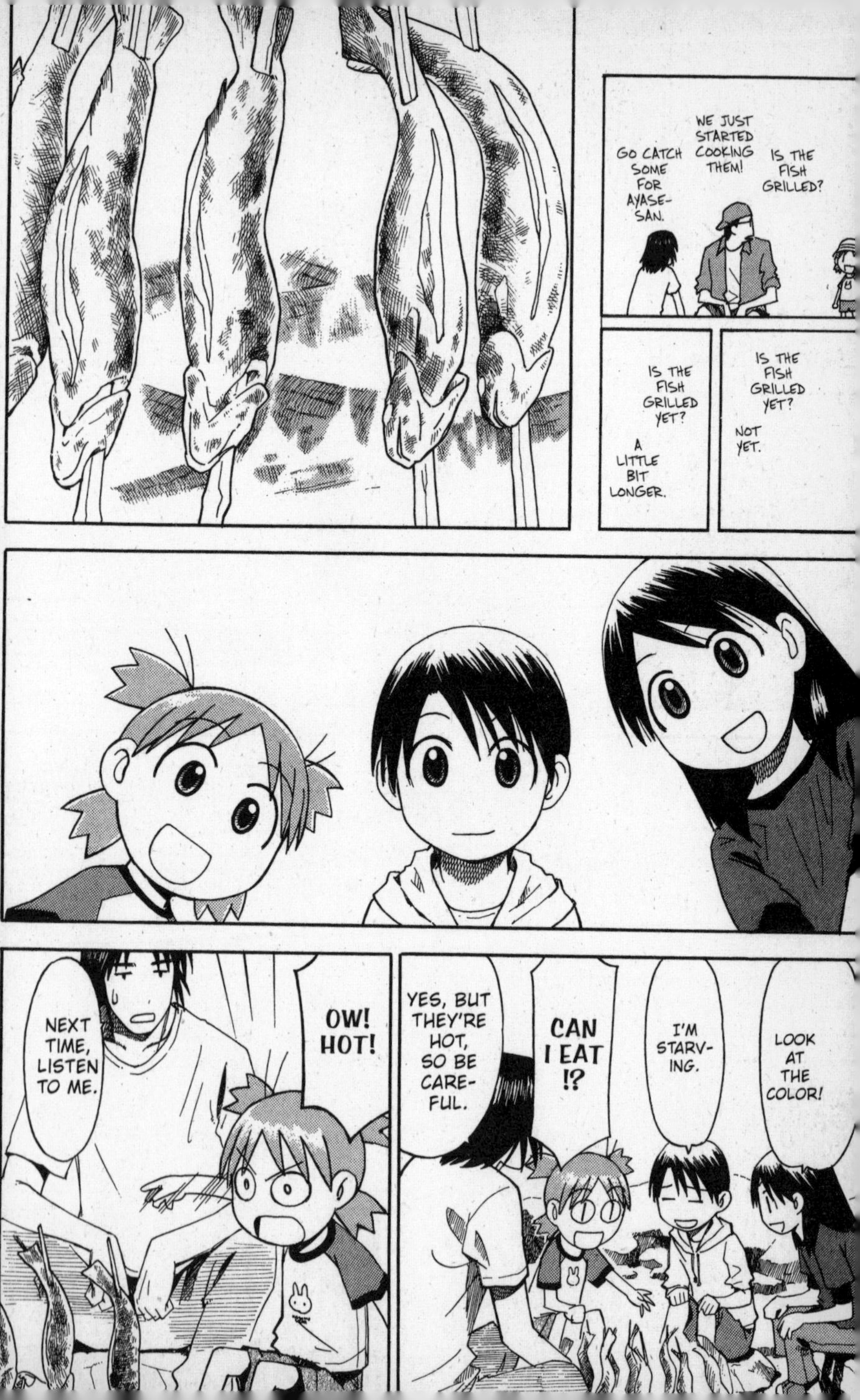
IS THE FISH GRILLED?
WE JUST STARTED COOKING THEM!
GO CATCH SOME FOR AYASE-SAN.
IS THE FISH GRILLED YET?
NOT YET.
IS THE FISH GRILLED YET?
A LITTLE BIT LONGER.
LOOK AT THE COLOR!
I'M STARV-ING.
CAN I EAT !?
YES, BUT THEY'RE HOT, SO BE CARE-FUL.
OW! HOT!
NEXT TIME, LISTEN TO ME.

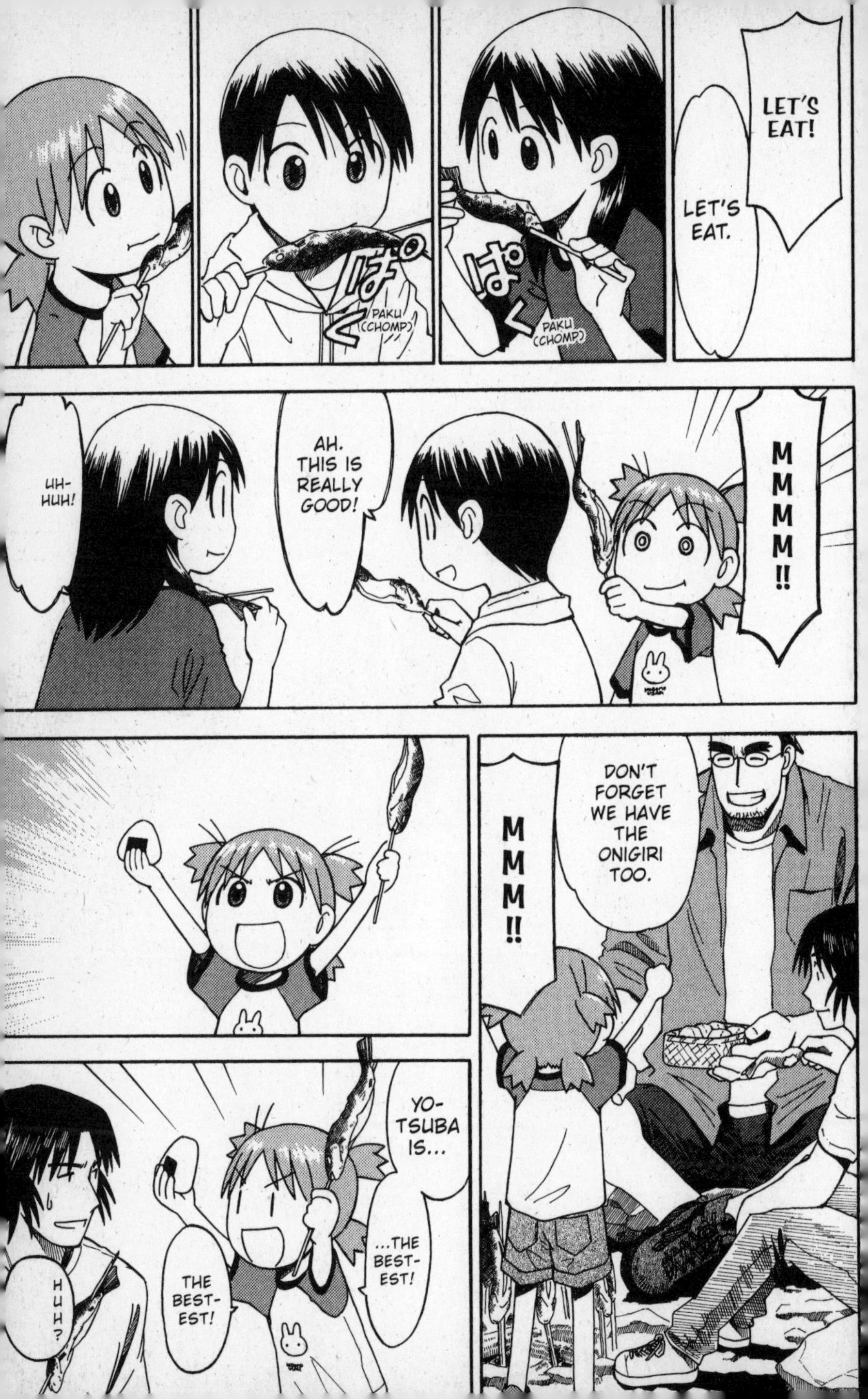
LET'S EAT!
LET'S EAT.
ぱく
PAKU (CHOMP)
ぱく
PAKU (CHOMP)
MMMM!!
AH. THIS IS REALLY GOOD!
UH-HUH!
DON'T FORGET WE HAVE THE ONIGIRI TOO.
MMM!!
YO-TSUBA IS...
...THE BEST-EST!
THE BEST-EST!
HUH?

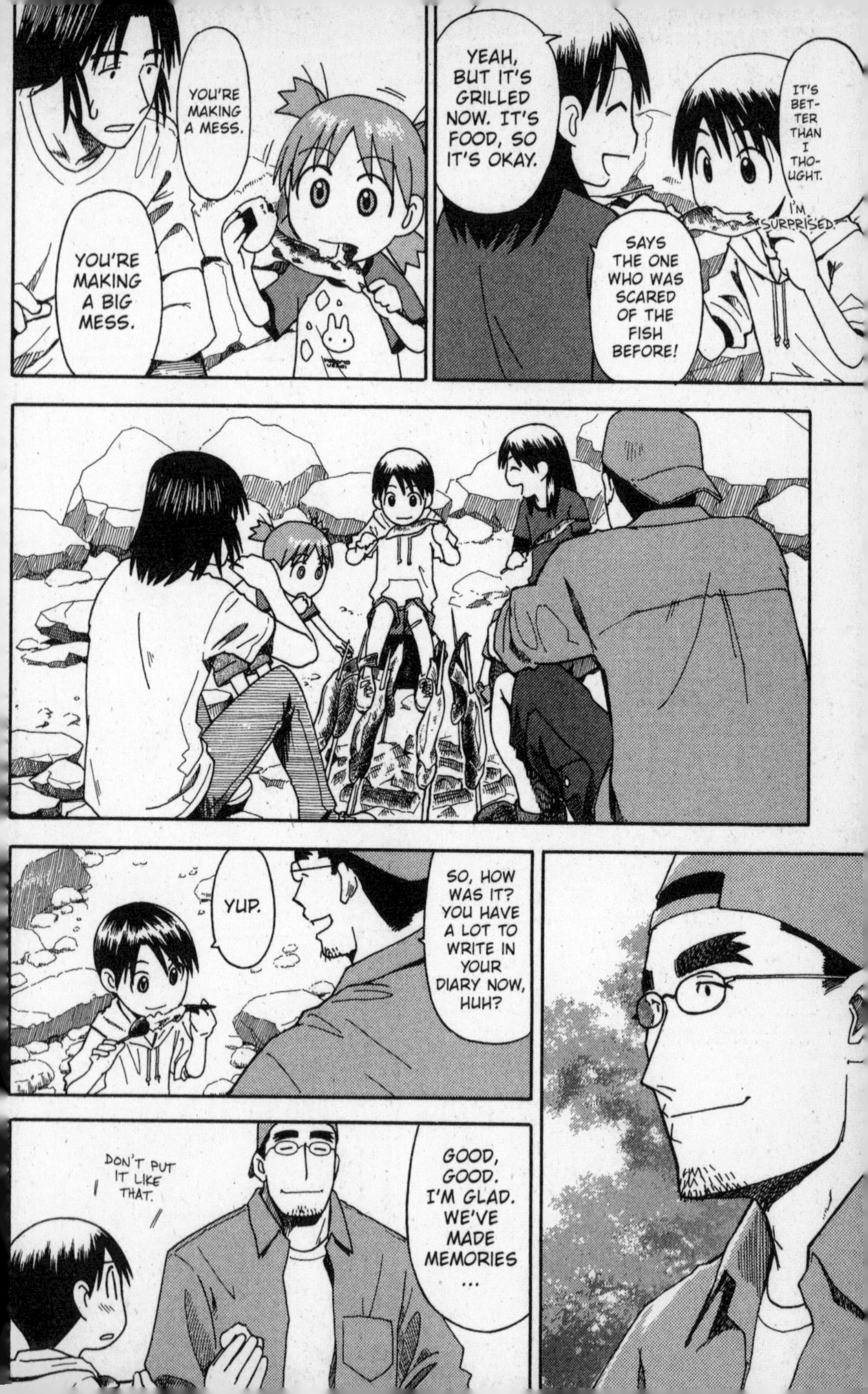
IT'S BETTER THAN I THOUGHT.
I'M SURPRISED.
YEAH, BUT IT'S GRILLED NOW. IT'S FOOD, SO IT'S OKAY.
SAYS THE ONE WHO WAS SCARED OF THE FISH BEFORE!
YOU'RE MAKING A MESS.
YOU'RE MAKING A BIG MESS.
SO, HOW WAS IT? YOU HAVE A LOT TO WRITE IN YOUR DIARY NOW, HUH?
YUP.
GOOD, GOOD. I'M GLAD. WE'VE MADE MEMORIES...
DON'T PUT IT LIKE THAT.

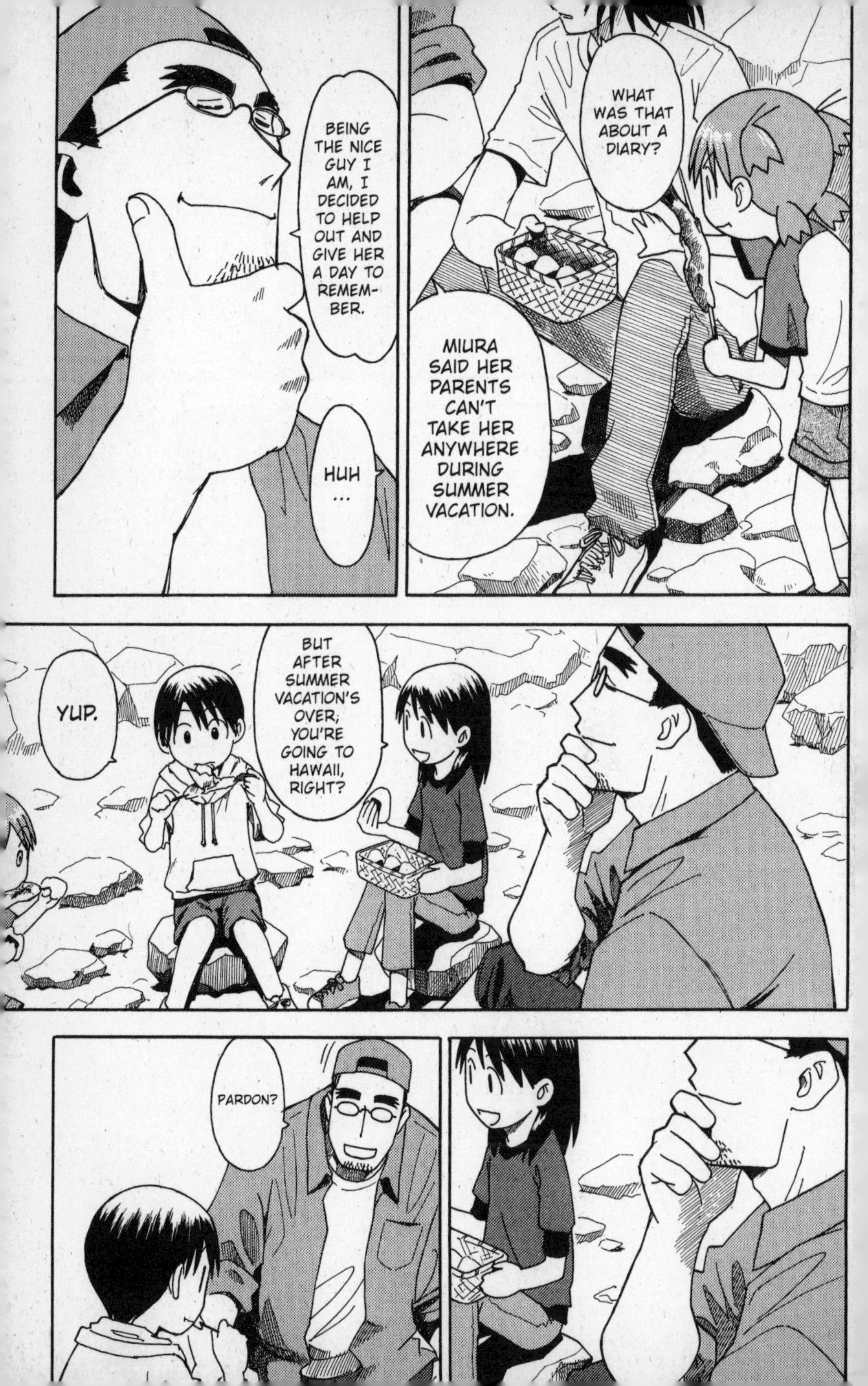
WHAT WAS THAT ABOUT A DIARY?
MIURA SAID HER PARENTS CAN'T TAKE HER ANYWHERE DURING SUMMER VACATION.
BEING THE NICE GUY I AM, I DECIDED TO HELP OUT AND GIVE HER A DAY TO REMEMBER.
HUH ...
BUT AFTER SUMMER VACATION'S OVER, YOU'RE GOING TO HAWAII, RIGHT?
YUP.
PARDON?

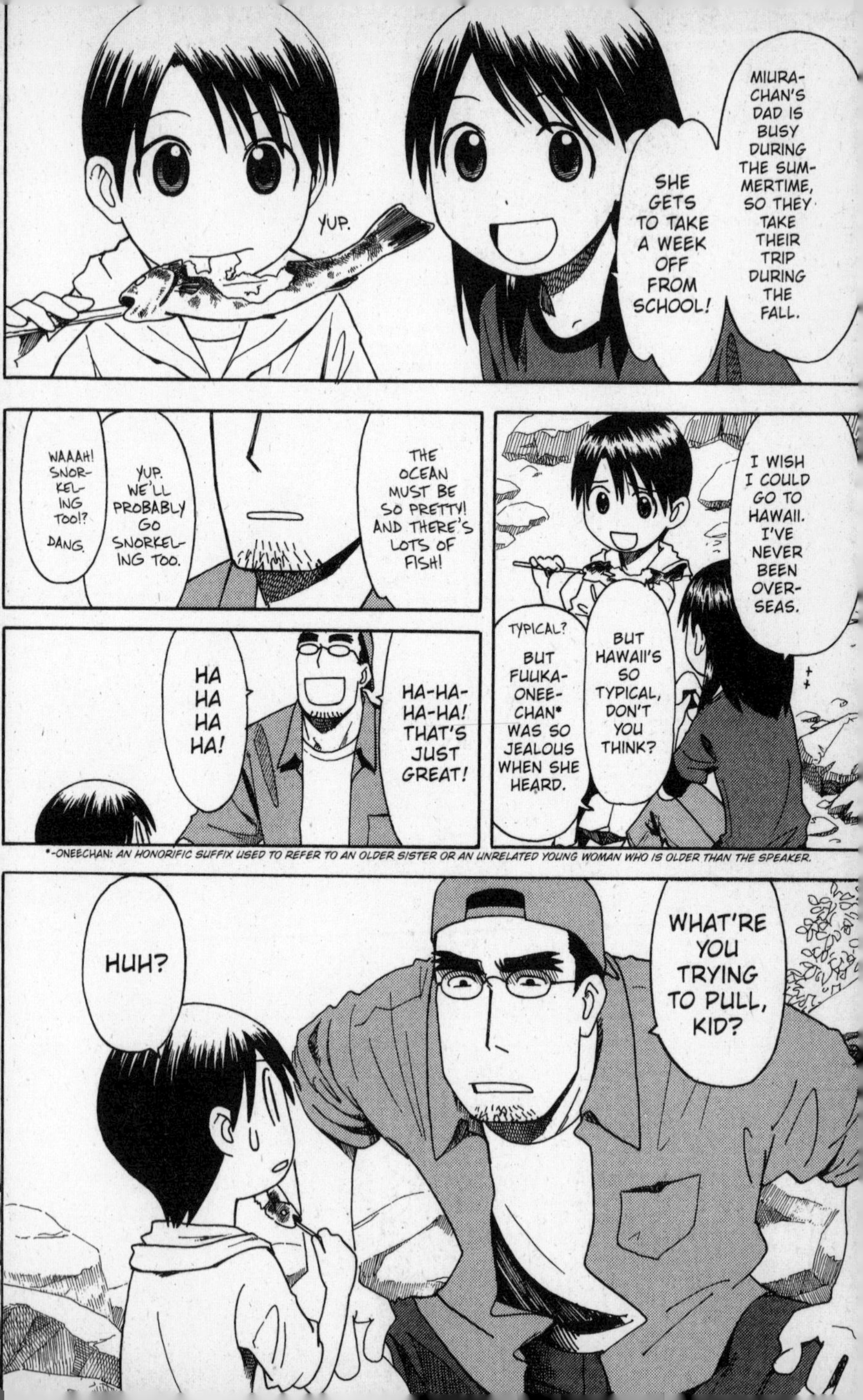
MIURA-CHAN'S DAD IS BUSY DURING THE SUMMERTIME, SO THEY TAKE THEIR TRIP DURING THE FALL.
SHE GETS TO TAKE A WEEK OFF FROM SCHOOL!
YUP.
I WISH I COULD GO TO HAWAII. I'VE NEVER BEEN OVERSEAS.
BUT HAWAII'S SO TYPICAL, DON'T YOU THINK?
TYPICAL?
BUT FUUKA-ONEE-CHAN* WAS SO JEALOUS WHEN SHE HEARD.
THE OCEAN MUST BE SO PRETTY! AND THERE'S LOTS OF FISH!
YUP. WE'LL PROBABLY GO SNORKELING TOO.
WAAAH! SNORKELING TOO!?
DANG.
HA-HA-HA-HA! THAT'S JUST GREAT!
HA HA HA HA!
WHAT'RE YOU TRYING TO PULL, KID?
HUH?

*-ONEECHAN: AN HONORIFIC SUFFIX USED TO REFER TO AN OLDER SISTER OR AN UNRELATED YOUNG WOMAN WHO IS OLDER THAN THE SPEAKER.

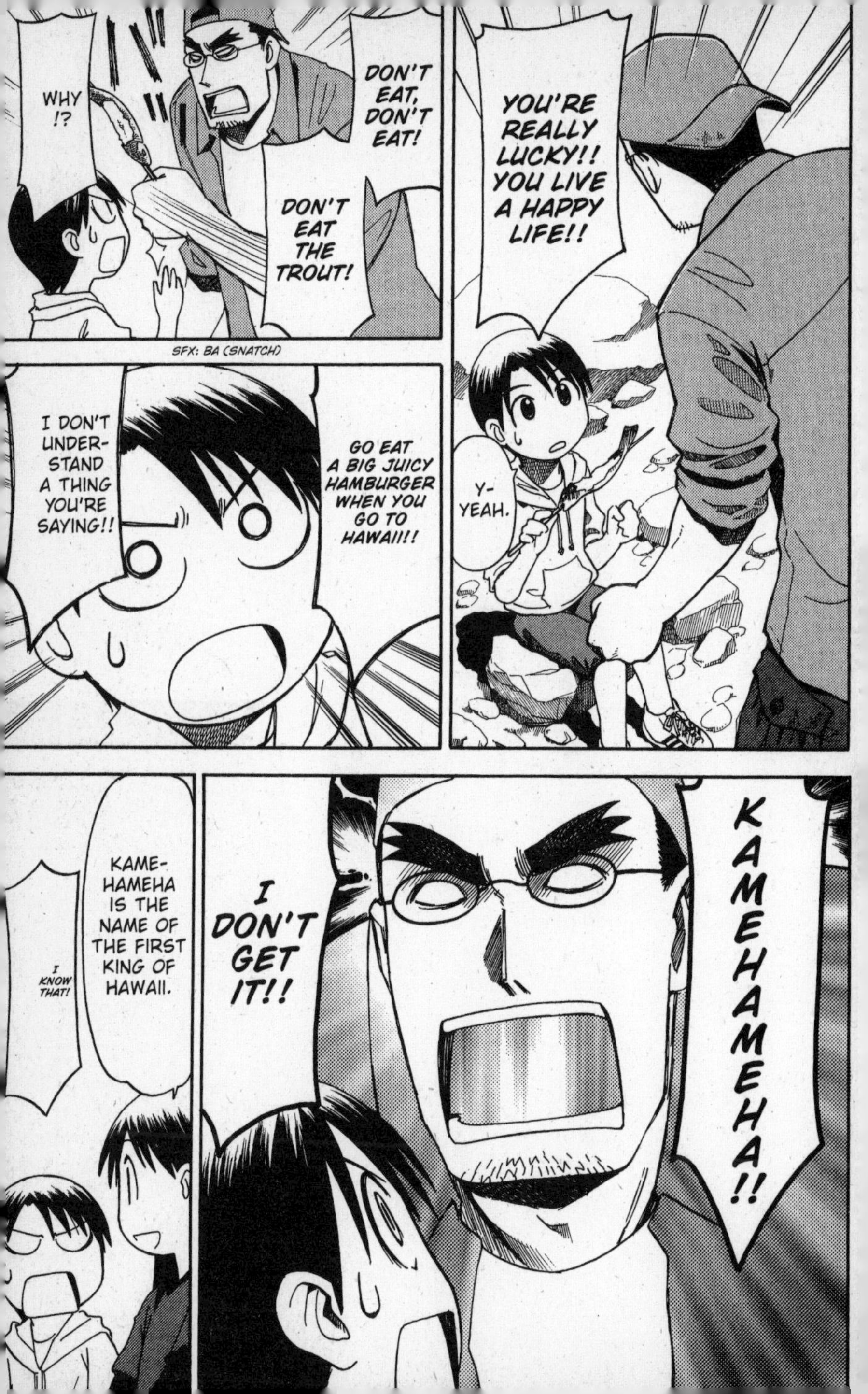
YOU'RE REALLY LUCKY!! YOU LIVE A HAPPY LIFE!!
Y-YEAH.
DON'T EAT, DON'T EAT!
DON'T EAT THE TROUT!
WHY!?
SFX: BA (SNATCH)
GO EAT A BIG JUICY HAMBURGER WHEN YOU GO TO HAWAII!!
I DON'T UNDER-STAND A THING YOU'RE SAYING!!
KAMEHAMEHA!!
I DON'T GET IT!!
KAME-HAMEHA IS THE NAME OF THE FIRST KING OF HAWAII.
I KNOW THAT!

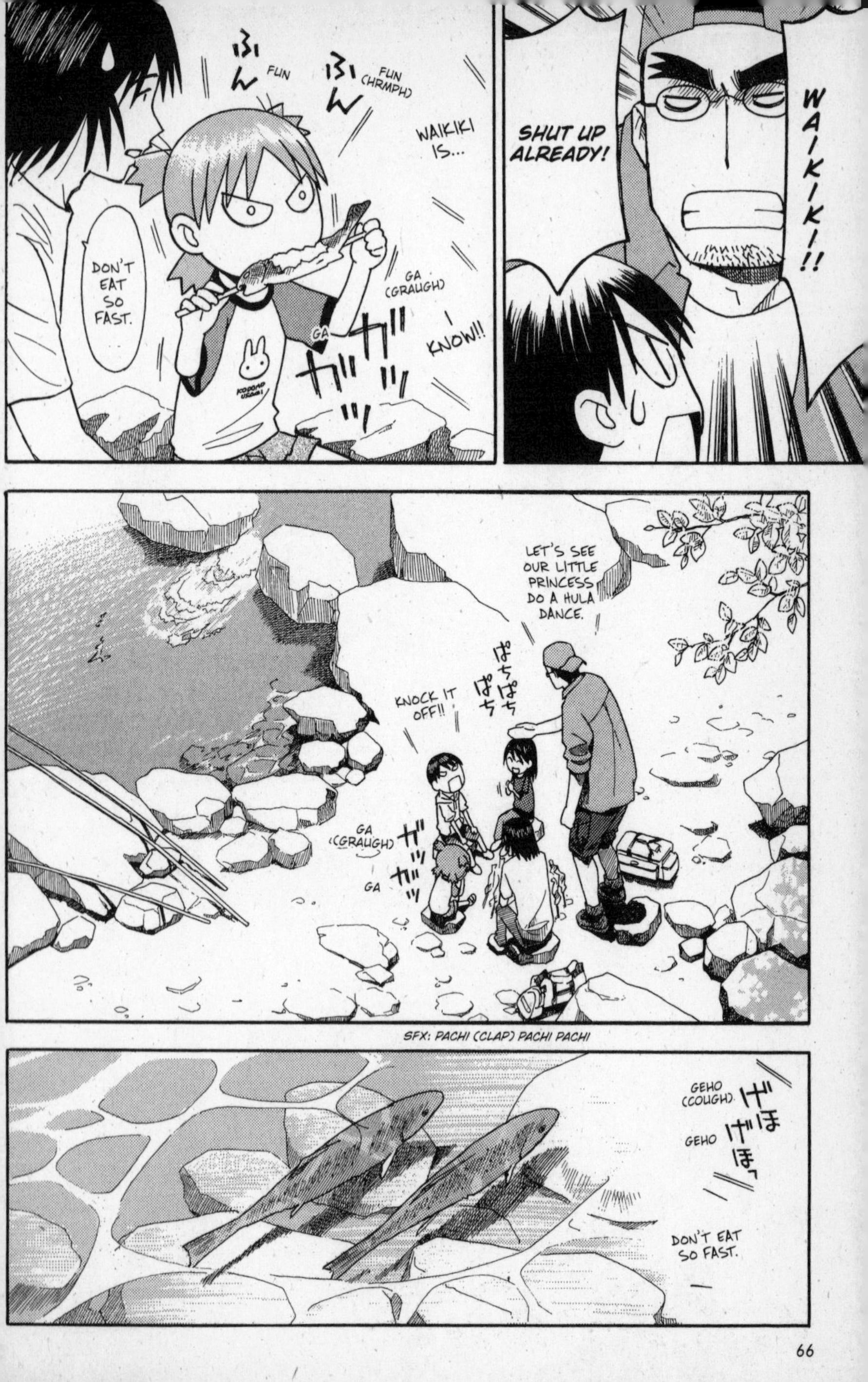
WAIKIKI!!
SHUT UP ALREADY!
ふん FUN
ふん FUN (HRMPH)
WAIKIKI IS...
DON'T EAT SO FAST.
GA (GRAUGH)
I KNOW!!
ガガッガッ GA
LET'S SEE OUR LITTLE PRINCESS DO A HULA DANCE.
ぱちぱちぱち
KNOCK IT OFF!!
GA (GRAUGH)
ガッガッ
GA
SFX: PACHI (CLAP) PACHI PACHI
GEHO (COUGH).
GEHO
げほげほっ
DON'T EAT SO FAST.

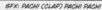

YOTSUBA&!

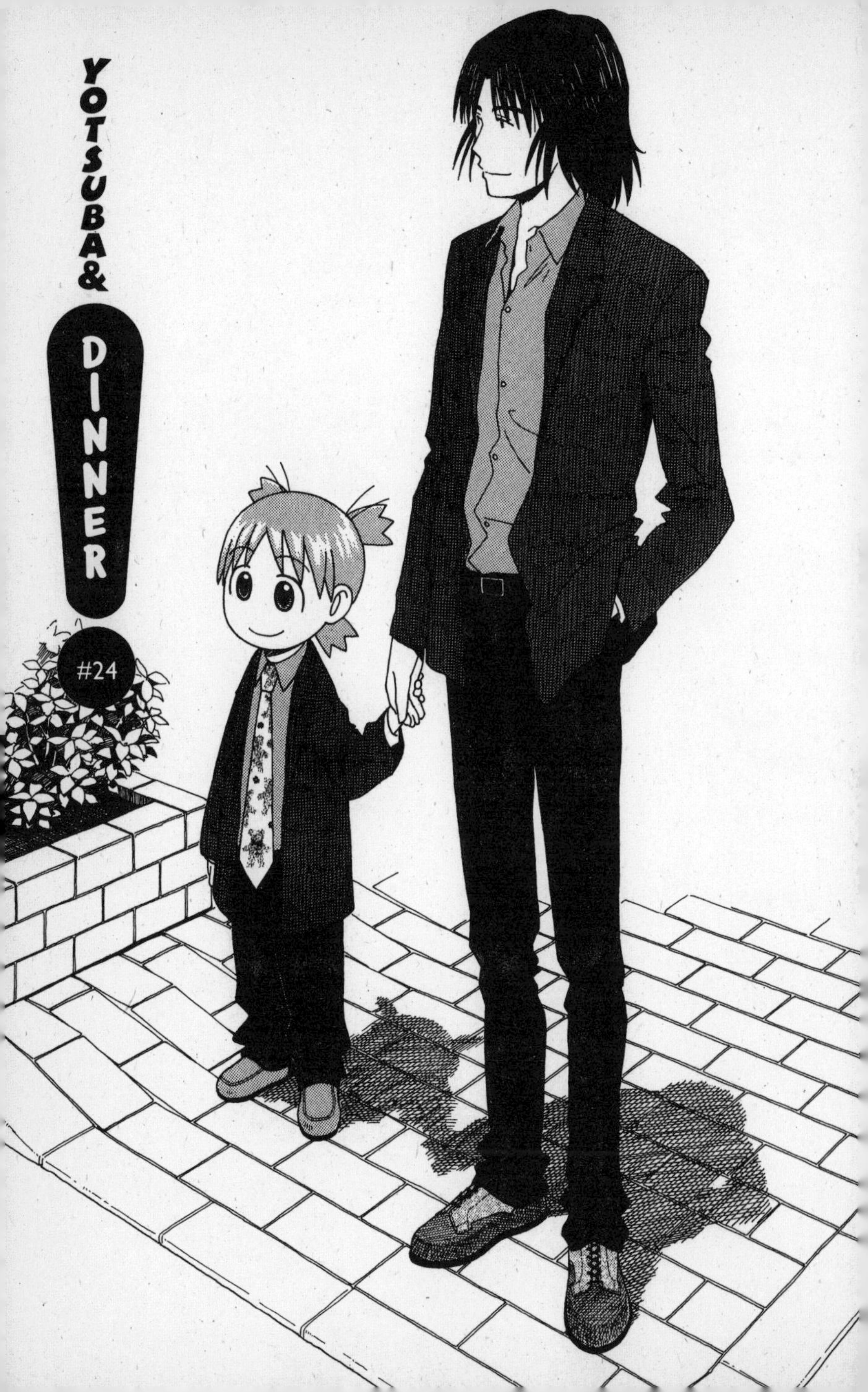
YOTSUBA&
DINNER
#24

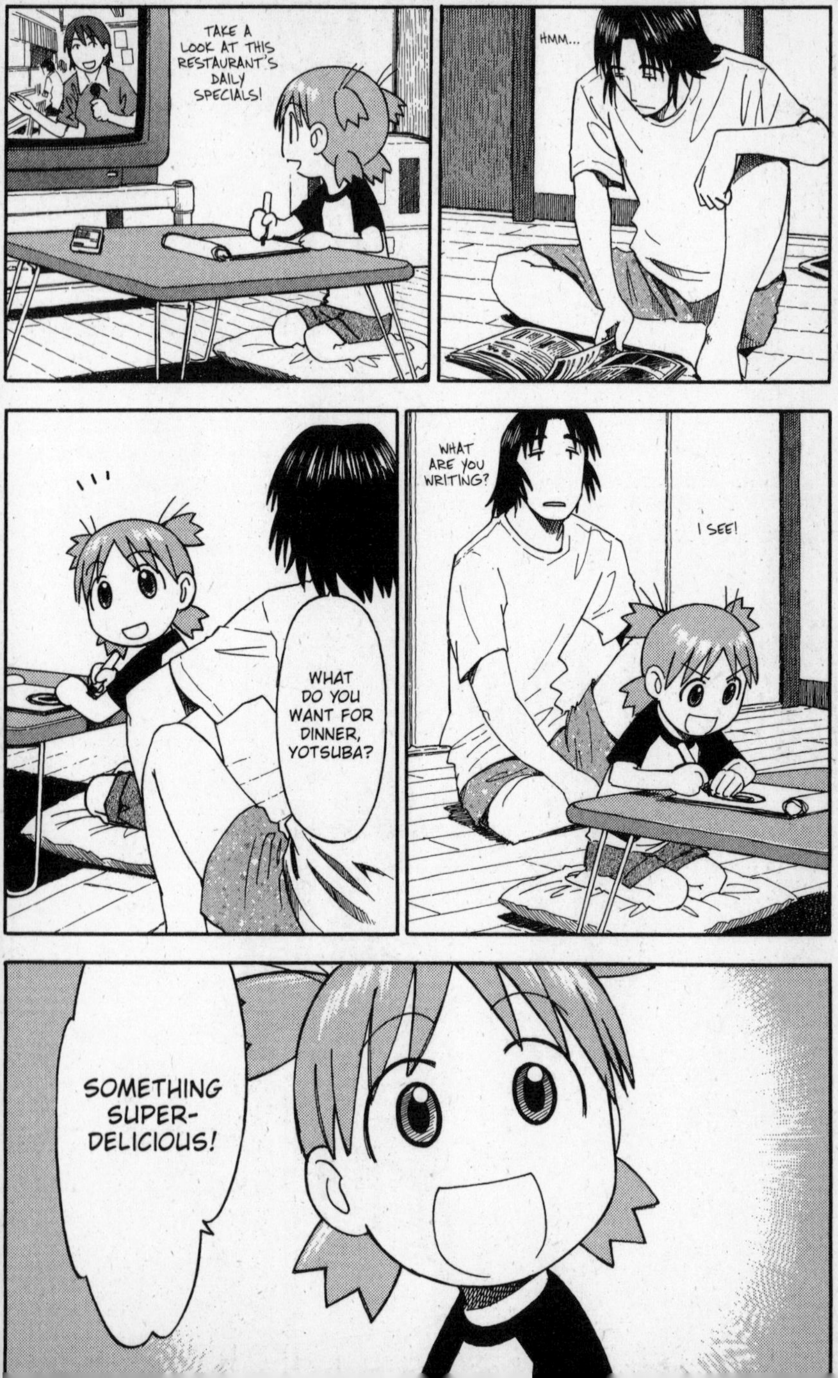
HMM...
TAKE A LOOK AT THIS RESTAURANT'S DAILY SPECIALS!
WHAT ARE YOU WRITING?
I SEE!
WHAT DO YOU WANT FOR DINNER, YOTSUBA?
SOMETHING SUPER-DELICIOUS!

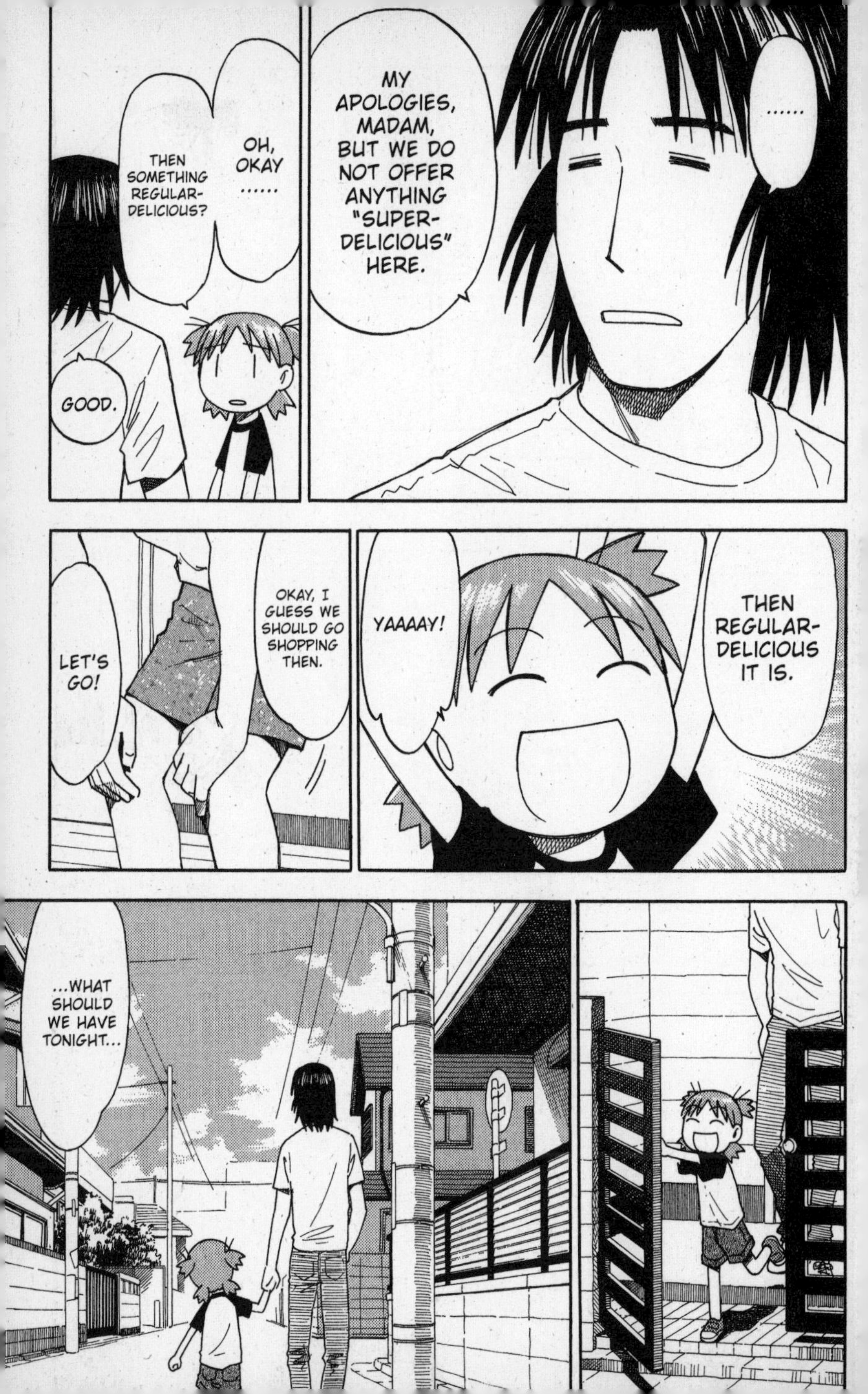
......
MY APOLOGIES, MADAM, BUT WE DO NOT OFFER ANYTHING "SUPER-DELICIOUS" HERE.
OH, OKAY ......
THEN SOMETHING REGULAR-DELICIOUS?
GOOD.
THEN REGULAR-DELICIOUS IT IS.
YAAAAY!
OKAY, I GUESS WE SHOULD GO SHOPPING THEN.
LET'S GO!
...WHAT SHOULD WE HAVE TONIGHT...

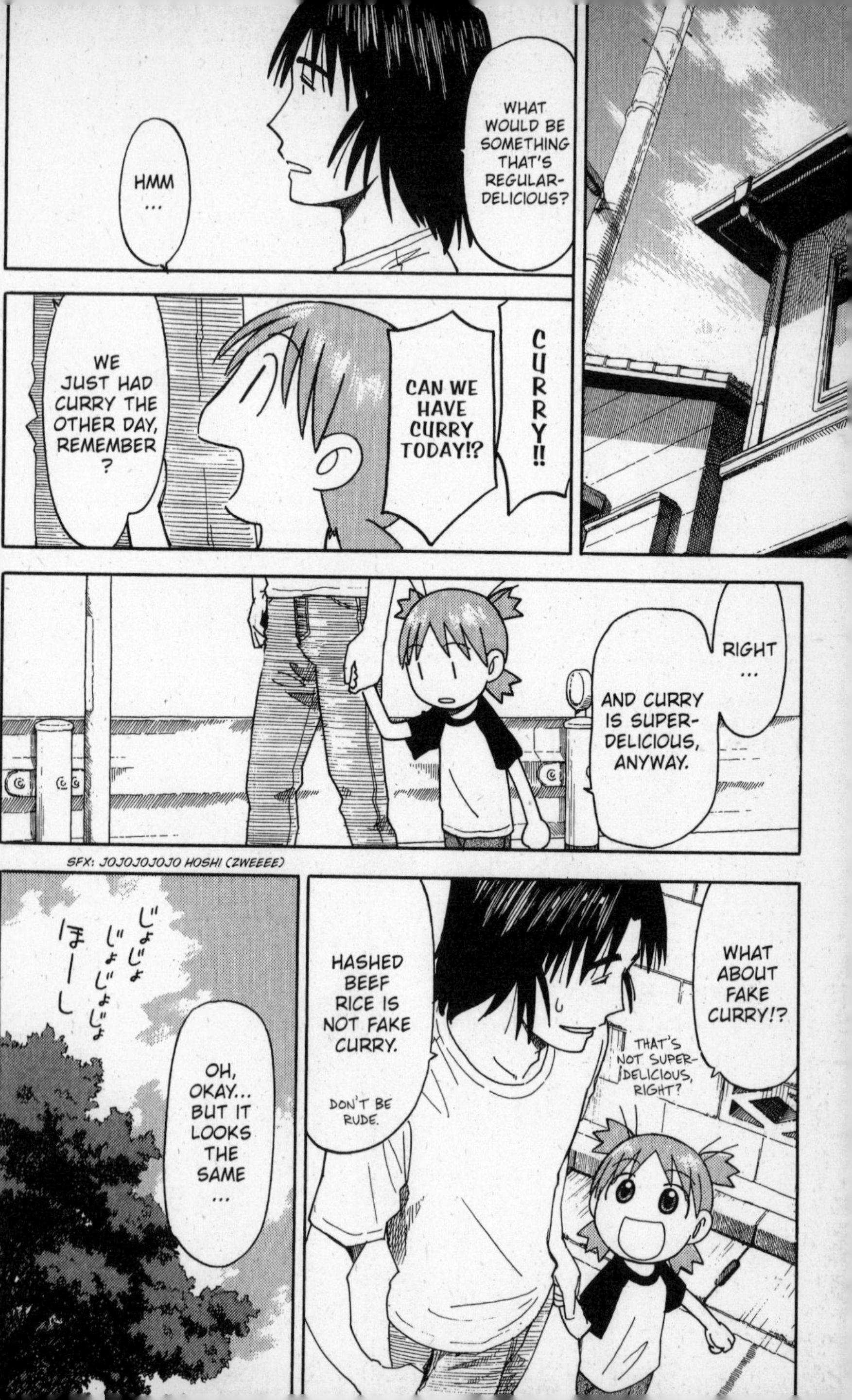
WHAT WOULD BE SOMETHING THAT'S REGULAR-DELICIOUS?
HMM...
CURRY!!
CAN WE HAVE CURRY TODAY!?
WE JUST HAD CURRY THE OTHER DAY, REMEMBER?
RIGHT...
AND CURRY IS SUPER-DELICIOUS, ANYWAY.
SFX: JOJOJOJOJO HOSHI (ZWEEEE)
WHAT ABOUT FAKE CURRY!?
THAT'S NOT SUPER-DELICIOUS, RIGHT?
HASHED BEEF RICE IS NOT FAKE CURRY.
DON'T BE RUDE.
OH, OKAY... BUT IT LOOKS THE SAME...
じょじょじょじょじょほーし

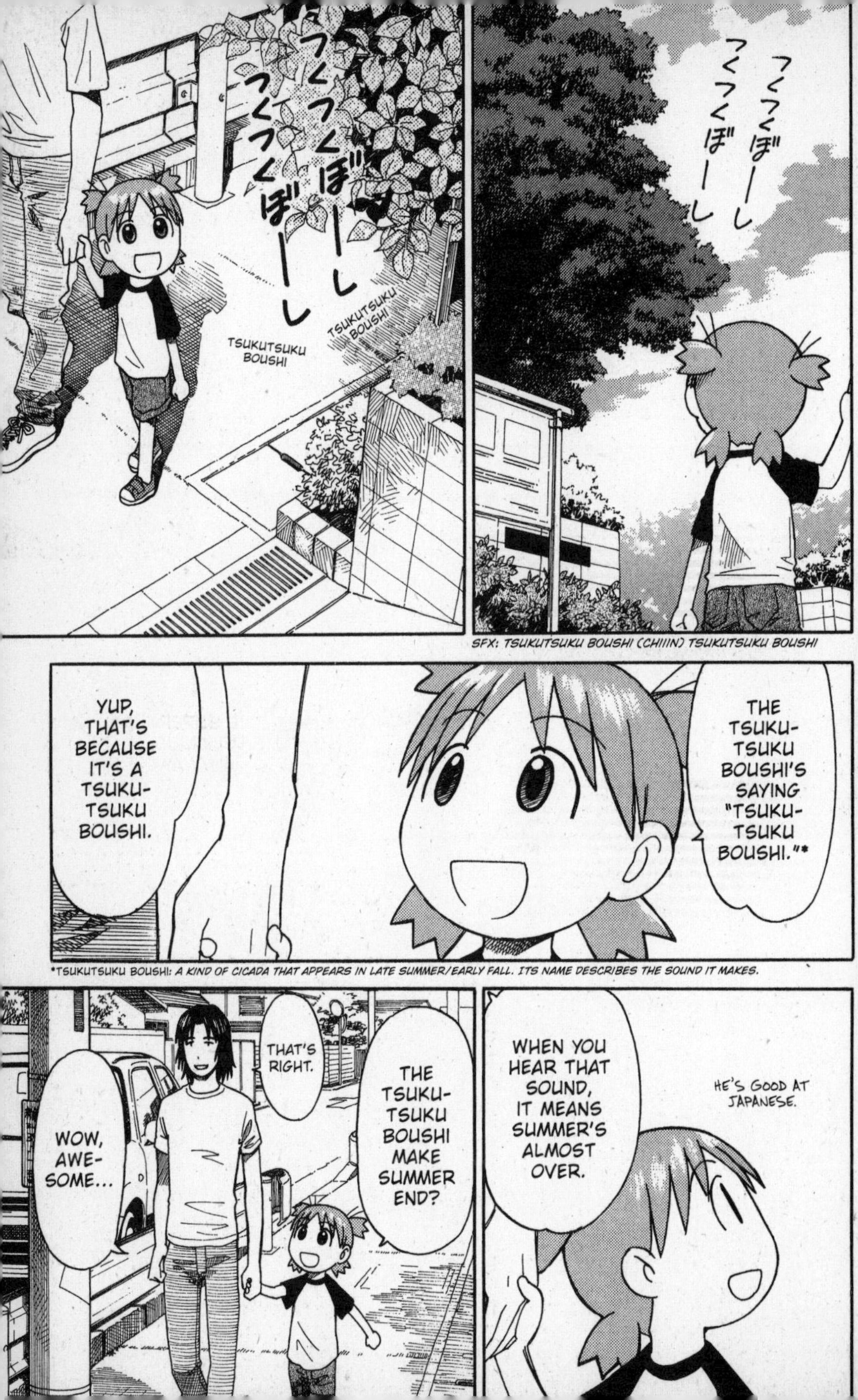
つくつくぼーし
つくつくぼーし
つくつくぼーし
つくつくぼーし
TSUKUTSUKU BOUSHI
TSUKUTSUKU BOUSHI
SFX: TSUKUTSUKU BOUSHI (CHIIIN) TSUKUTSUKU BOUSHI
THE TSUKU-TSUKU BOUSHI'S SAYING "TSUKU-TSUKU BOUSHI."*
YUP, THAT'S BECAUSE IT'S A TSUKU-TSUKU BOUSHI.
*TSUKUTSUKU BOUSHI: A KIND OF CICADA THAT APPEARS IN LATE SUMMER/EARLY FALL. ITS NAME DESCRIBES THE SOUND IT MAKES.
WHEN YOU HEAR THAT SOUND, IT MEANS SUMMER'S ALMOST OVER.
HE'S GOOD AT JAPANESE.
THE TSUKU-TSUKU BOUSHI MAKE SUMMER END?
THAT'S RIGHT.
WOW, AWE-SOME...

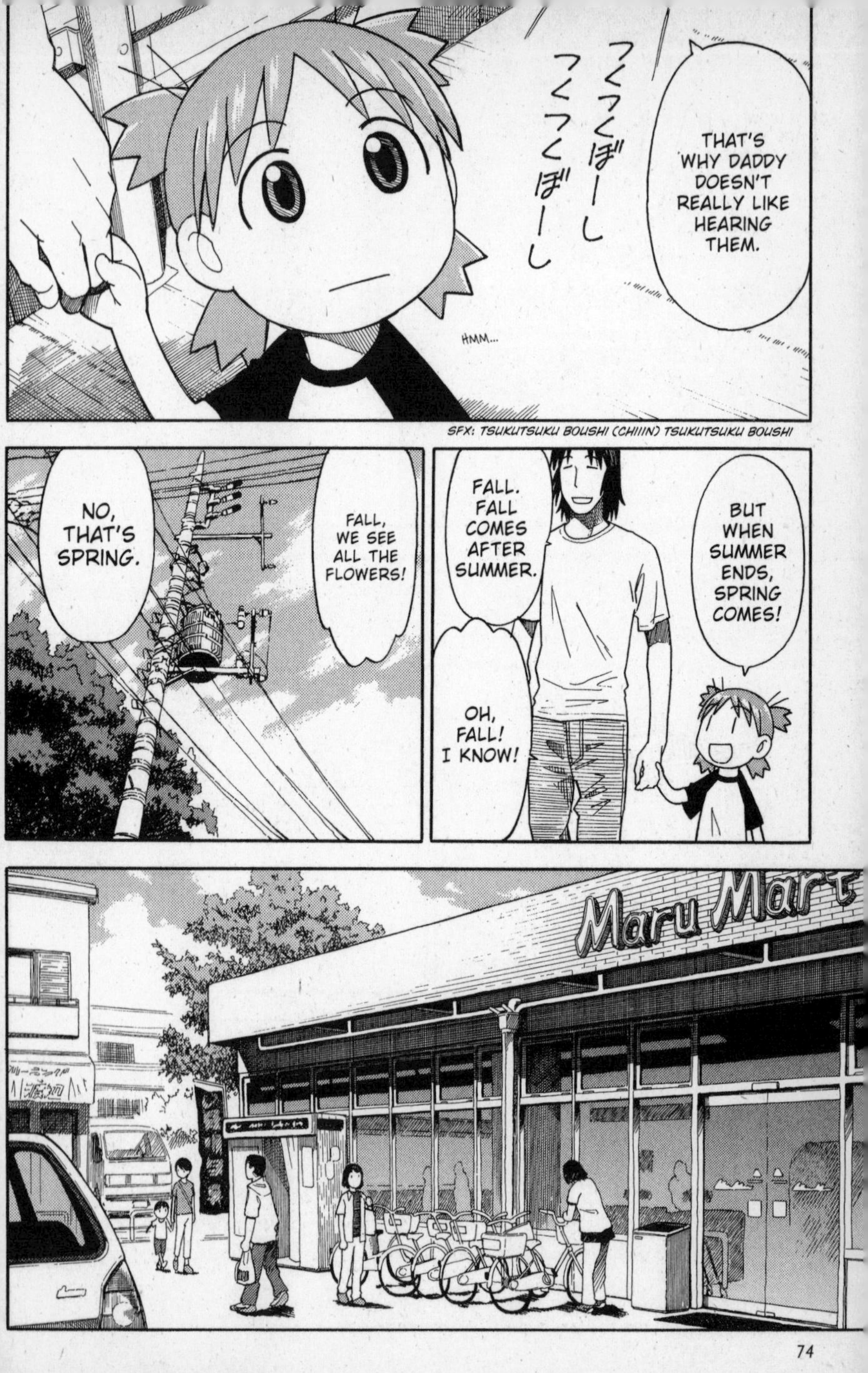
THAT'S WHY DADDY DOESN'T REALLY LIKE HEARING THEM.
つくつくぼーし
つくつくぼーし
HMM...
SFX: TSUKUTSUKU BOUSHI (CHIIIN) TSUKUTSUKU BOUSHI
BUT WHEN SUMMER ENDS, SPRING COMES!
FALL. FALL COMES AFTER SUMMER.
OH, FALL! I KNOW!
FALL, WE SEE ALL THE FLOWERS!
NO, THAT'S SPRING.
Maru Mart

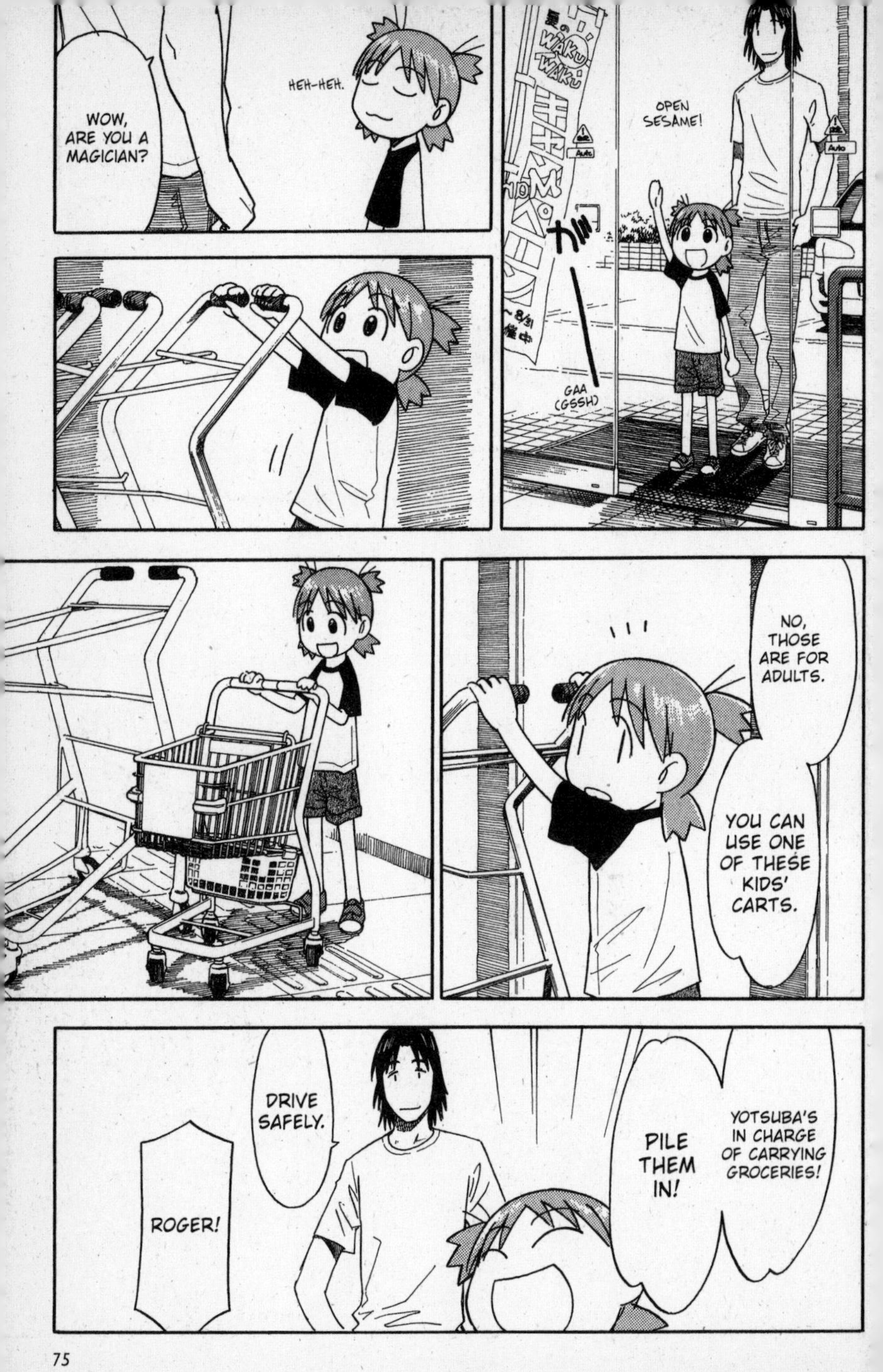
OPEN SESAME!
GAA (GSSH)
WOW, ARE YOU A MAGICIAN?
HEH-HEH.
NO, THOSE ARE FOR ADULTS.
YOU CAN USE ONE OF THESE KIDS' CARTS.
YOTSUBA'S IN CHARGE OF CARRYING GROCERIES!
PILE THEM IN!
DRIVE SAFELY.
ROGER!

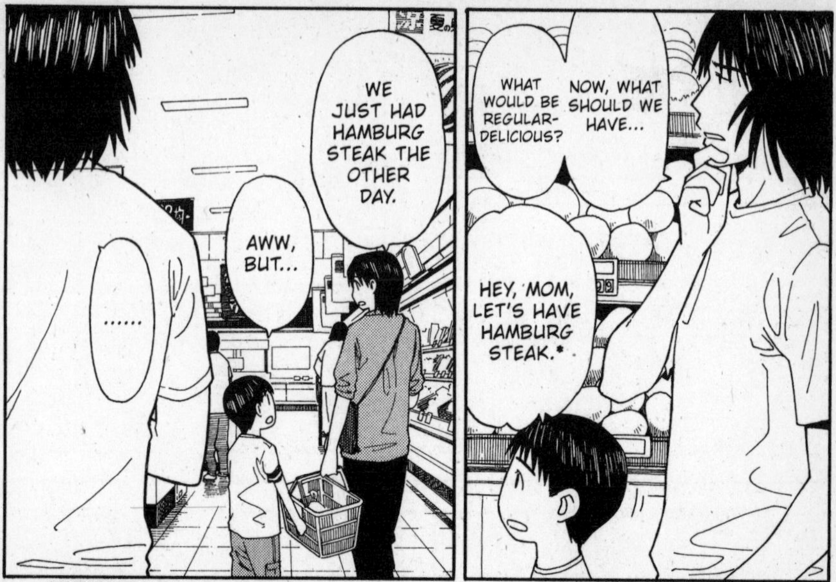
NOW, WHAT SHOULD WE HAVE...
WHAT WOULD BE REGULAR-DELICIOUS?
HEY, MOM, LET'S HAVE HAMBURG STEAK.*
WE JUST HAD HAMBURG STEAK THE OTHER DAY.
AWW, BUT...
......

*HAMBURG STEAK: THE JAPANESE VERSION OF SALISBURY STEAK, MADE WITH BEEF/PORK, EGGS, ONIONS, AND BREADCRUMBS.

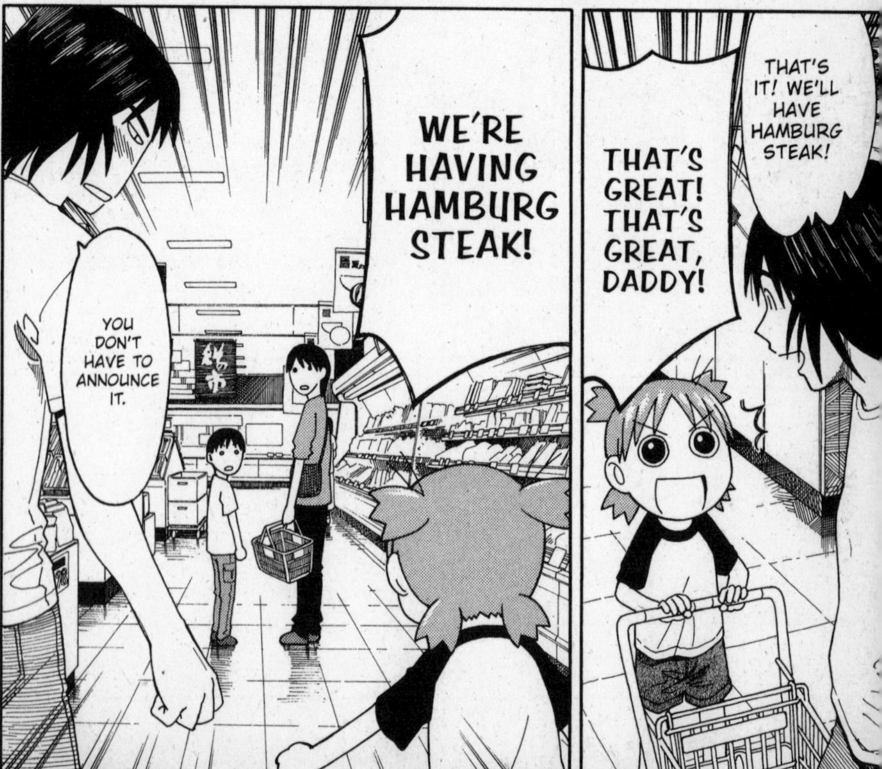
THAT'S IT! WE'LL HAVE HAMBURG STEAK!
THAT'S GREAT! THAT'S GREAT, DADDY!
WE'RE HAVING HAMBURG STEAK!
YOU DON'T HAVE TO ANNOUNCE IT.

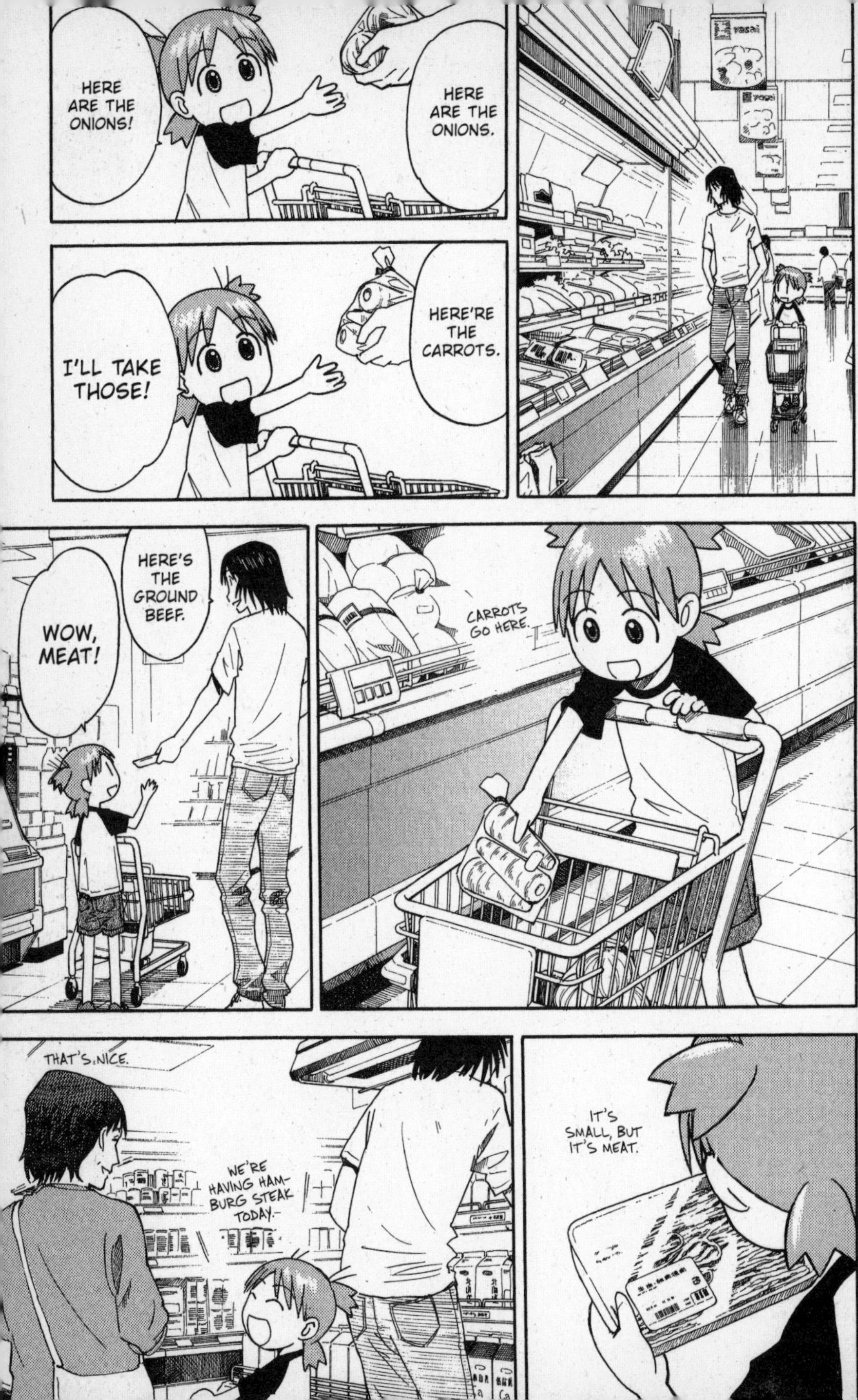
HERE ARE THE ONIONS.
HERE ARE THE ONIONS!
HERE'RE THE CARROTS.
I'LL TAKE THOSE!
CARROTS GO HERE.
HERE'S THE GROUND BEEF.
WOW, MEAT!
IT'S SMALL, BUT IT'S MEAT.
WE'RE HAVING HAMBURG STEAK TODAY.
THAT'S NICE.

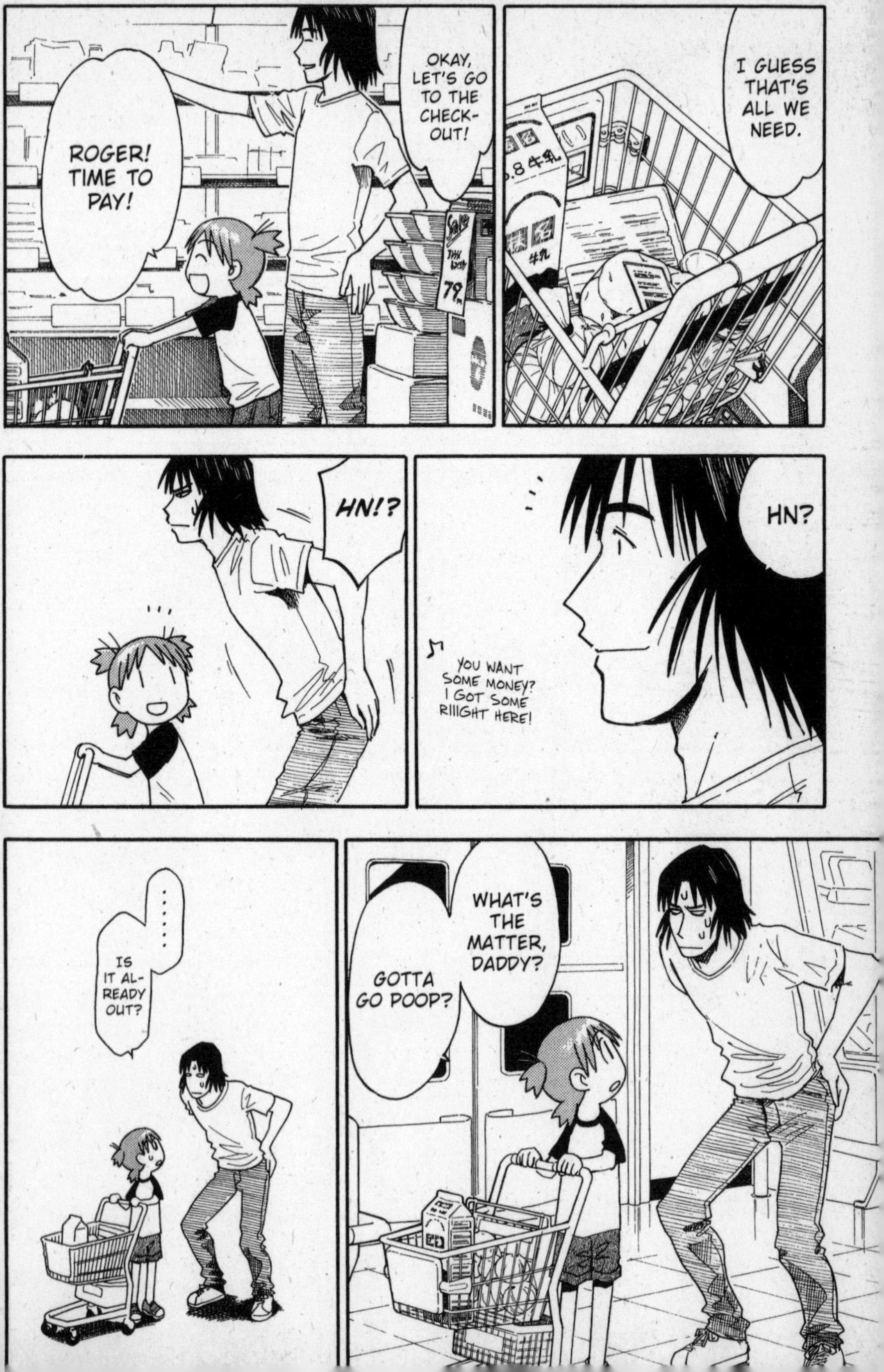
I GUESS THAT'S ALL WE NEED.
OKAY, LET'S GO TO THE CHECK-OUT!
ROGER! TIME TO PAY!
HN?
YOU WANT SOME MONEY? I GOT SOME RIIIGHT HERE!
HN!?
WHAT'S THE MATTER, DADDY?
GOTTA GO POOP?
......
IS IT AL-READY OUT?

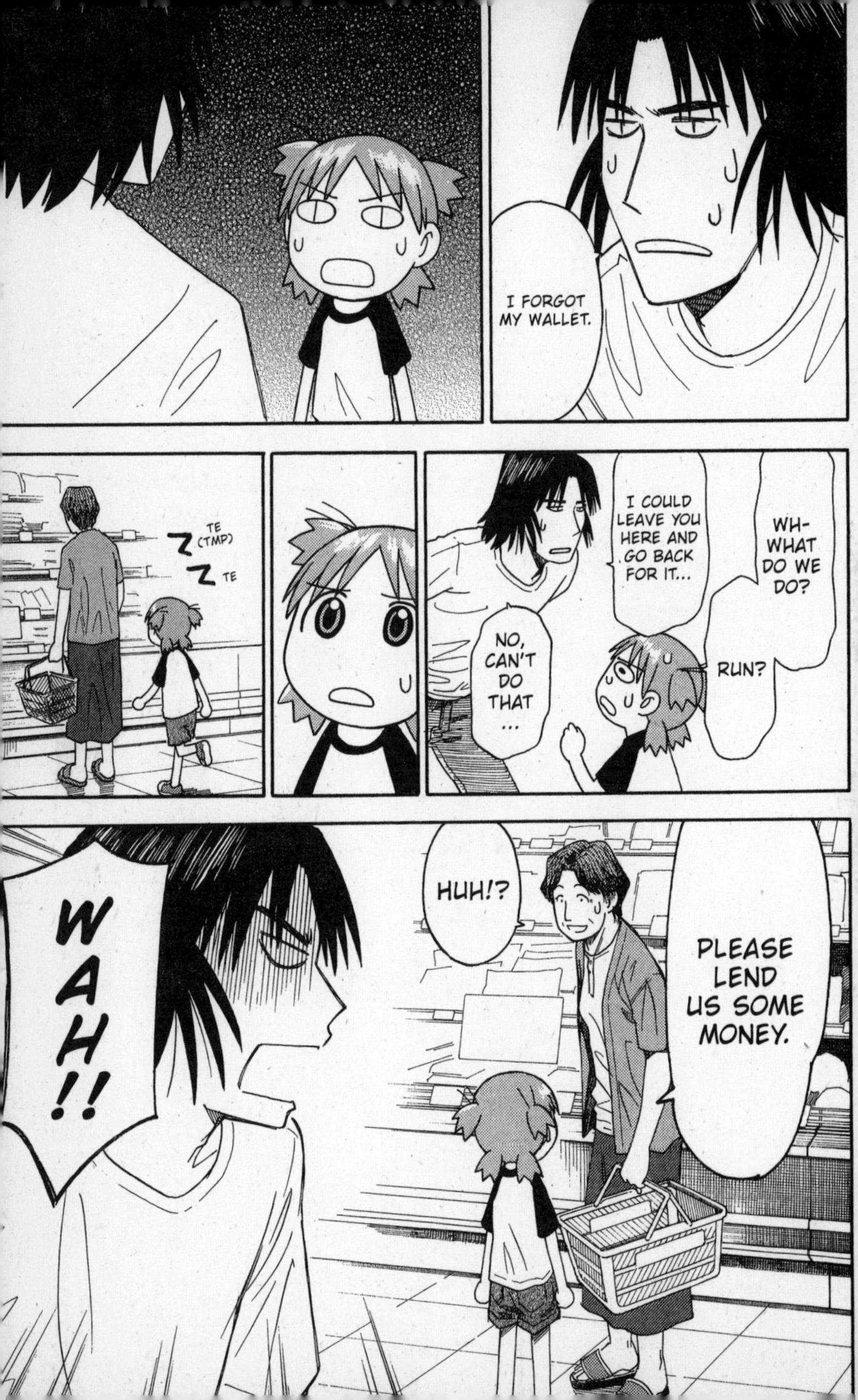
I FORGOT MY WALLET.
WH- WHAT DO WE DO?
I COULD LEAVE YOU HERE AND GO BACK FOR IT...
RUN?
NO, CAN'T DO THAT ...
TE (TMP)
TE
PLEASE LEND US SOME MONEY.
HUH!?
WAH!!

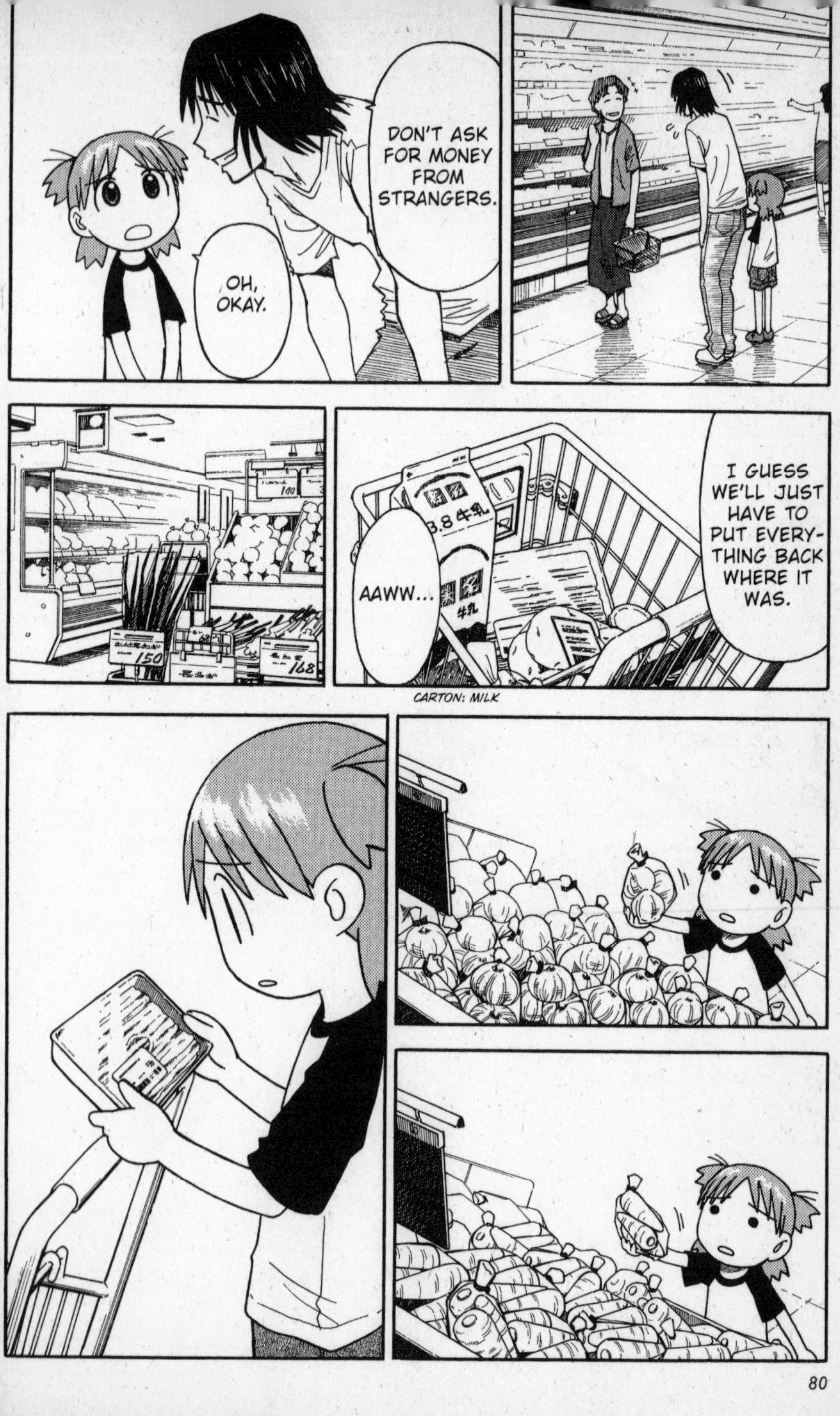
DON'T ASK FOR MONEY FROM STRANGERS.
OH, OKAY.
I GUESS WE'LL JUST HAVE TO PUT EVERY-THING BACK WHERE IT WAS.
AAWW...
CARTON: MILK

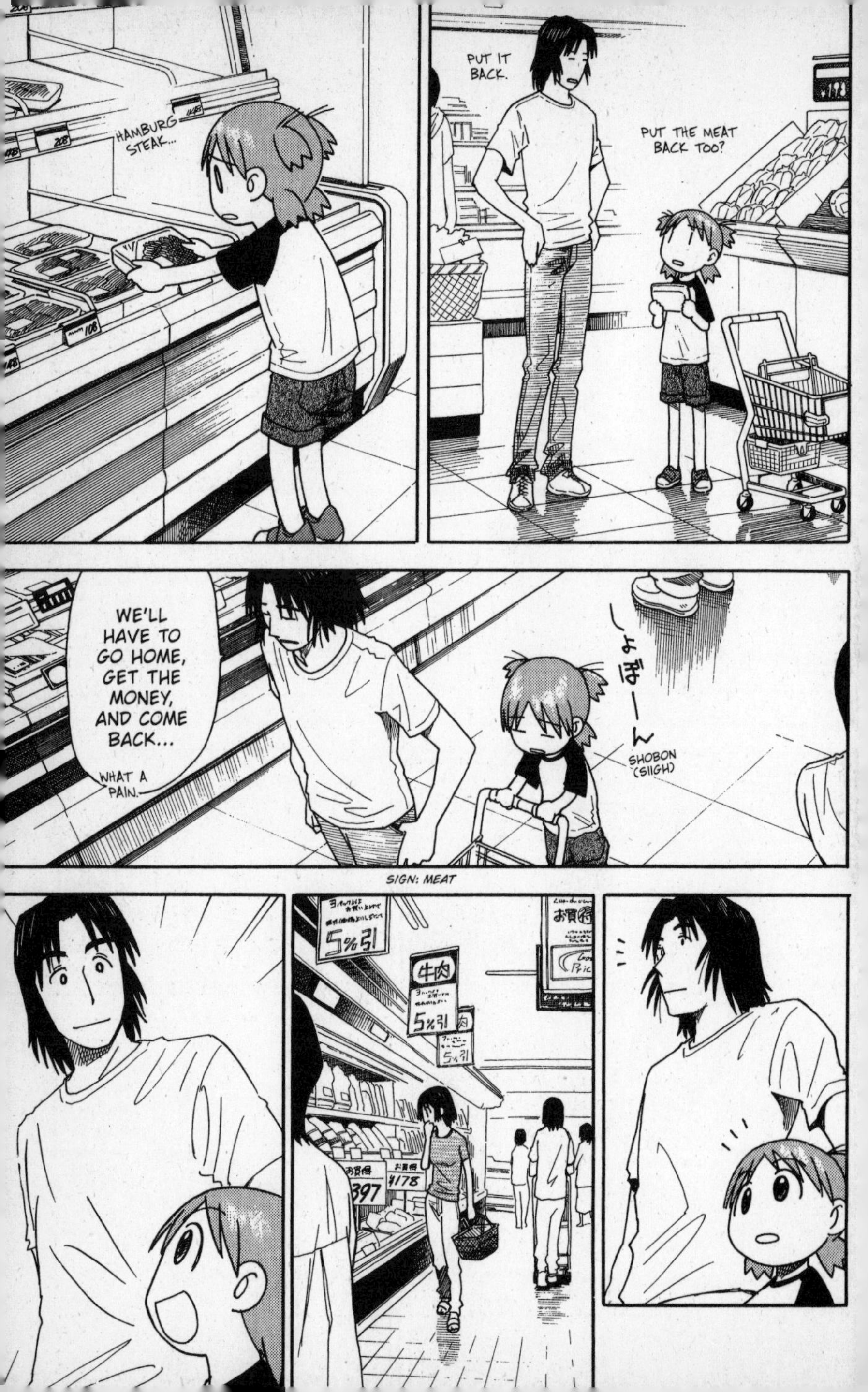
PUT IT BACK.
PUT THE MEAT BACK TOO?
HAMBURG STEAK...
WE'LL HAVE TO GO HOME, GET THE MONEY, AND COME BACK...
WHAT A PAIN.
しょぼーん
SHOBON (SIIGH)
SIGN: MEAT
5%引
牛肉
5%引
肉
5%引
お買得
お買得
397
¥178

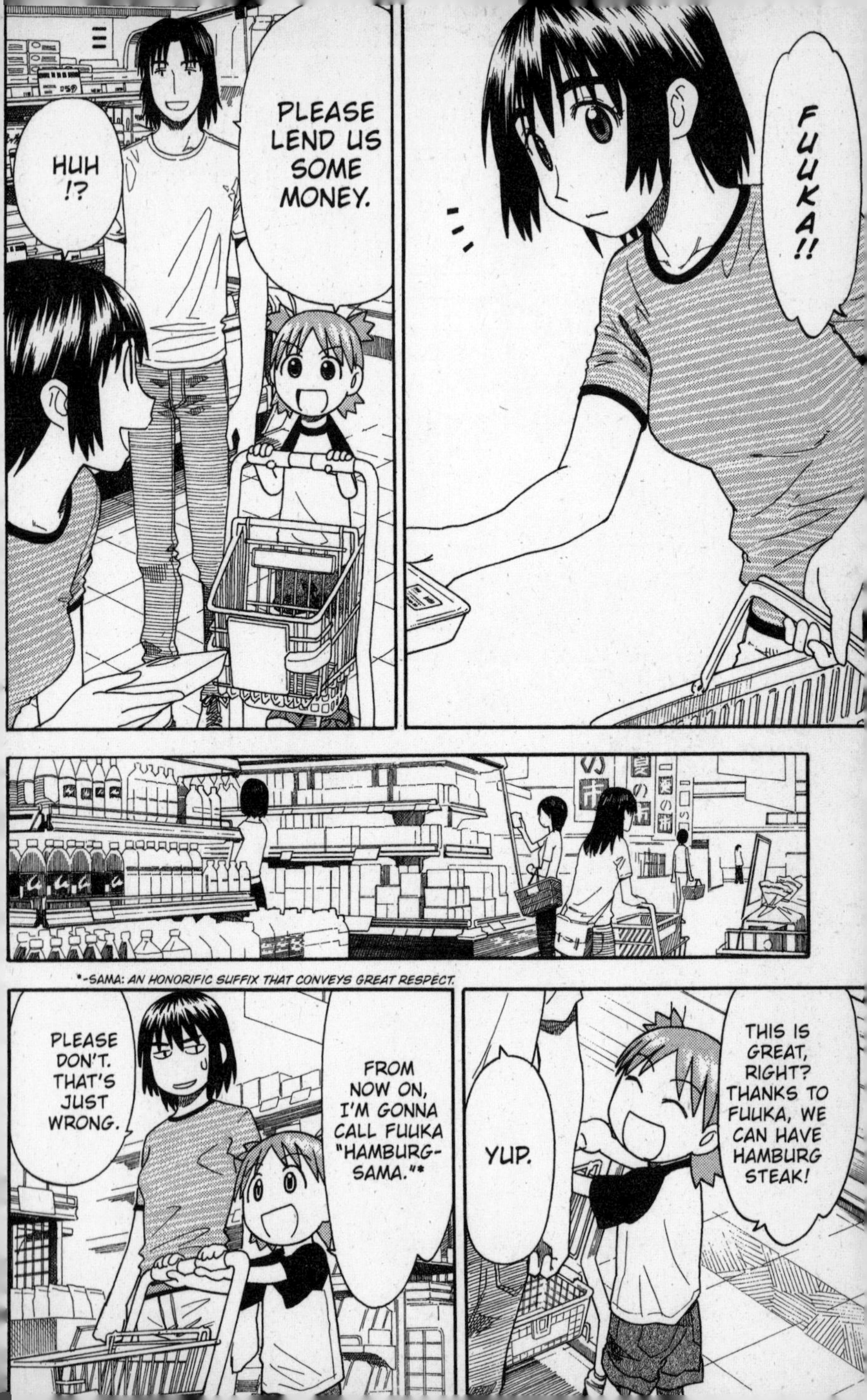
FUUKA!!
PLEASE LEND US SOME MONEY.
HUH !?
THIS IS GREAT, RIGHT? THANKS TO FUUKA, WE CAN HAVE HAMBURG STEAK!
YUP.
FROM NOW ON, I'M GONNA CALL FUUKA "HAMBURG-SAMA."*
PLEASE DON'T. THAT'S JUST WRONG.

*-SAMA: AN HONORIFIC SUFFIX THAT CONVEYS GREAT RESPECT.

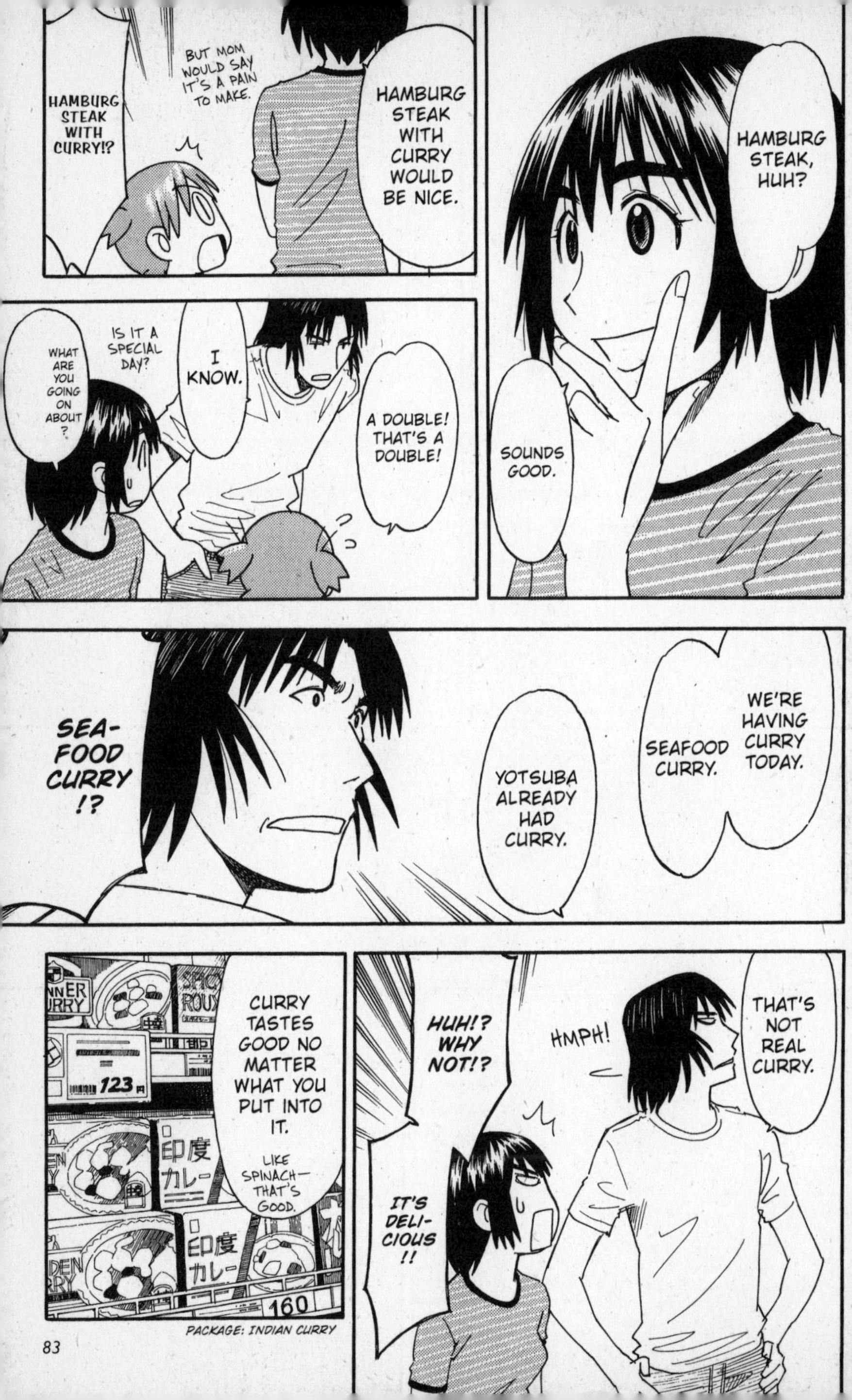
HAMBURG STEAK, HUH?
SOUNDS GOOD.
HAMBURG STEAK WITH CURRY WOULD BE NICE.
BUT MOM WOULD SAY IT'S A PAIN TO MAKE.
HAMBURG STEAK WITH CURRY!?
A DOUBLE! THAT'S A DOUBLE!
I KNOW.
IS IT A SPECIAL DAY?
WHAT ARE YOU GOING ON ABOUT?
WE'RE HAVING CURRY TODAY.
SEAFOOD CURRY.
YOTSUBA ALREADY HAD CURRY.
SEA-FOOD CURRY!?
THAT'S NOT REAL CURRY.
HMPH!
HUH!? WHY NOT!?
IT'S DELICIOUS!!
CURRY TASTES GOOD NO MATTER WHAT YOU PUT INTO IT.
LIKE SPINACH— THAT'S GOOD.
印度カレー
160

PACKAGE: INDIAN CURRY

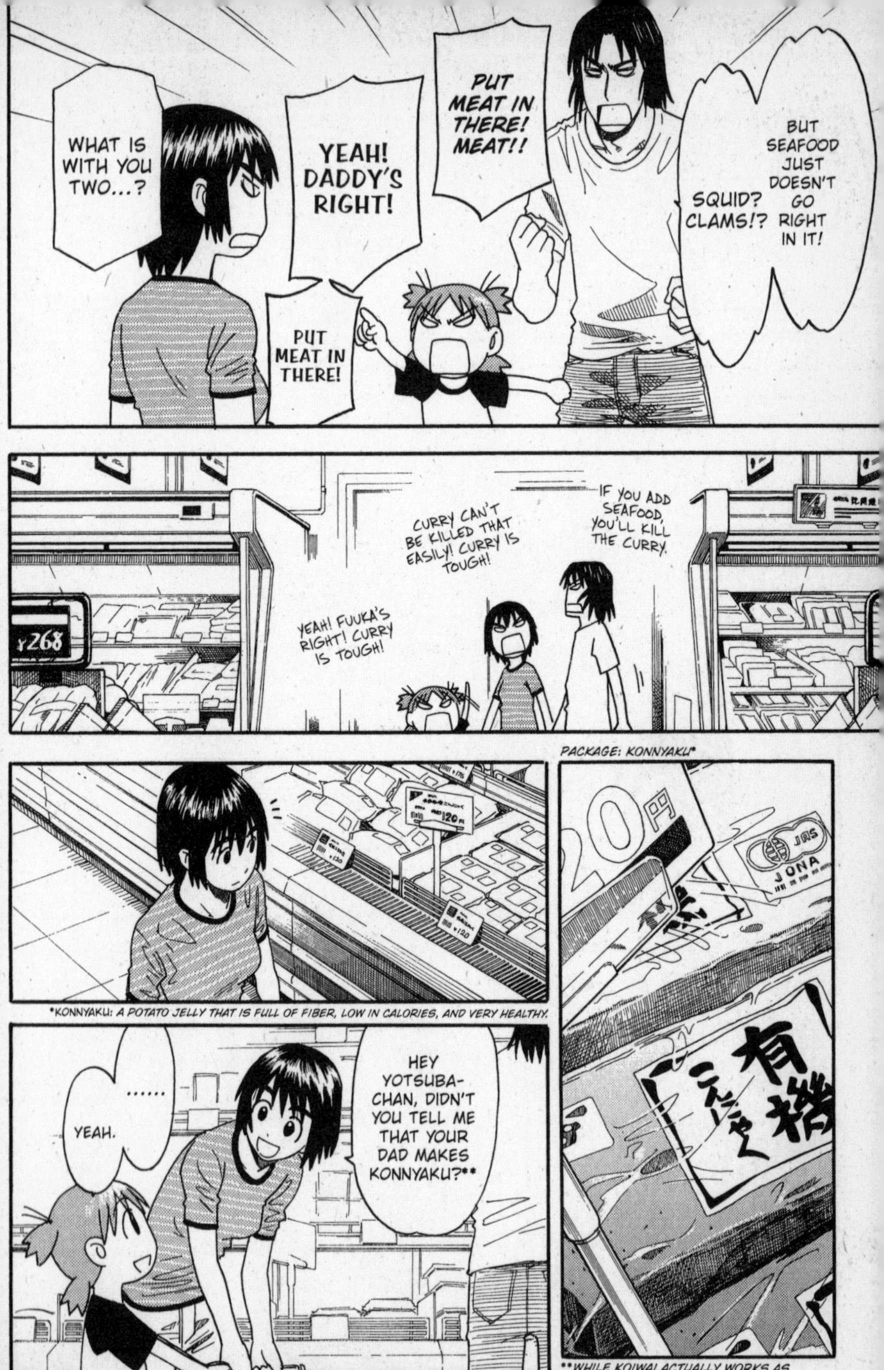
BUT SEAFOOD JUST DOESN'T GO RIGHT IN IT!
SQUID? CLAMS!?
PUT MEAT IN THERE! MEAT!!
YEAH! DADDY'S RIGHT!
PUT MEAT IN THERE!
WHAT IS WITH YOU TWO...?
IF YOU ADD SEAFOOD, YOU'LL KILL THE CURRY.
CURRY CAN'T BE KILLED THAT EASILY! CURRY IS TOUGH!
YEAH! FUUKA'S RIGHT! CURRY IS TOUGH!
¥268
PACKAGE: KONNYAKU*
20円
JAS
JONA
有機
こんにゃく
¥120
¥120
HEY YOTSUBA-CHAN, DIDN'T YOU TELL ME THAT YOUR DAD MAKES KONNYAKU?**
......
YEAH.

*KONNYAKU: A POTATO JELLY THAT IS FULL OF FIBER, LOW IN CALORIES, AND VERY HEALTHY.

**WHILE KOIWAI ACTUALLY WORKS AS A TRANSLATOR, FUUKA THINKS HE MAKES KONNYAKU. READ CHAPTER 7 OF VOLUME 1 TO SEE WHY!

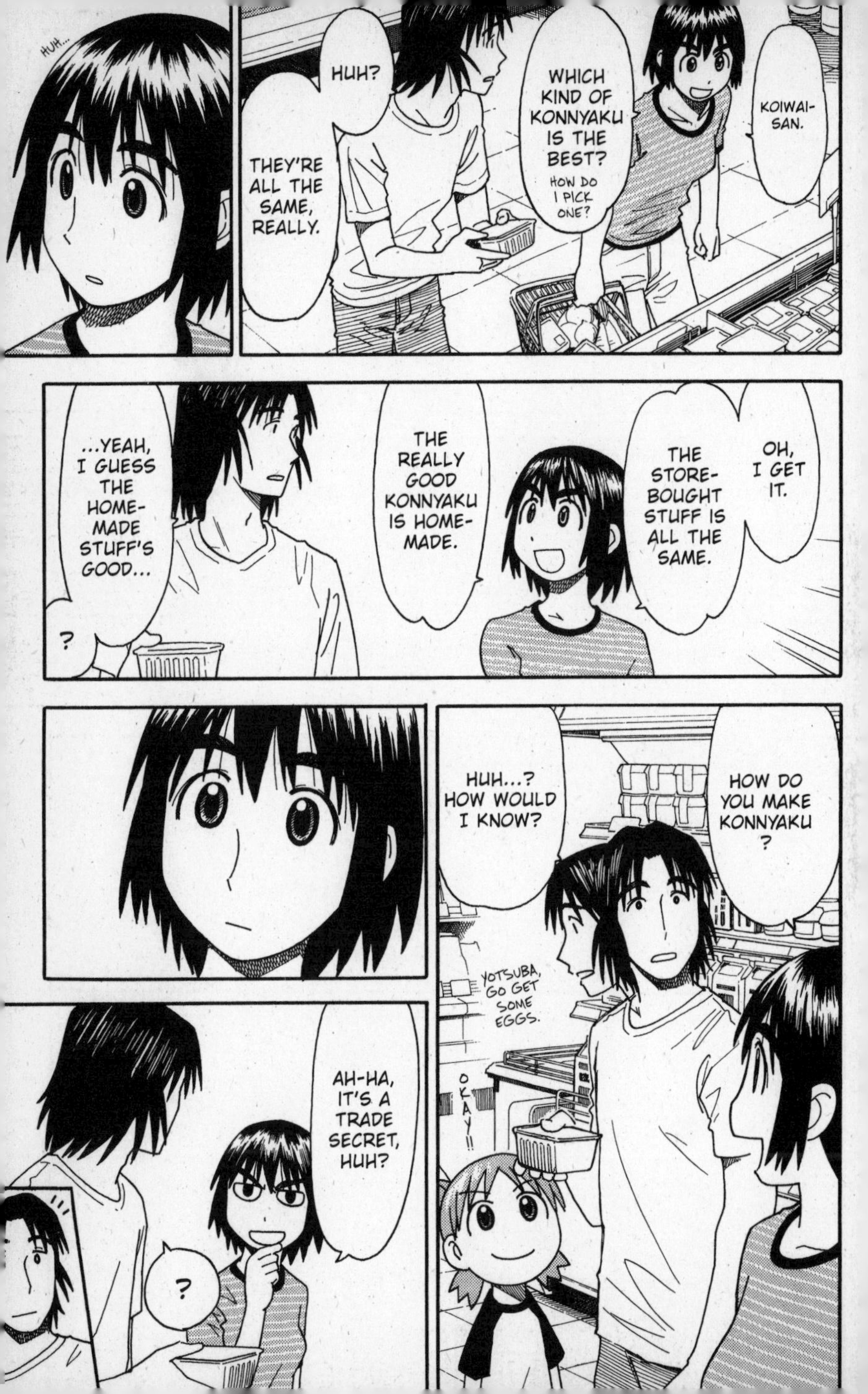
KOIWAI-SAN.
WHICH KIND OF KONNYAKU IS THE BEST?
HOW DO I PICK ONE?
HUH?
THEY'RE ALL THE SAME, REALLY.
HUH...
OH, I GET IT.
THE STORE-BOUGHT STUFF IS ALL THE SAME.
THE REALLY GOOD KONNYAKU IS HOME-MADE.
...YEAH, I GUESS THE HOME-MADE STUFF'S GOOD...
?
HOW DO YOU MAKE KONNYAKU?
HUH...? HOW WOULD I KNOW?
YOTSUBA, GO GET SOME EGGS.
OKAY!!
AH-HA, IT'S A TRADE SECRET, HUH?
?

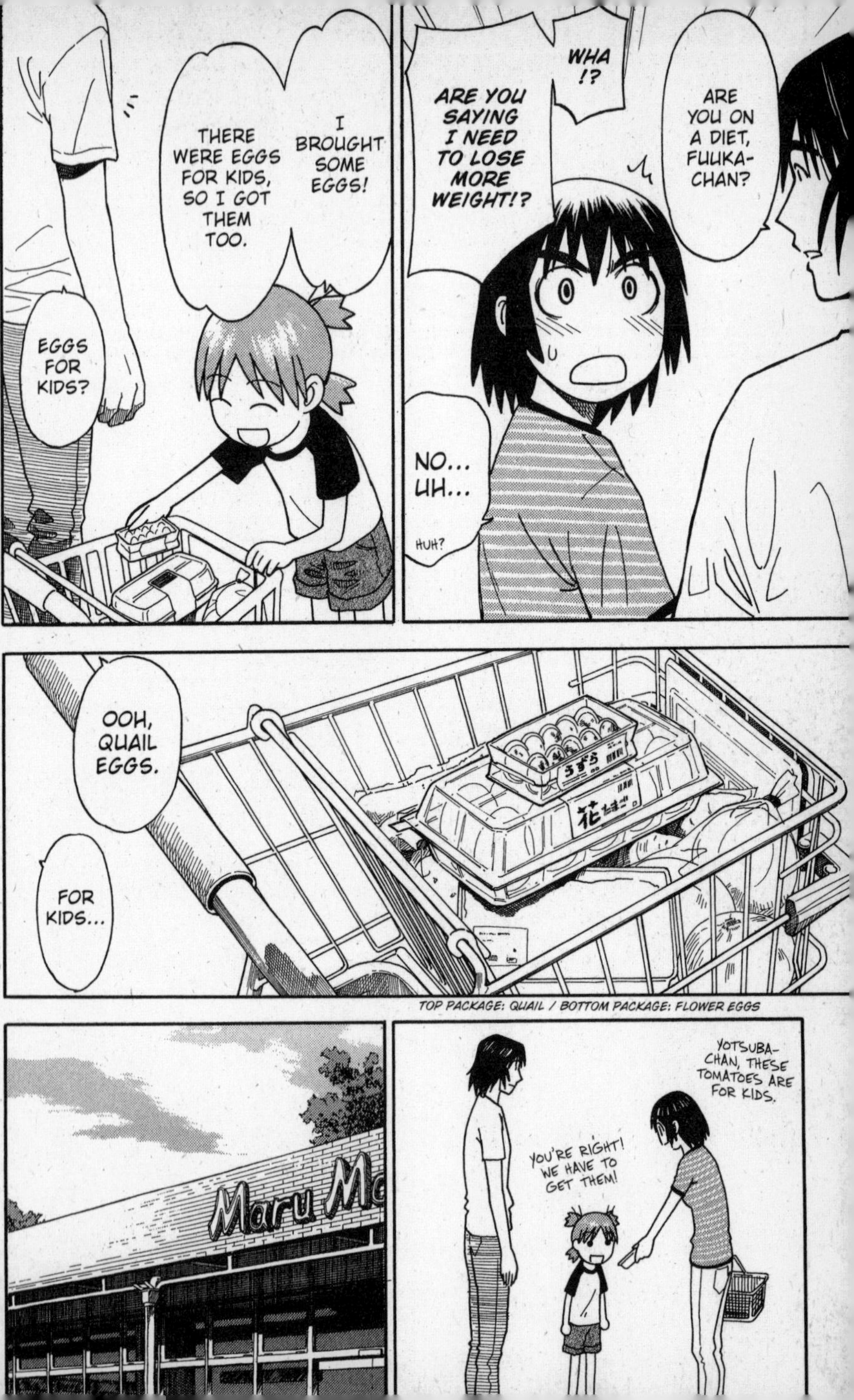
ARE YOU ON A DIET, FUUKA-CHAN?
WHA !?
ARE YOU SAYING I NEED TO LOSE MORE WEIGHT!?
NO... UH...
HUH?
I BROUGHT SOME EGGS!
THERE WERE EGGS FOR KIDS, SO I GOT THEM TOO.
EGGS FOR KIDS?
OOH, QUAIL EGGS.
FOR KIDS...
うずら
花たまご
YOTSUBA-CHAN, THESE TOMATOES ARE FOR KIDS.
YOU'RE RIGHT! WE HAVE TO GET THEM!
Maru Mo
TOP PACKAGE: QUAIL / BOTTOM PACKAGE: FLOWER EGGS

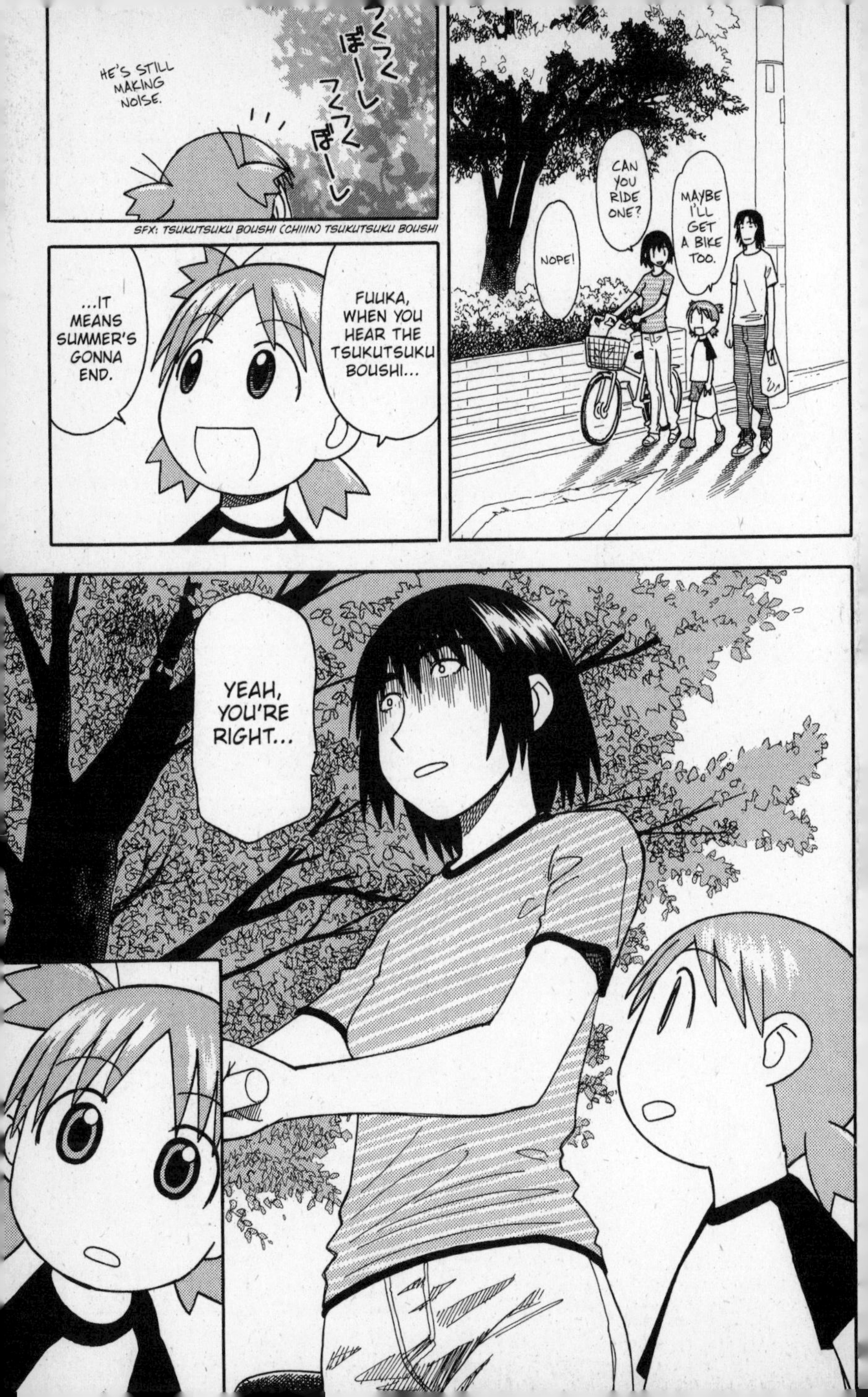
MAYBE I'LL GET A BIKE TOO.
CAN YOU RIDE ONE?
NOPE!
つくつくぼーし
つくつくぼーし
HE'S STILL MAKING NOISE.
SFX: TSUKUTSUKU BOUSHI (CHIIIN) TSUKUTSUKU BOUSHI
FUUKA, WHEN YOU HEAR THE TSUKUTSUKU BOUSHI...
...IT MEANS SUMMER'S GONNA END.
YEAH, YOU'RE RIGHT...

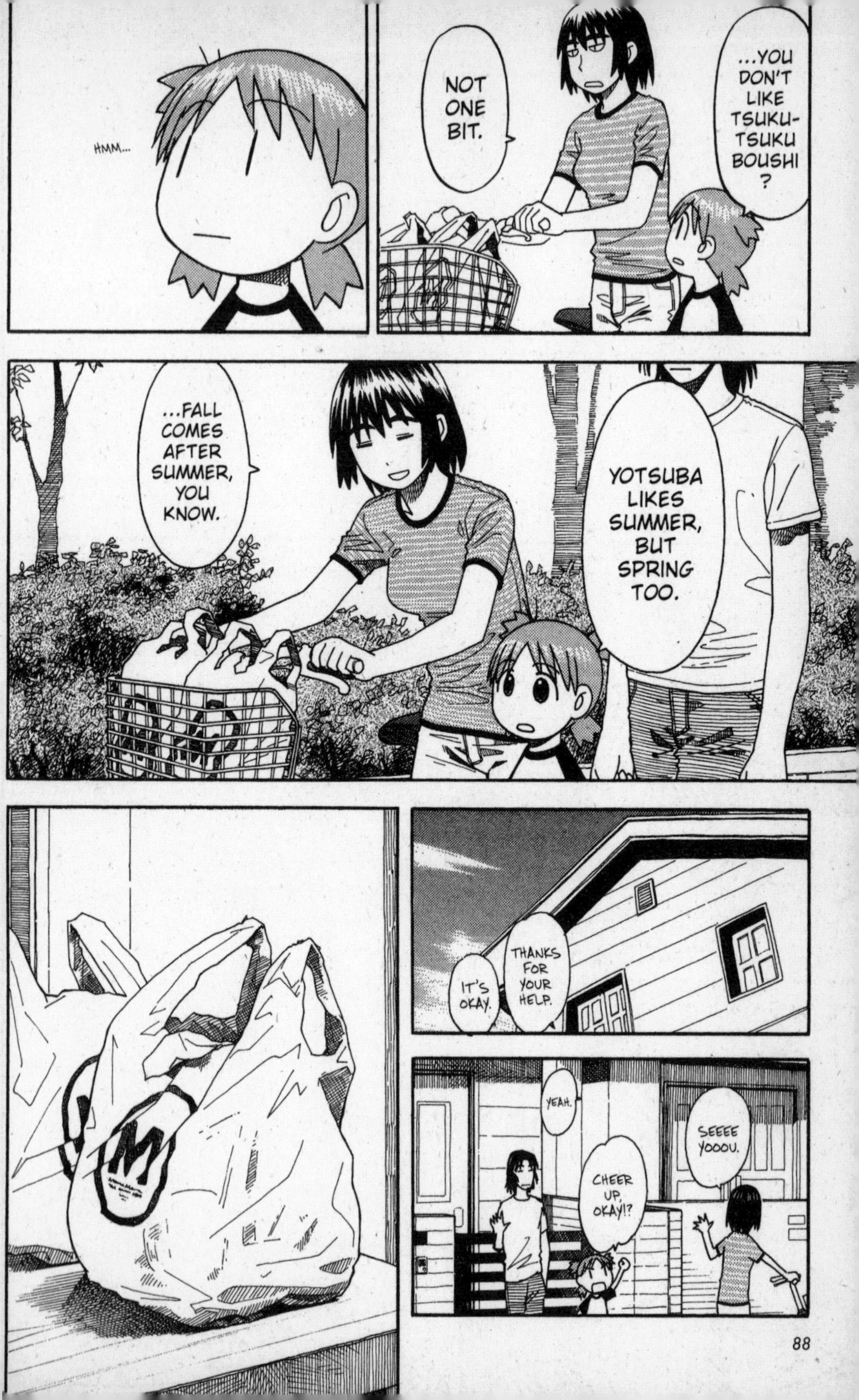
...YOU DON'T LIKE TSUKU-TSUKU BOUSHI?
NOT ONE BIT.
HMM...
YOTSUBA LIKES SUMMER, BUT SPRING TOO.
...FALL COMES AFTER SUMMER, YOU KNOW.
THANKS FOR YOUR HELP.
IT'S OKAY.
SEEEE YOOOU.
YEAH.
CHEER UP, OKAY!?

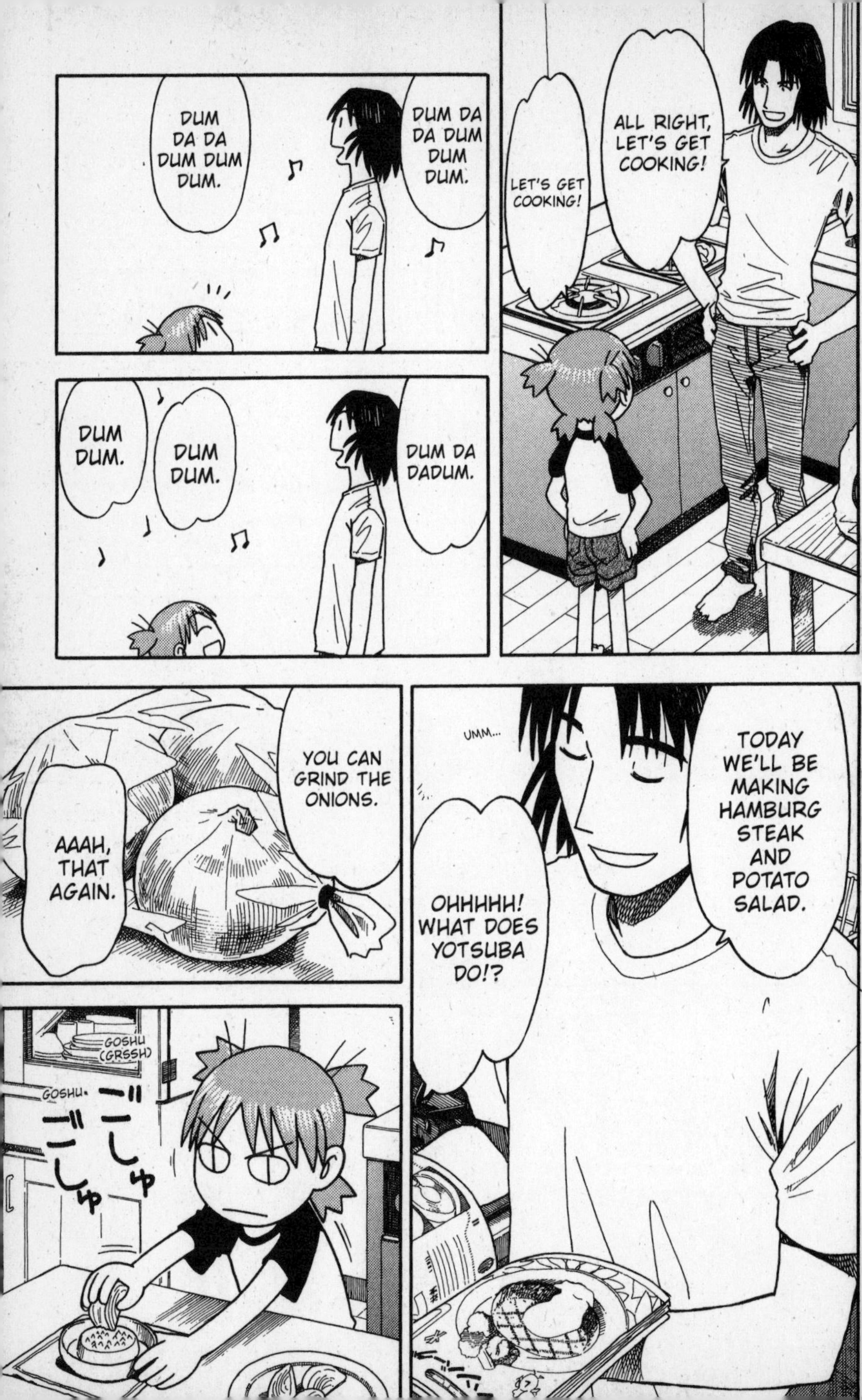
ALL RIGHT, LET'S GET COOKING!
LET'S GET COOKING!
DUM DA DA DUM DUM DUM.
DUM DA DA DUM DUM DUM.
DUM DA DADUM.
DUM DUM.
DUM DUM.
TODAY WE'LL BE MAKING HAMBURG STEAK AND POTATO SALAD.
UMM...
OHHHHH! WHAT DOES YOTSUBA DO!?
YOU CAN GRIND THE ONIONS.
AAAH, THAT AGAIN.
GOSHU (GRSSH)
GOSHU.
ごしゅ
ごしゅ

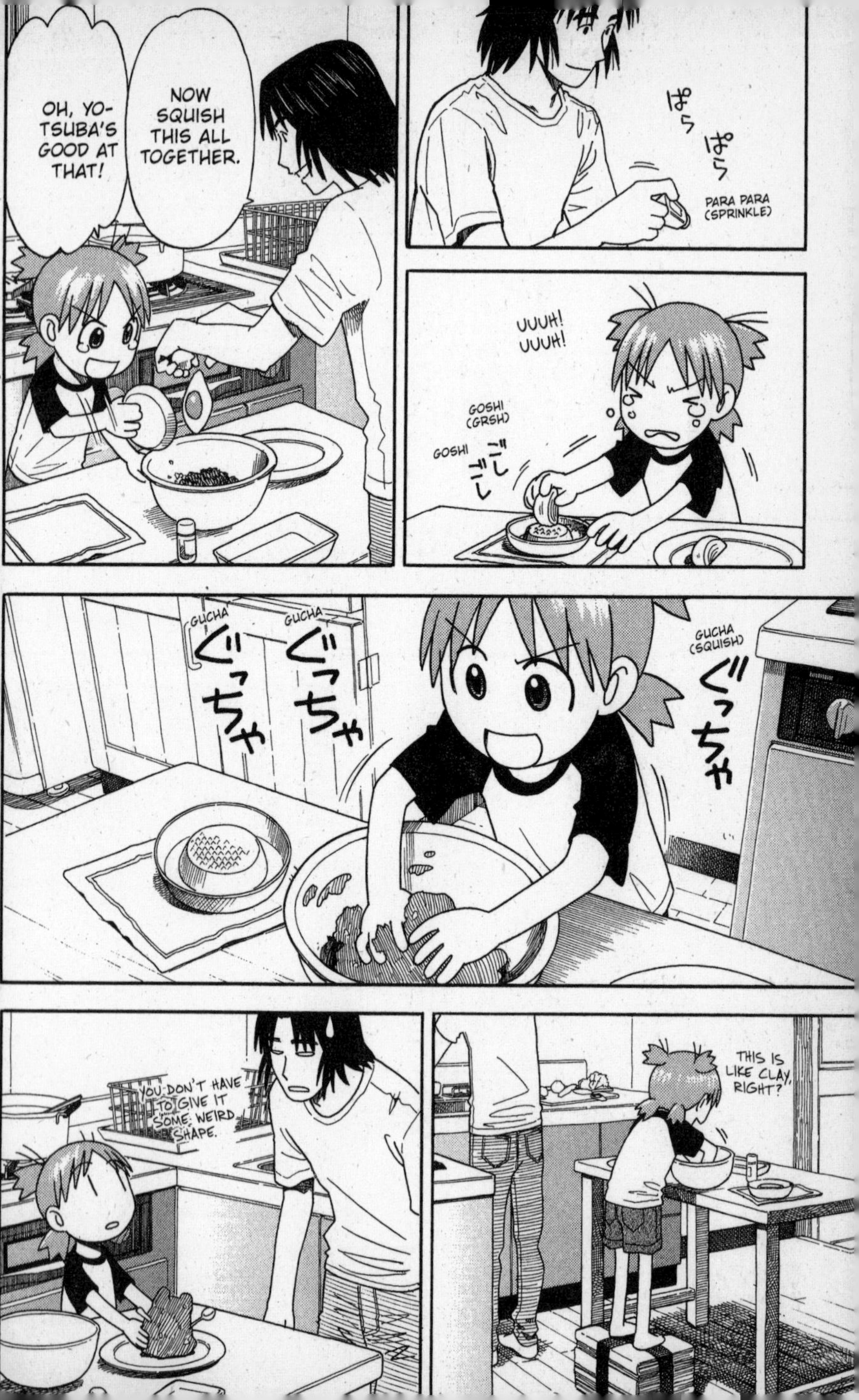
ぱら ぱら
PARA PARA (SPRINKLE)
UUUH! UUUH!
GOSHI (GRSH)
ごし
GOSHI
ごし
NOW SQUISH THIS ALL TOGETHER.
OH, YO-TSUBA'S GOOD AT THAT!
GUCHA (SQUISH)
ぐっちゃ
GUCHA
ぐっちゃ
GUCHA
ぐっちゃ
THIS IS LIKE CLAY, RIGHT?
YOU DON'T HAVE TO GIVE IT SOME WEIRD SHAPE.

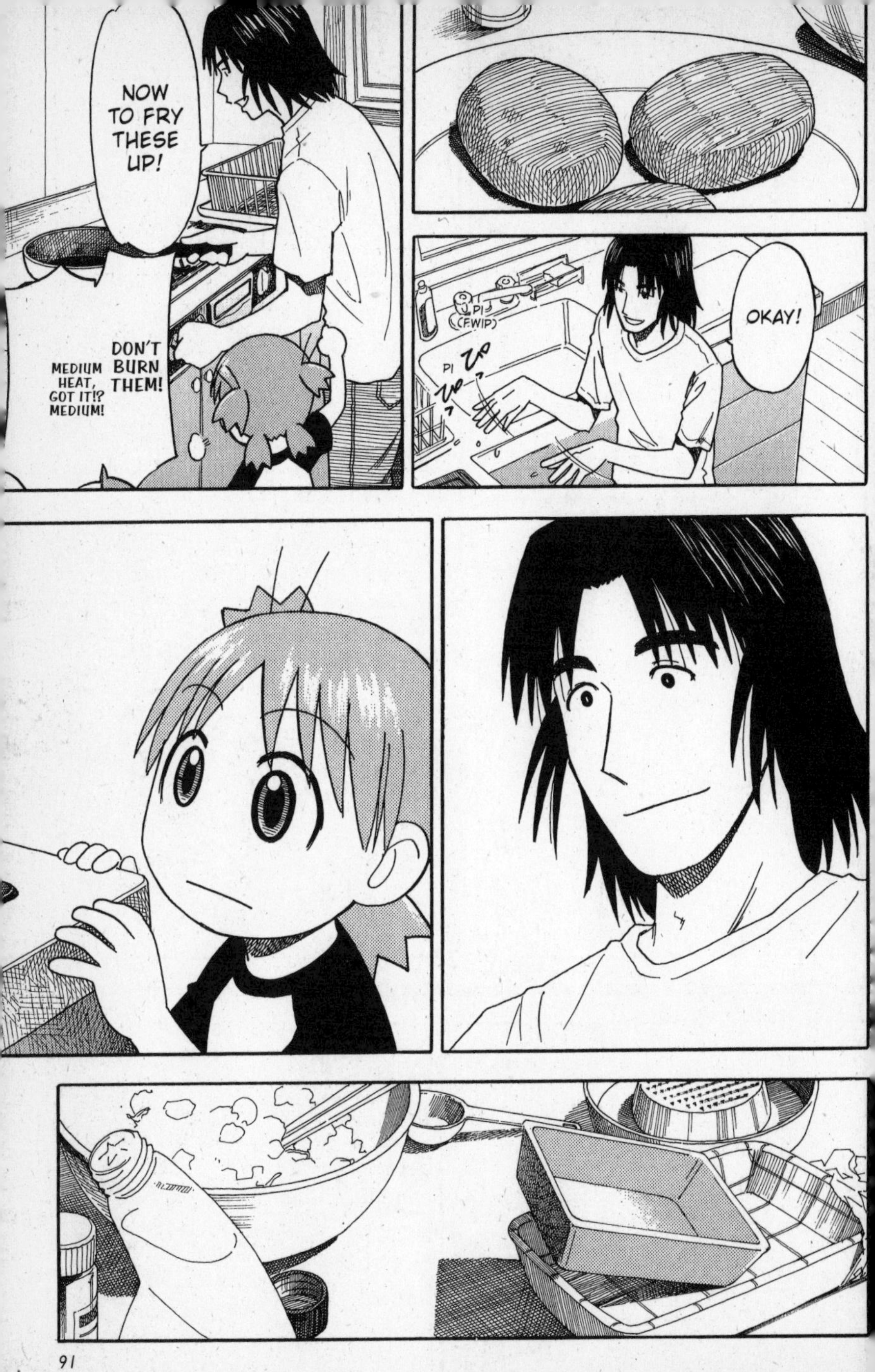
OKAY!
PI
(FWIP)
PI
NOW TO FRY THESE UP!
DON'T BURN THEM!
MEDIUM HEAT, GOT IT!? MEDIUM!

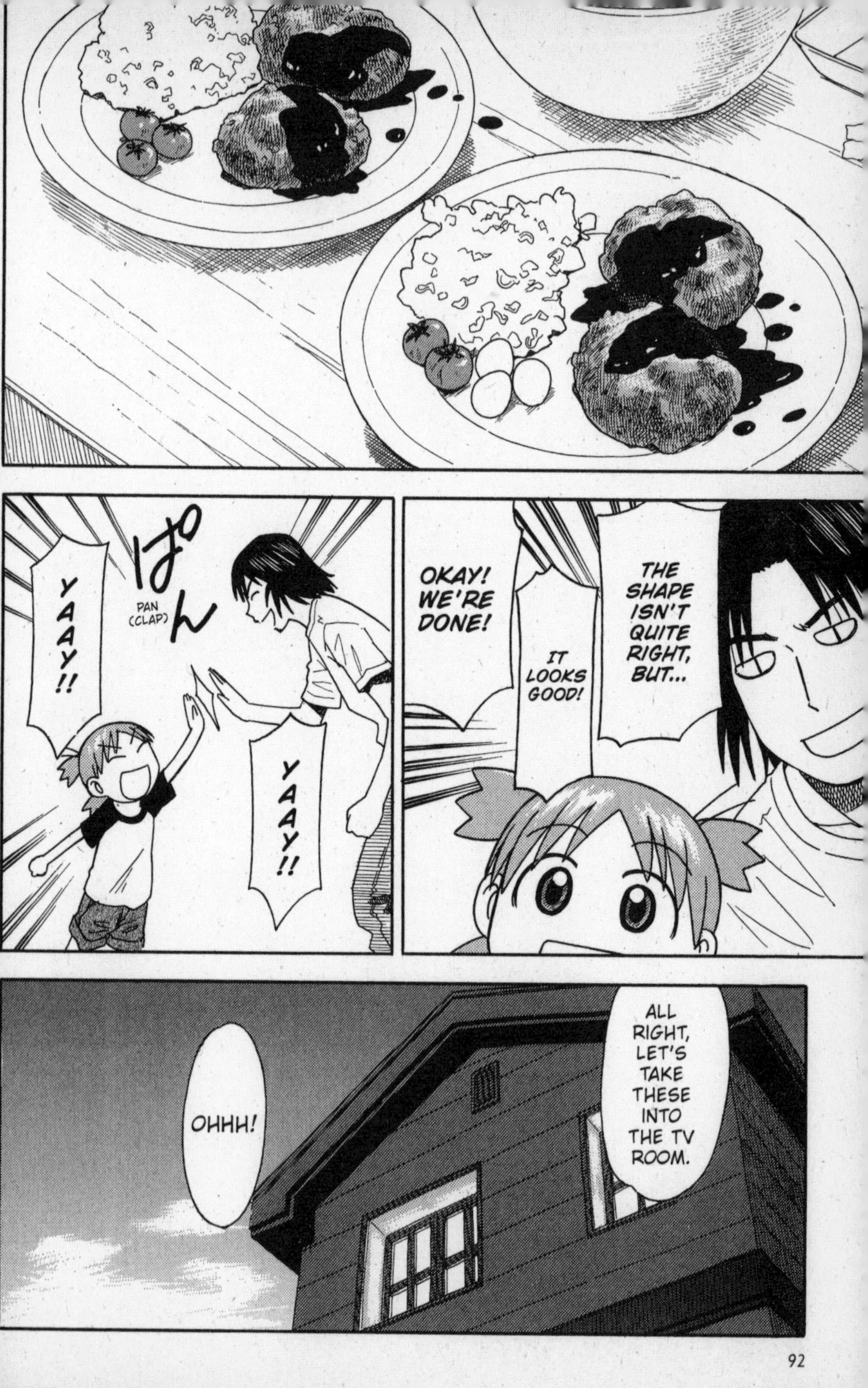
THE SHAPE ISN'T QUITE RIGHT, BUT...
IT LOOKS GOOD!
OKAY! WE'RE DONE!
ぱん
PAN (CLAP)
YAAAY!!
YAAAY!!
ALL RIGHT, LET'S TAKE THESE INTO THE TV ROOM.
OHHH!

YOTSUBA&!

YOTSUBA& 4-PANEL COMICS

INTERMISSION

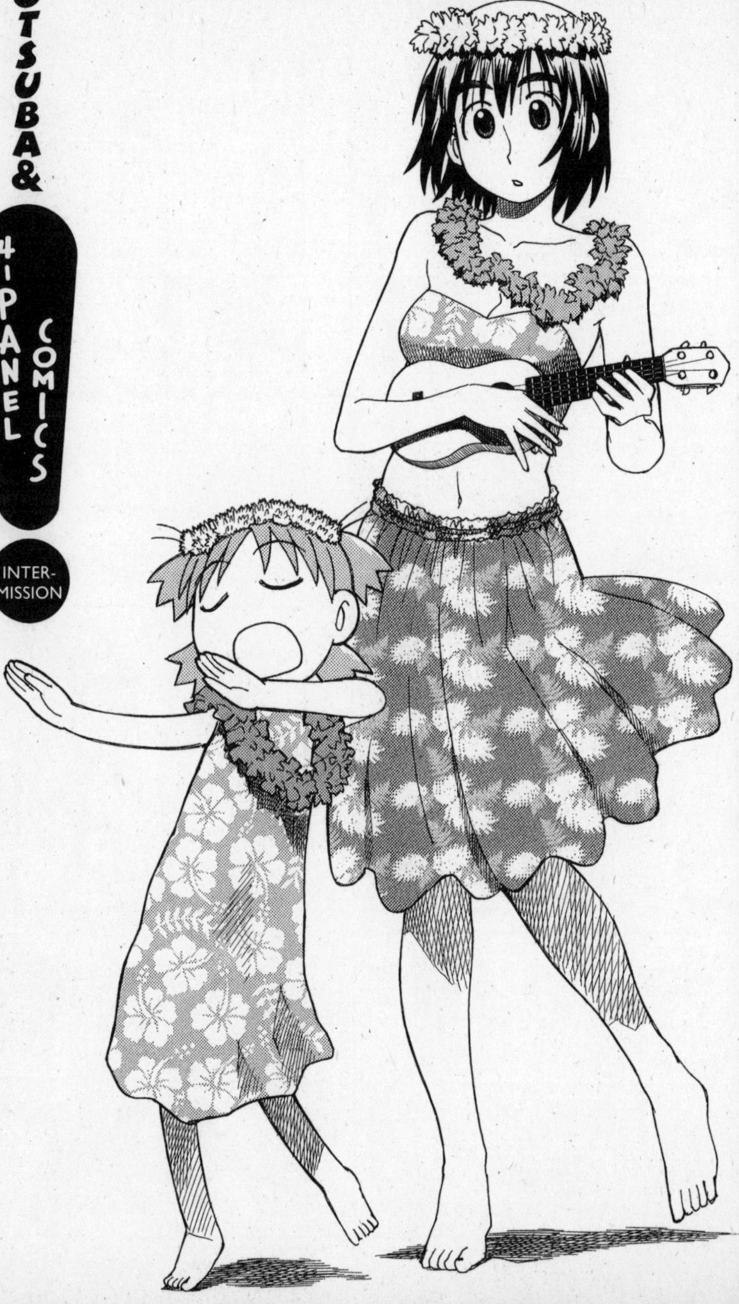

TRUE IDENTITY

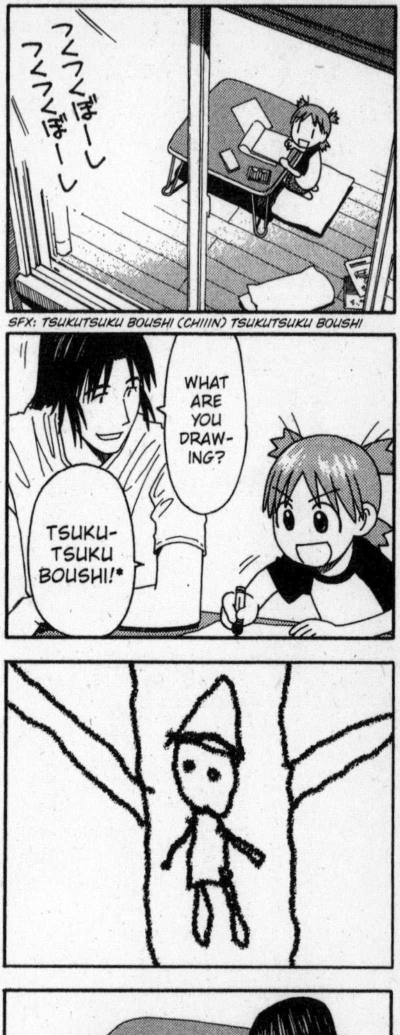

つくつくぼーし
つくつくぼーし
SFX: TSUKUTSUKU BOUSHI (CHIIIN) TSUKUTSUKU BOUSHI
WHAT ARE YOU DRAWING?
TSUKU-TSUKU BOUSHI!*

FLYING

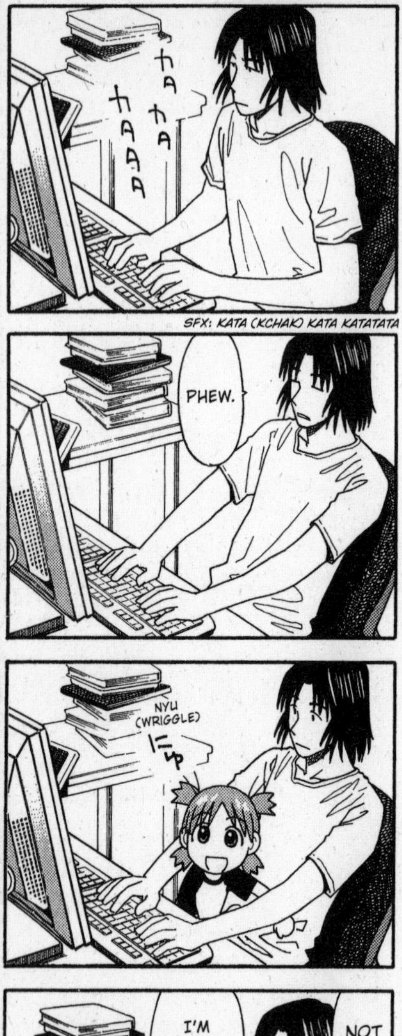

カタ
カタ
カタタタ
SFX: KATA (KCHAK) KATA KATATATA
PHEW.
NYU (WRIGGLE)
にゅ
NOT YET.
I'M NOT DONE WORKING YET.
HUH?

*TSUKUTSUKU BOUSHI *LITERALLY MEANS* "POKE-POKE HAT," *WHICH IS WHY YOTSUBA THINKS IT'S REFERRING TO A POINTY HAT.*

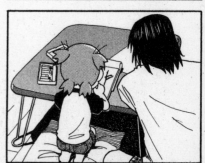

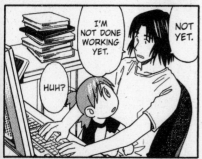

GET READY, GET SET...

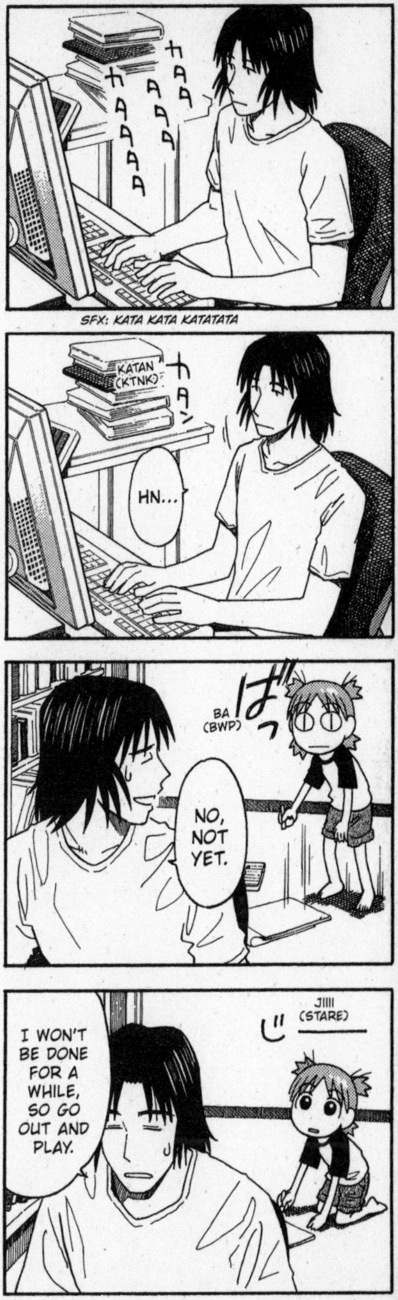
SFX: KATA KATA KATATATA
KATAN (KTNK)
HN...
BA (BWP)
NO, NOT YET.
JIIII (STARE)
I WON'T BE DONE FOR A WHILE, SO GO OUT AND PLAY.

KICKOFF

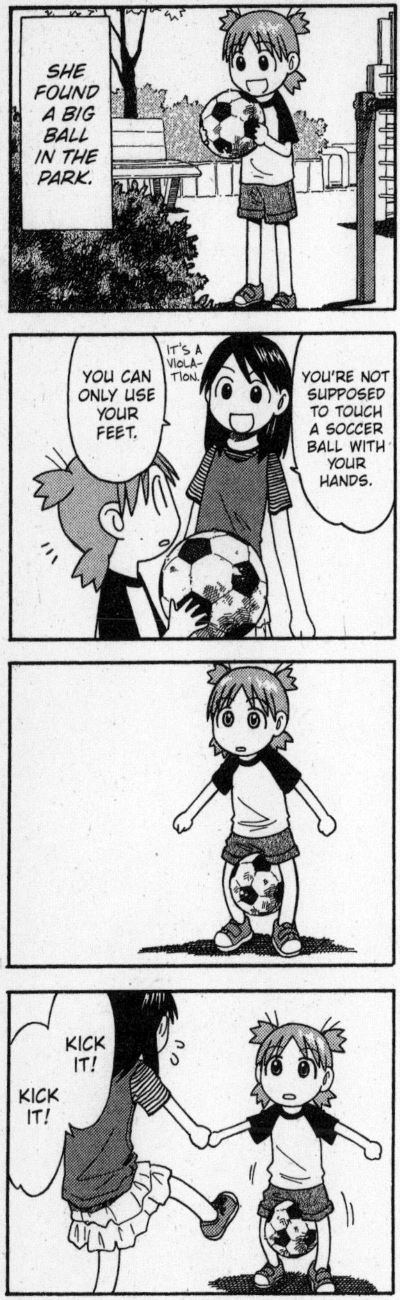
SHE FOUND A BIG BALL IN THE PARK.
YOU'RE NOT SUPPOSED TO TOUCH A SOCCER BALL WITH YOUR HANDS.
IT'S A VIOLATION.
YOU CAN ONLY USE YOUR FEET.
KICK IT!
KICK IT!

GOAL

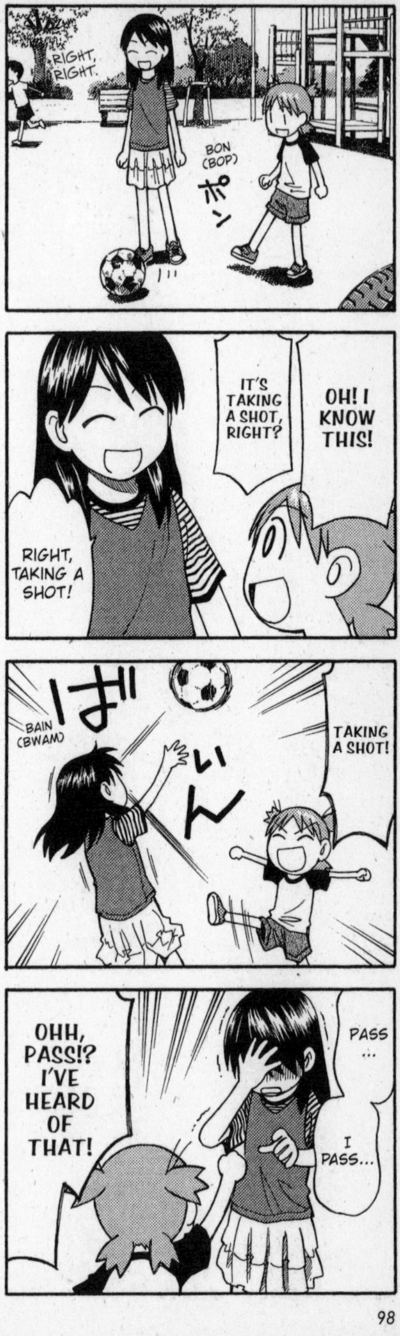
RIGHT, RIGHT.
BON (BOP)
ポン
OH! I KNOW THIS!
IT'S TAKING A SHOT, RIGHT?
RIGHT, TAKING A SHOT!
TAKING A SHOT!
ばいん
BAIN (BWAM)
PASS ...
I PASS...
OHH, PASS!? I'VE HEARD OF THAT!

OBEY THE RULES

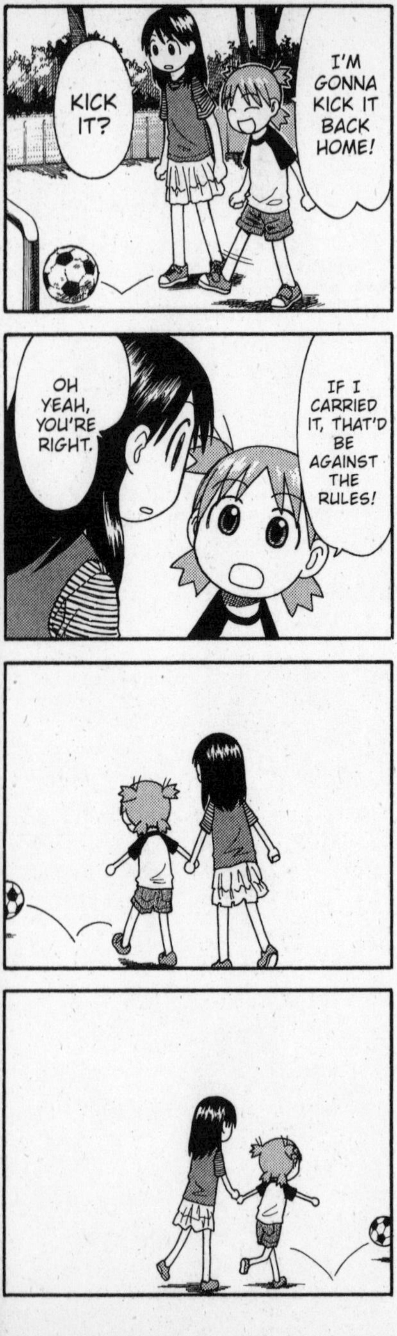
I'M GONNA KICK IT BACK HOME!
KICK IT?
IF I CARRIED IT, THAT'D BE AGAINST THE RULES!
OH YEAH, YOU'RE RIGHT.

HAND OF GOD

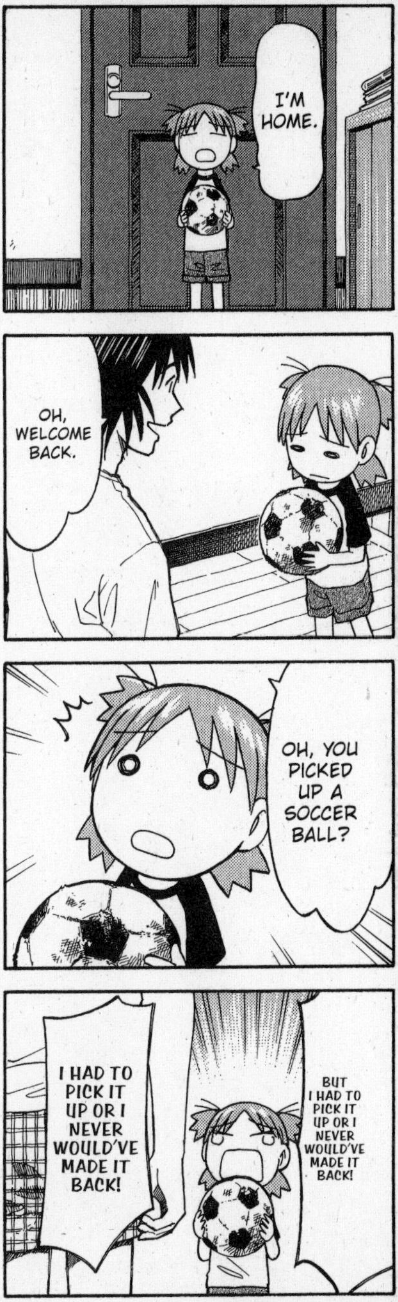
I'M HOME.
OH, WELCOME BACK.
OH, YOU PICKED UP A SOCCER BALL?
BUT I HAD TO PICK IT UP OR I NEVER WOULD'VE MADE IT BACK!
I HAD TO PICK IT UP OR I NEVER WOULD'VE MADE IT BACK!

CRUEL

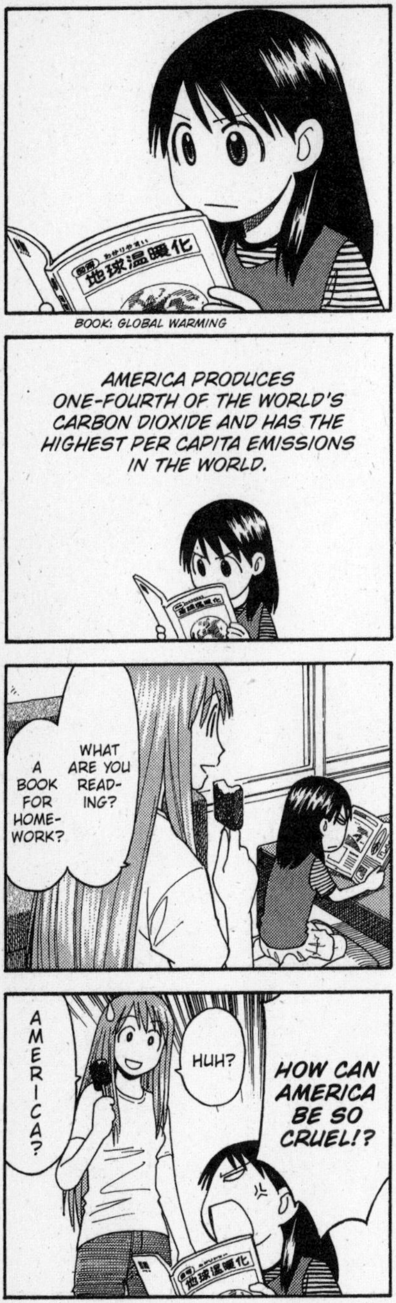
BOOK: GLOBAL WARMING
AMERICA PRODUCES ONE-FOURTH OF THE WORLD'S CARBON DIOXIDE AND HAS THE HIGHEST PER CAPITA EMISSIONS IN THE WORLD.
WHAT ARE YOU READING?
A BOOK FOR HOMEWORK?
HOW CAN AMERICA BE SO CRUEL!?
HUH?
AMERICA?

ACTUALLY, IT'S BROWN.

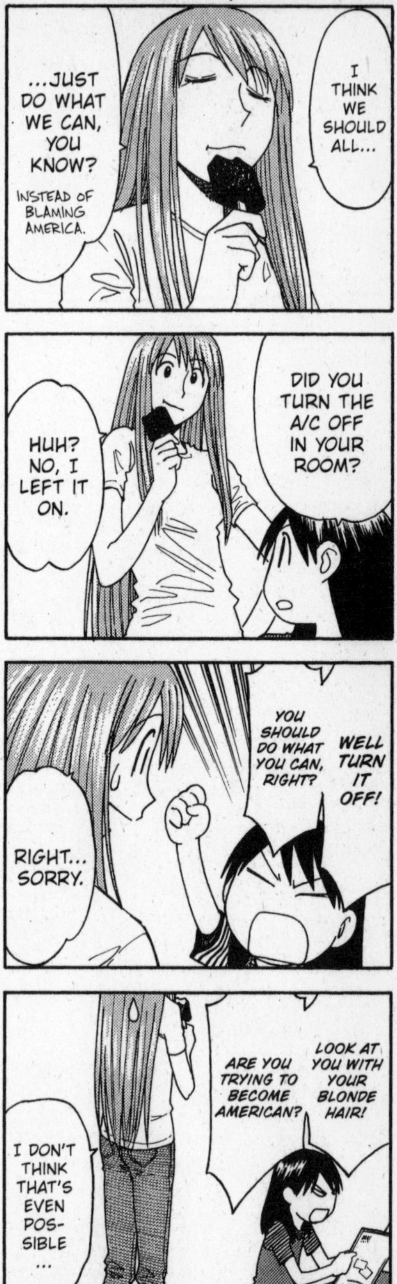
I THINK WE SHOULD ALL...
...JUST DO WHAT WE CAN, YOU KNOW?
INSTEAD OF BLAMING AMERICA.
DID YOU TURN THE A/C OFF IN YOUR ROOM?
HUH? NO, I LEFT IT ON.
WELL TURN IT OFF!
YOU SHOULD DO WHAT YOU CAN, RIGHT?
RIGHT... SORRY.
LOOK AT YOU WITH YOUR BLONDE HAIR!
ARE YOU TRYING TO BECOME AMERICAN?
I DON'T THINK THAT'S EVEN POS-SIBLE...

DIFFICULT QUESTION

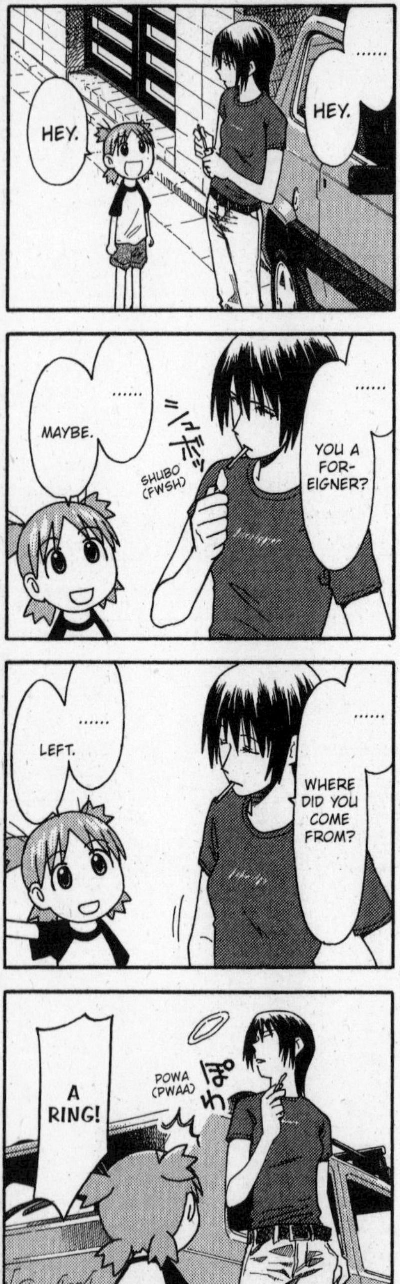
......
HEY.
HEY.
......
YOU A FOR-EIGNER?
シュボッ
SHUBO (FWSH)
......
MAYBE.
......
WHERE DID YOU COME FROM?
......
LEFT.
ぽわ
POWA (PWAA)
A RING!

I DON'T GET IT

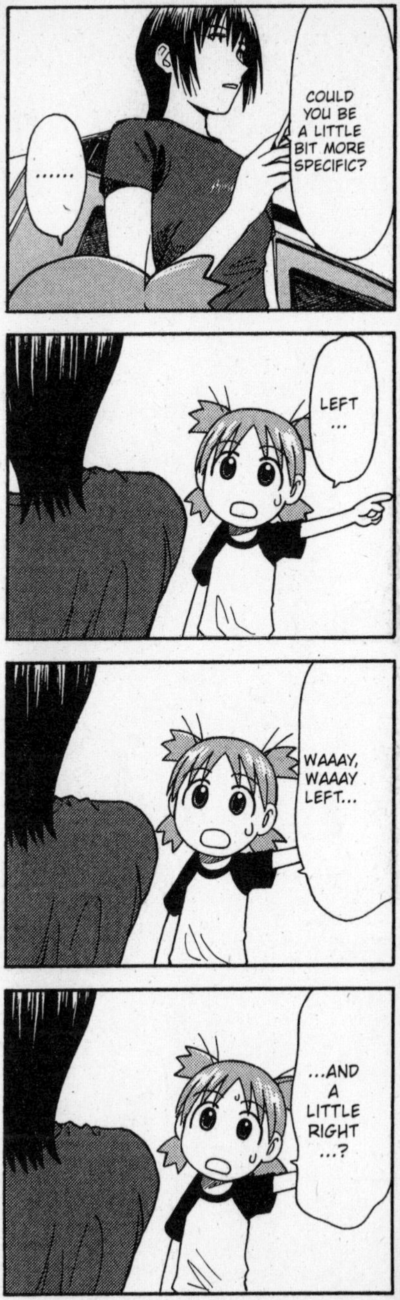
COULD YOU BE A LITTLE BIT MORE SPECIFIC?
......
LEFT ...
WAAAY, WAAAY LEFT...
...AND A LITTLE RIGHT ...?

WHERE ARE YOU GOING?

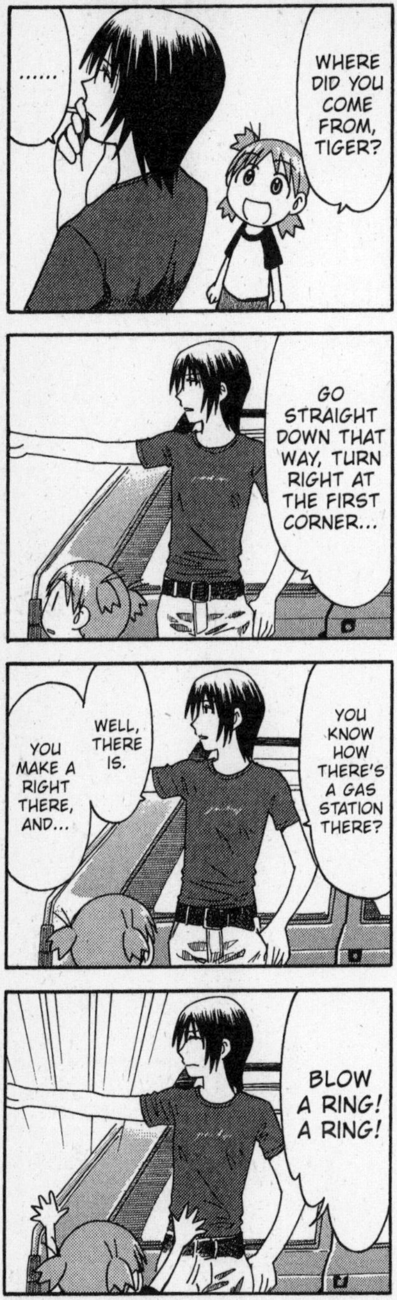
WHERE DID YOU COME FROM, TIGER?
......
GO STRAIGHT DOWN THAT WAY, TURN RIGHT AT THE FIRST CORNER...
YOU KNOW HOW THERE'S A GAS STATION THERE?
WELL, THERE IS.
YOU MAKE A RIGHT THERE, AND...
BLOW A RING! A RING!

THE SPANKING

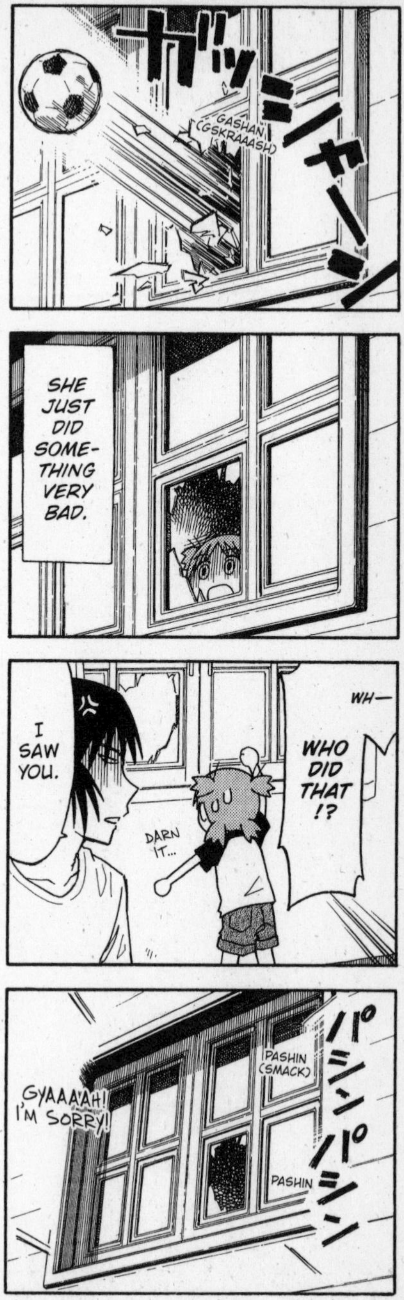
GASHAN (GSKRAAASH)
SHE JUST DID SOME-THING VERY BAD.
WH—
WHO DID THAT !?
I SAW YOU.
DARN IT...
PASHIN (SMACK)
PASHIN
GYAAAAH! I'M SORRY!

I DID SOMETHING BAD

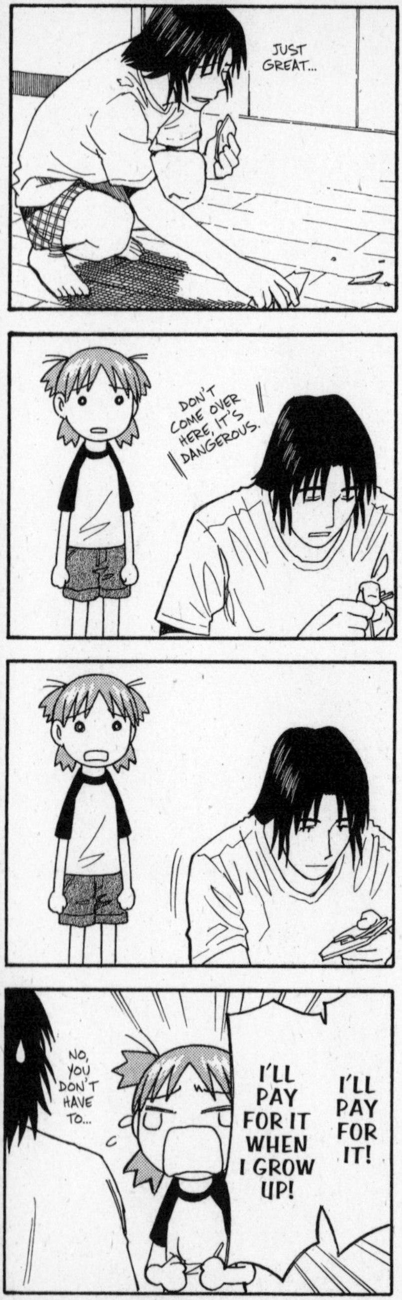
JUST GREAT...
DON'T COME OVER HERE, IT'S DANGEROUS.
I'LL PAY FOR IT!
I'LL PAY FOR IT WHEN I GROW UP!
NO, YOU DON'T HAVE TO...

YOTSUBA&!

YOTSUBA& YOUTH

#25

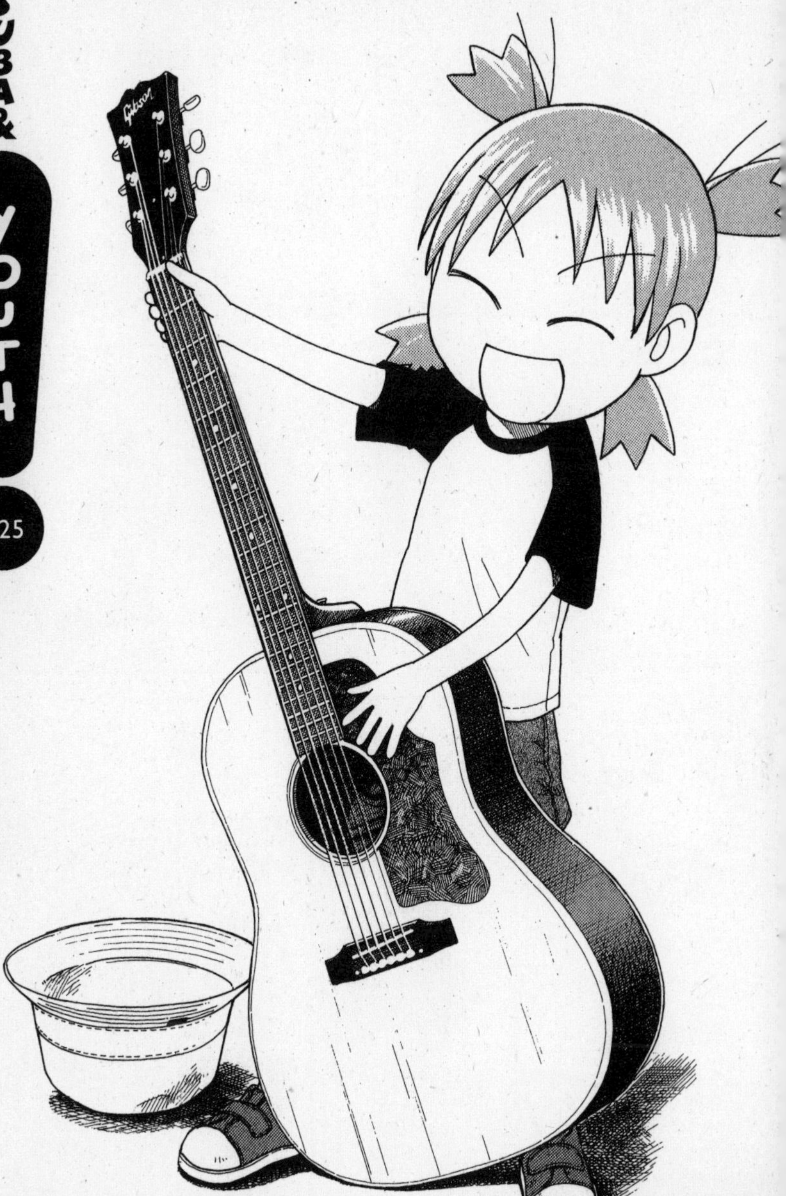
Gibson

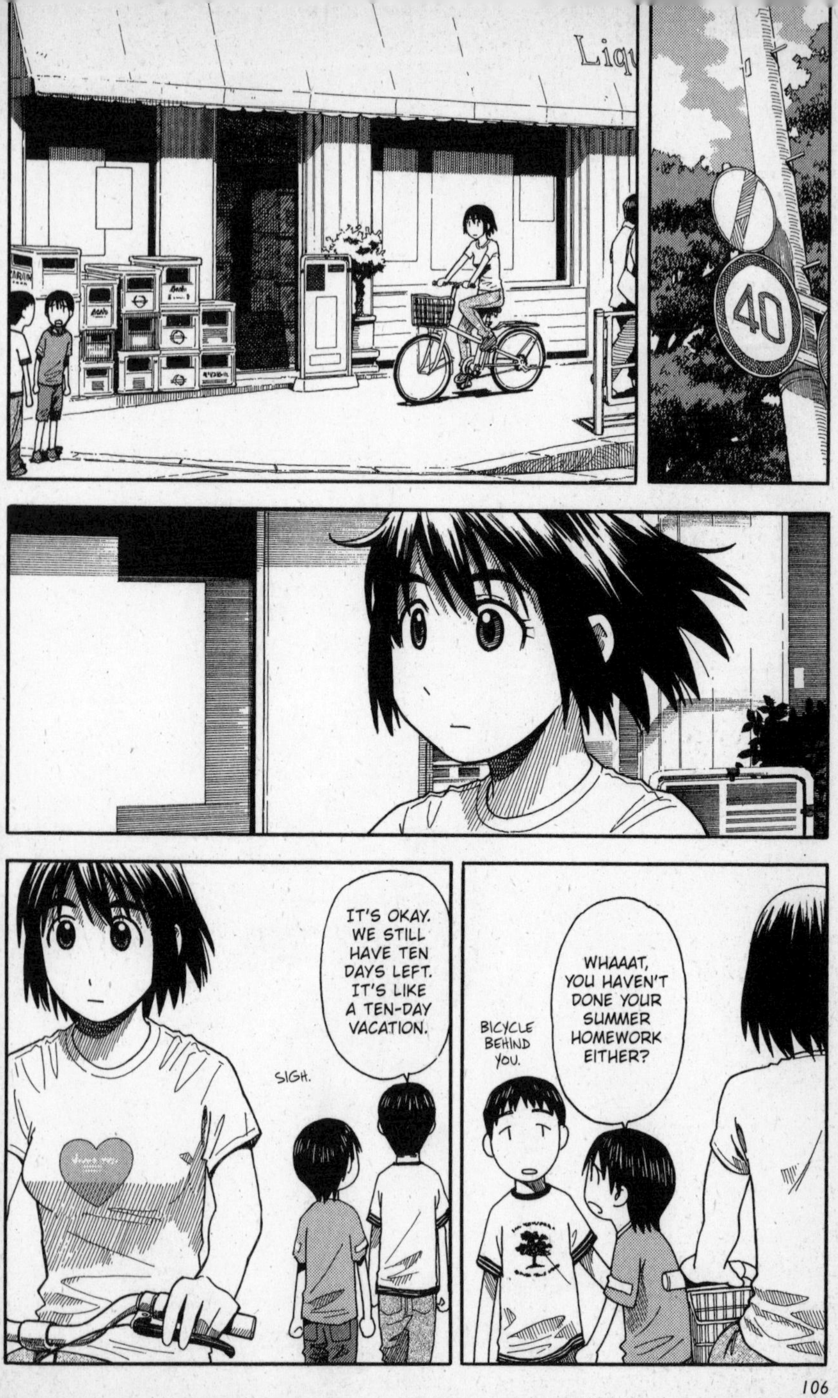
40
Liqu
WHAAAT, YOU HAVEN'T DONE YOUR SUMMER HOMEWORK EITHER?
BICYCLE BEHIND YOU.
IT'S OKAY. WE STILL HAVE TEN DAYS LEFT. IT'S LIKE A TEN-DAY VACATION.
SIGH.

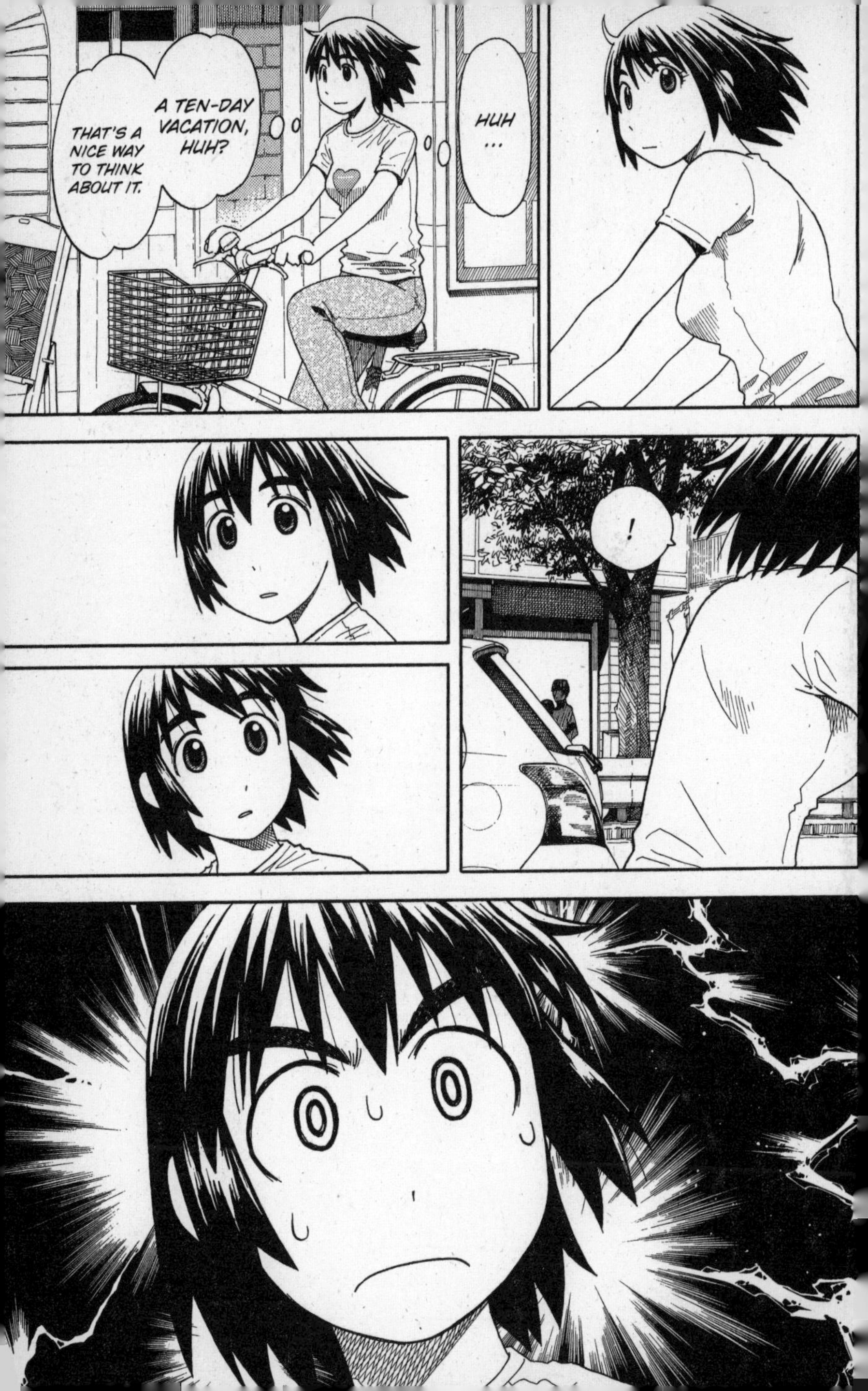
HUH ...
A TEN-DAY VACATION, HUH?
THAT'S A NICE WAY TO THINK ABOUT IT.
!

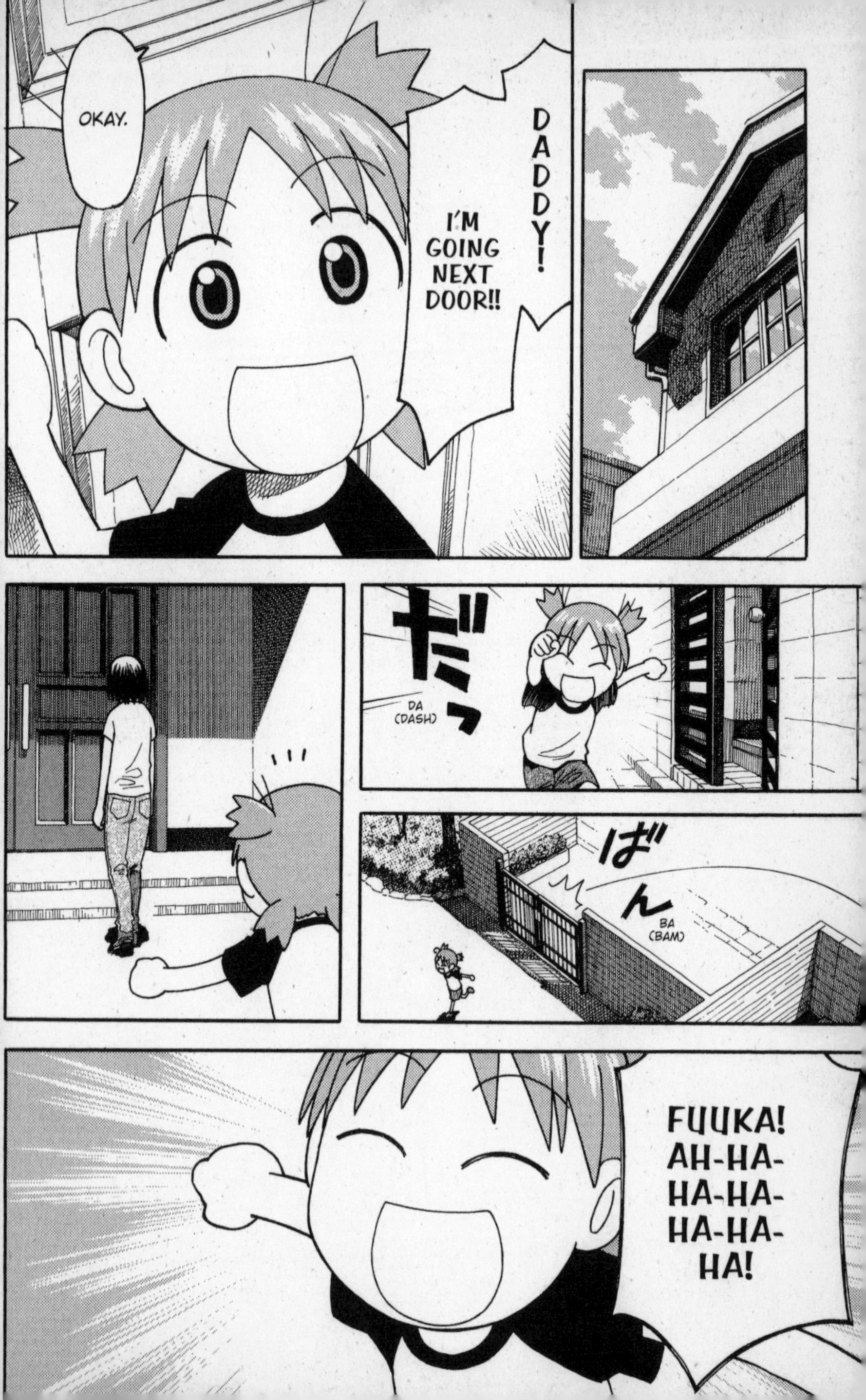
DADDY!
I'M GOING NEXT DOOR!!
OKAY.
ダッ
DA (DASH)
ばん
BA (BAM)
FUUKA! AH-HA-HA-HA-HA-HA-HA!

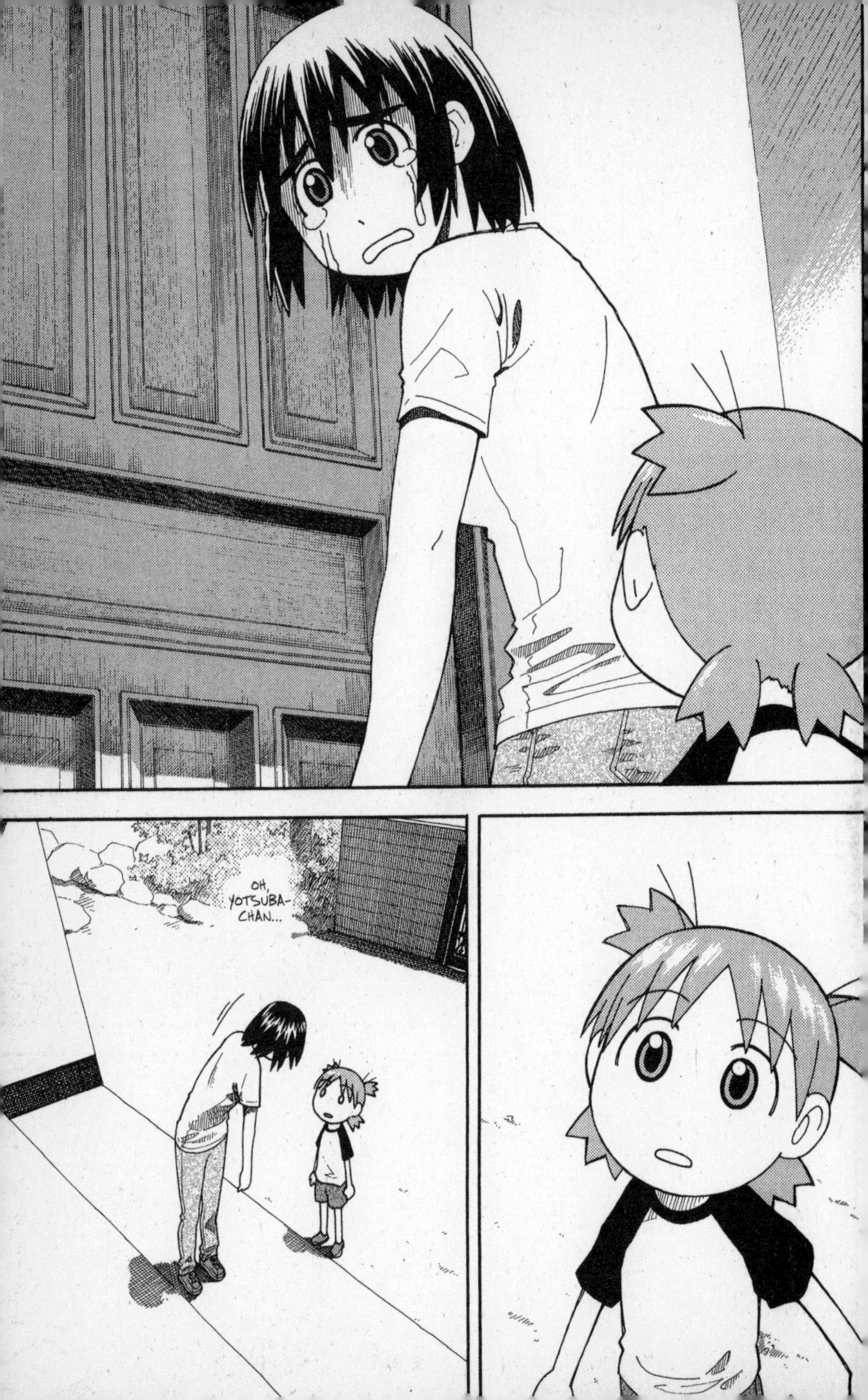
OH, YOTSUBA-CHAN...

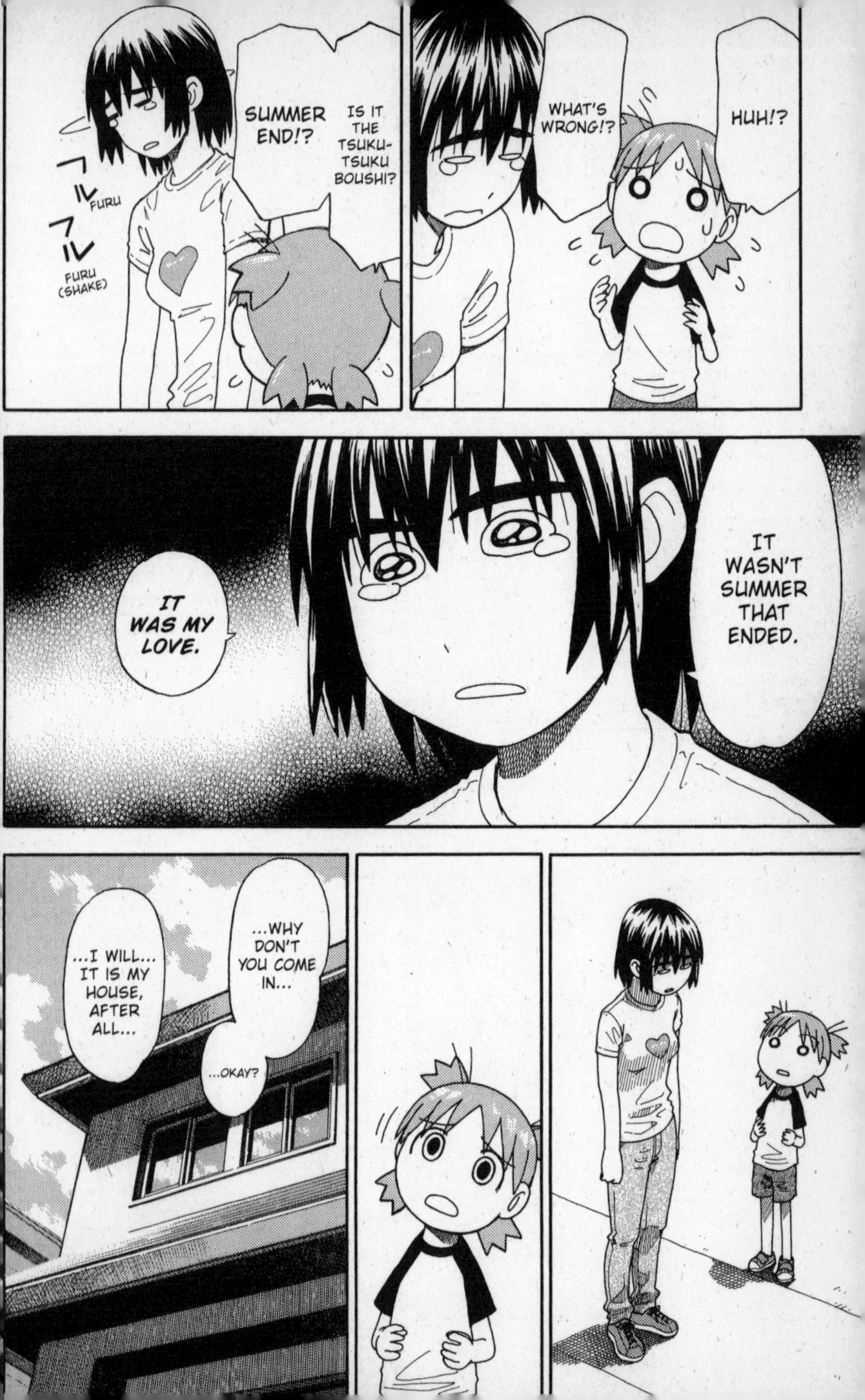
HUH!?
WHAT'S WRONG!?
IS IT THE TSUKU-TSUKU BOUSHI?
SUMMER END!?
フル FURU
フル FURU (SHAKE)
IT WASN'T SUMMER THAT ENDED.
IT WAS MY LOVE.
...WHY DON'T YOU COME IN...
...OKAY?
...I WILL... IT IS MY HOUSE, AFTER ALL...

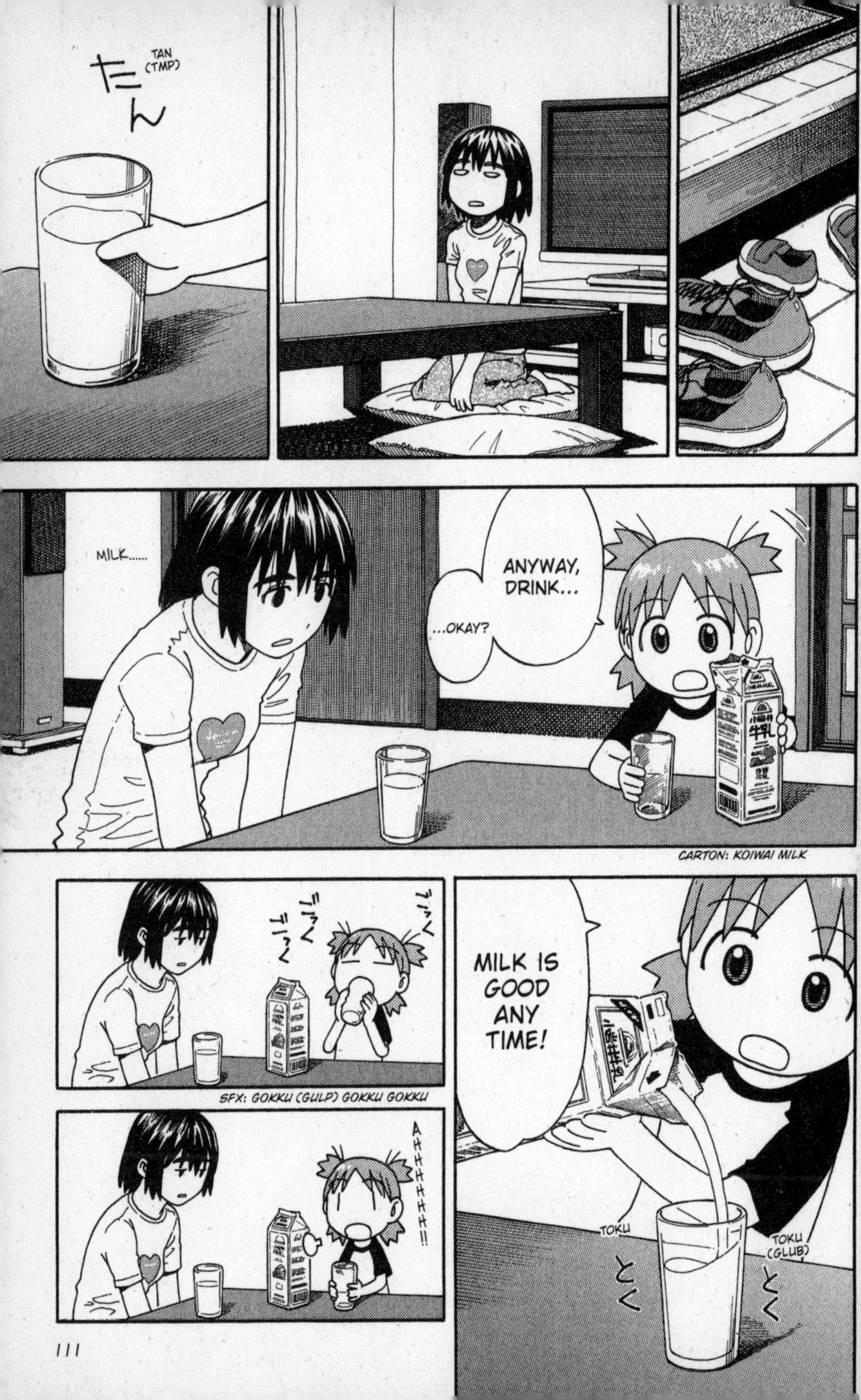
たん
TAN (TMP)
ANYWAY, DRINK...
...OKAY?
MILK......
CARTON: KOIWAI MILK
MILK IS GOOD ANY TIME!
TOKU (GLUB)
TOKU
とくとく
ごっく ごっく ごっく
SFX: GOKKU (GULP) GOKKU GOKKU
AHHHHHHH!!

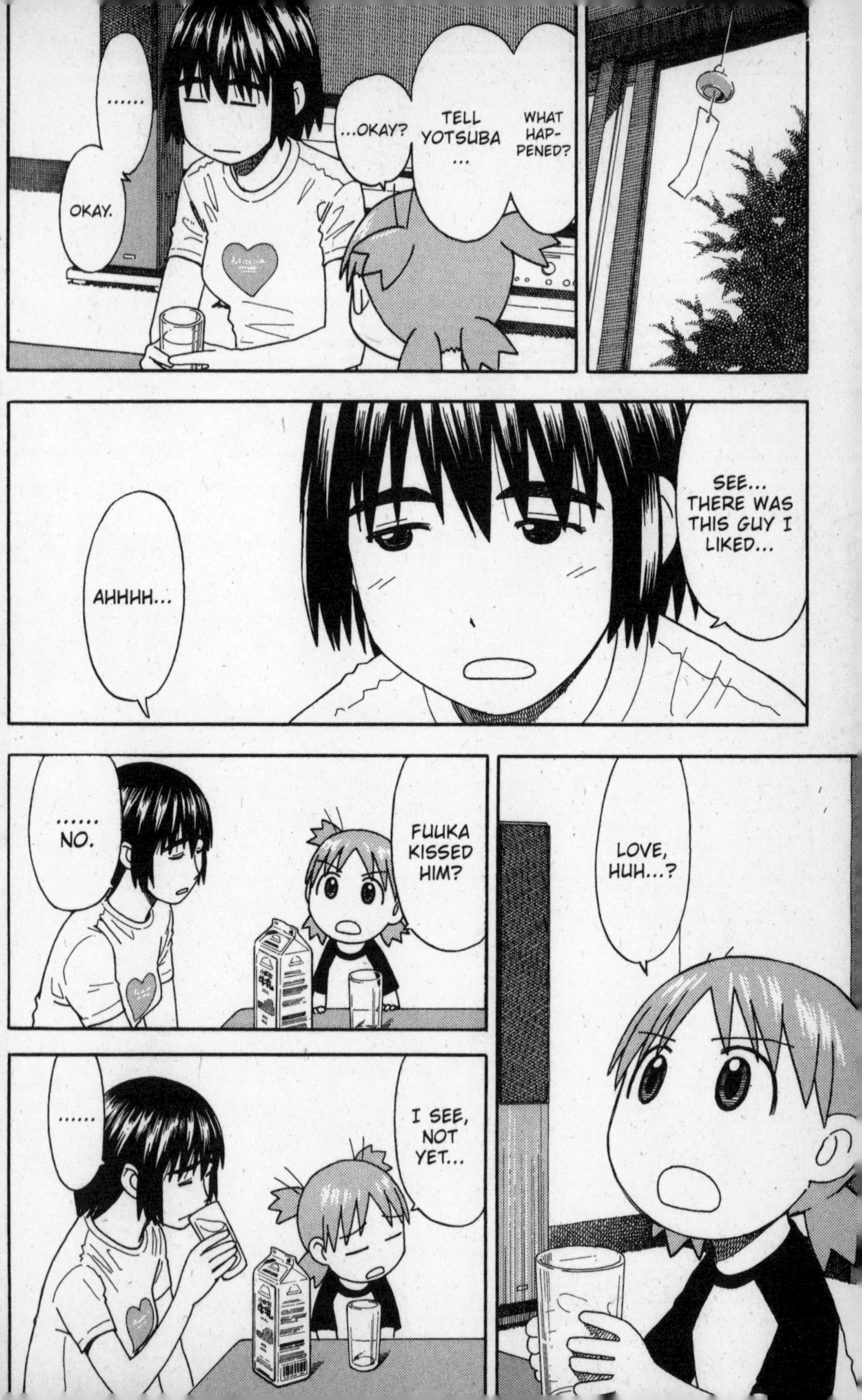
WHAT HAPPENED?
TELL YOTSUBA ...
...OKAY?
......
OKAY.
SEE... THERE WAS THIS GUY I LIKED...
AHHHH...
LOVE, HUH...?
FUUKA KISSED HIM?
...... NO.
I SEE, NOT YET...
......

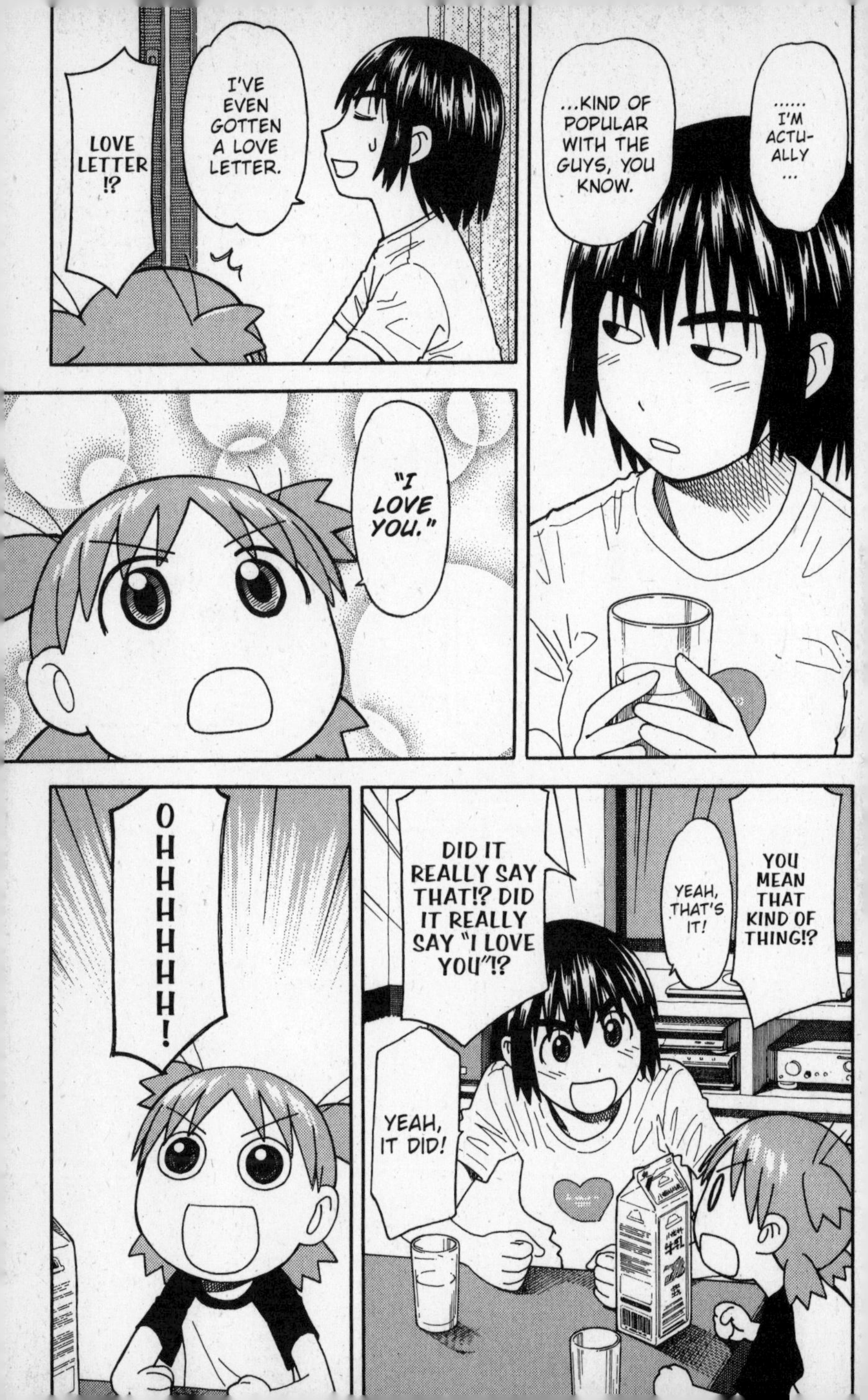
......I'M ACTU-ALLY...
...KIND OF POPULAR WITH THE GUYS, YOU KNOW.
I'VE EVEN GOTTEN A LOVE LETTER.
LOVE LETTER!?
"I LOVE YOU."
YOU MEAN THAT KIND OF THING!?
YEAH, THAT'S IT!
DID IT REALLY SAY THAT!? DID IT REALLY SAY "I LOVE YOU"!?
YEAH, IT DID!
OHHHHHHH!

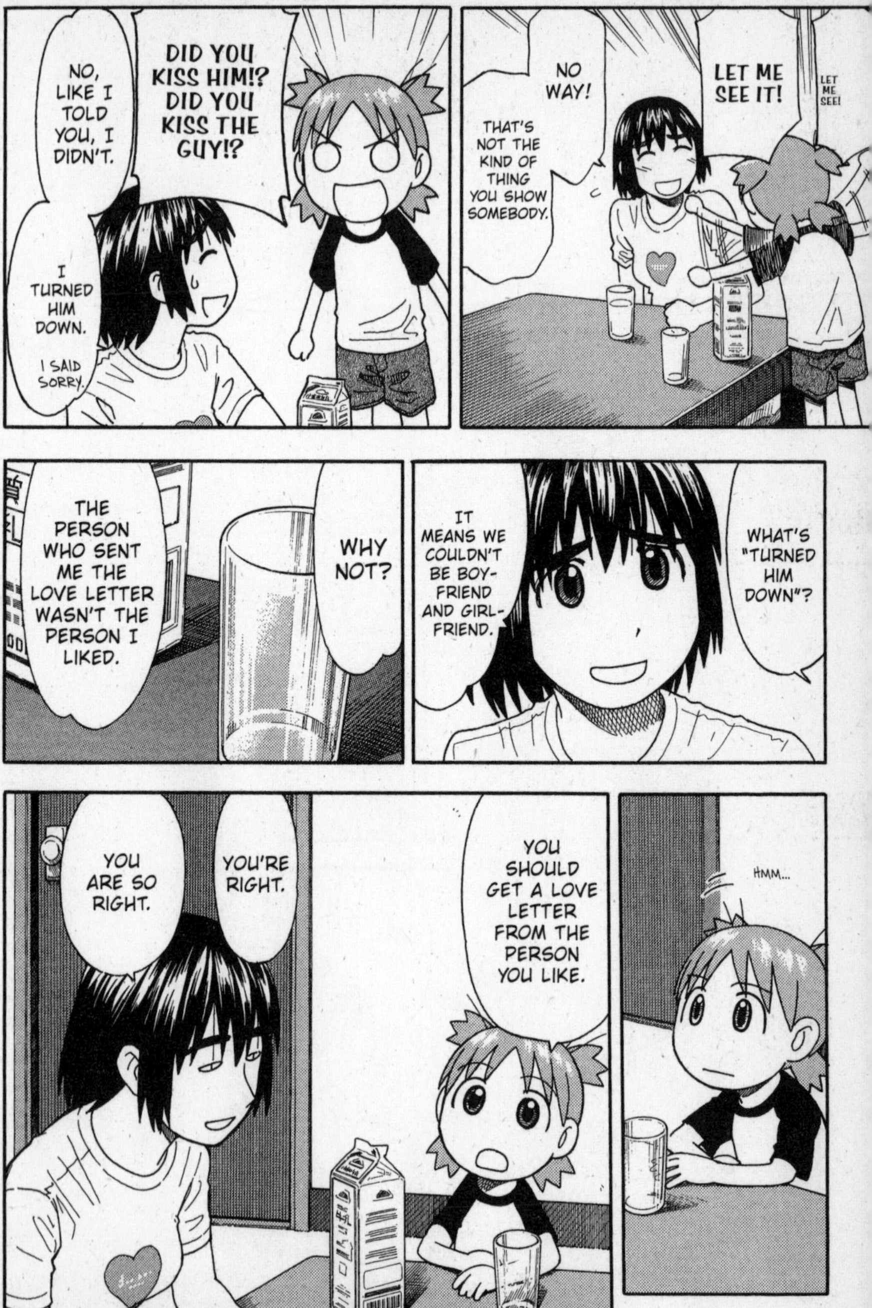
LET ME SEE IT!
LET ME SEE!
NO WAY!
THAT'S NOT THE KIND OF THING YOU SHOW SOMEBODY.
DID YOU KISS HIM!? DID YOU KISS THE GUY!?
NO, LIKE I TOLD YOU, I DIDN'T.
I TURNED HIM DOWN.
I SAID SORRY.
WHAT'S "TURNED HIM DOWN"?
IT MEANS WE COULDN'T BE BOY-FRIEND AND GIRL-FRIEND.
WHY NOT?
THE PERSON WHO SENT ME THE LOVE LETTER WASN'T THE PERSON I LIKED.
HMM...
YOU SHOULD GET A LOVE LETTER FROM THE PERSON YOU LIKE.
YOU'RE RIGHT.
YOU ARE SO RIGHT.

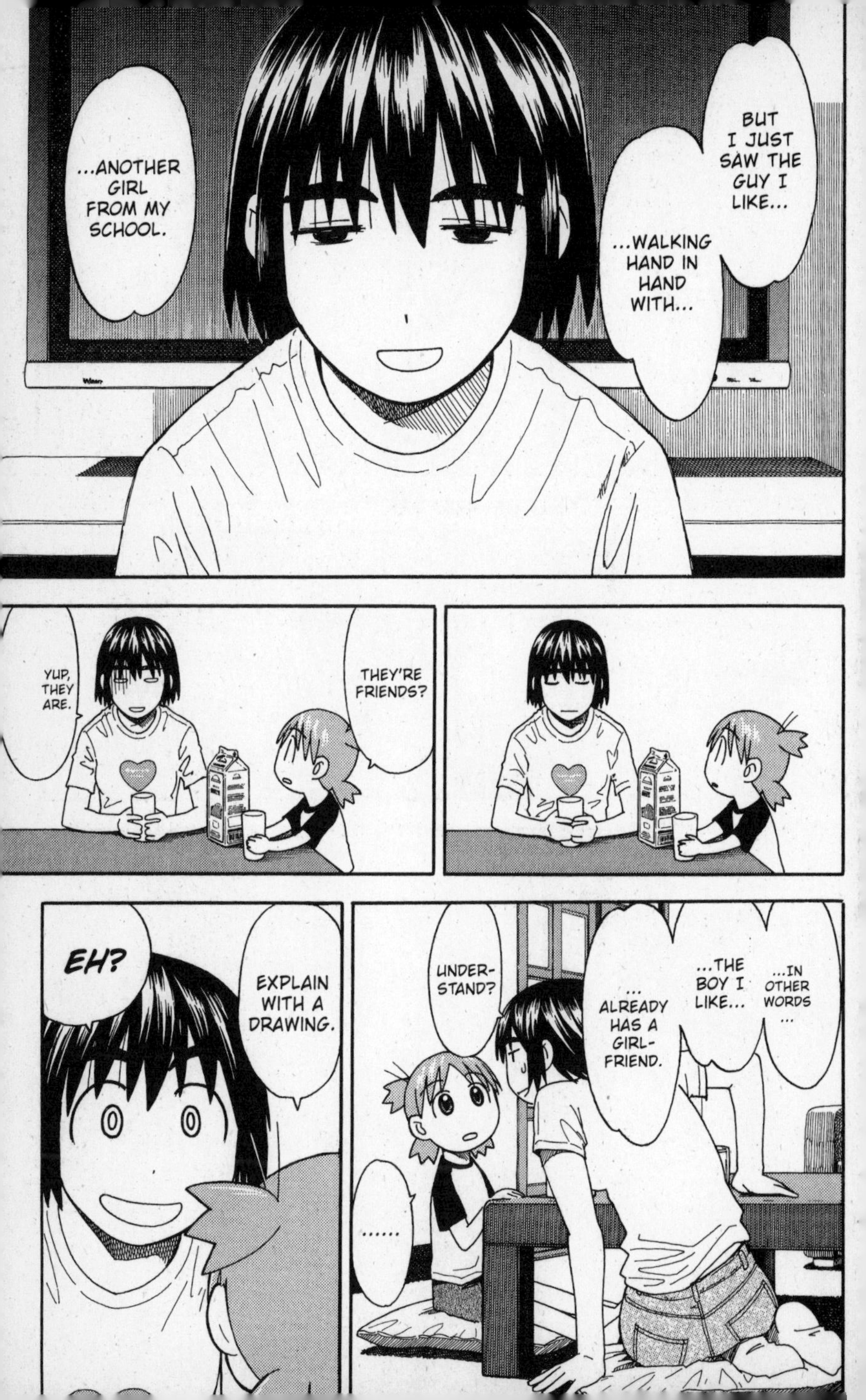
BUT I JUST SAW THE GUY I LIKE...
...WALKING HAND IN HAND WITH...
...ANOTHER GIRL FROM MY SCHOOL.
THEY'RE FRIENDS?
YUP, THEY ARE.
...IN OTHER WORDS...
...THE BOY I LIKE...
... ALREADY HAS A GIRL-FRIEND.
UNDER-STAND?
......
EXPLAIN WITH A DRAWING.
EH?

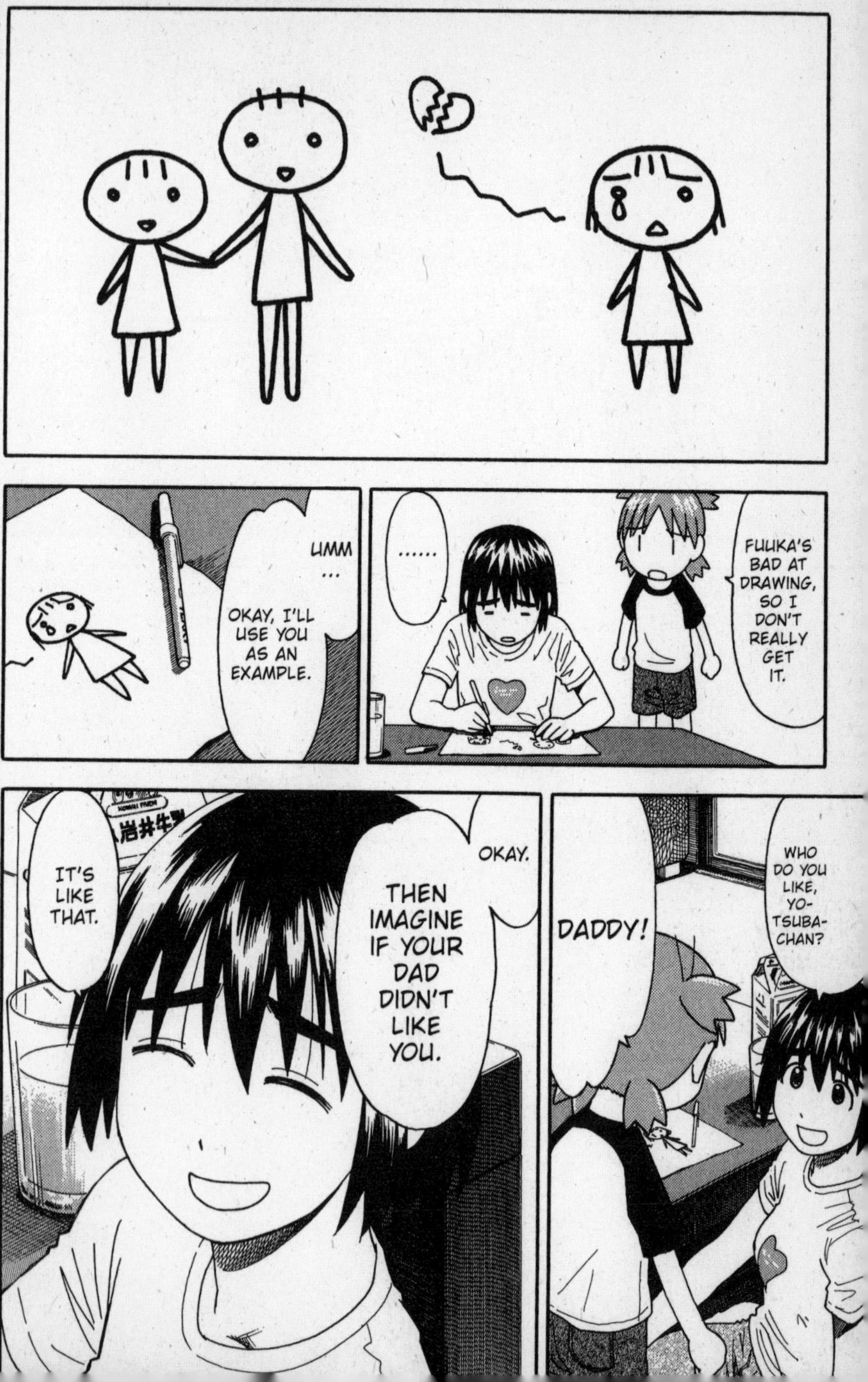
FUUKA'S BAD AT DRAWING, SO I DON'T REALLY GET IT.
......
UMM ...
OKAY, I'LL USE YOU AS AN EXAMPLE.
WHO DO YOU LIKE, YO-TSUBA-CHAN?
DADDY!
OKAY.
THEN IMAGINE IF YOUR DAD DIDN'T LIKE YOU.
IT'S LIKE THAT.

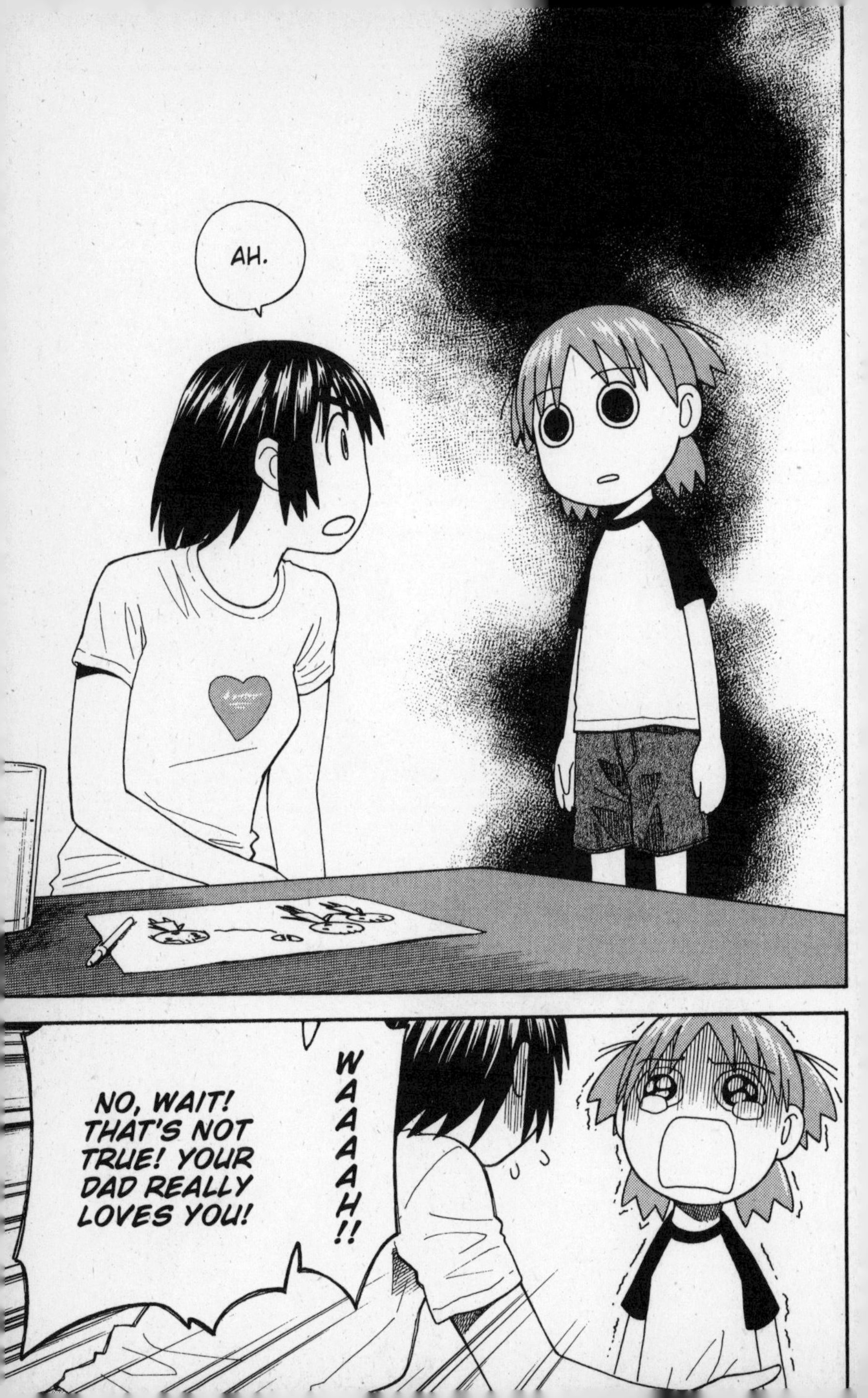
AH.
WAAAAAH!!
NO, WAIT! THAT'S NOT TRUE! YOUR DAD REALLY LOVES YOU!

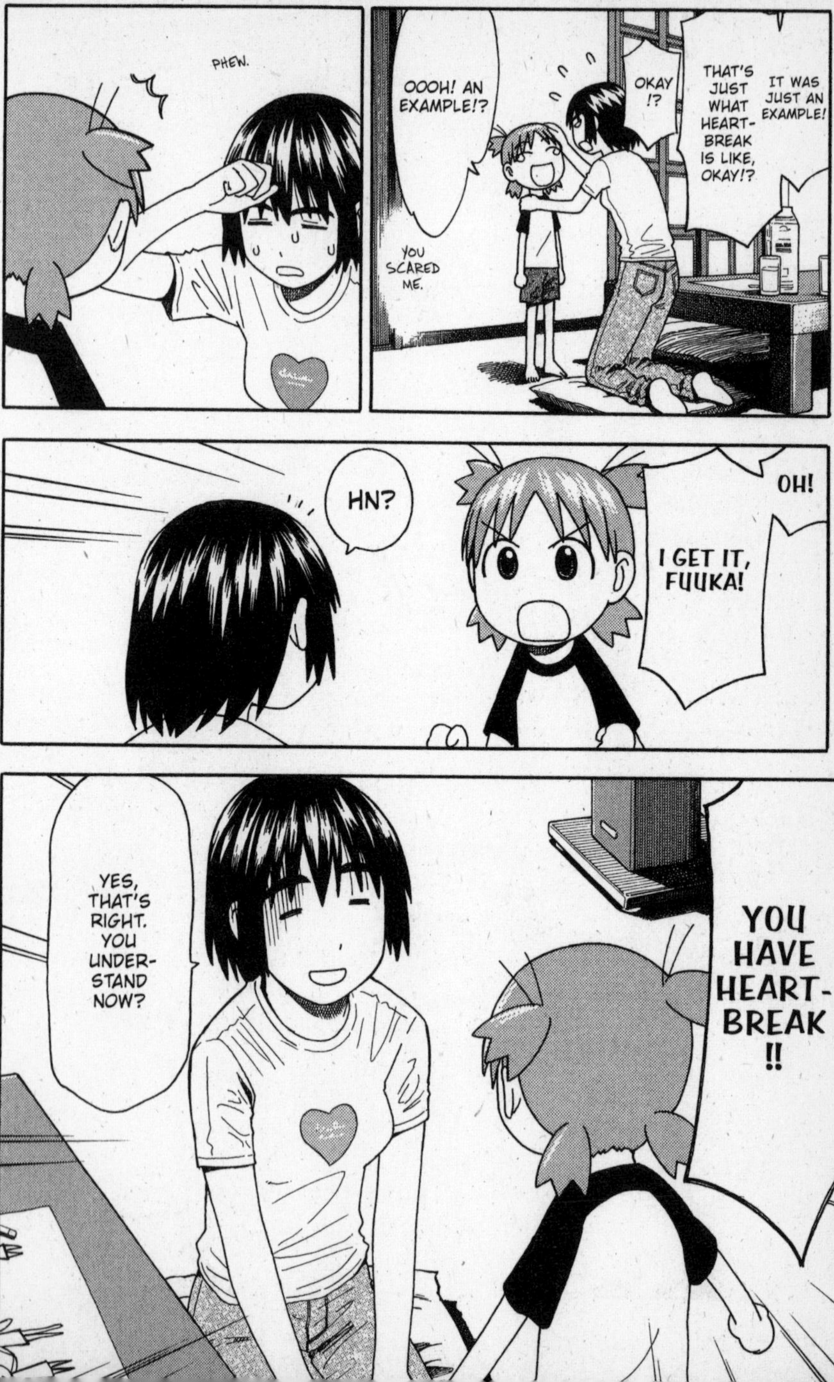
IT WAS JUST AN EXAMPLE!
THAT'S JUST WHAT HEART-BREAK IS LIKE, OKAY!?
OKAY !?
OOOH! AN EXAMPLE!?
YOU SCARED ME.
PHEW.
OH!
I GET IT, FUUKA!
HN?
YOU HAVE HEART-BREAK !!
YES, THAT'S RIGHT. YOU UNDER-STAND NOW?

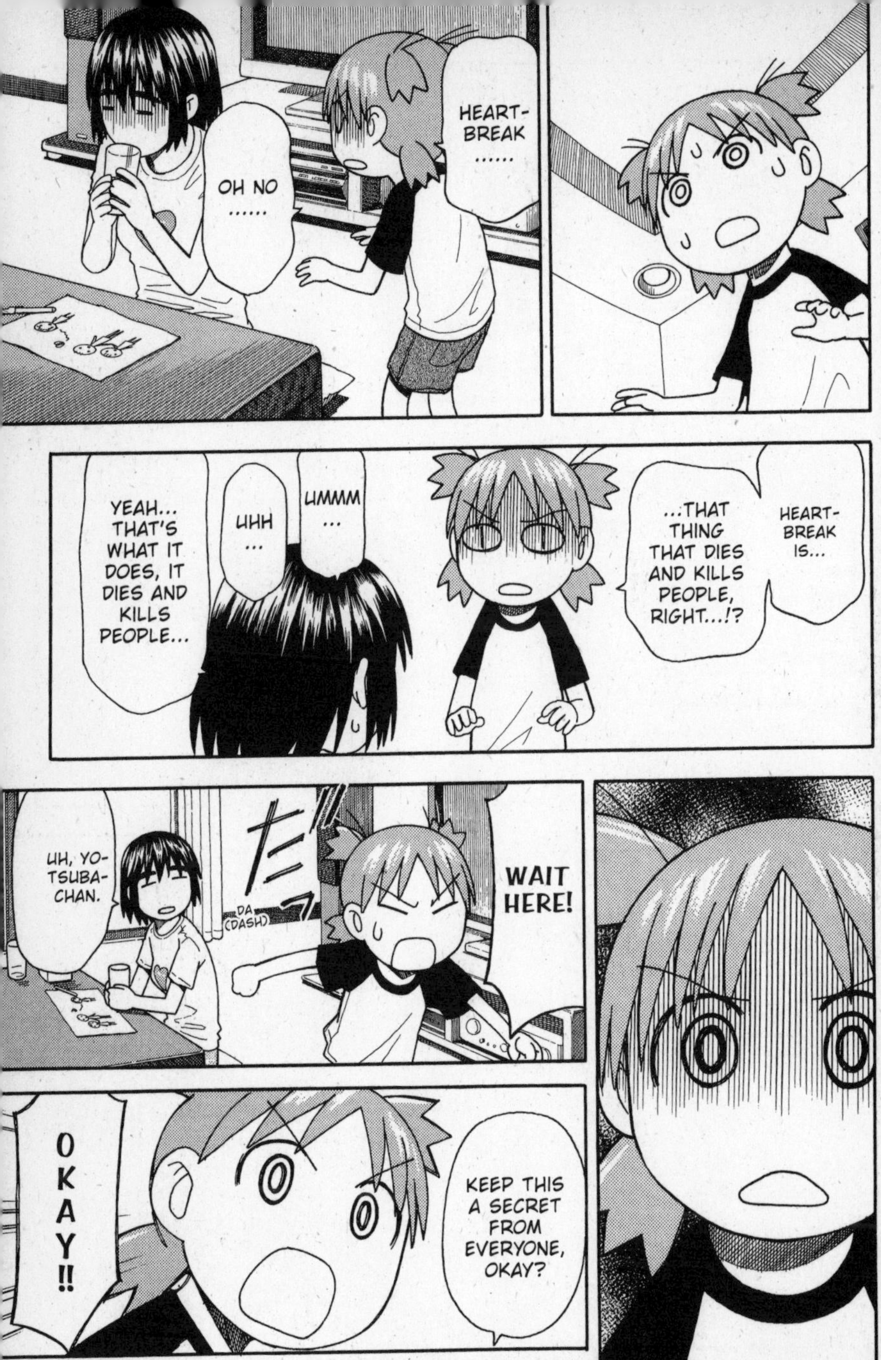
HEART-BREAK ......
OH NO ......
HEART-BREAK IS...
...THAT THING THAT DIES AND KILLS PEOPLE, RIGHT...!?
UMMM ...
UHH ...
YEAH... THAT'S WHAT IT DOES, IT DIES AND KILLS PEOPLE...
WAIT HERE!
DA (DASH)
UH, YO-TSUBA-CHAN.
KEEP THIS A SECRET FROM EVERYONE, OKAY?
OKAY!!

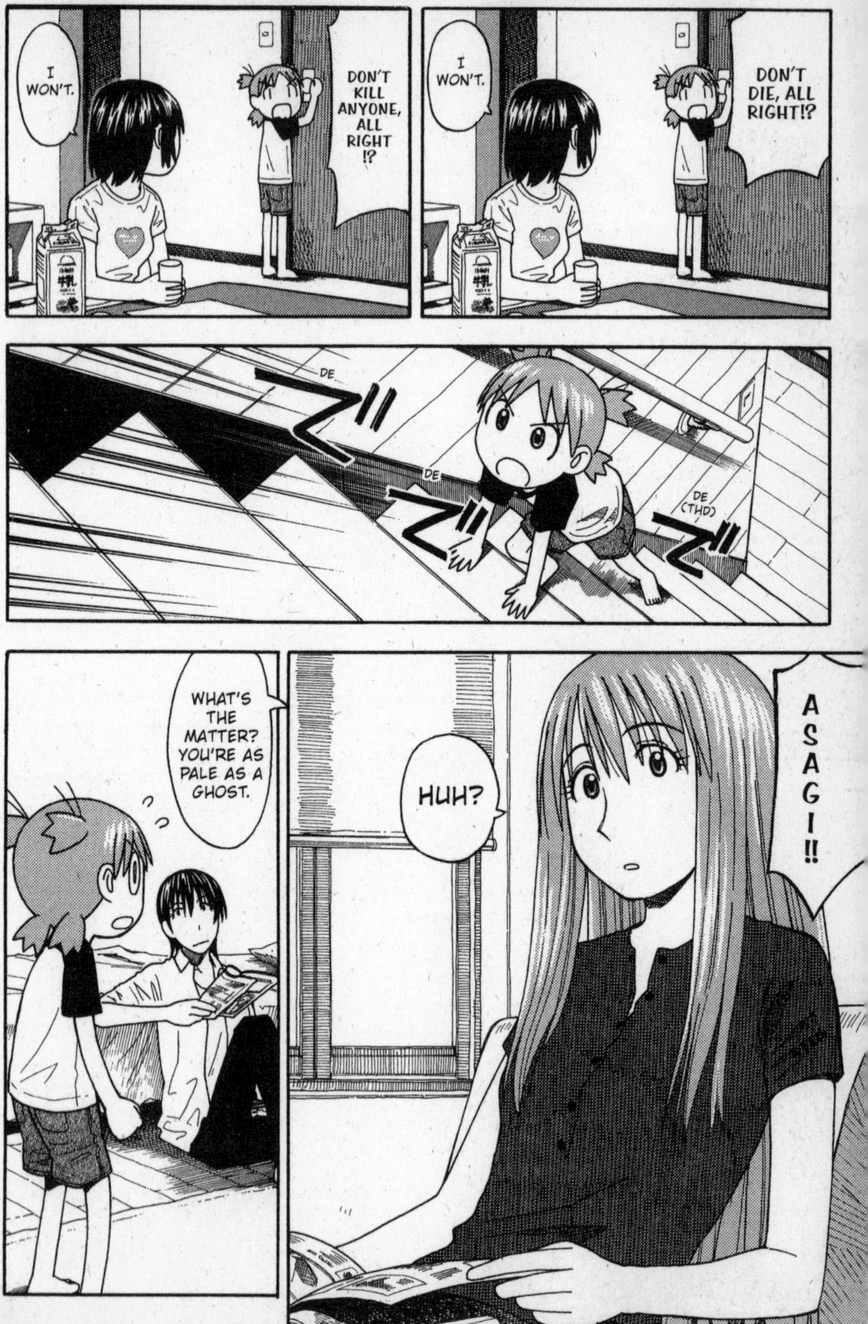
DON'T DIE, ALL RIGHT!?
I WON'T.
DON'T KILL ANYONE, ALL RIGHT !?
I WON'T.
DE
DE
DE (THD)
ASAGI!!
HUH?
WHAT'S THE MATTER? YOU'RE AS PALE AS A GHOST.

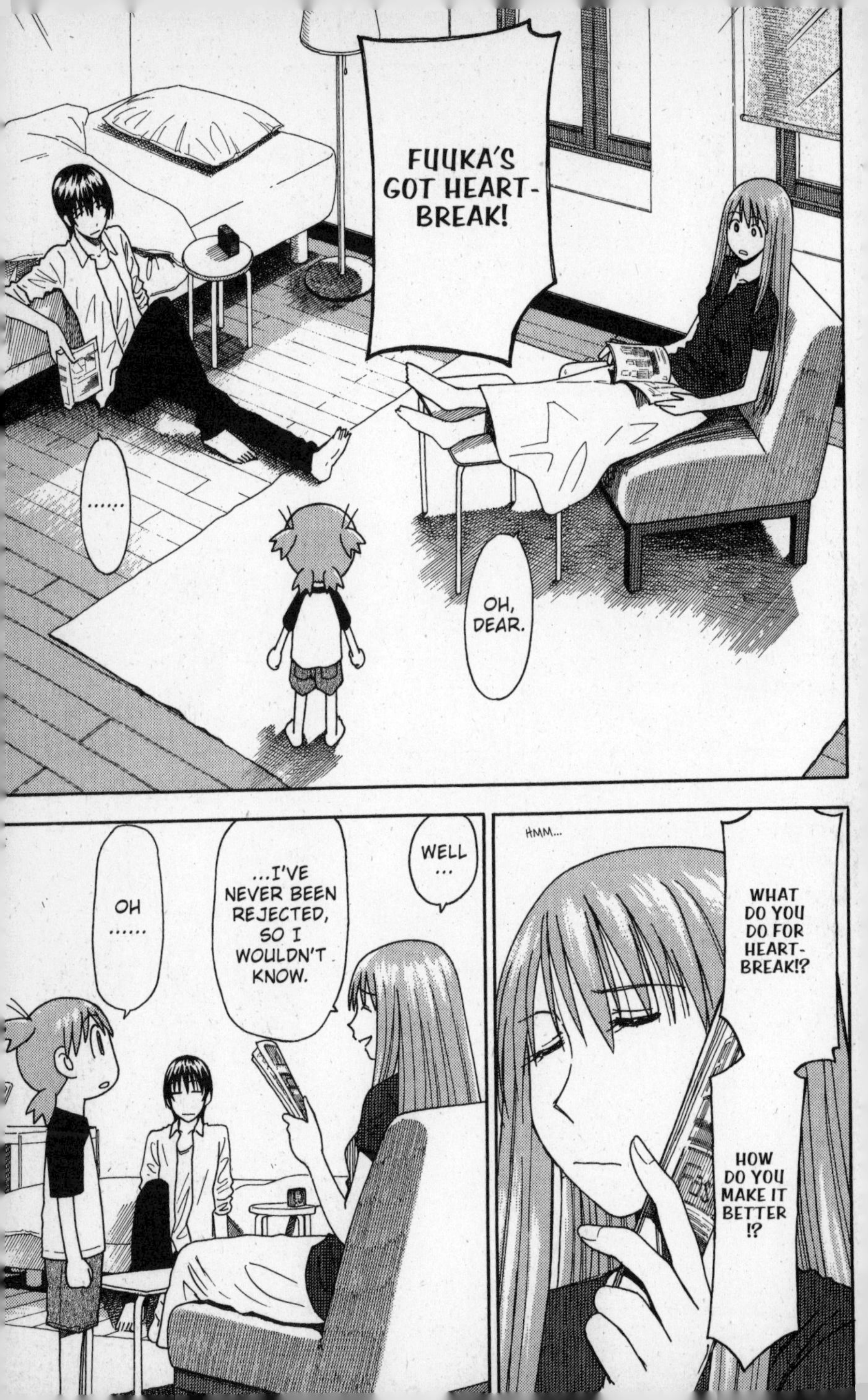
FUUKA'S GOT HEART-BREAK!
OH, DEAR.
......
HMM...
WHAT DO YOU DO FOR HEART-BREAK!?
HOW DO YOU MAKE IT BETTER!?
WELL...
...I'VE NEVER BEEN REJECTED, SO I WOULDN'T KNOW.
OH ......

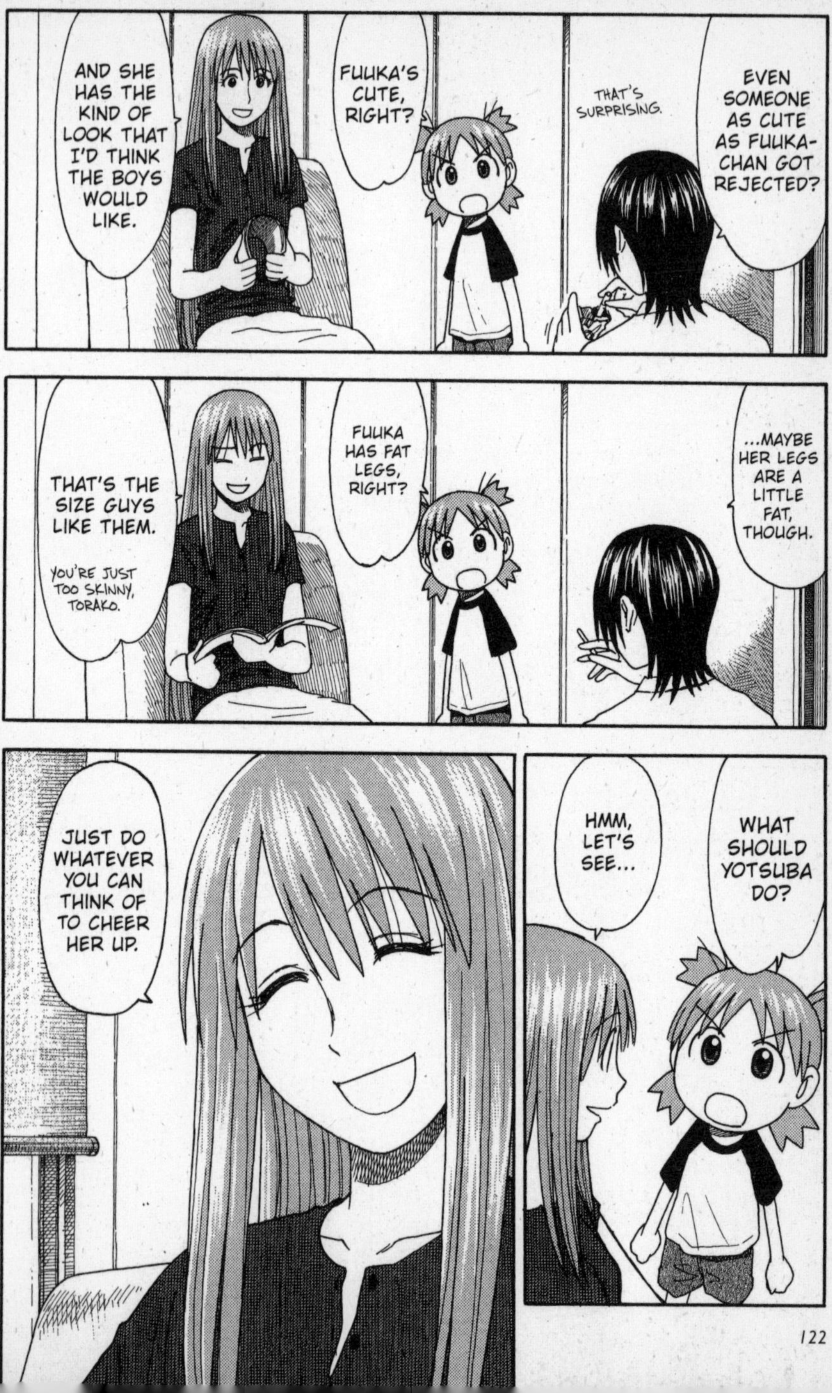
EVEN SOMEONE AS CUTE AS FUUKA-CHAN GOT REJECTED?
THAT'S SURPRISING.
FUUKA'S CUTE, RIGHT?
AND SHE HAS THE KIND OF LOOK THAT I'D THINK THE BOYS WOULD LIKE.
...MAYBE HER LEGS ARE A LITTLE FAT, THOUGH.
FUUKA HAS FAT LEGS, RIGHT?
THAT'S THE SIZE GUYS LIKE THEM.
YOU'RE JUST TOO SKINNY, TORAKO.
WHAT SHOULD YOTSUBA DO?
HMM, LET'S SEE...
JUST DO WHATEVER YOU CAN THINK OF TO CHEER HER UP.

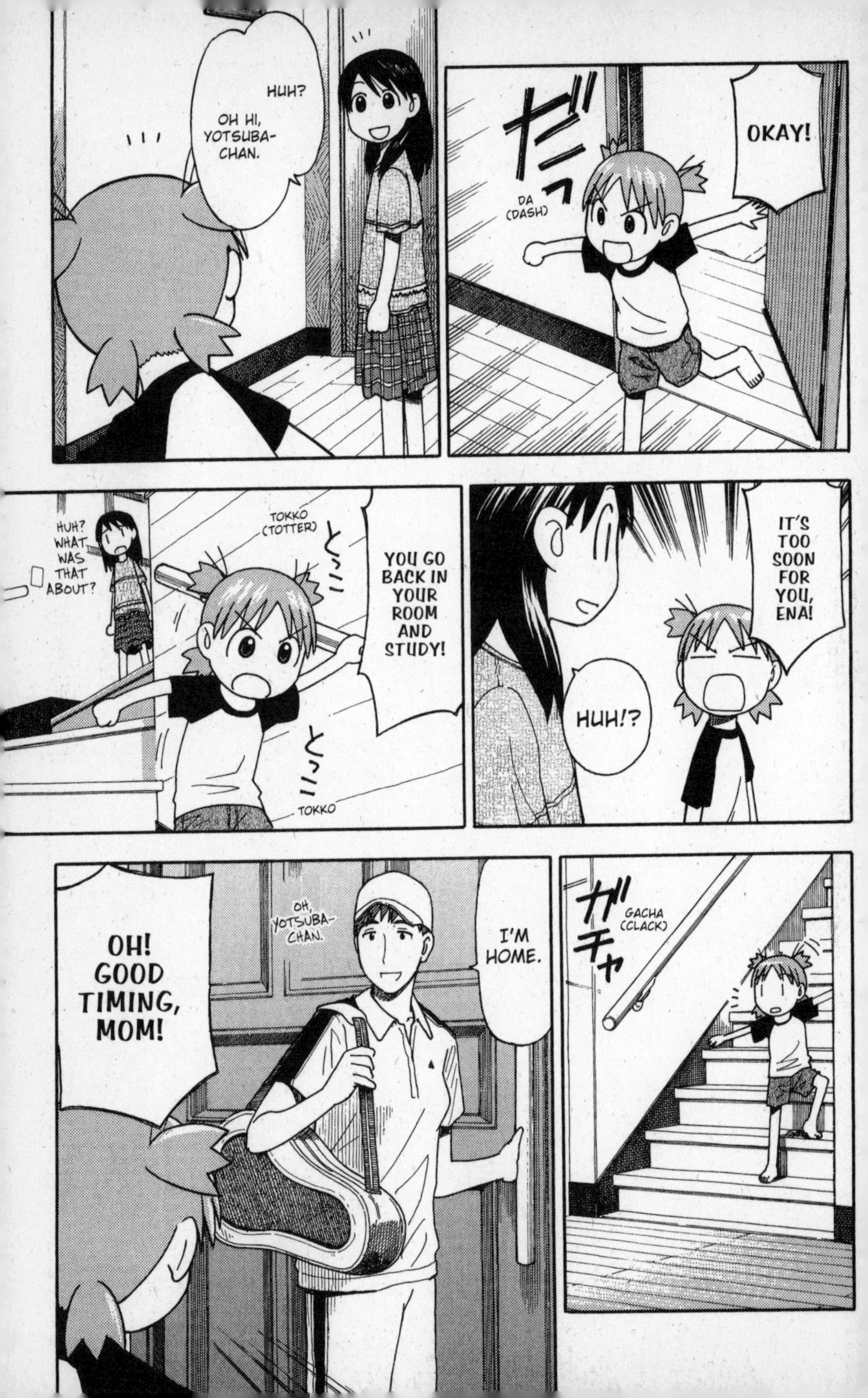
OKAY!
DA (DASH)
HUH?
OH HI, YOTSUBA-CHAN.
IT'S TOO SOON FOR YOU, ENA!
HUH!?
YOU GO BACK IN YOUR ROOM AND STUDY!
TOKKO (TOTTER)
TOKKO
HUH? WHAT WAS THAT ABOUT?
GACHA (CLACK)
I'M HOME.
OH, YOTSUBA-CHAN.
OH! GOOD TIMING, MOM!

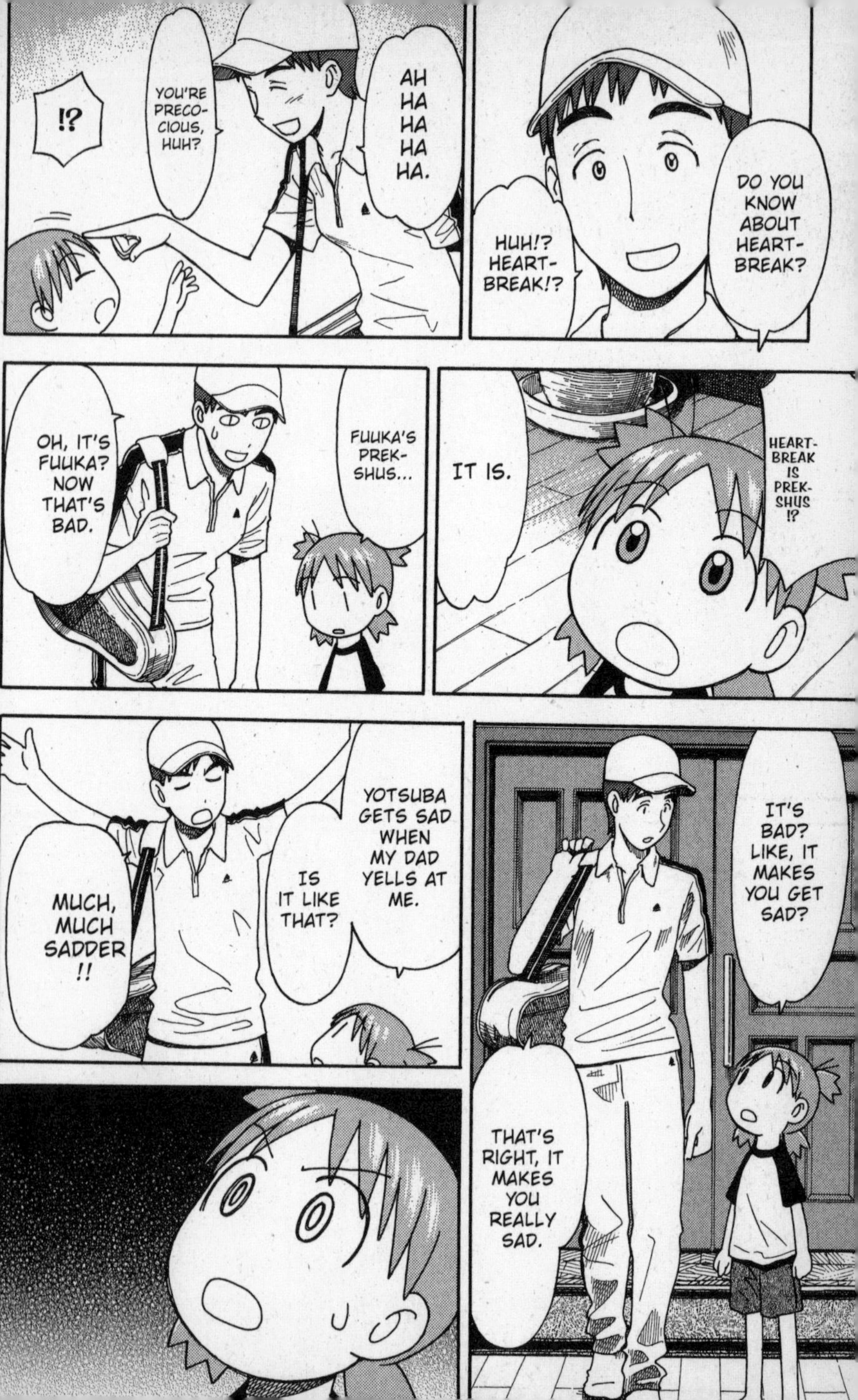
DO YOU KNOW ABOUT HEART-BREAK?
HUH!? HEART-BREAK!?
AH HA HA HA HA.
YOU'RE PRECO-CIOUS, HUH?
!?
HEART-BREAK IS PREK-SHUS!?
IT IS.
FUUKA'S PREK-SHUS...
OH, IT'S FUUKA? NOW THAT'S BAD.
IT'S BAD? LIKE, IT MAKES YOU GET SAD?
THAT'S RIGHT, IT MAKES YOU REALLY SAD.
YOTSUBA GETS SAD WHEN MY DAD YELLS AT ME.
IS IT LIKE THAT?
MUCH, MUCH SADDER !!

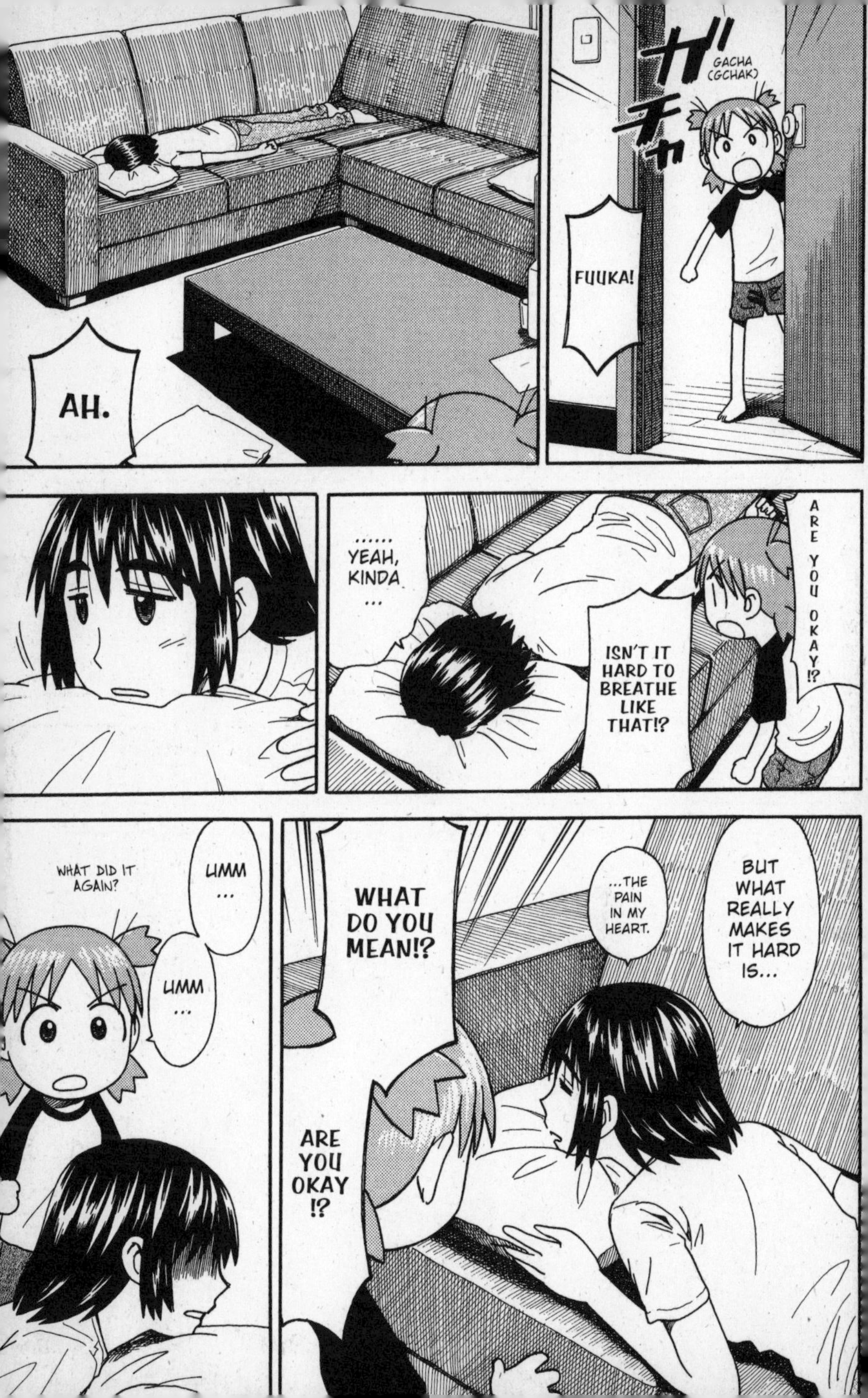
ガチャ
GACHA (GCHAK)
FUUKA!
AH.
ARE YOU OKAY!?
ISN'T IT HARD TO BREATHE LIKE THAT!?
……YEAH, KINDA …
BUT WHAT REALLY MAKES IT HARD IS…
…THE PAIN IN MY HEART.
WHAT DO YOU MEAN!?
ARE YOU OKAY !?
UMM …
WHAT DID IT AGAIN?
UMM …

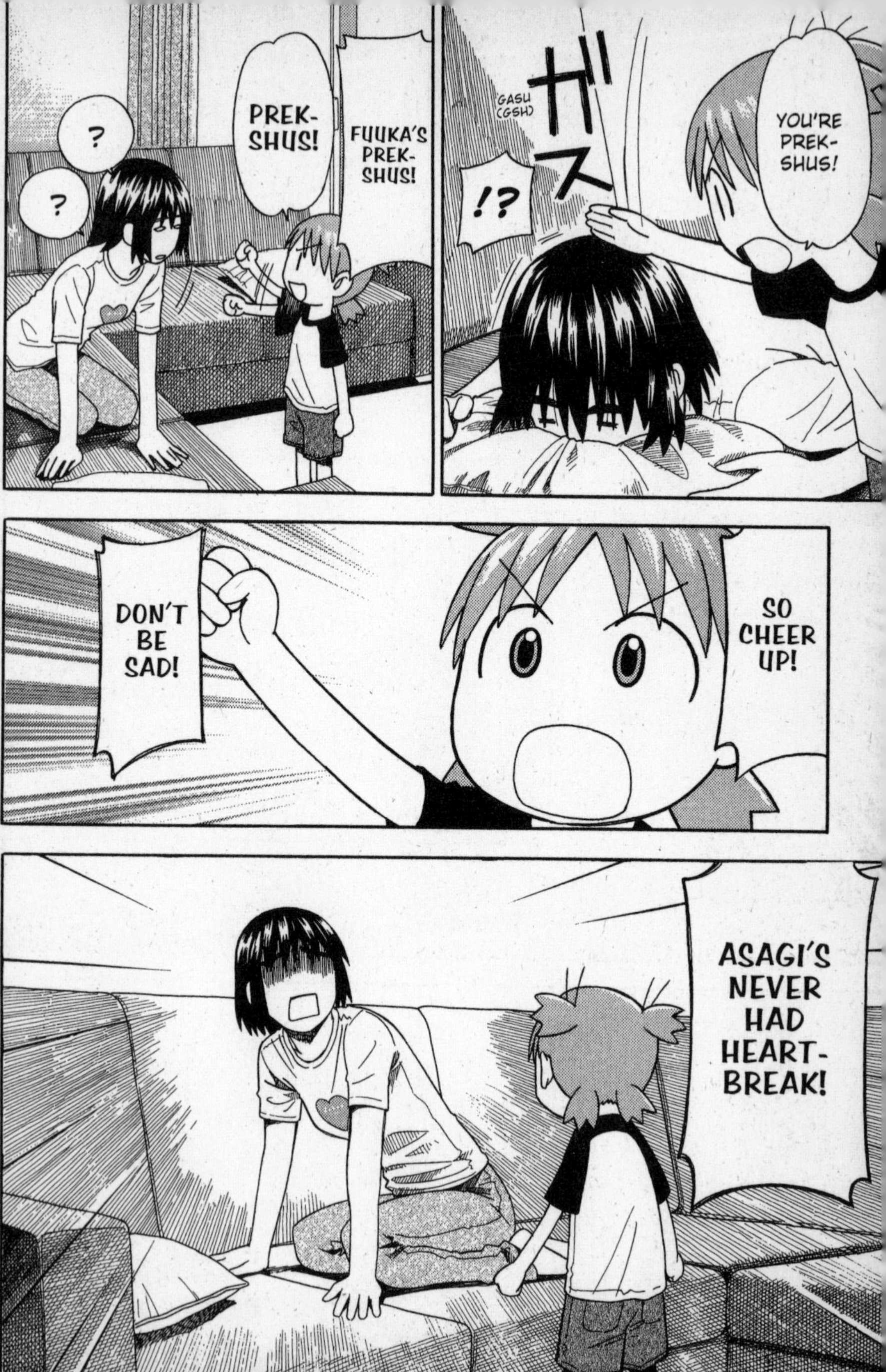
YOU'RE PREK-SHUS!
ガス
GASU (GSH)
!?
FUUKA'S PREK-SHUS!
PREK-SHUS!
?
?
SO CHEER UP!
DON'T BE SAD!
ASAGI'S NEVER HAD HEART-BREAK!

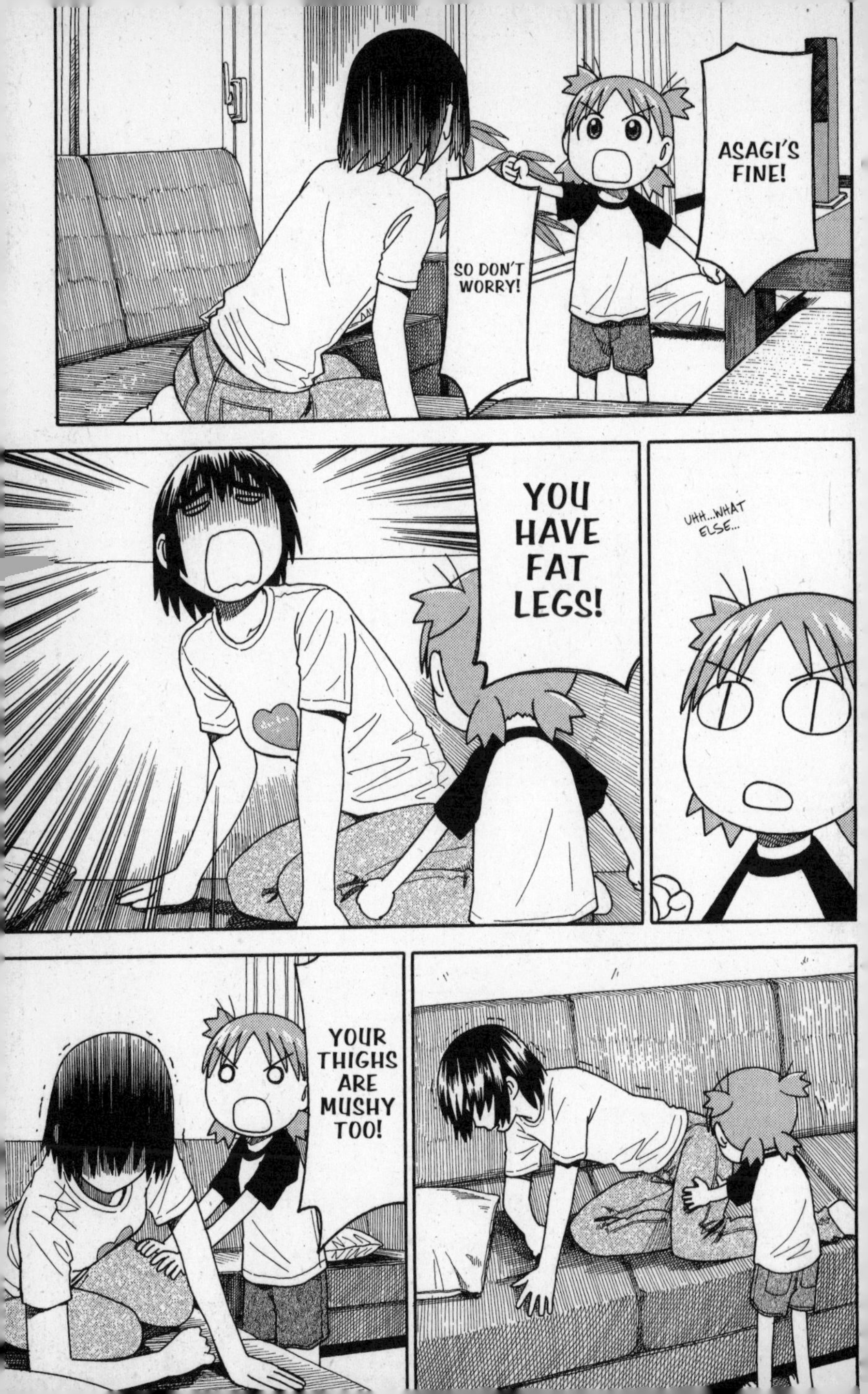
ASAGI'S FINE!
SO DON'T WORRY!
UHH...WHAT ELSE...
YOU HAVE FAT LEGS!
YOUR THIGHS ARE MUSHY TOO!

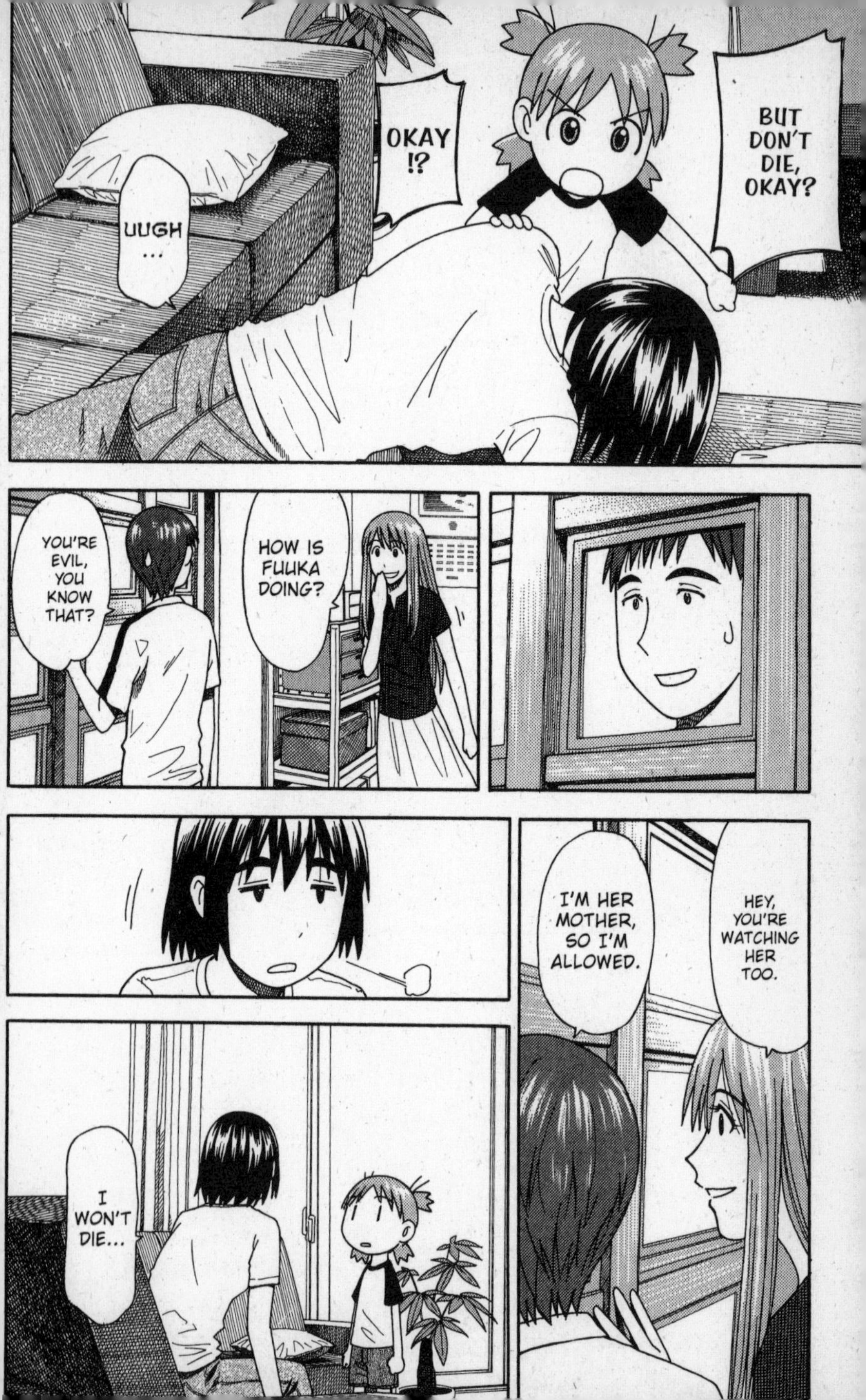
BUT DON'T DIE, OKAY?
OKAY !?
UUGH ...
HOW IS FUUKA DOING?
YOU'RE EVIL, YOU KNOW THAT?
HEY, YOU'RE WATCHING HER TOO.
I'M HER MOTHER, SO I'M ALLOWED.
I WON'T DIE...

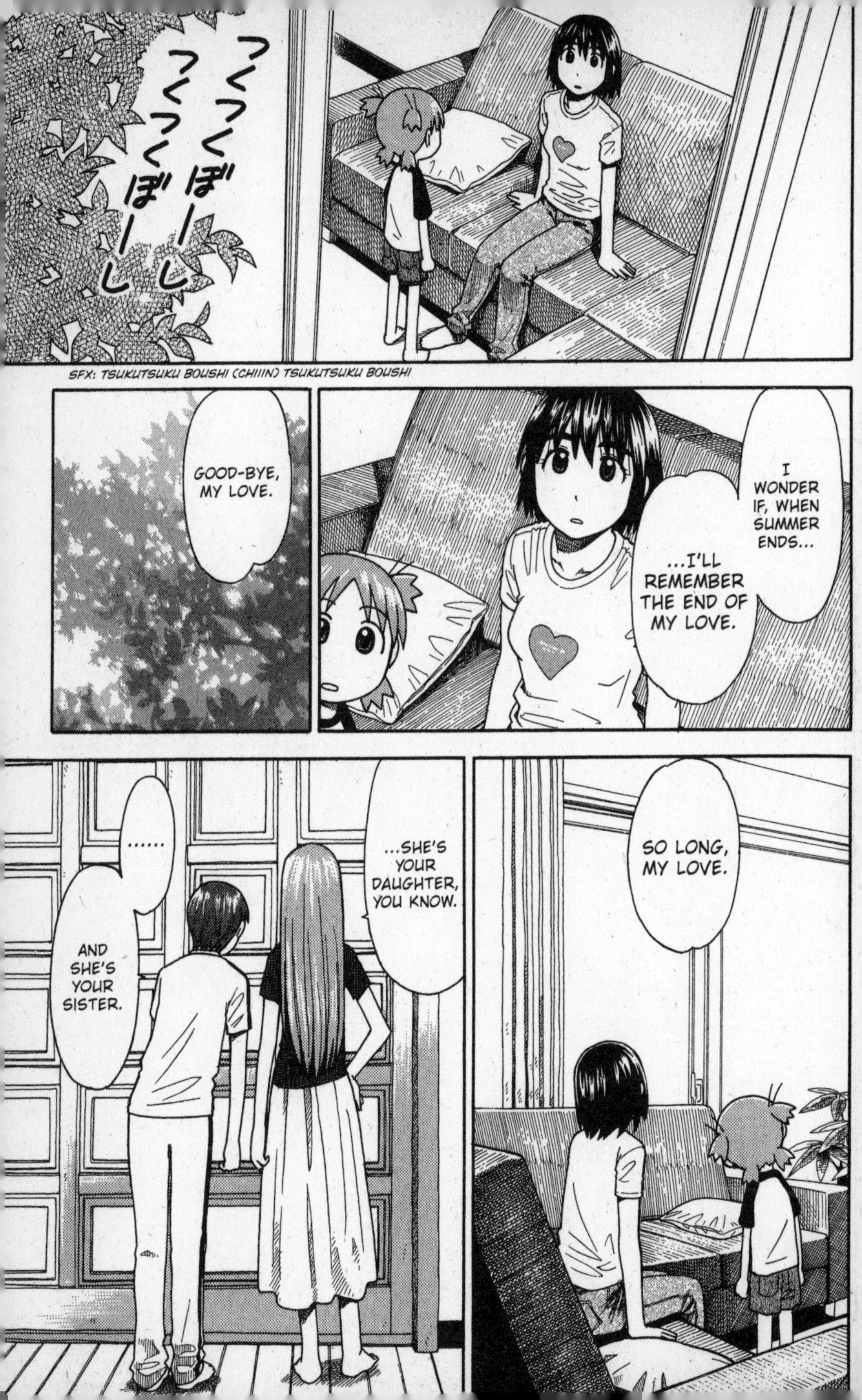
つくつくぼーし
つくつくぼーし
SFX: TSUKUTSUKU BOUSHI (CHIIIN) TSUKUTSUKU BOUSHI
I WONDER IF, WHEN SUMMER ENDS...
...I'LL REMEMBER THE END OF MY LOVE.
GOOD-BYE, MY LOVE.
SO LONG, MY LOVE.
...SHE'S YOUR DAUGHTER, YOU KNOW.
......
AND SHE'S YOUR SISTER.

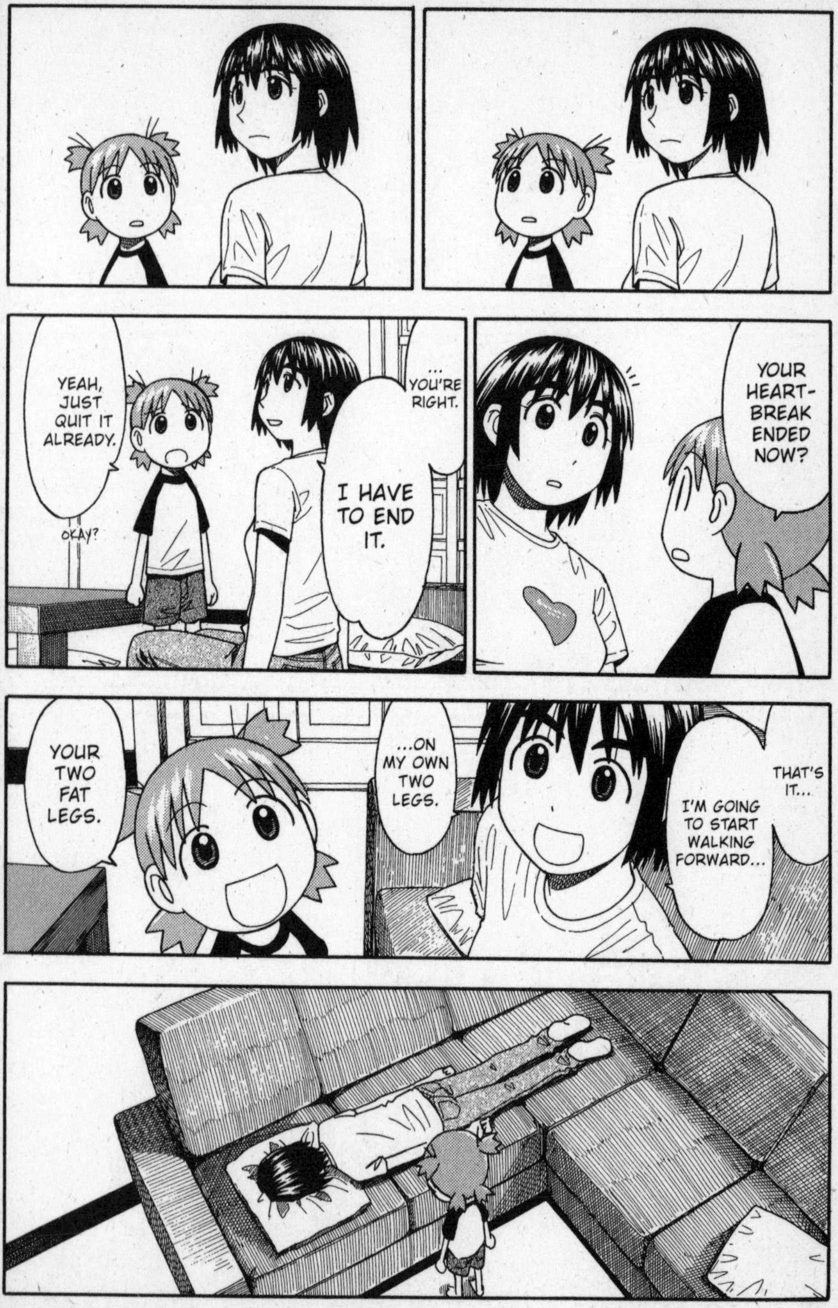
YOUR HEART-BREAK ENDED NOW?
... YOU'RE RIGHT.
I HAVE TO END IT.
YEAH, JUST QUIT IT ALREADY.
OKAY?
THAT'S IT...
I'M GOING TO START WALKING FORWARD...
...ON MY OWN TWO LEGS.
YOUR TWO FAT LEGS.

YOTSUBA&!

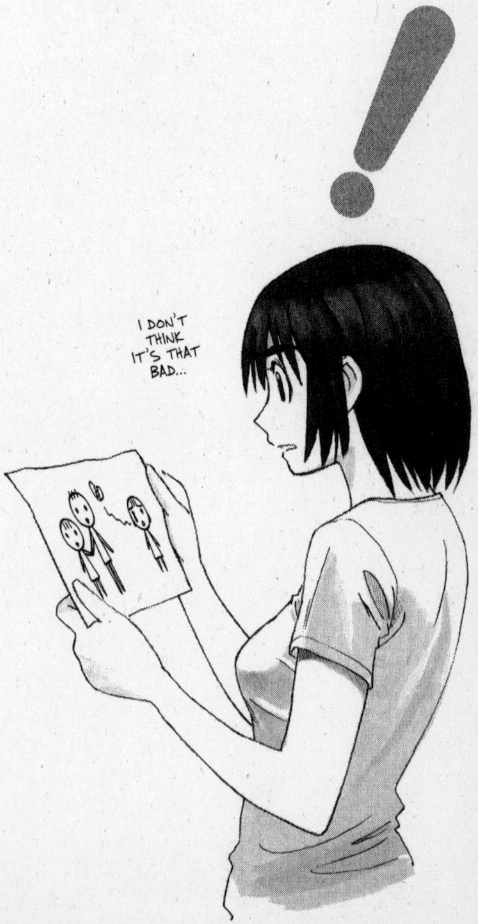
I DON'T THINK IT'S THAT BAD...

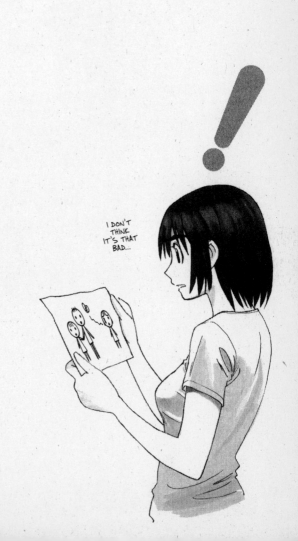

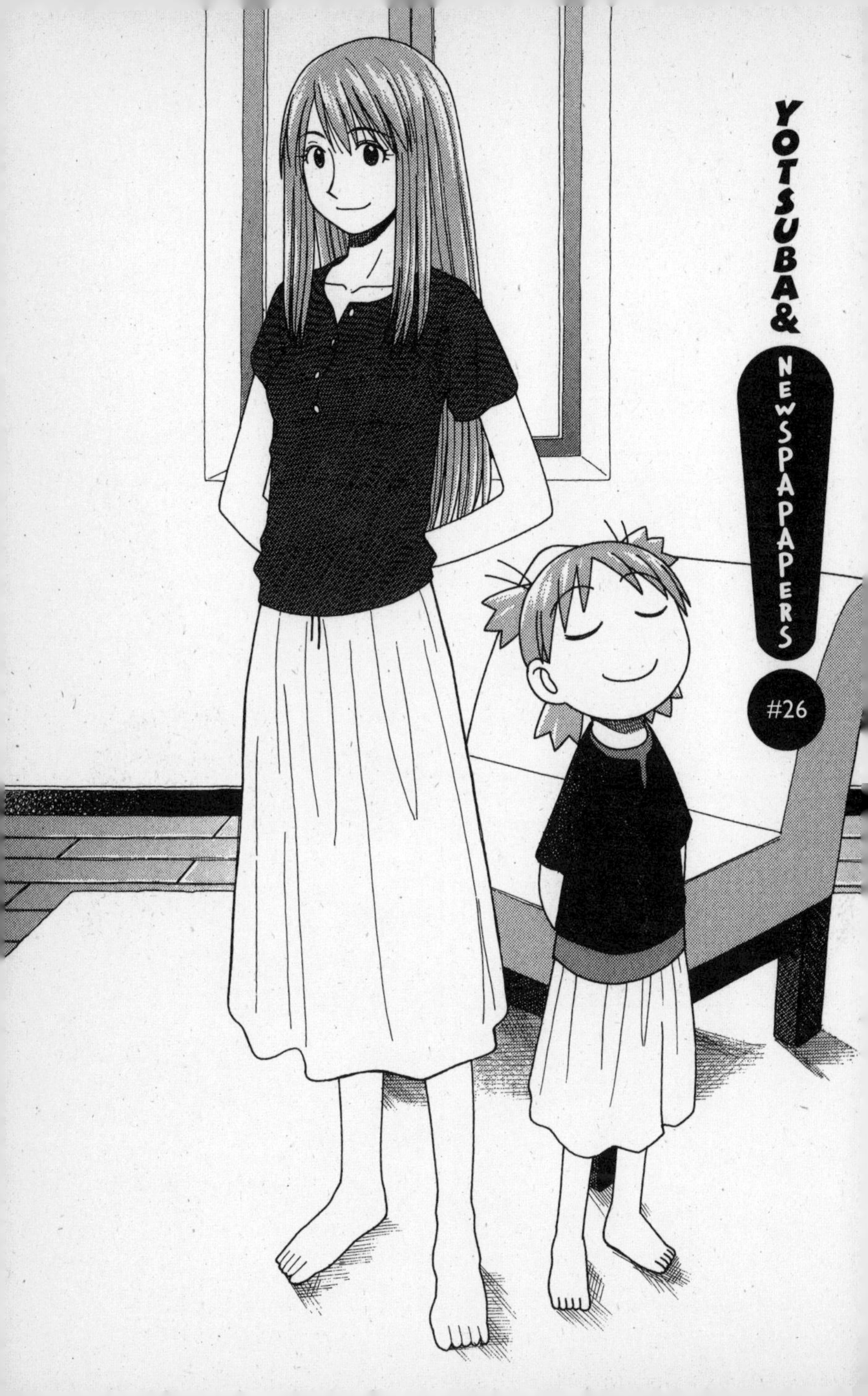
YOTSUBA&
NEWSPAPERS
#26

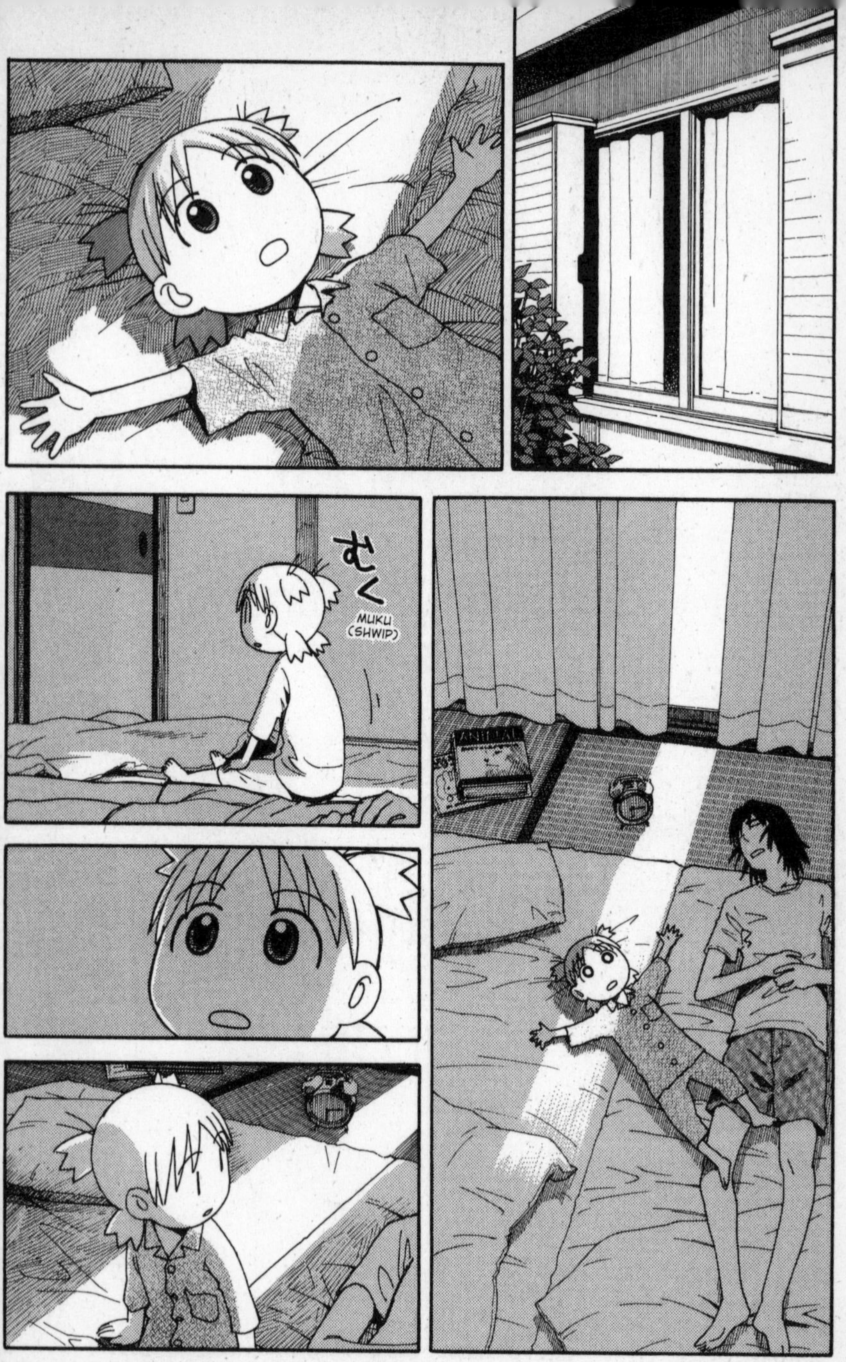
むく
MUKU
(SHWIP)

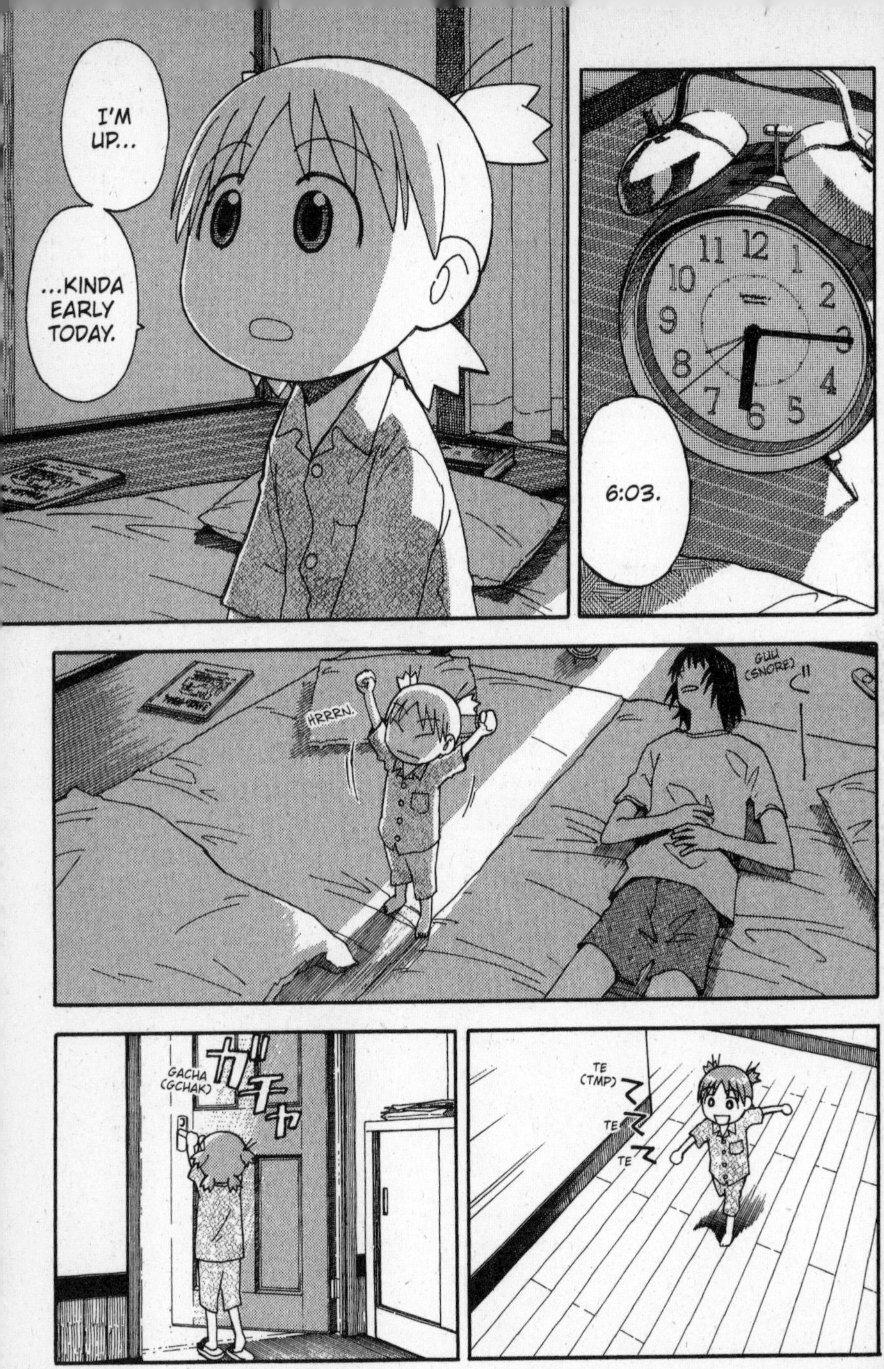
6:03.
I'M UP...
...KINDA EARLY TODAY.
GUU (SNORE)
HRRRN.
TE (TMP)
TE
TE
ガチャ
GACHA (GCHAK)

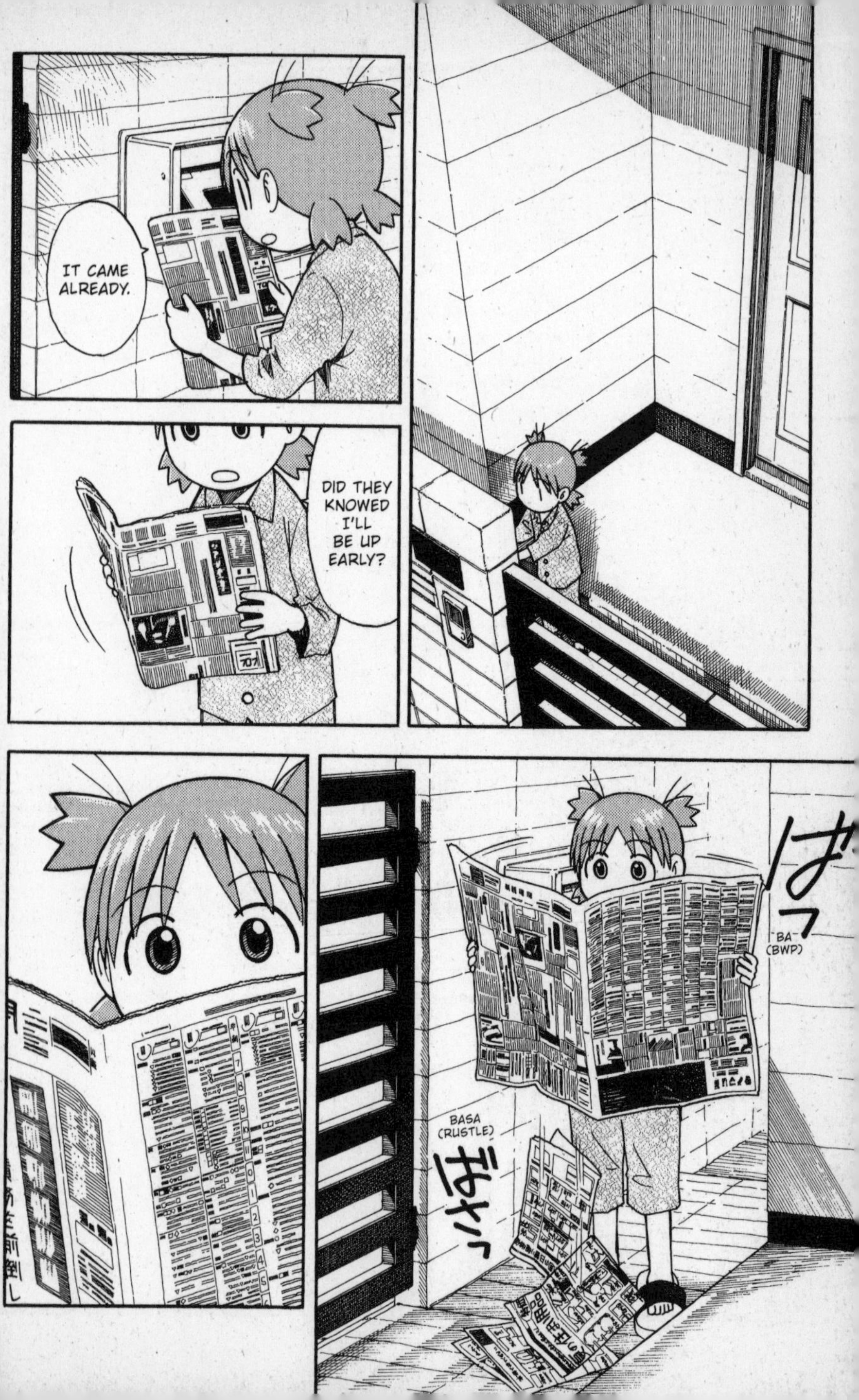
IT CAME ALREADY.
DID THEY KNOWED I'LL BE UP EARLY?
ぱっ
BA (BWP)
BASA (RUSTLE)
ばさっ

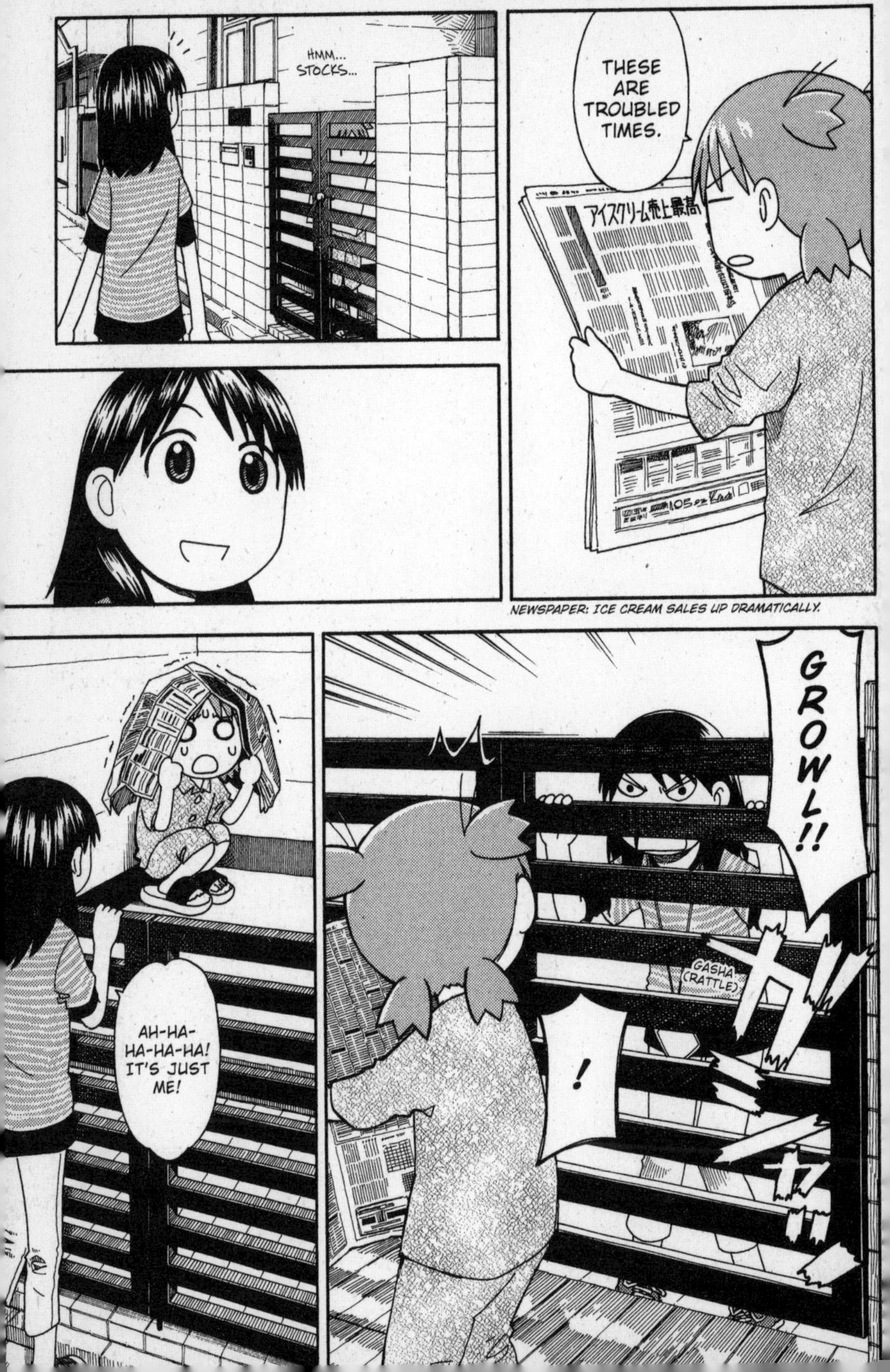
THESE ARE TROUBLED TIMES.
アイスクリーム売上最高
HMM... STOCKS...
NEWSPAPER: ICE CREAM SALES UP DRAMATICALLY.
GROWL!!
GASHA (RATTLE)
!
AH-HA-HA-HA-HA! IT'S JUST ME!

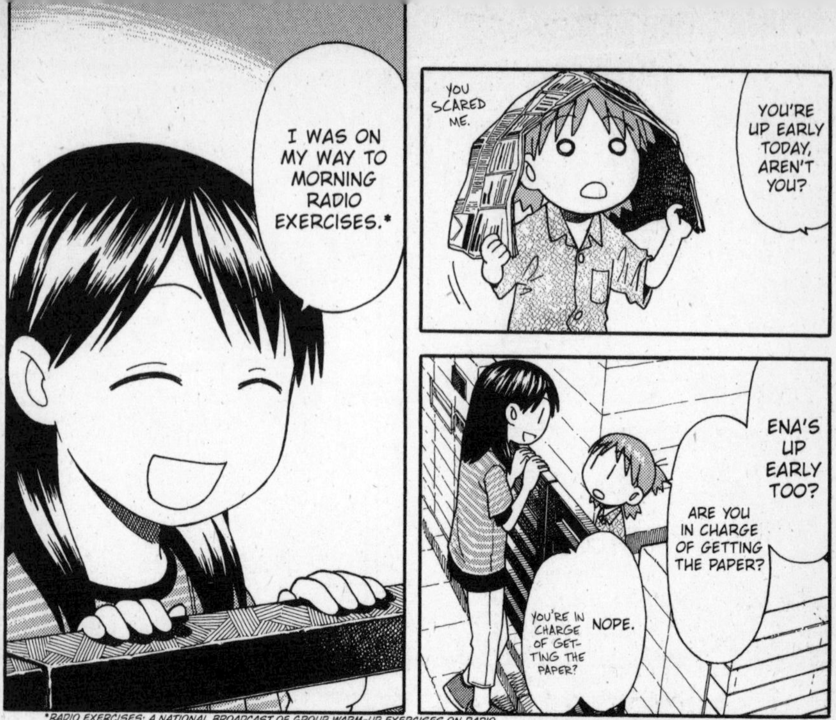
YOU'RE UP EARLY TODAY, AREN'T YOU?
YOU SCARED ME.
ENA'S UP EARLY TOO?
ARE YOU IN CHARGE OF GETTING THE PAPER?
NOPE.
YOU'RE IN CHARGE OF GET-TING THE PAPER?
I WAS ON MY WAY TO MORNING RADIO EXERCISES.*

*RADIO EXERCISES: A NATIONAL BROADCAST OF GROUP WARM-UP EXERCISES ON RADIO AND TELEVISION IN JAPAN TO ENCOURAGE HEALTH, WELL-BEING, AND COMMUNITY.

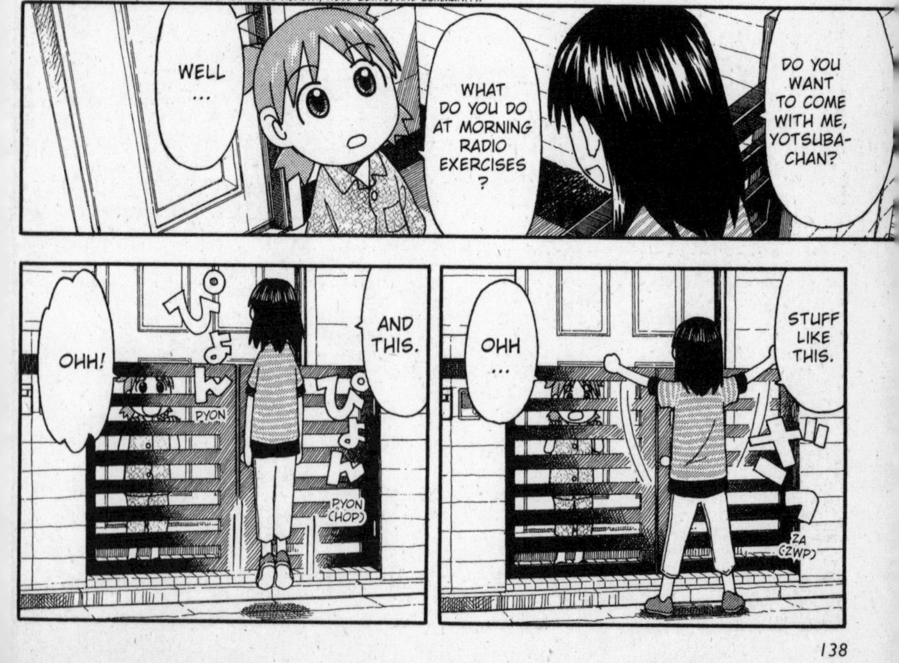
DO YOU WANT TO COME WITH ME, YOTSUBA-CHAN?
WHAT DO YOU DO AT MORNING RADIO EXERCISES ?
WELL ...
STUFF LIKE THIS.
OHH ...
ZA (ZWP)
AND THIS.
PYON (HOP)
PYON
OHH!

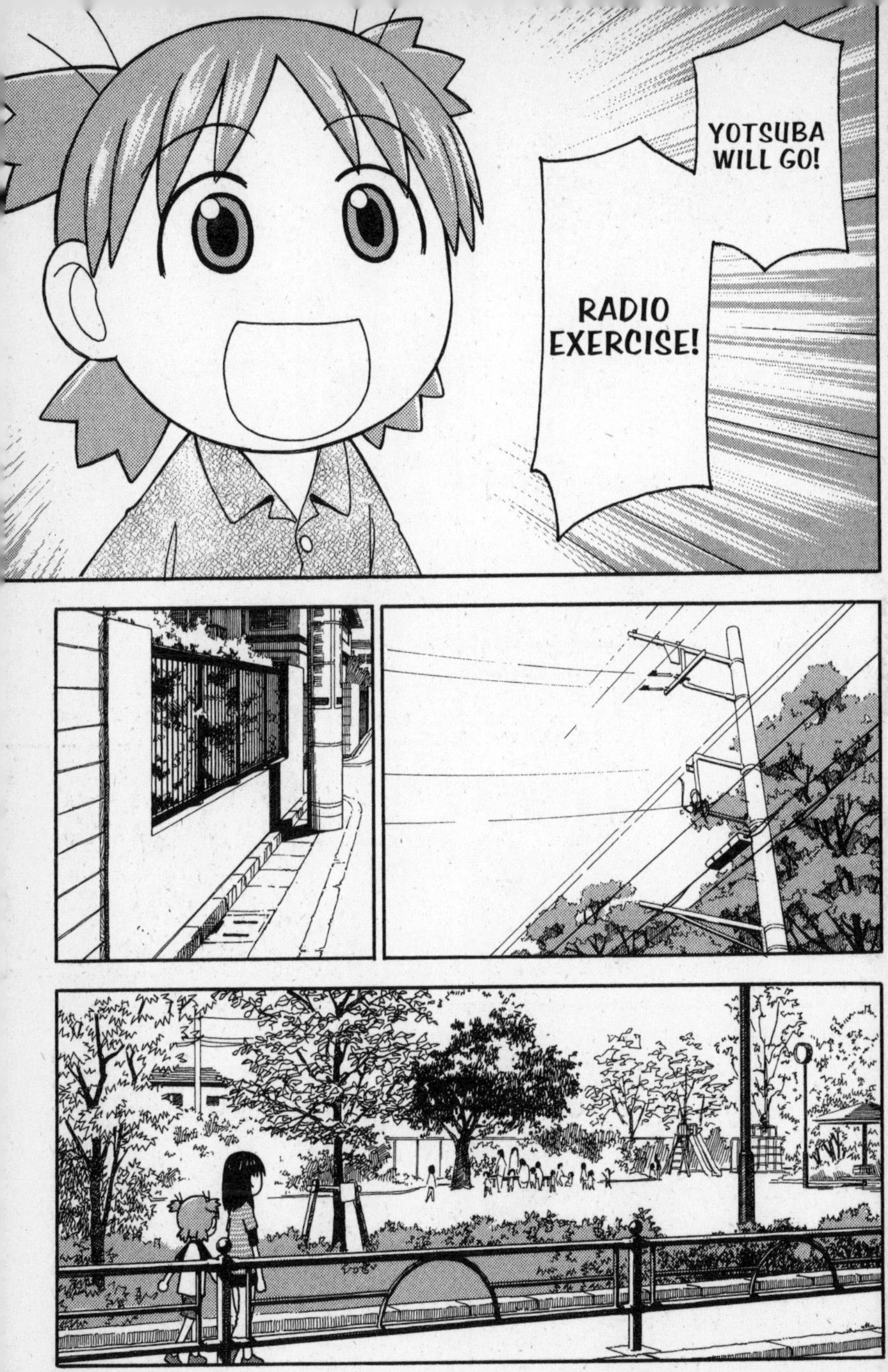
YOTSUBA WILL GO!
RADIO EXERCISE!

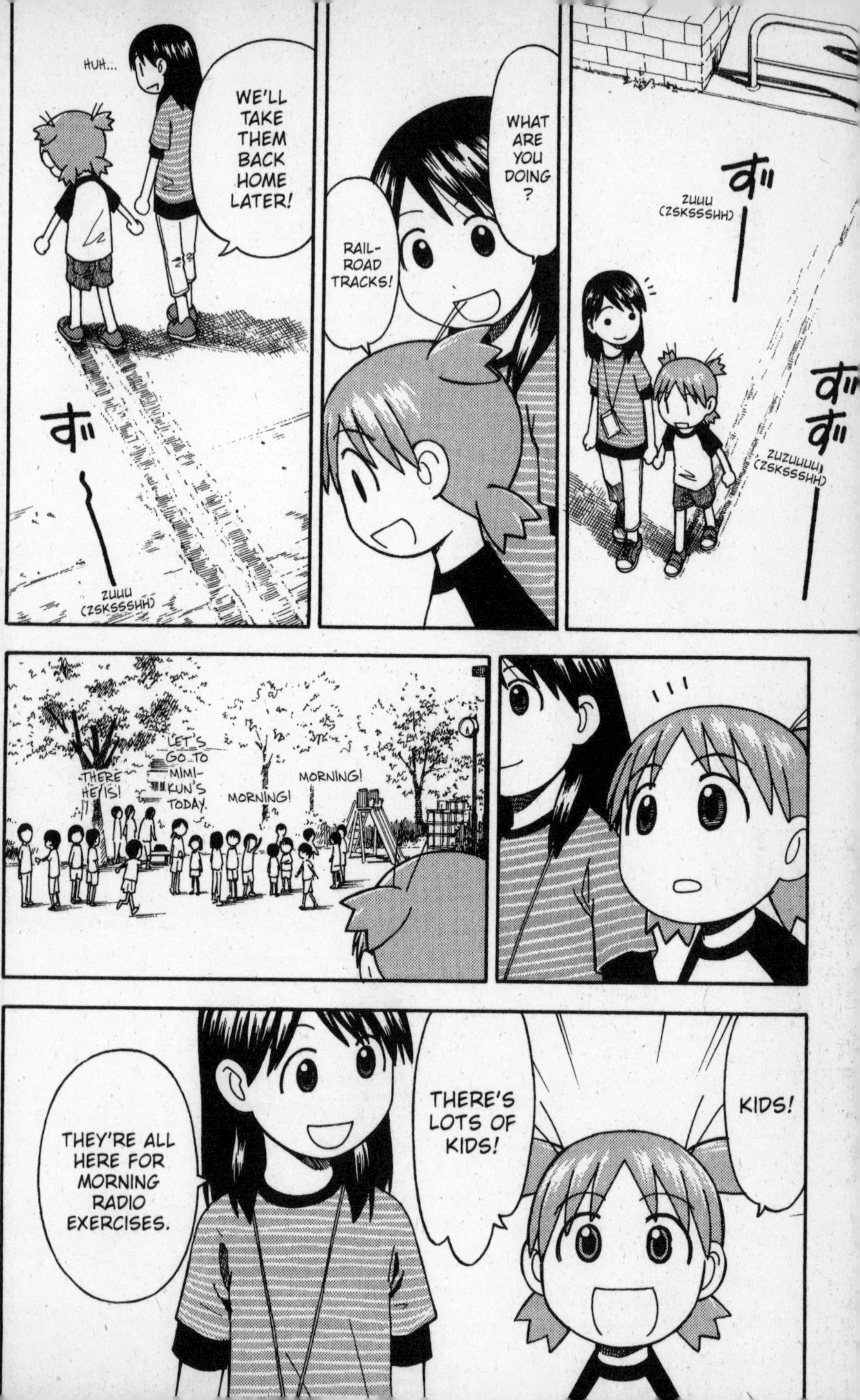
ずず
ZUZUUUU (ZSKSSSHH)
ず
ZUUU (ZSKSSSHH)
WHAT ARE YOU DOING?
RAIL-ROAD TRACKS!
WE'LL TAKE THEM BACK HOME LATER!
HUH...
ず
ZUUU (ZSKSSSHH)
MORNING!
MORNING!
LET'S GO TO MIMI-KUN'S TODAY.
THERE HE IS!
KIDS!
THERE'S LOTS OF KIDS!
THEY'RE ALL HERE FOR MORNING RADIO EXERCISES.

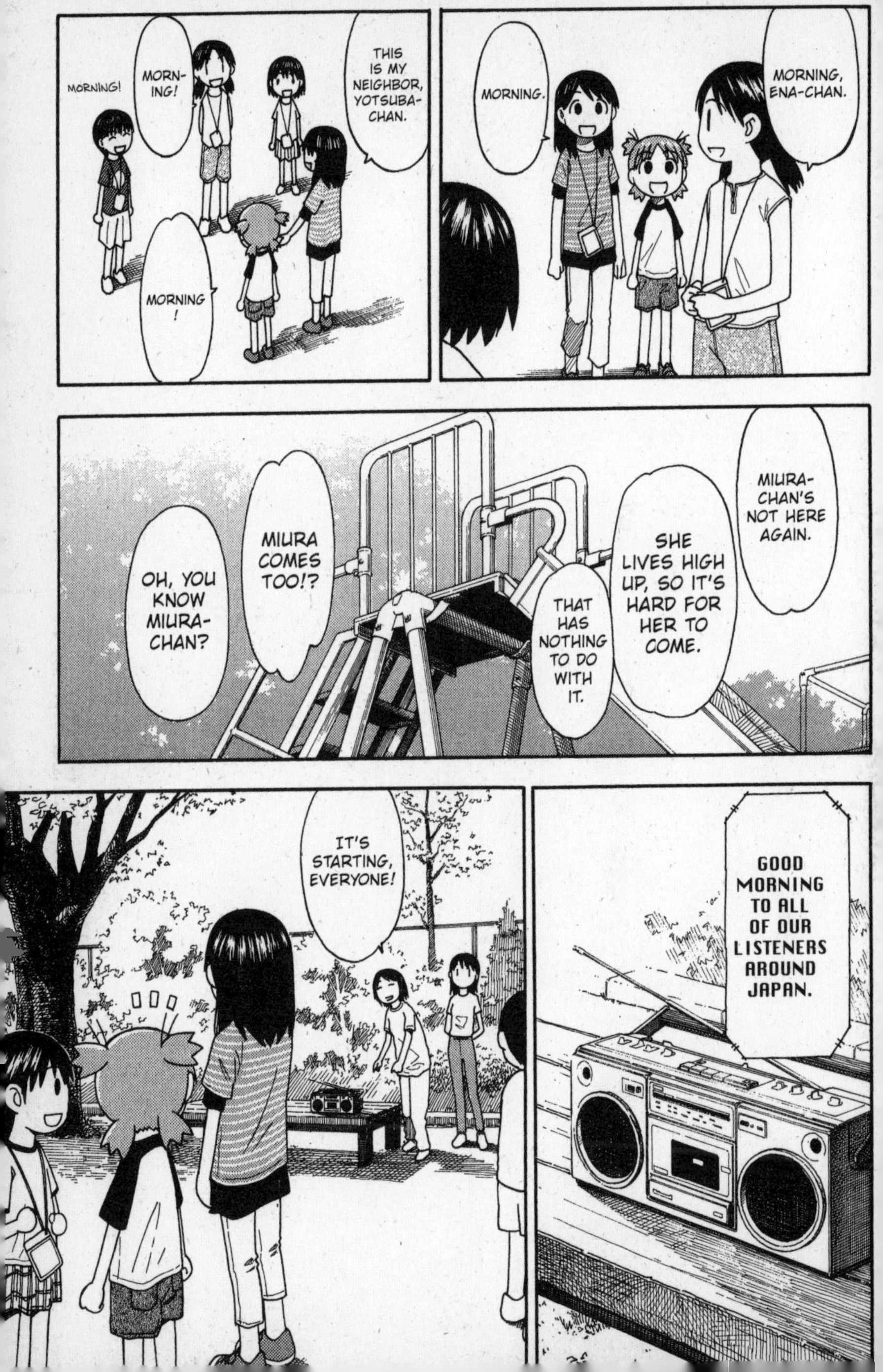
MORNING, ENA-CHAN.
MORNING.
THIS IS MY NEIGHBOR, YOTSUBA-CHAN.
MORN-ING!
MORNING!
MORNING!
MIURA-CHAN'S NOT HERE AGAIN.
SHE LIVES HIGH UP, SO IT'S HARD FOR HER TO COME.
THAT HAS NOTHING TO DO WITH IT.
MIURA COMES TOO!?
OH, YOU KNOW MIURA-CHAN?
GOOD MORNING TO ALL OF OUR LISTENERS AROUND JAPAN.
IT'S STARTING, EVERYONE!

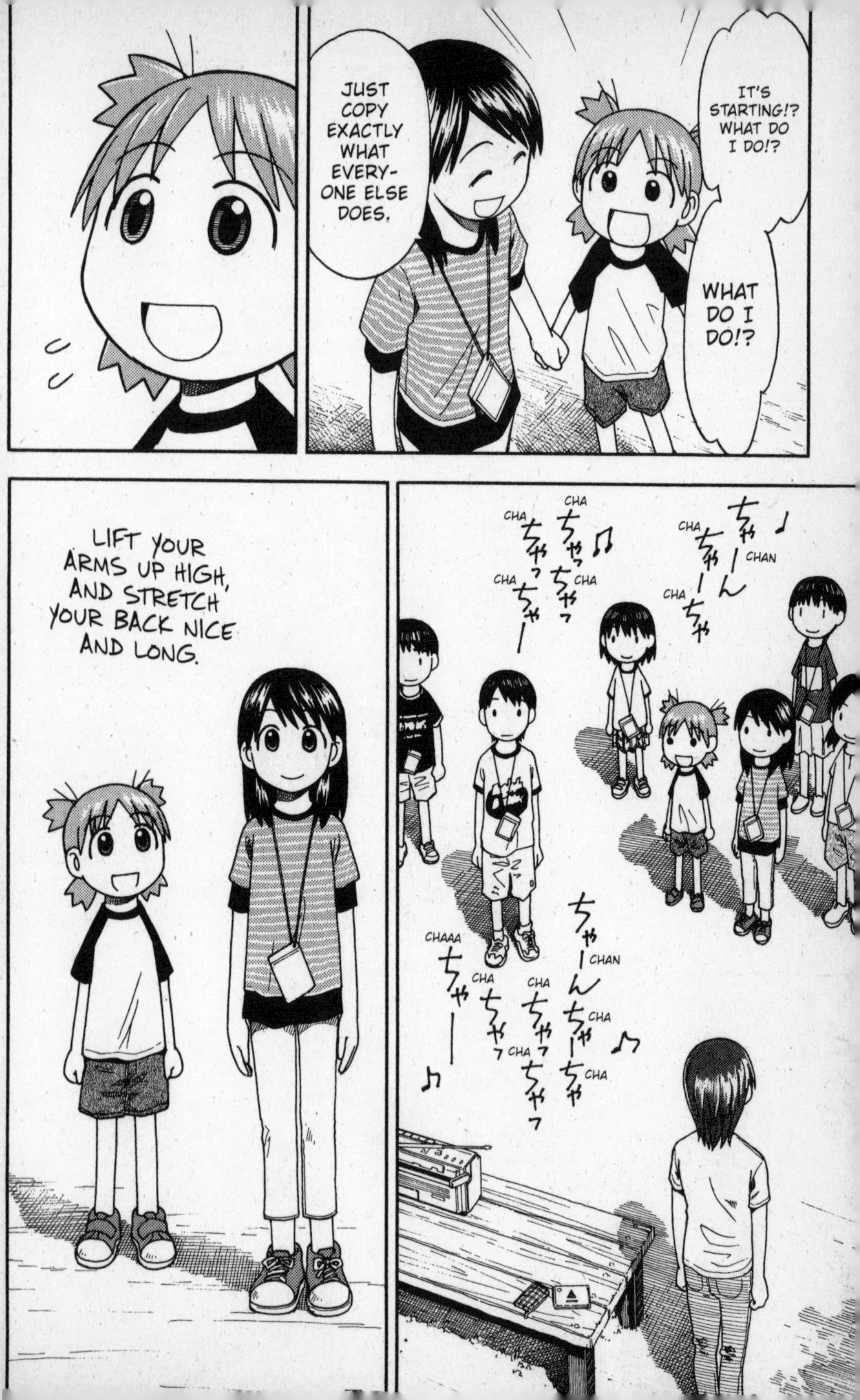
IT'S STARTING!? WHAT DO I DO!?
WHAT DO I DO!?
JUST COPY EXACTLY WHAT EVERY-ONE ELSE DOES.
ちゃーんちゃーちゃ
CHA CHAN CHA
ちゃっちゃっ
CHA CHA
ちゃっちゃっちゃー
CHA CHA
ちゃーんちゃーちゃ
CHAN CHA CHA
ちゃっちゃっ
CHA CHA
ちゃっ
CHA
ちゃー
CHAAA
LIFT YOUR ARMS UP HIGH, AND STRETCH YOUR BACK NICE AND LONG.

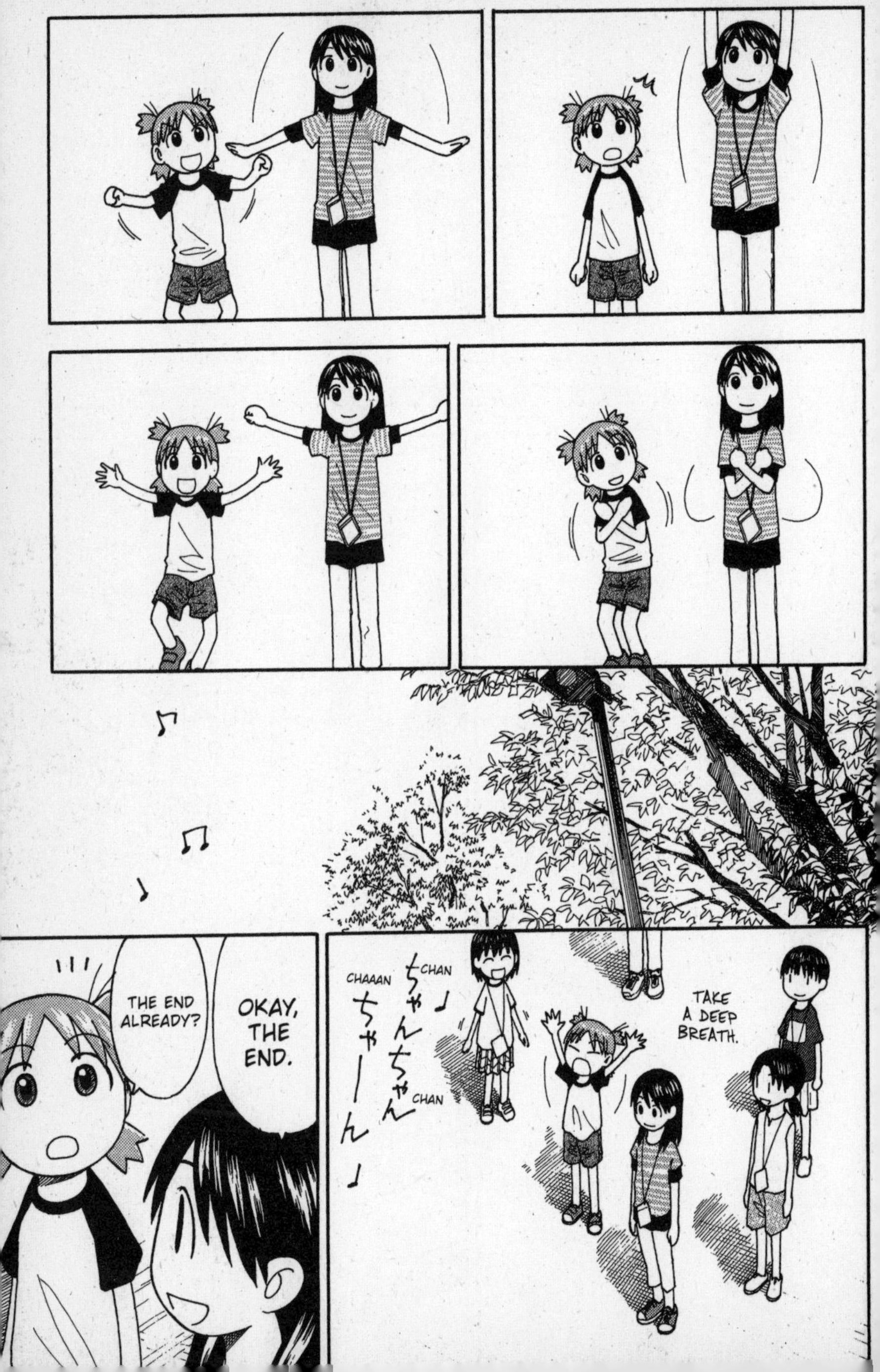
TAKE A DEEP BREATH.
ちゃんちゃん
CHAN
CHAN
ちゃーん
CHAAAN
OKAY, THE END.
THE END ALREADY?

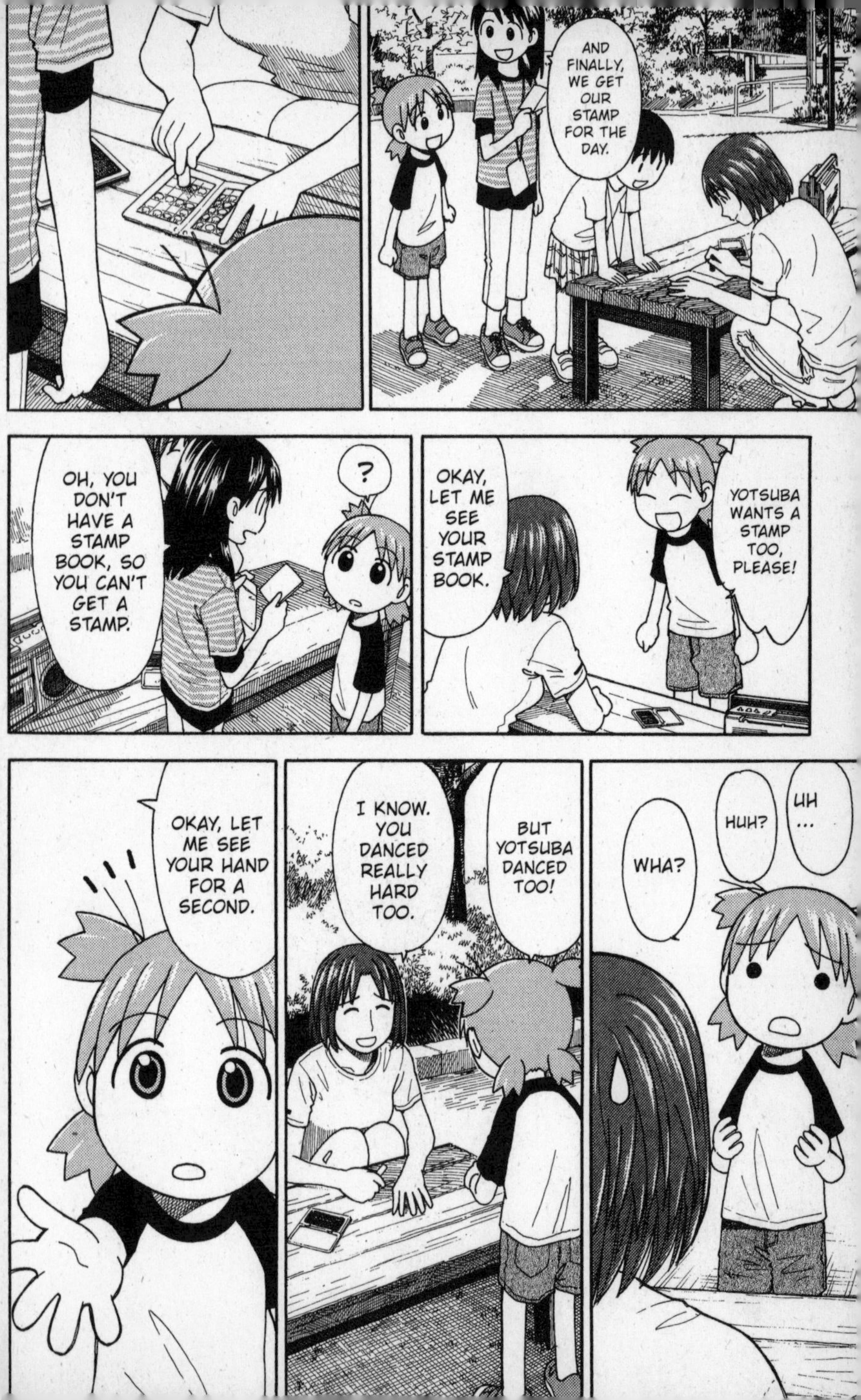
AND FINALLY, WE GET OUR STAMP FOR THE DAY.
YOTSUBA WANTS A STAMP TOO, PLEASE!
OKAY, LET ME SEE YOUR STAMP BOOK.
?
OH, YOU DON'T HAVE A STAMP BOOK, SO YOU CAN'T GET A STAMP.
UH ...
HUH?
WHA?
BUT YOTSUBA DANCED TOO!
I KNOW. YOU DANCED REALLY HARD TOO.
OKAY, LET ME SEE YOUR HAND FOR A SECOND.

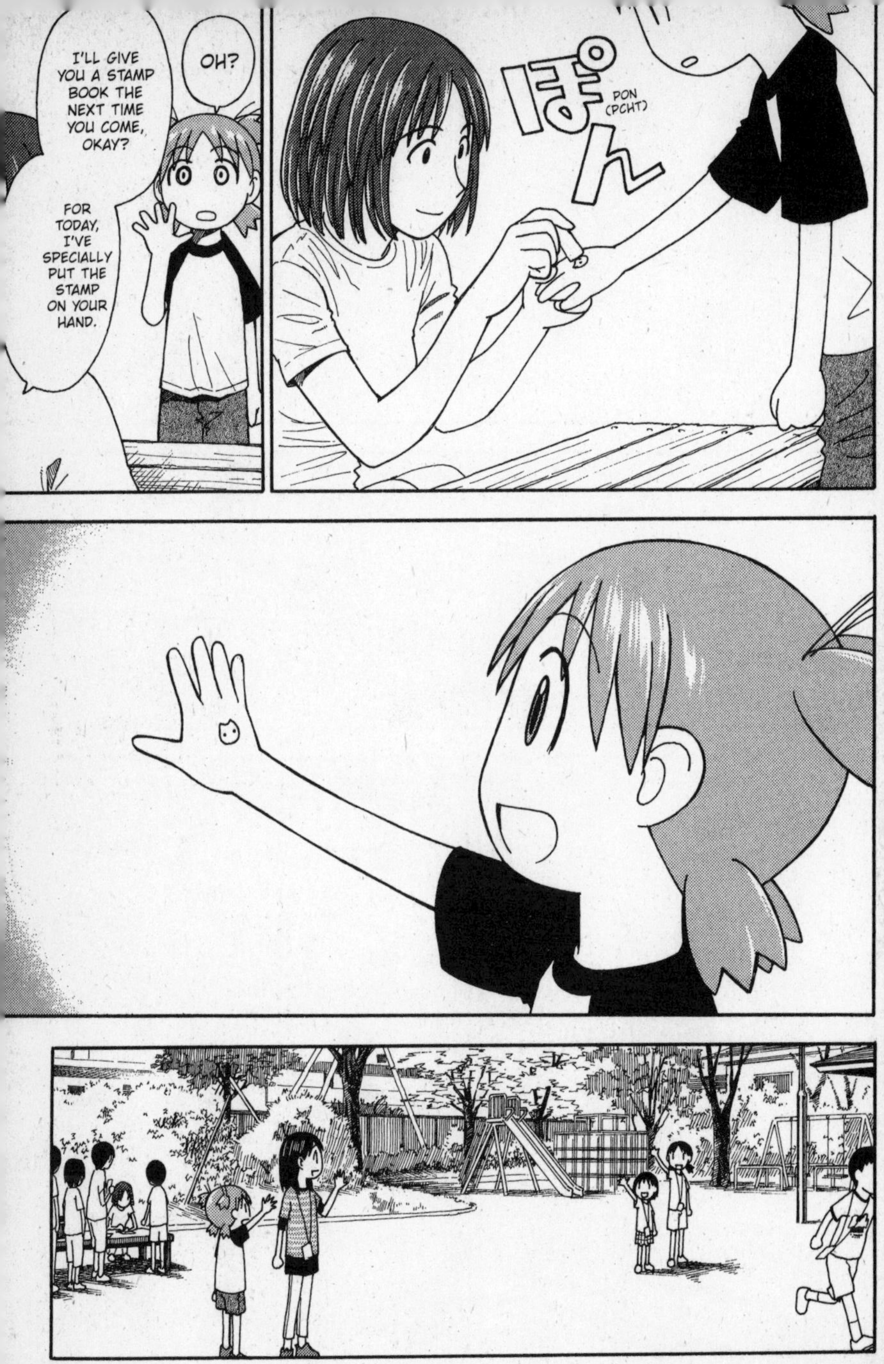
ぽん
PON (PCHT)
OH?
I'LL GIVE YOU A STAMP BOOK THE NEXT TIME YOU COME, OKAY?
FOR TODAY, I'VE SPECIALLY PUT THE STAMP ON YOUR HAND.

ずー
ZUUU

ずー
ZUUU
(ZSKSSSSHH)

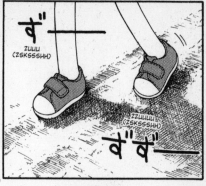

ず—
ZUUU
(ZSKSSSSHH)

ずず—
ZZUUUU
(ZSKSSSSHH)

YUP!

IT'S
SPECIAL!

ず
ZUUU

THAT'S NICE, SHE
GAVE YOU
A STAMP.

ず
ZUUU
(ZSKSSSSHH)

ブ
ル
ル
BURURURURU
(VROOOM)

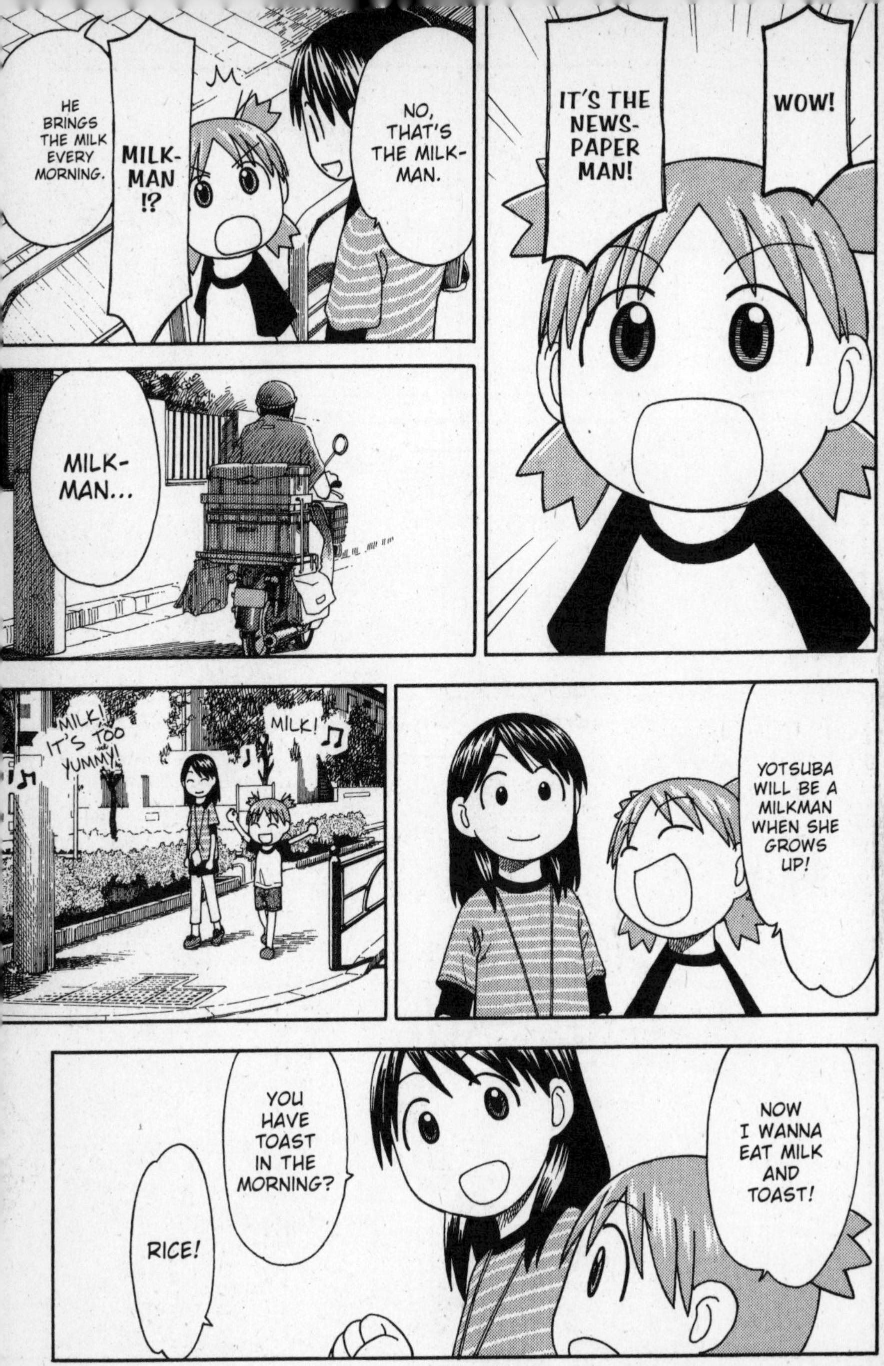
WOW!
IT'S THE NEWS-PAPER MAN!
NO, THAT'S THE MILK-MAN.
MILK-MAN!?
HE BRINGS THE MILK EVERY MORNING.
MILK-MAN...
YOTSUBA WILL BE A MILKMAN WHEN SHE GROWS UP!
MILK!
MILK! IT'S TOO YUMMY!
NOW I WANNA EAT MILK AND TOAST!
YOU HAVE TOAST IN THE MORNING?
RICE!

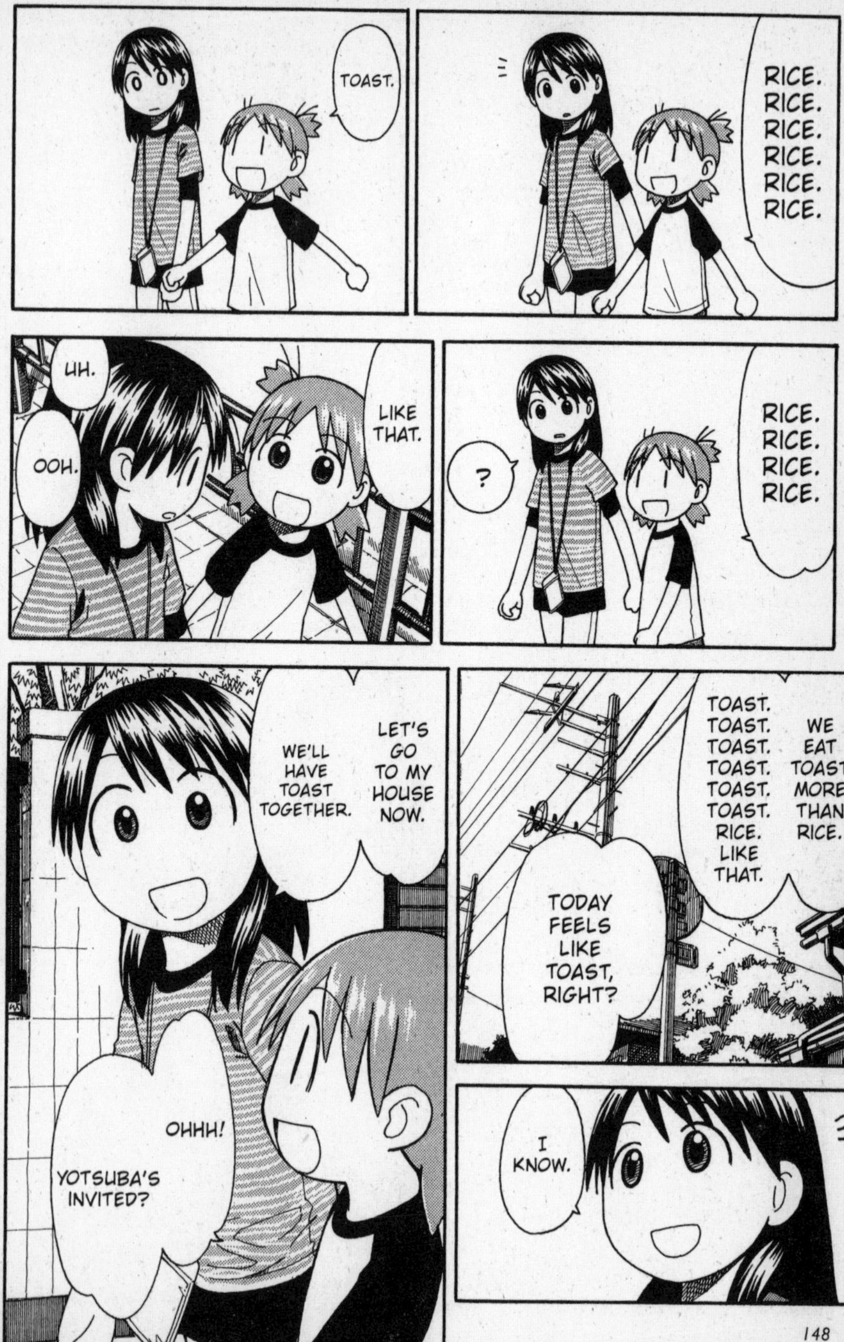
RICE. RICE. RICE. RICE. RICE. RICE.
TOAST.
RICE. RICE. RICE. RICE.
?
LIKE THAT.
UH.
OOH.
WE EAT TOAST MORE THAN RICE.
TOAST. TOAST. TOAST. TOAST. TOAST. TOAST. RICE. LIKE THAT.
TODAY FEELS LIKE TOAST, RIGHT?
I KNOW.
LET'S GO TO MY HOUSE NOW.
WE'LL HAVE TOAST TOGETHER.
OHHH!
YOTSUBA'S INVITED?

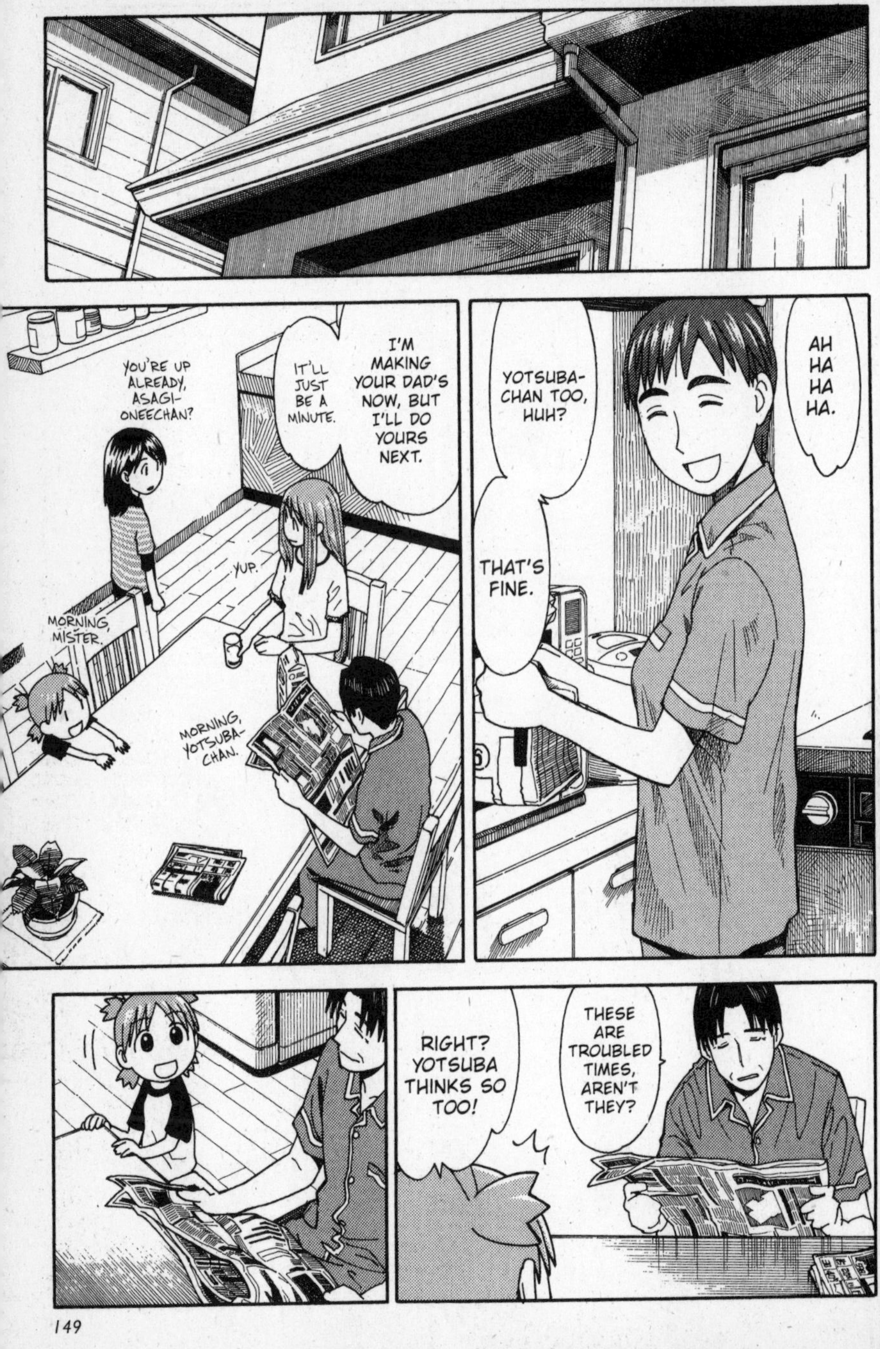
AH HA HA HA.
YOTSUBA-CHAN TOO, HUH?
THAT'S FINE.
I'M MAKING YOUR DAD'S NOW, BUT I'LL DO YOURS NEXT.
IT'LL JUST BE A MINUTE.
YOU'RE UP ALREADY, ASAGI-ONEECHAN?
YUP.
MORNING, MISTER.
MORNING, YOTSUBA-CHAN.
THESE ARE TROUBLED TIMES, AREN'T THEY?
RIGHT? YOTSUBA THINKS SO TOO!

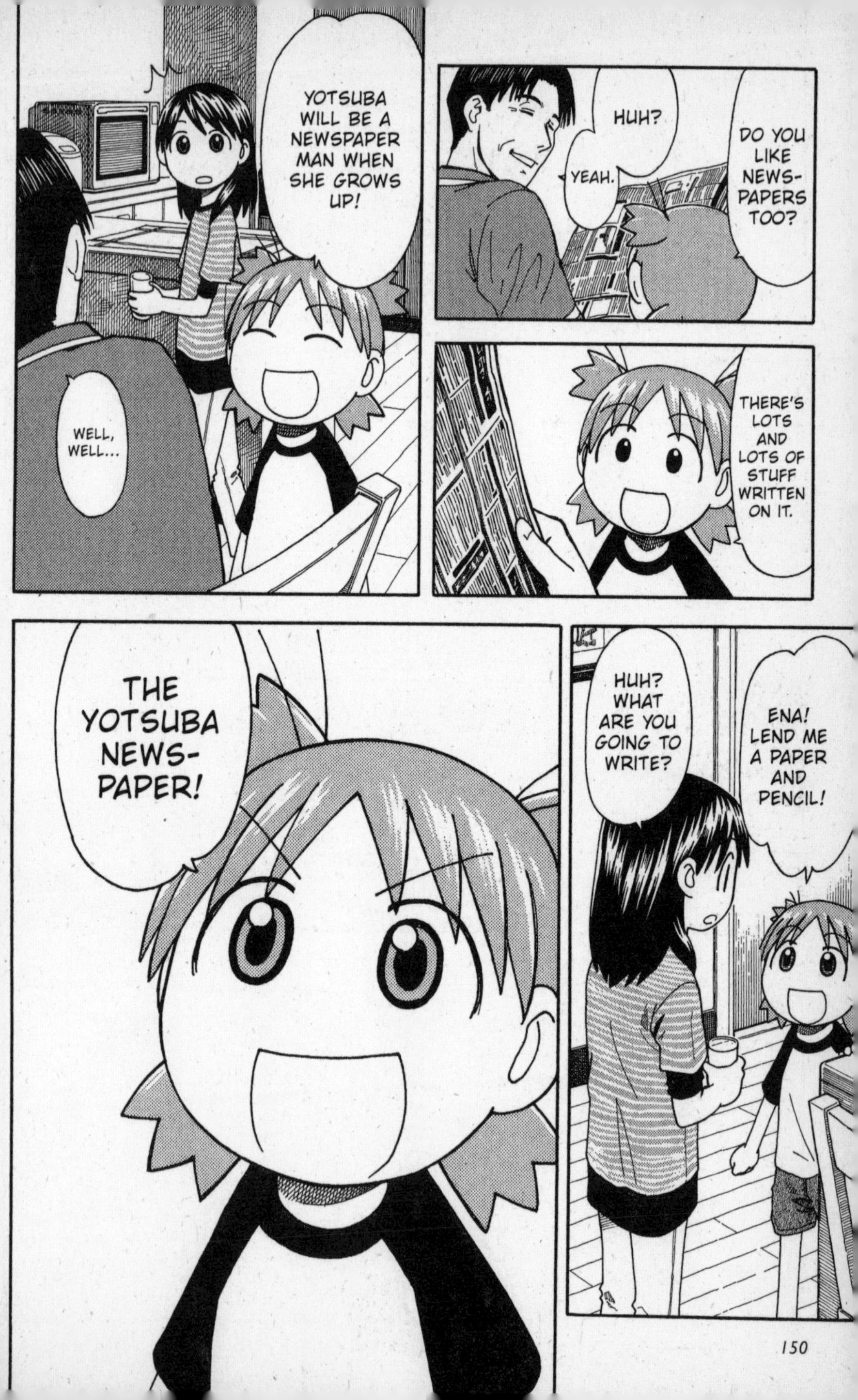
DO YOU LIKE NEWS-PAPERS TOO?
HUH?
YEAH.
THERE'S LOTS AND LOTS OF STUFF WRITTEN ON IT.
YOTSUBA WILL BE A NEWSPAPER MAN WHEN SHE GROWS UP!
WELL, WELL...
ENA! LEND ME A PAPER AND PENCIL!
HUH? WHAT ARE YOU GOING TO WRITE?
THE YOTSUBA NEWS-PAPER!

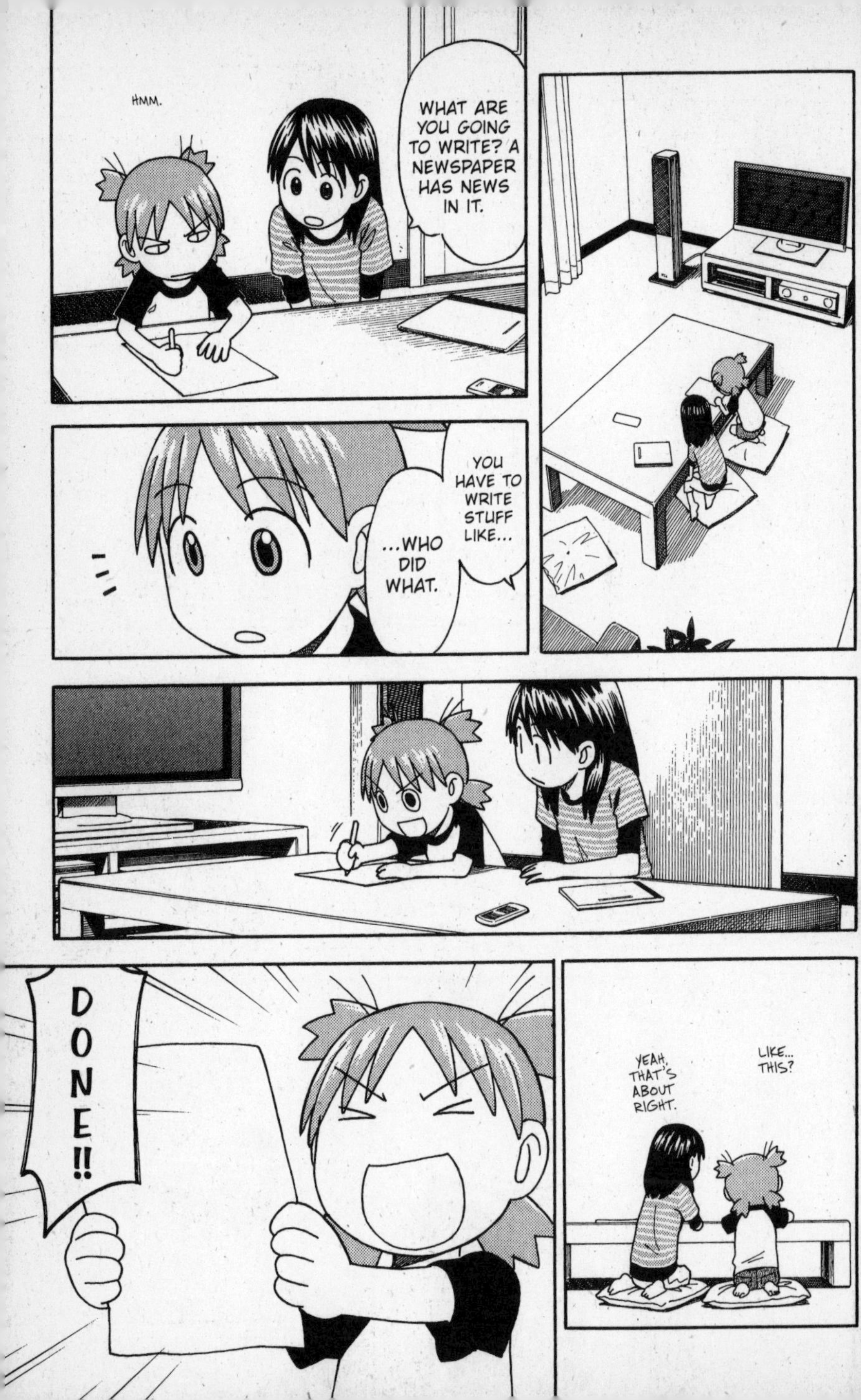
WHAT ARE YOU GOING TO WRITE? A NEWSPAPER HAS NEWS IN IT.
HMM.
YOU HAVE TO WRITE STUFF LIKE...
...WHO DID WHAT.
LIKE... THIS?
YEAH, THAT'S ABOUT RIGHT.
DONE!!

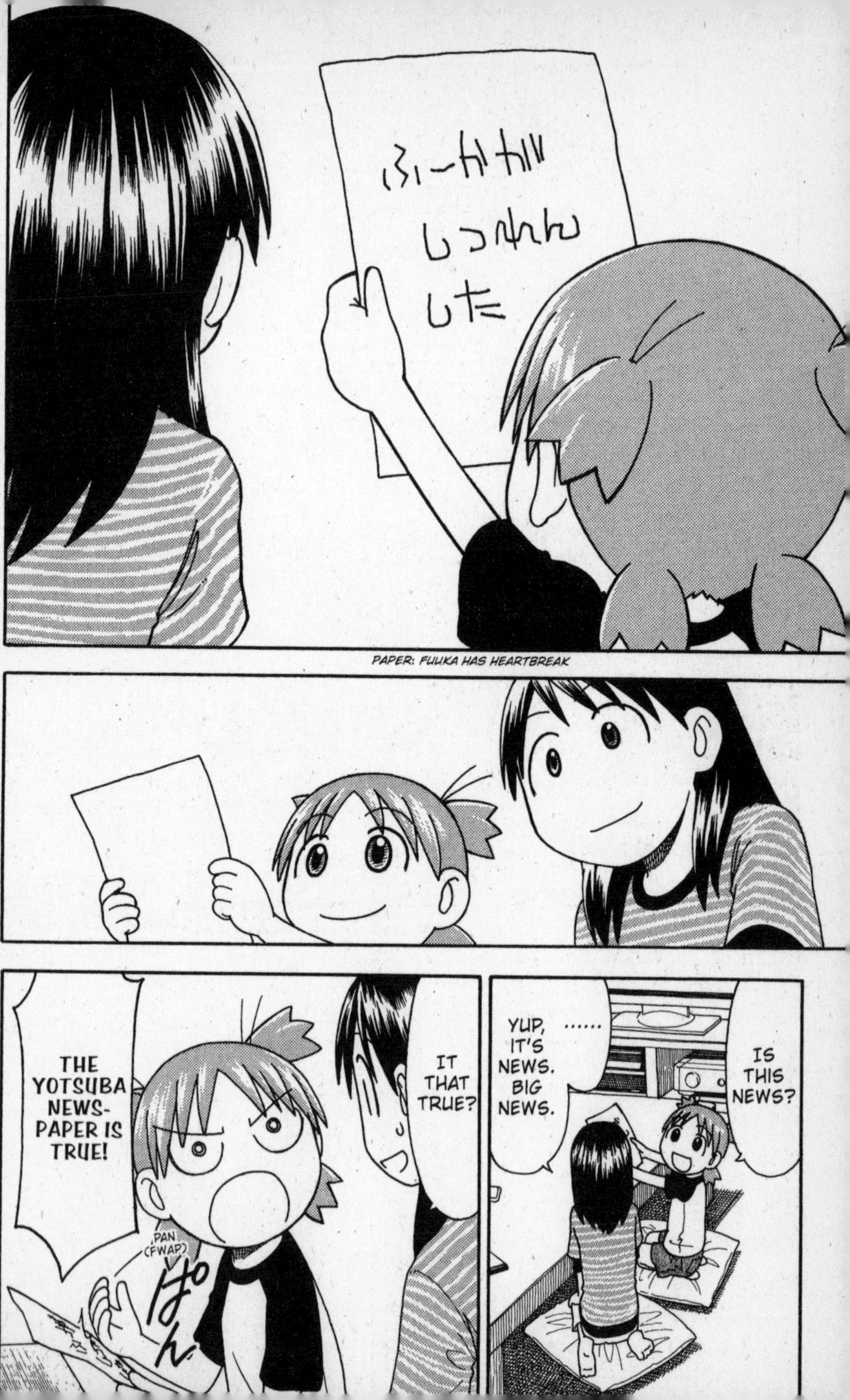

ふーかが
しつれん
した
PAPER: FUUKA HAS HEARTBREAK
IS THIS NEWS?
......
YUP, IT'S NEWS. BIG NEWS.
IT THAT TRUE?
THE YOTSUBA NEWS-PAPER IS TRUE!
ぱん
PAN (FWAP)

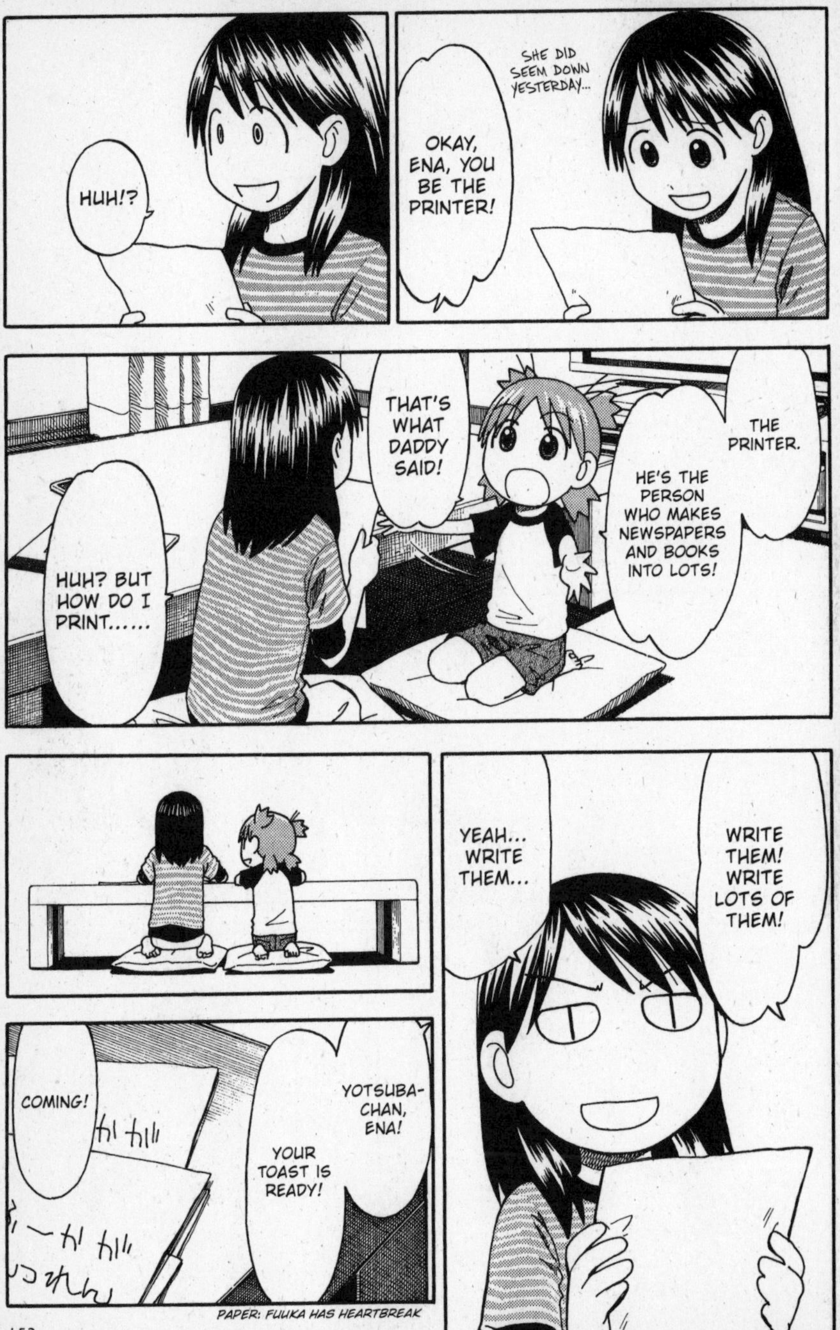
SHE DID SEEM DOWN YESTERDAY...
OKAY, ENA, YOU BE THE PRINTER!
HUH!?
THE PRINTER.
HE'S THE PERSON WHO MAKES NEWSPAPERS AND BOOKS INTO LOTS!
THAT'S WHAT DADDY SAID!
HUH? BUT HOW DO I PRINT......
WRITE THEM! WRITE LOTS OF THEM!
YEAH... WRITE THEM...
YOTSUBA-CHAN, ENA!
YOUR TOAST IS READY!
COMING!
PAPER: FUUKA HAS HEARTBREAK

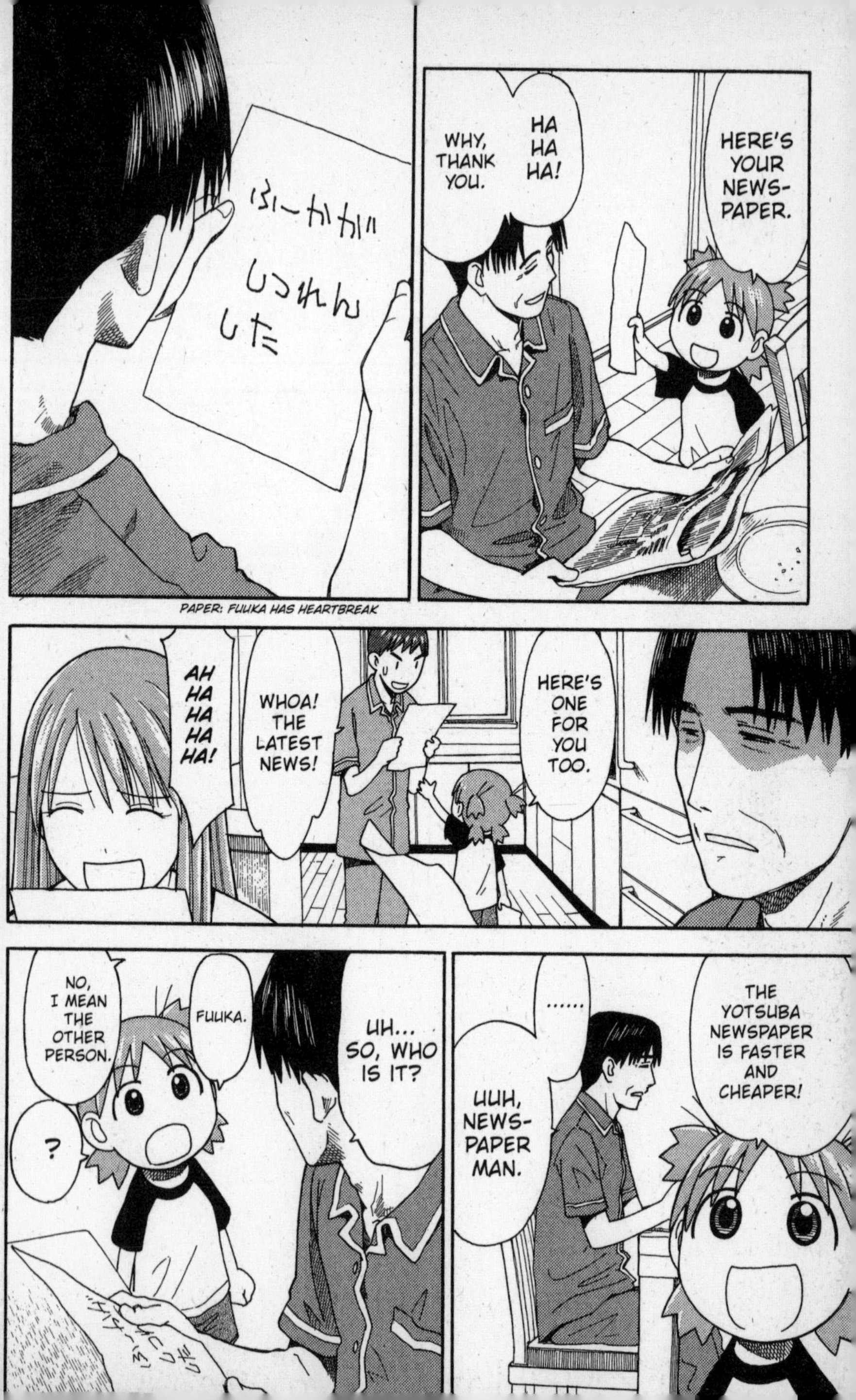
HERE'S YOUR NEWS-PAPER.
HA HA HA!
WHY, THANK YOU.
ふーかが しつれんした
PAPER: FUUKA HAS HEARTBREAK
HERE'S ONE FOR YOU TOO.
WHOA! THE LATEST NEWS!
AH HA HA HA HA HA!
THE YOTSUBA NEWSPAPER IS FASTER AND CHEAPER!
......
UUH, NEWS-PAPER MAN.
UH... SO, WHO IS IT?
FUUKA.
NO, I MEAN THE OTHER PERSON.
?

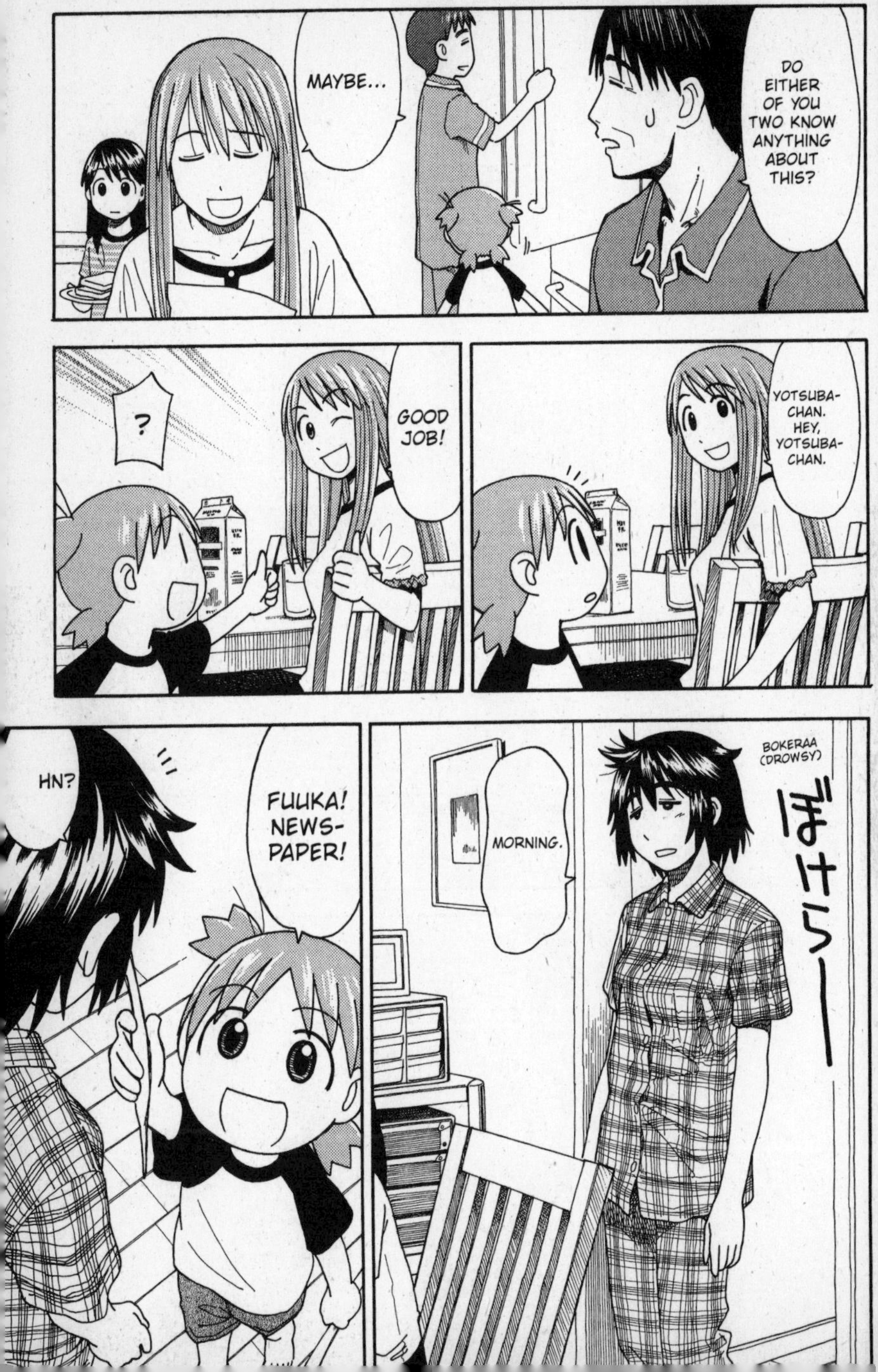
DO EITHER OF YOU TWO KNOW ANYTHING ABOUT THIS?
MAYBE...
YOTSUBA-CHAN. HEY, YOTSUBA-CHAN.
GOOD JOB!
?
BOKERAA (DROWSY)
ぼけらー
MORNING.
FUUKA! NEWS-PAPER!
HN?

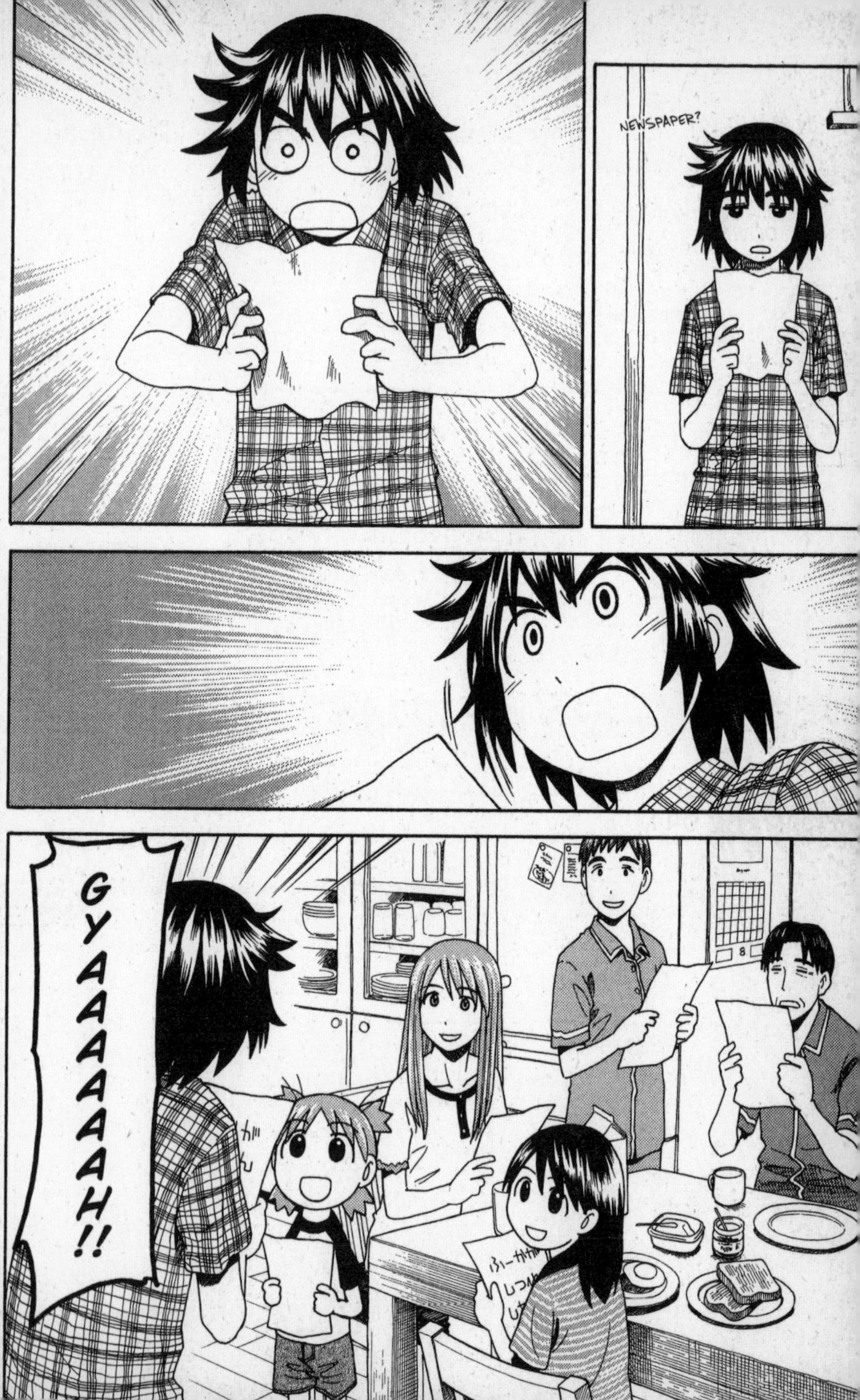
NEWSPAPER?
GYAAAAAAH!!

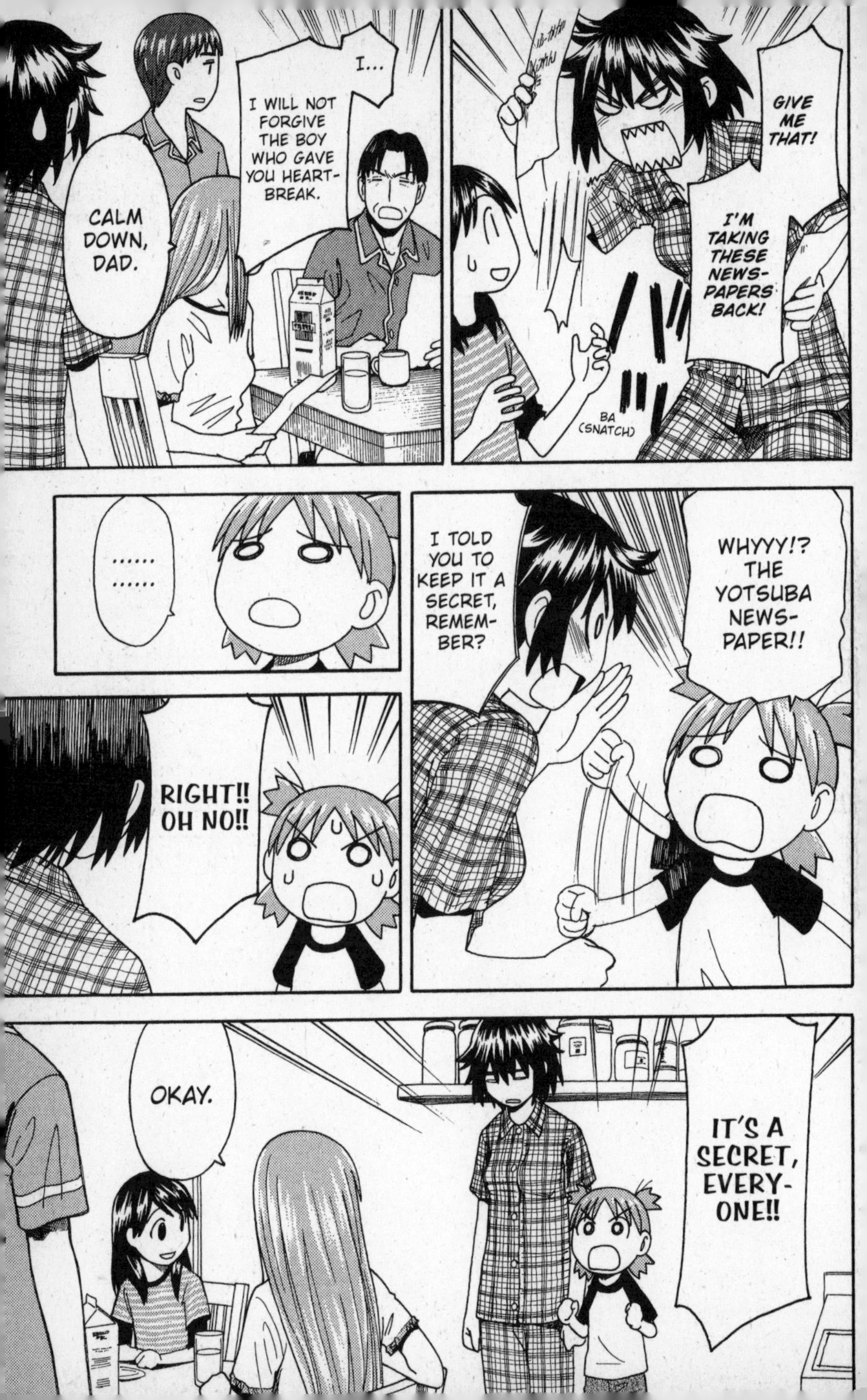
GIVE ME THAT!
I'M TAKING THESE NEWS-PAPERS BACK!
BA (SNATCH)
I...
I WILL NOT FORGIVE THE BOY WHO GAVE YOU HEART-BREAK.
CALM DOWN, DAD.
WHYYY!? THE YOTSUBA NEWS-PAPER!!
I TOLD YOU TO KEEP IT A SECRET, REMEMBER?
....
RIGHT!! OH NO!!
IT'S A SECRET, EVERY-ONE!!
OKAY.

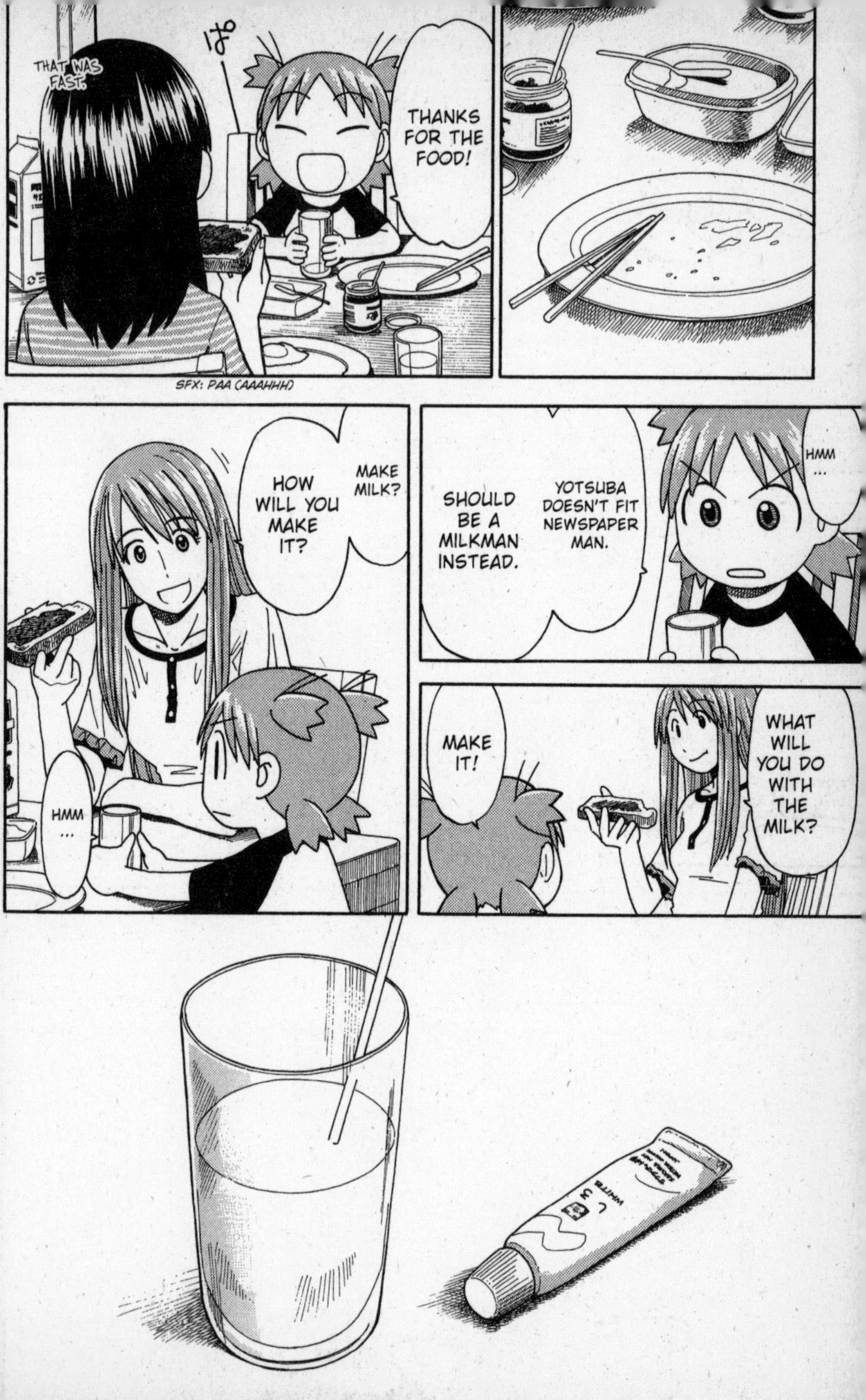

THANKS FOR THE FOOD!
ぱ
THAT WAS FAST.
SFX: PAA (AAAHHH)
HMM ...
YOTSUBA DOESN'T FIT NEWSPAPER MAN.
SHOULD BE A MILKMAN INSTEAD.
WHAT WILL YOU DO WITH THE MILK?
MAKE IT!
MAKE MILK?
HOW WILL YOU MAKE IT?
HMM ...

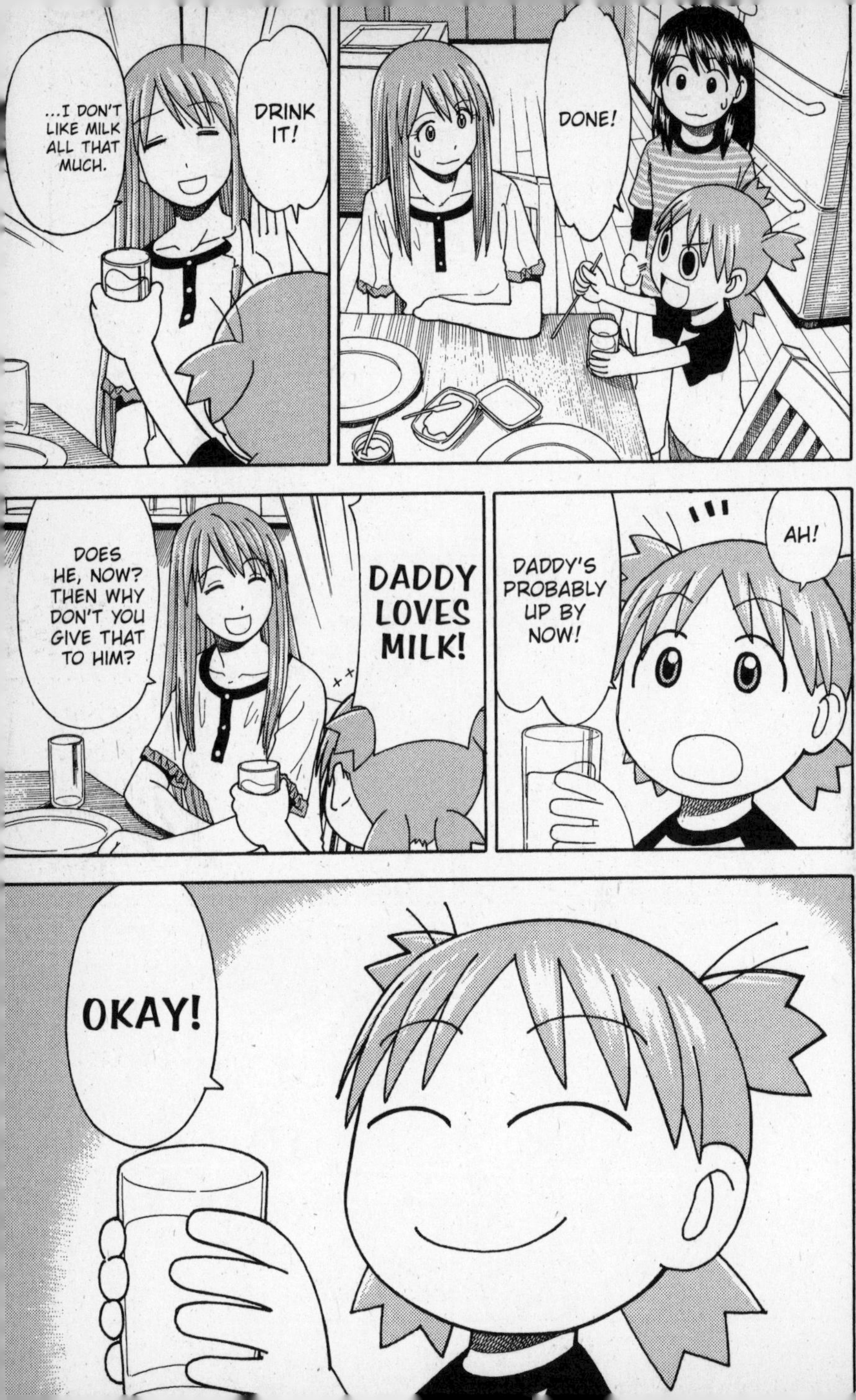
DONE!
DRINK IT!
...I DON'T LIKE MILK ALL THAT MUCH.
AH!
DADDY'S PROBABLY UP BY NOW!
DADDY LOVES MILK!
DOES HE, NOW? THEN WHY DON'T YOU GIVE THAT TO HIM?
OKAY!

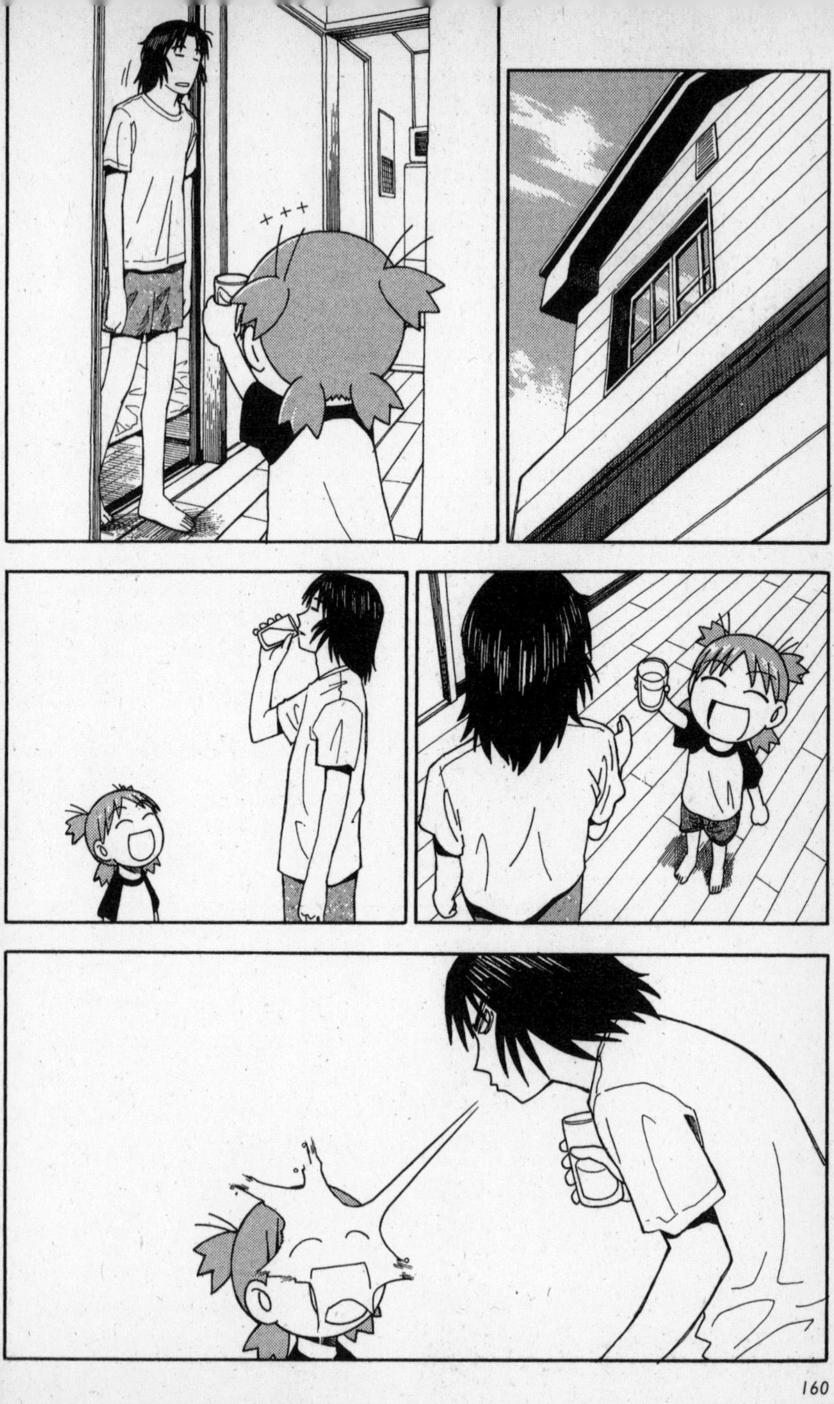

YOTSUBA&!

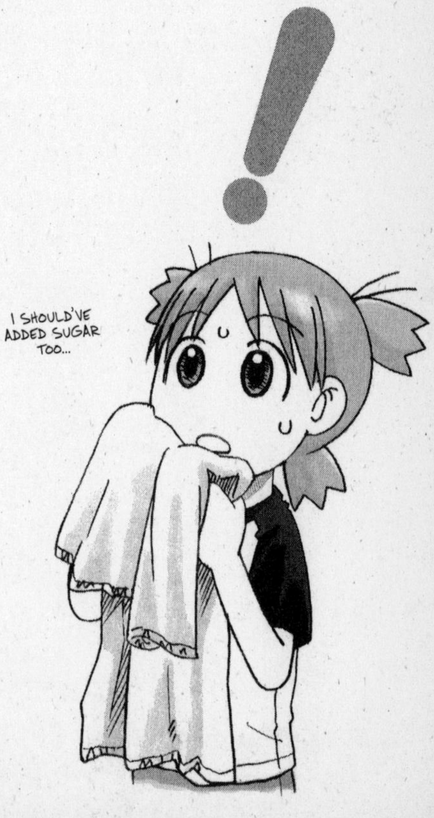
I SHOULD'VE ADDED SUGAR TOO...

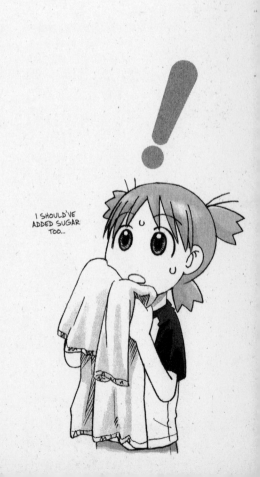

YOTSUBA&
TSUKUTSUKU BOUSHI
#27

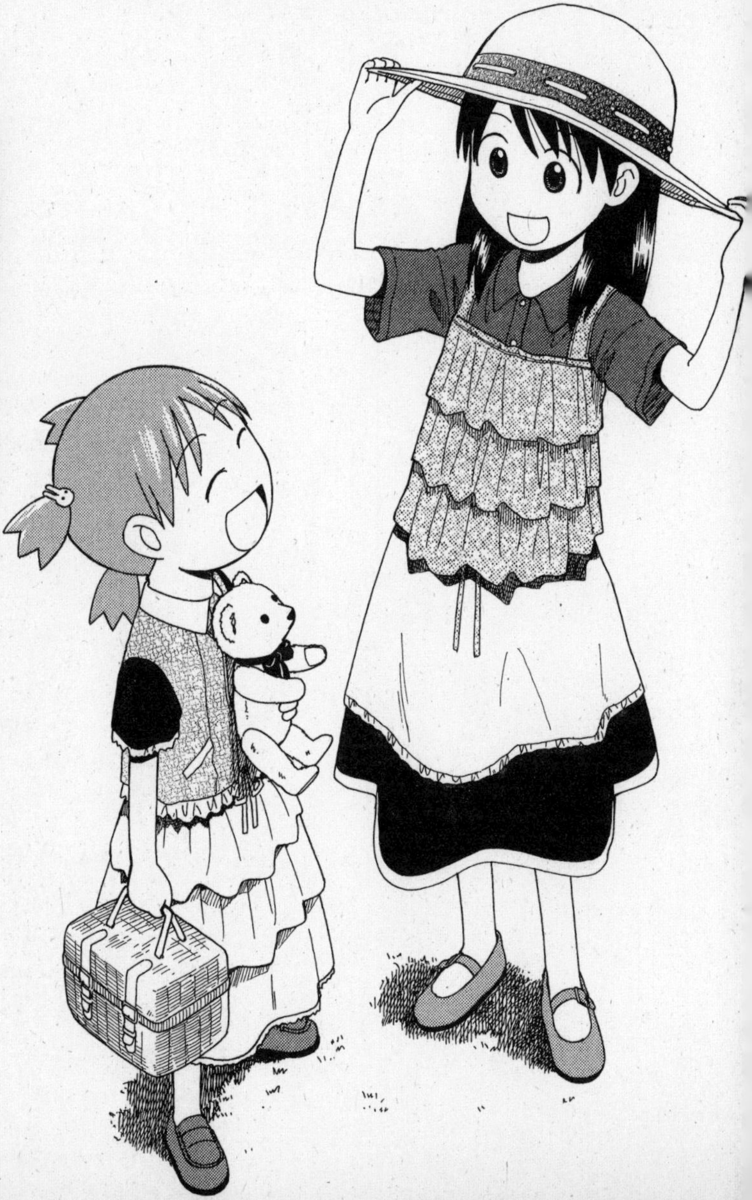

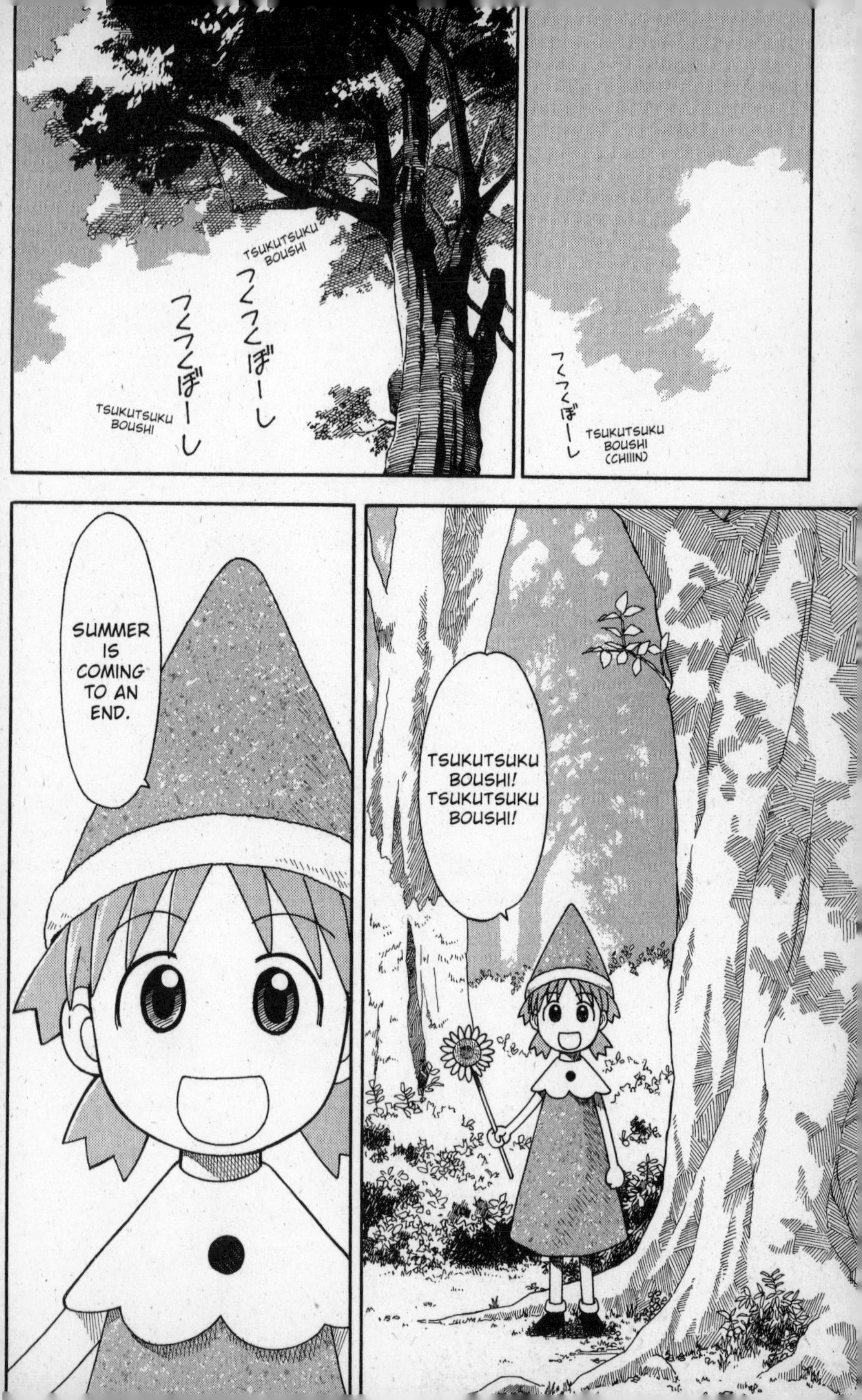
つくつくぼーし
TSUKUTSUKU BOUSHI (CHIIIN)
TSUKUTSUKU BOUSHI
つくつくぼーし
つくつくぼーし
TSUKUTSUKU BOUSHI
TSUKUTSUKU BOUSHI! TSUKUTSUKU BOUSHI!
SUMMER IS COMING TO AN END.

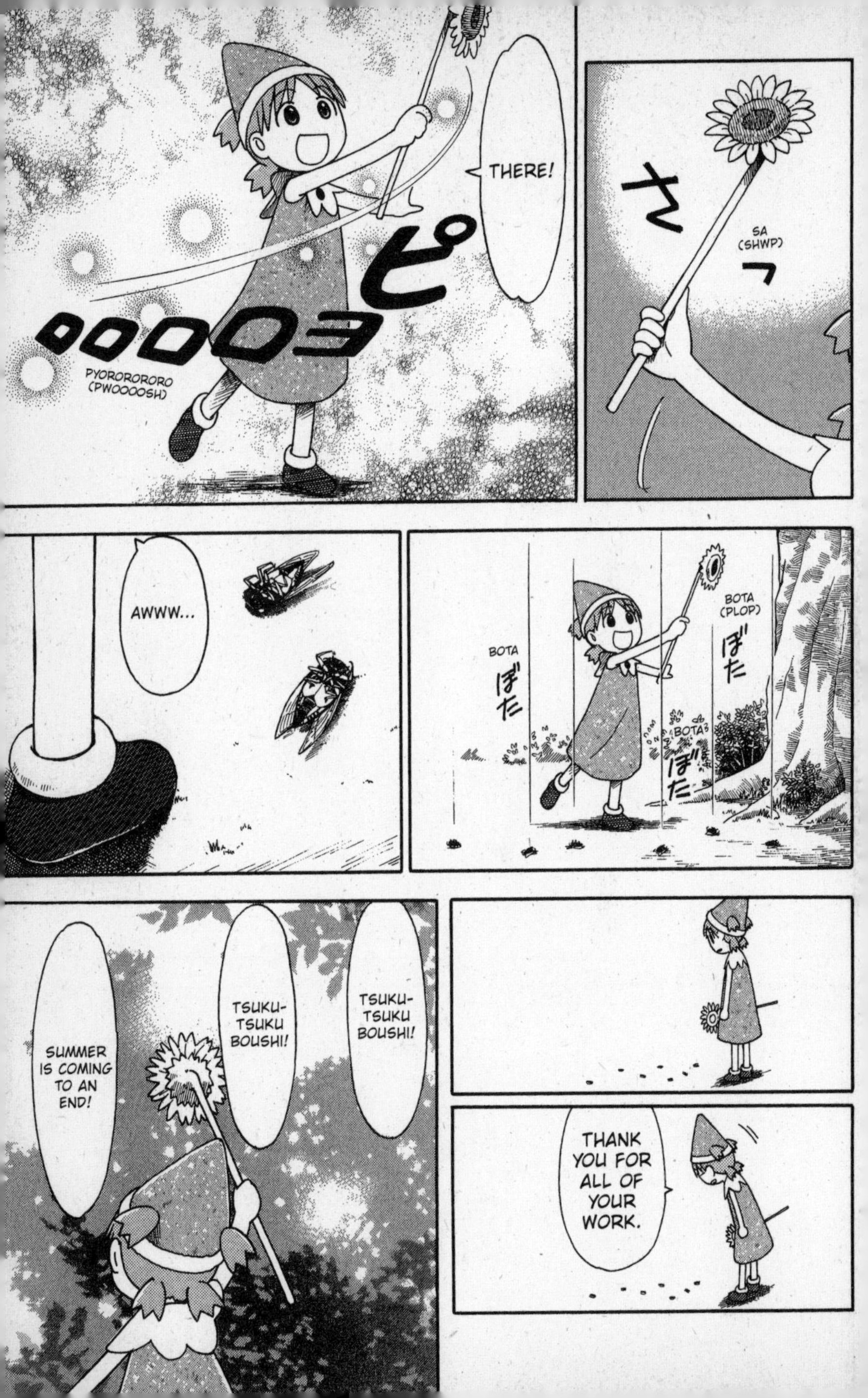
さ
SA
(SHWP)
THERE!
ピョロロロロ
PYORORORORO
(PWOOOOSH)
BOTA
(PLOP)
ぼた
BOTA
ぼた
BOTA
ぼた
AWWW...
THANK YOU FOR ALL OF YOUR WORK.
TSUKU-TSUKU BOUSHI!
TSUKU-TSUKU BOUSHI!
SUMMER IS COMING TO AN END!

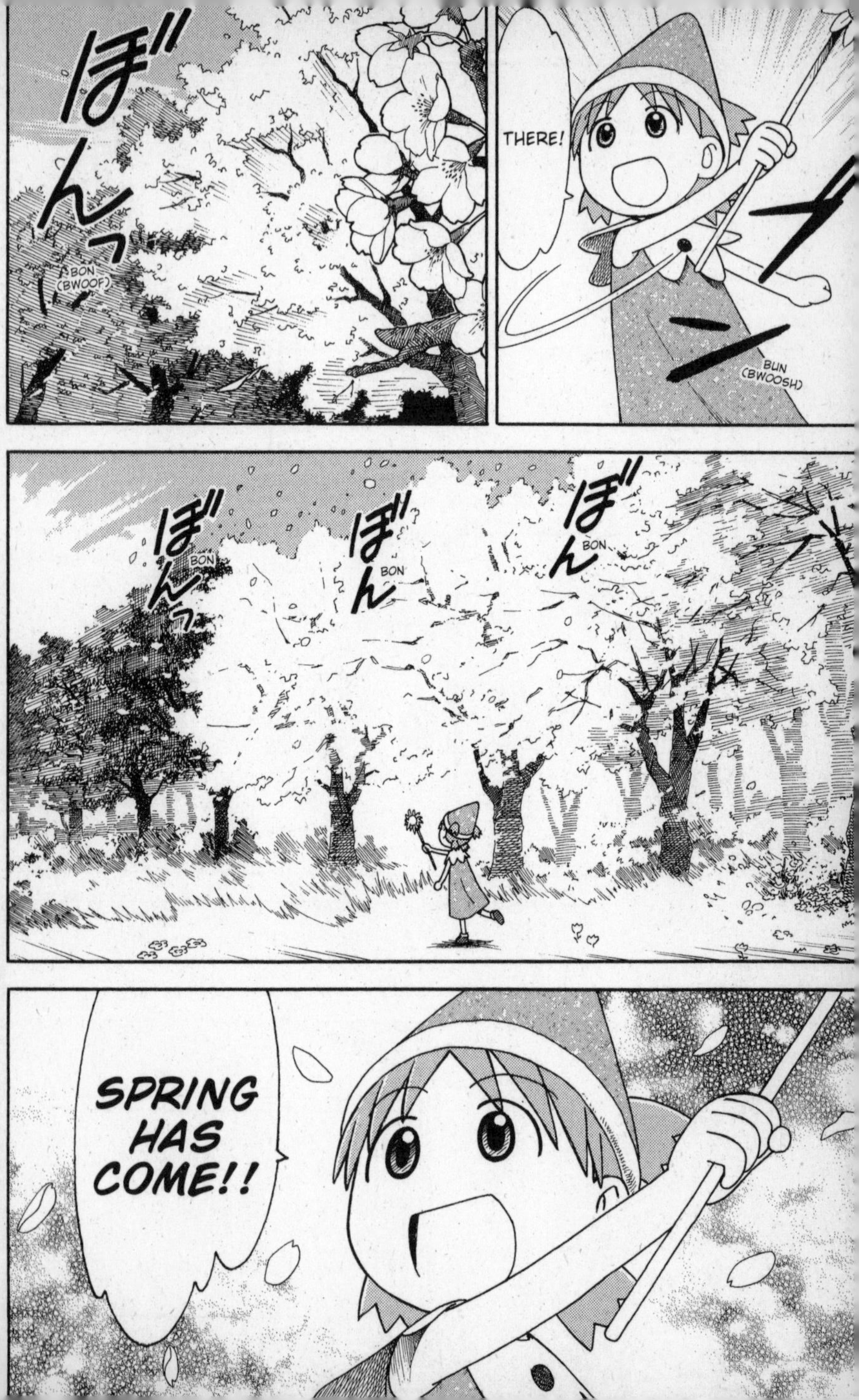
THERE!
BUN (BWOOSH)
ぼんっ
BON (BWOOF)
ぼん
BON
ぼん
BON
ぼんっ
BON
SPRING HAS COME!!

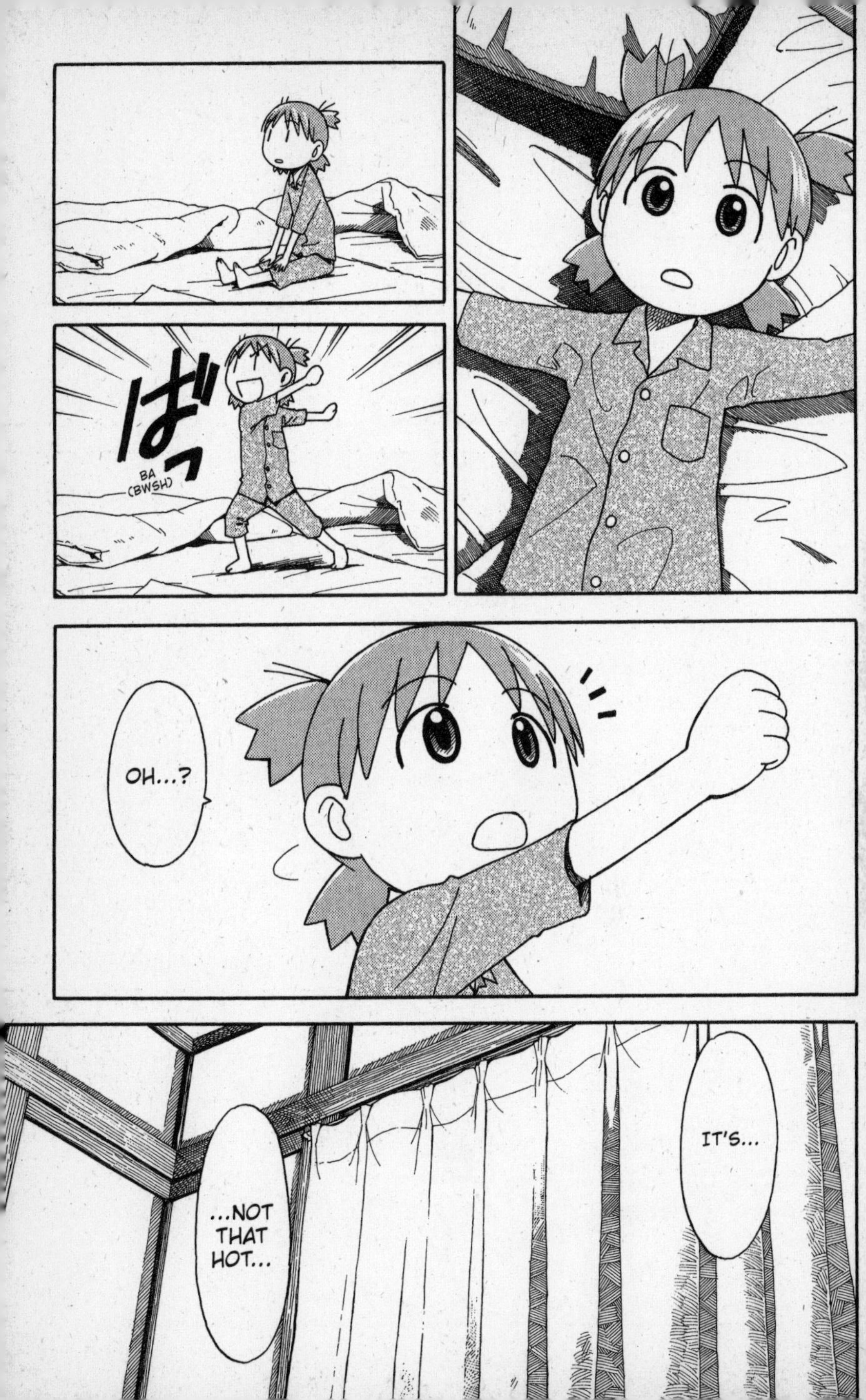
ばっ
BA (BWSH)
OH...?
IT'S...
...NOT THAT HOT...

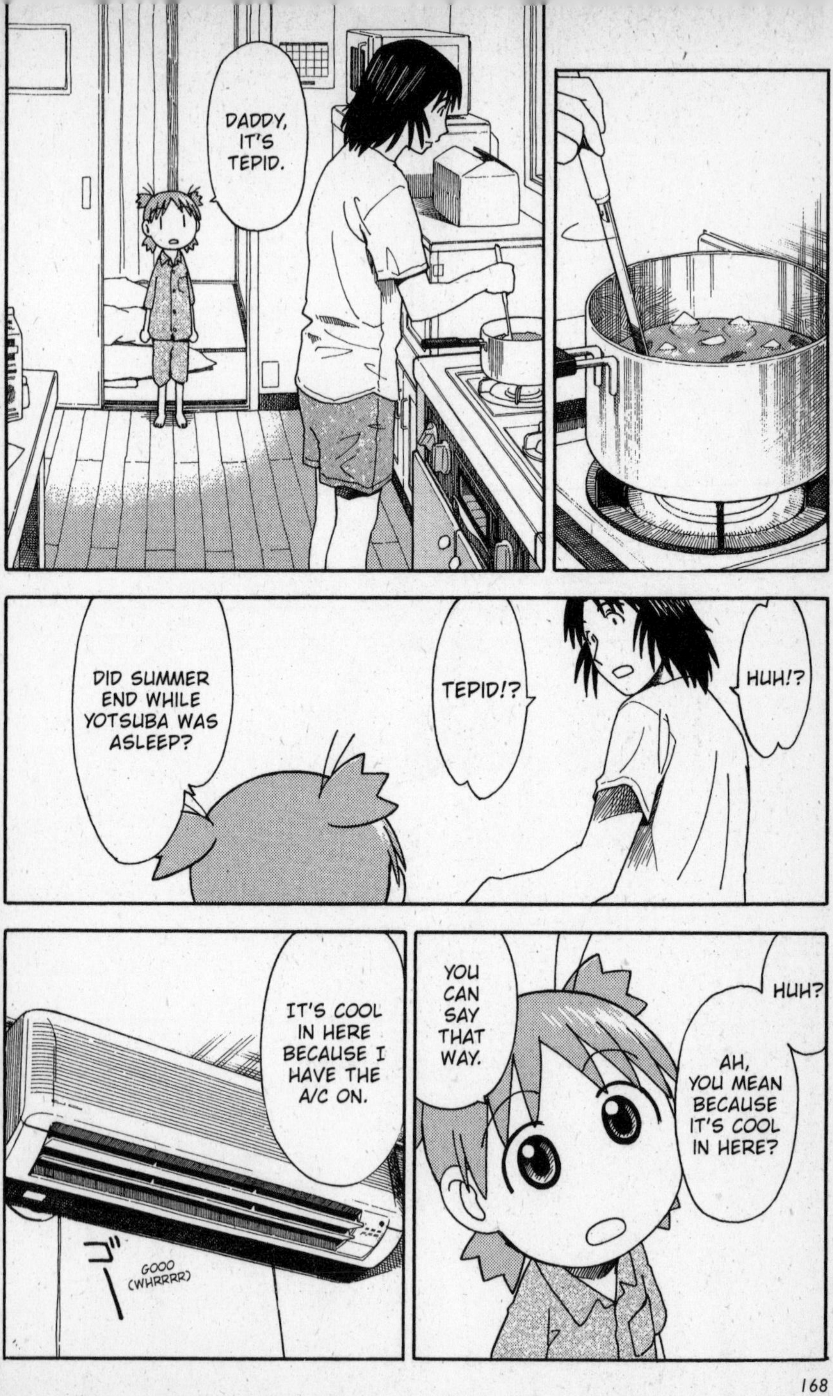
DADDY, IT'S TEPID.
HUH!?
TEPID!?
DID SUMMER END WHILE YOTSUBA WAS ASLEEP?
HUH?
AH, YOU MEAN BECAUSE IT'S COOL IN HERE?
YOU CAN SAY THAT WAY.
IT'S COOL IN HERE BECAUSE I HAVE THE A/C ON.
ゴー
GOOO (WHRRRR)

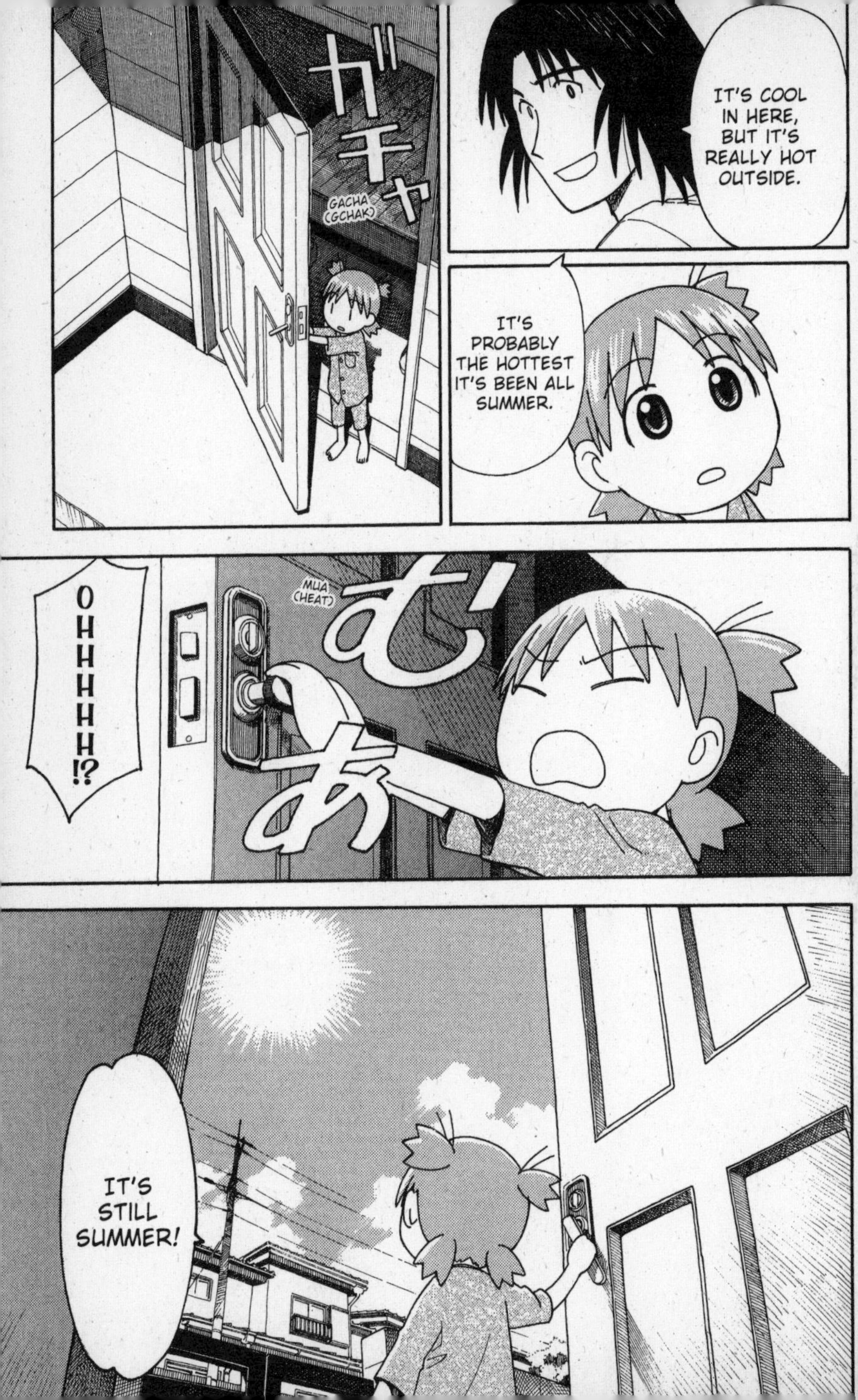
IT'S COOL IN HERE, BUT IT'S REALLY HOT OUTSIDE.
IT'S PROBABLY THE HOTTEST IT'S BEEN ALL SUMMER.
ガチャ
GACHA (GCHAK)
むあ
MUA (HEAT)
OHHHHHH!?
IT'S STILL SUMMER!

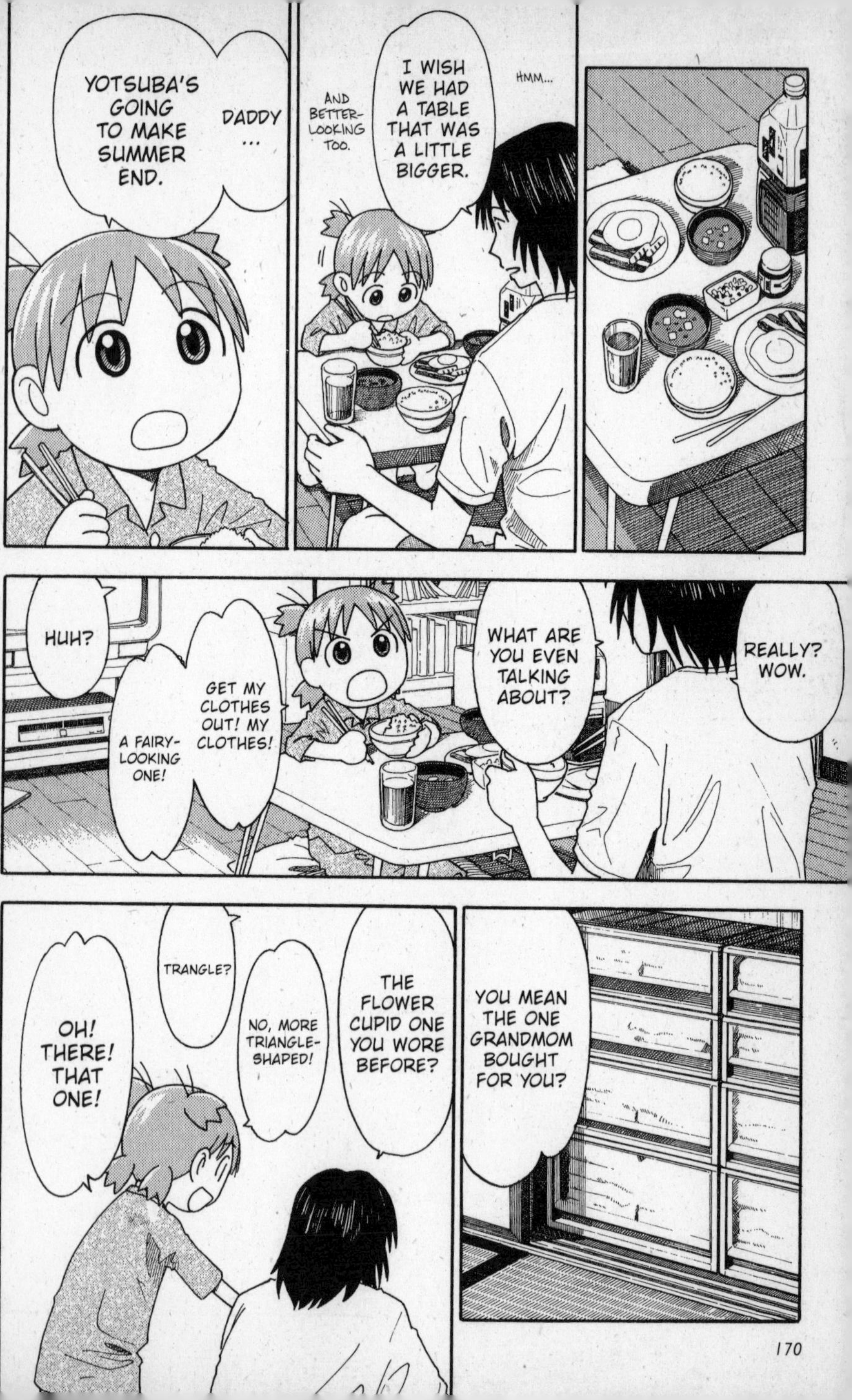
HMM...
I WISH WE HAD A TABLE THAT WAS A LITTLE BIGGER.
AND BETTER-LOOKING TOO.
DADDY ...
YOTSUBA'S GOING TO MAKE SUMMER END.
REALLY? WOW.
WHAT ARE YOU EVEN TALKING ABOUT?
GET MY CLOTHES OUT! MY CLOTHES!
A FAIRY-LOOKING ONE!
HUH?
YOU MEAN THE ONE GRANDMOM BOUGHT FOR YOU?
THE FLOWER CUPID ONE YOU WORE BEFORE?
NO, MORE TRIANGLE-SHAPED!
TRANGLE?
OH! THERE! THAT ONE!

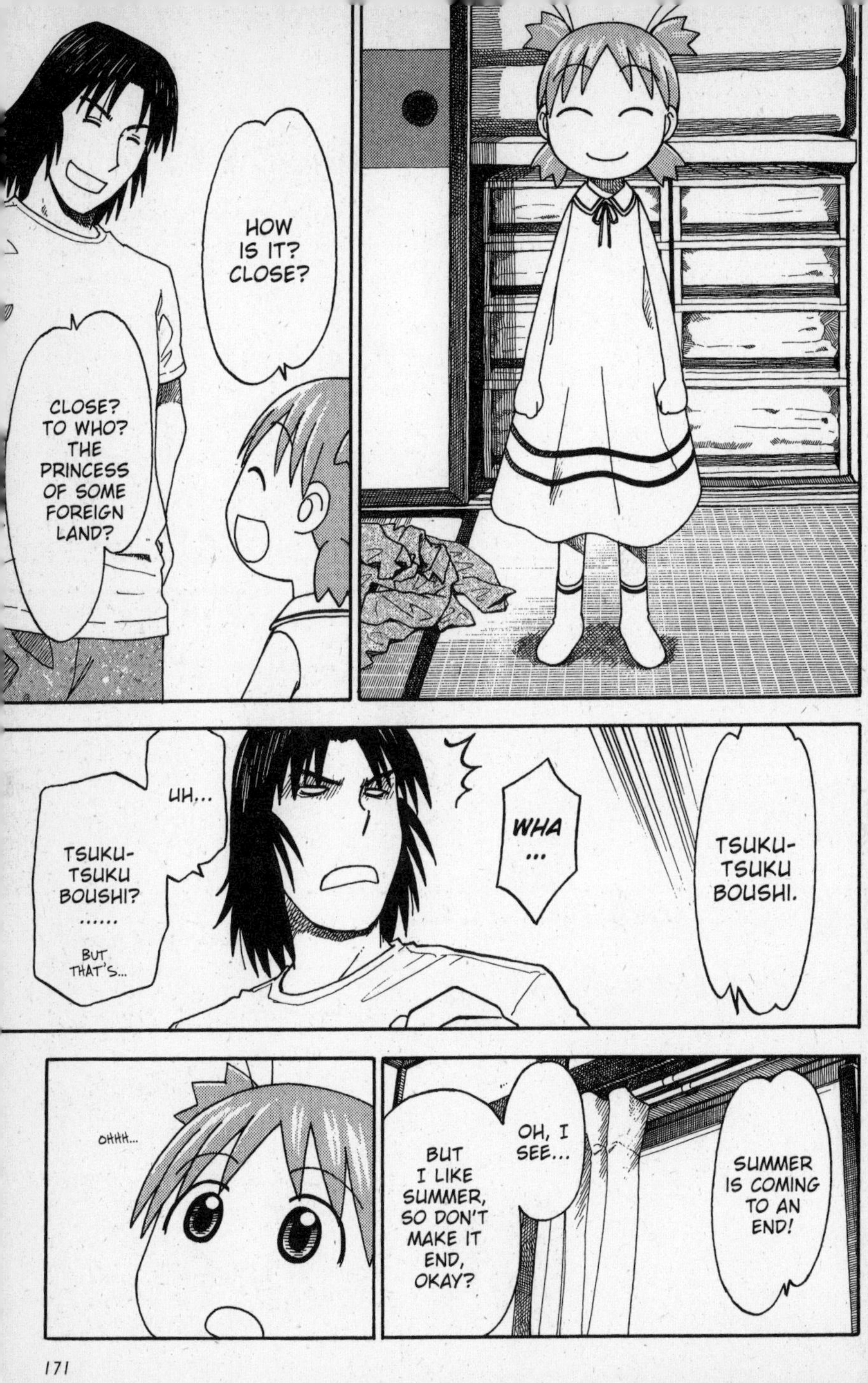
HOW IS IT? CLOSE?
CLOSE? TO WHO? THE PRINCESS OF SOME FOREIGN LAND?
TSUKU-TSUKU BOUSHI.
WHA...
UH...
TSUKU-TSUKU BOUSHI? ......
BUT THAT'S...
SUMMER IS COMING TO AN END!
OH, I SEE...
BUT I LIKE SUMMER, SO DON'T MAKE IT END, OKAY?
OHHH...

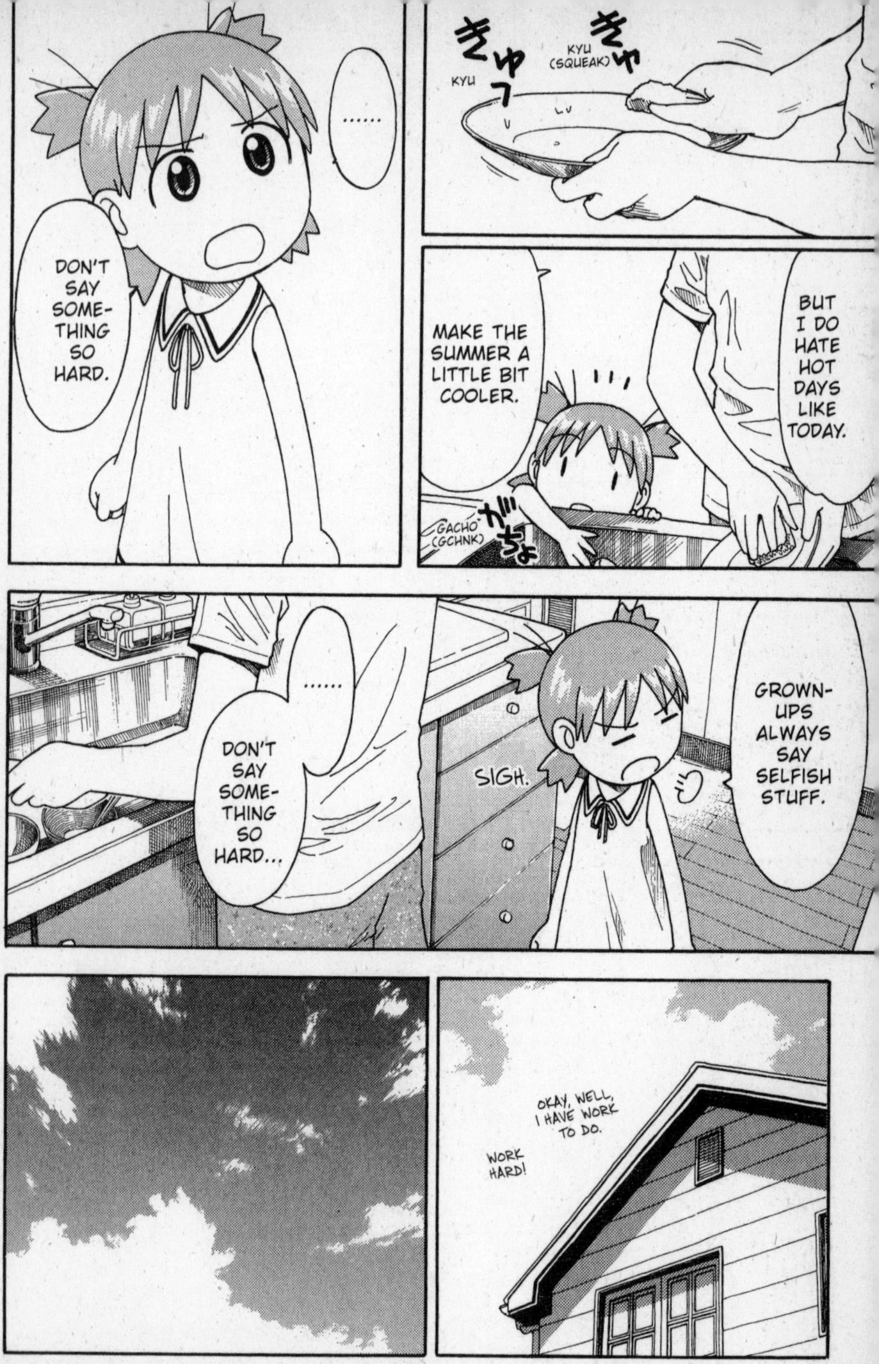
きゅ
KYU (SQUEAK)
きゅっ
KYU
BUT I DO HATE HOT DAYS LIKE TODAY.
MAKE THE SUMMER A LITTLE BIT COOLER.
がちょ
GACHO (GCHNK)
......
DON'T SAY SOME-THING SO HARD.
GROWN-UPS ALWAYS SAY SELFISH STUFF.
SIGH.
......
DON'T SAY SOME-THING SO HARD...
OKAY, WELL, I HAVE WORK TO DO.
WORK HARD!

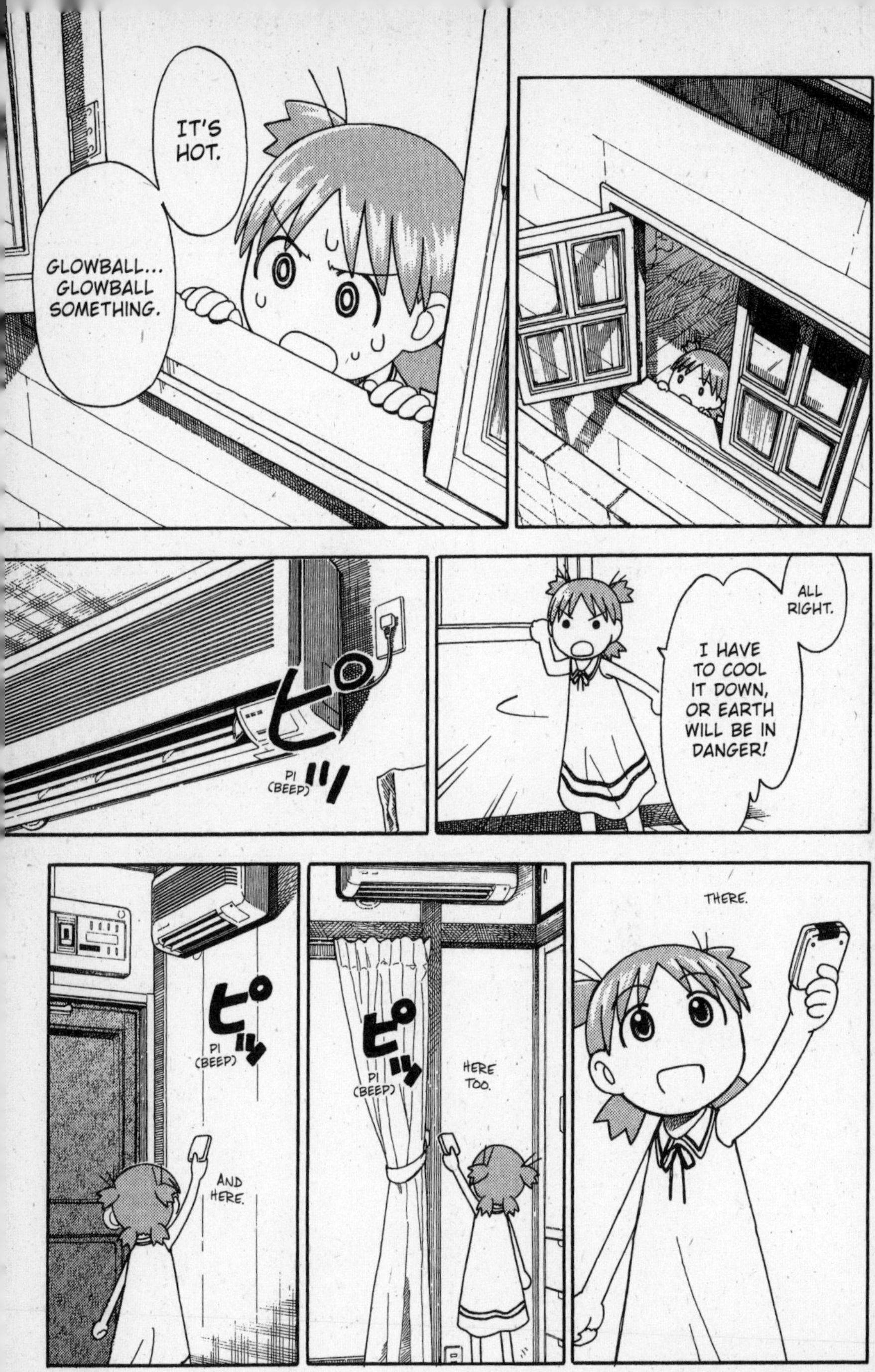
IT'S HOT.
GLOWBALL... GLOWBALL SOMETHING.
ALL RIGHT.
I HAVE TO COOL IT DOWN, OR EARTH WILL BE IN DANGER!
ピッ
PI (BEEP)
THERE.
ピッ
PI (BEEP)
HERE TOO.
ピッ
PI (BEEP)
AND HERE.

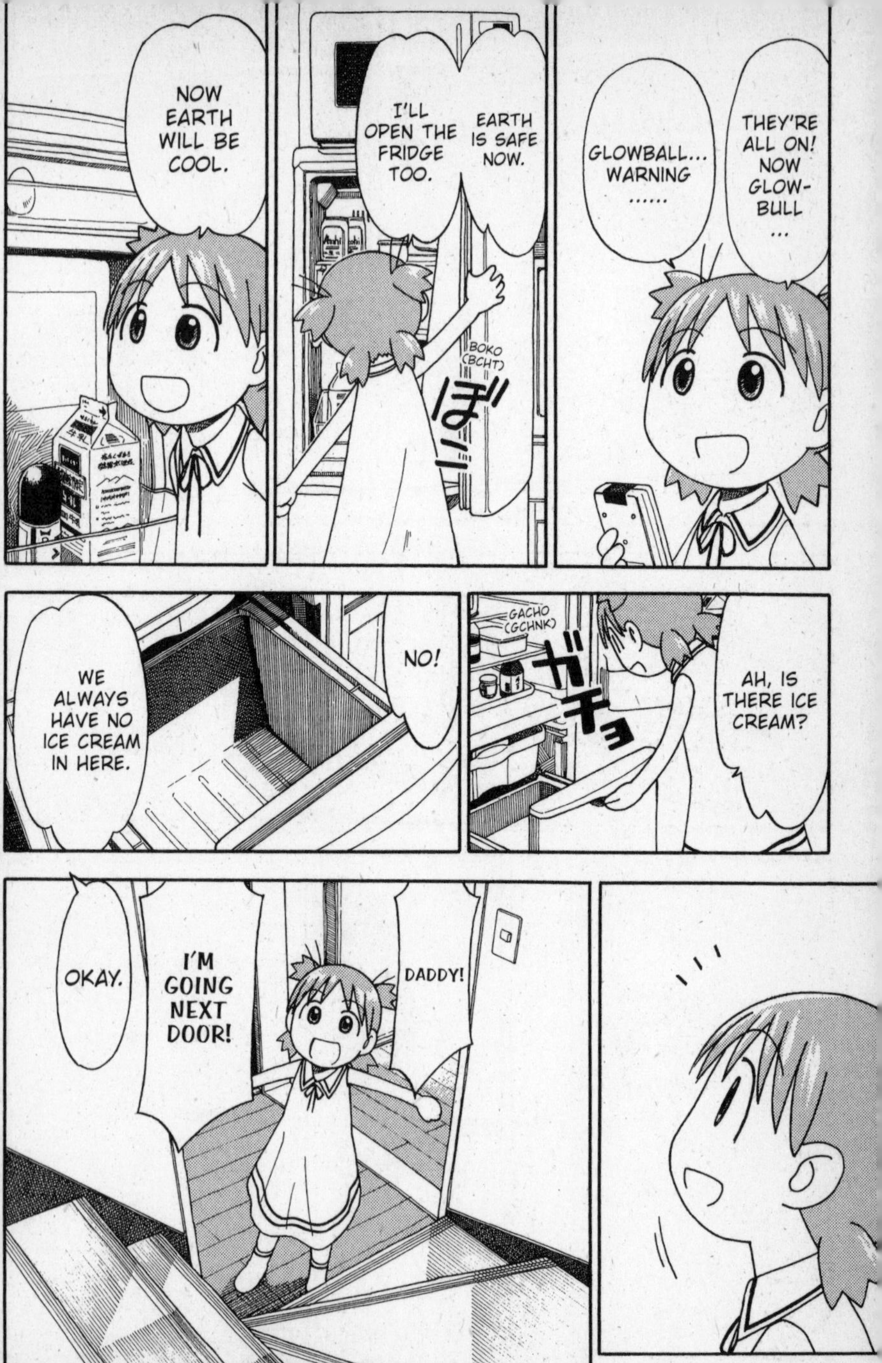
THEY'RE ALL ON! NOW GLOW-BULL ...
GLOWBALL... WARNING ......
EARTH IS SAFE NOW.
I'LL OPEN THE FRIDGE TOO.
BOKO (BCHT)
ぼこ
NOW EARTH WILL BE COOL.
AH, IS THERE ICE CREAM?
GACHO (GCHNK)
ガチョ
NO!
WE ALWAYS HAVE NO ICE CREAM IN HERE.
DADDY!
I'M GOING NEXT DOOR!
OKAY.

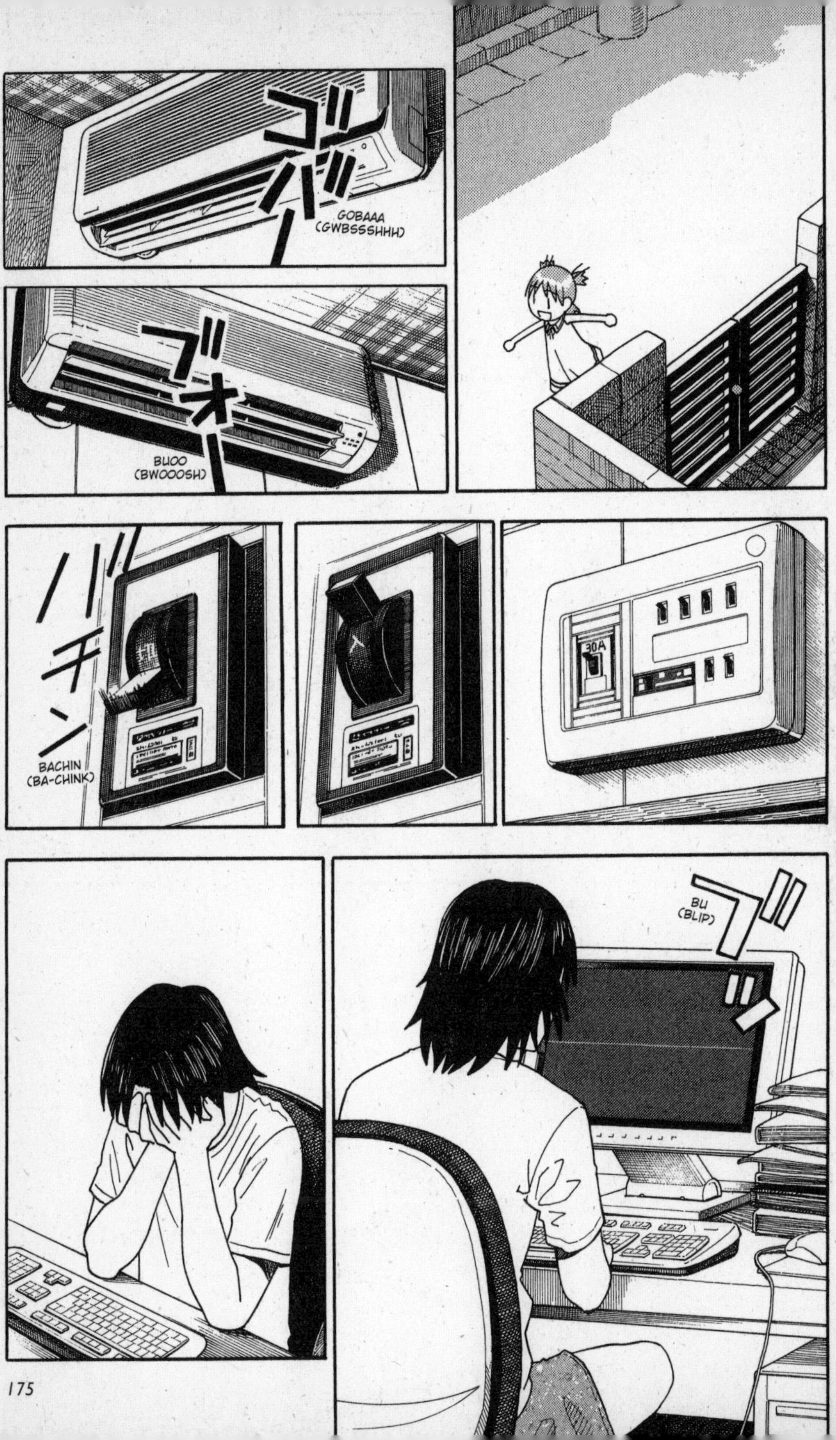
GOBAAA
(GWBSSSHHH)
BUOO
(BWOOOSH)
BACHIN
(BA-CHINK)
BU
(BLIP)

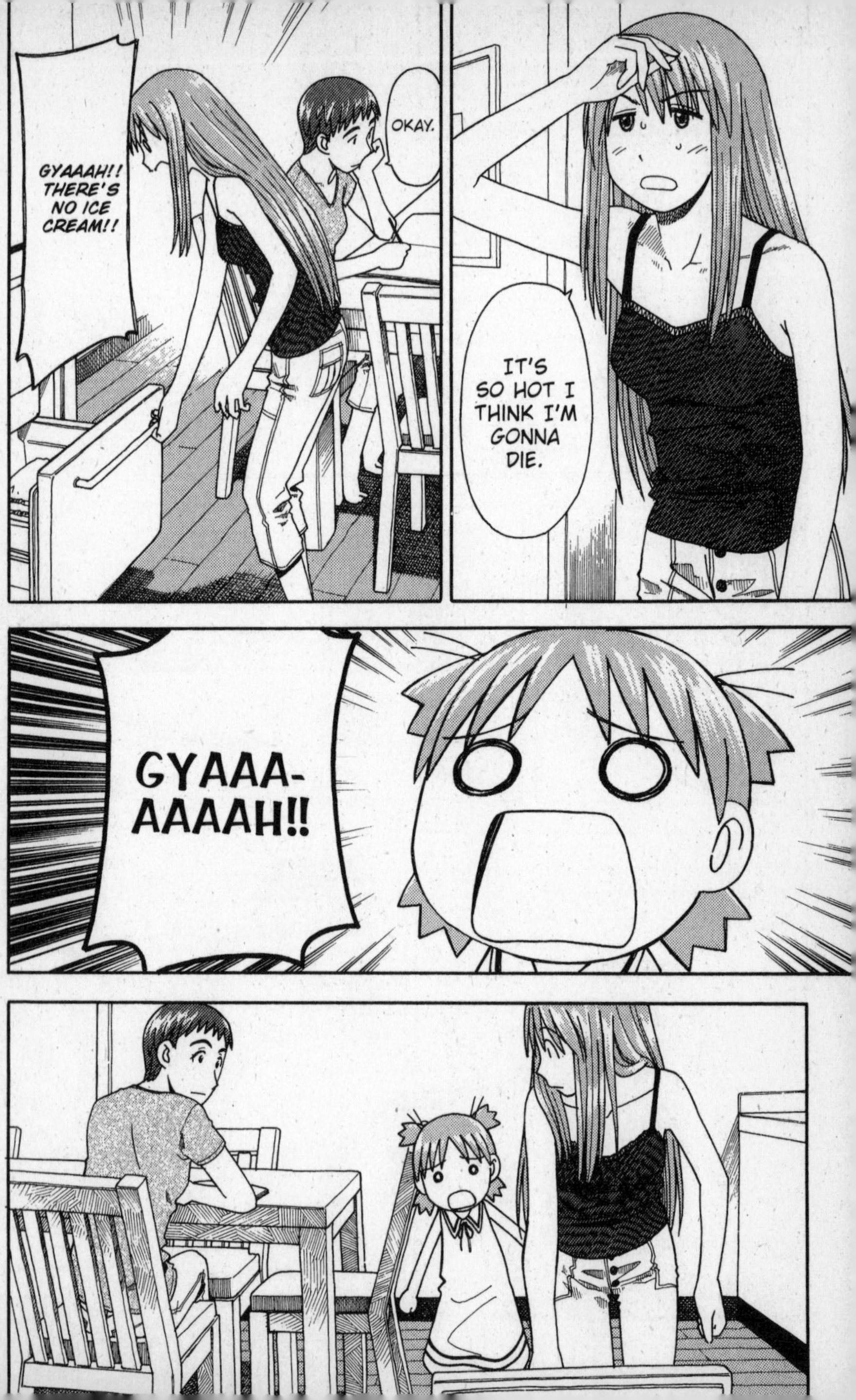
IT'S SO HOT I THINK I'M GONNA DIE.
OKAY.
GYAAAH!! THERE'S NO ICE CREAM!!
GYAAA-AAAAH!!

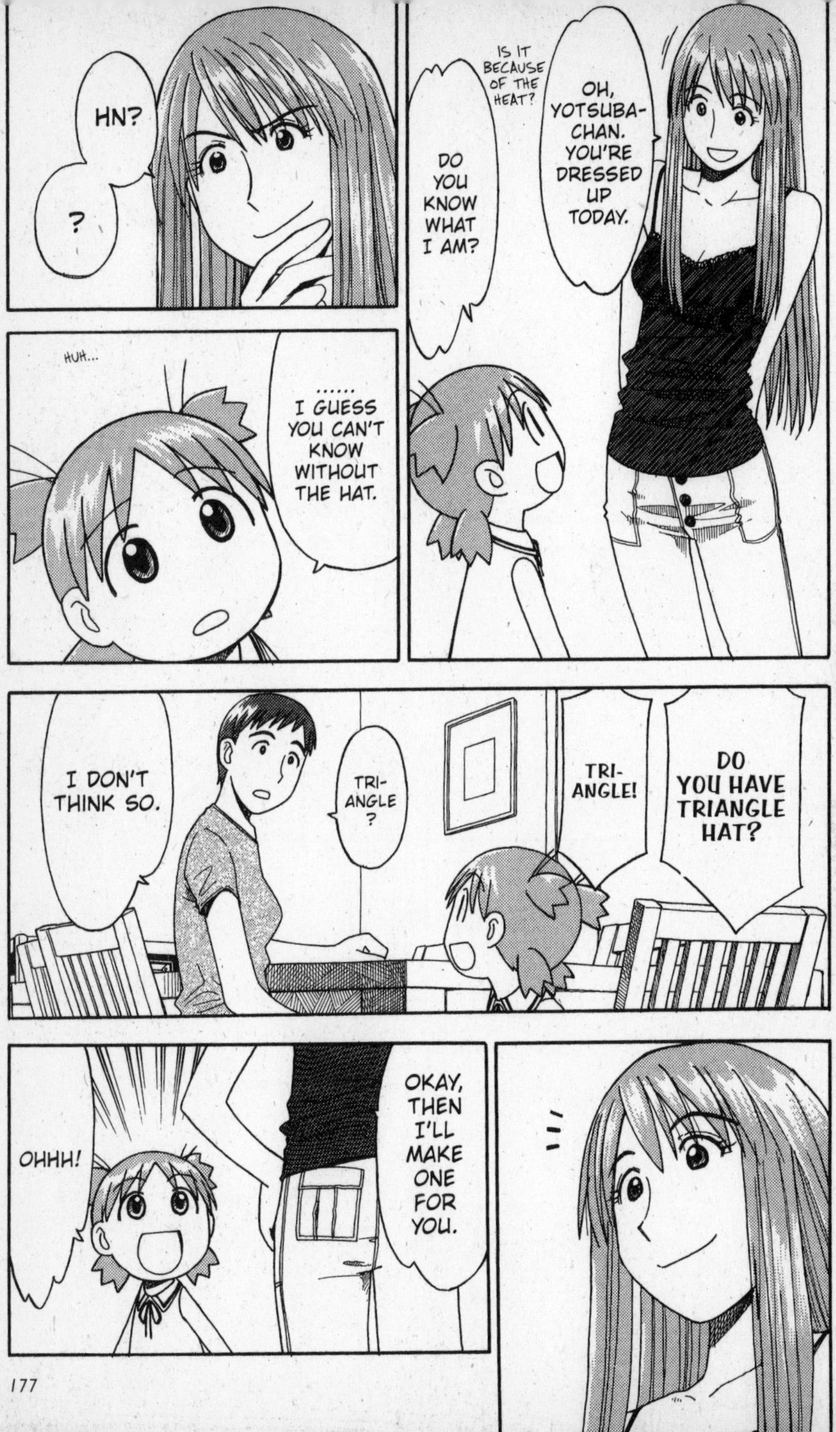
OH, YOTSUBA-CHAN. YOU'RE DRESSED UP TODAY.
IS IT BECAUSE OF THE HEAT?
DO YOU KNOW WHAT I AM?
HN?
?
...... I GUESS YOU CAN'T KNOW WITHOUT THE HAT.
HUH...
DO YOU HAVE TRIANGLE HAT?
TRI-ANGLE!
TRI-ANGLE ?
I DON'T THINK SO.
OKAY, THEN I'LL MAKE ONE FOR YOU.
OHHH!

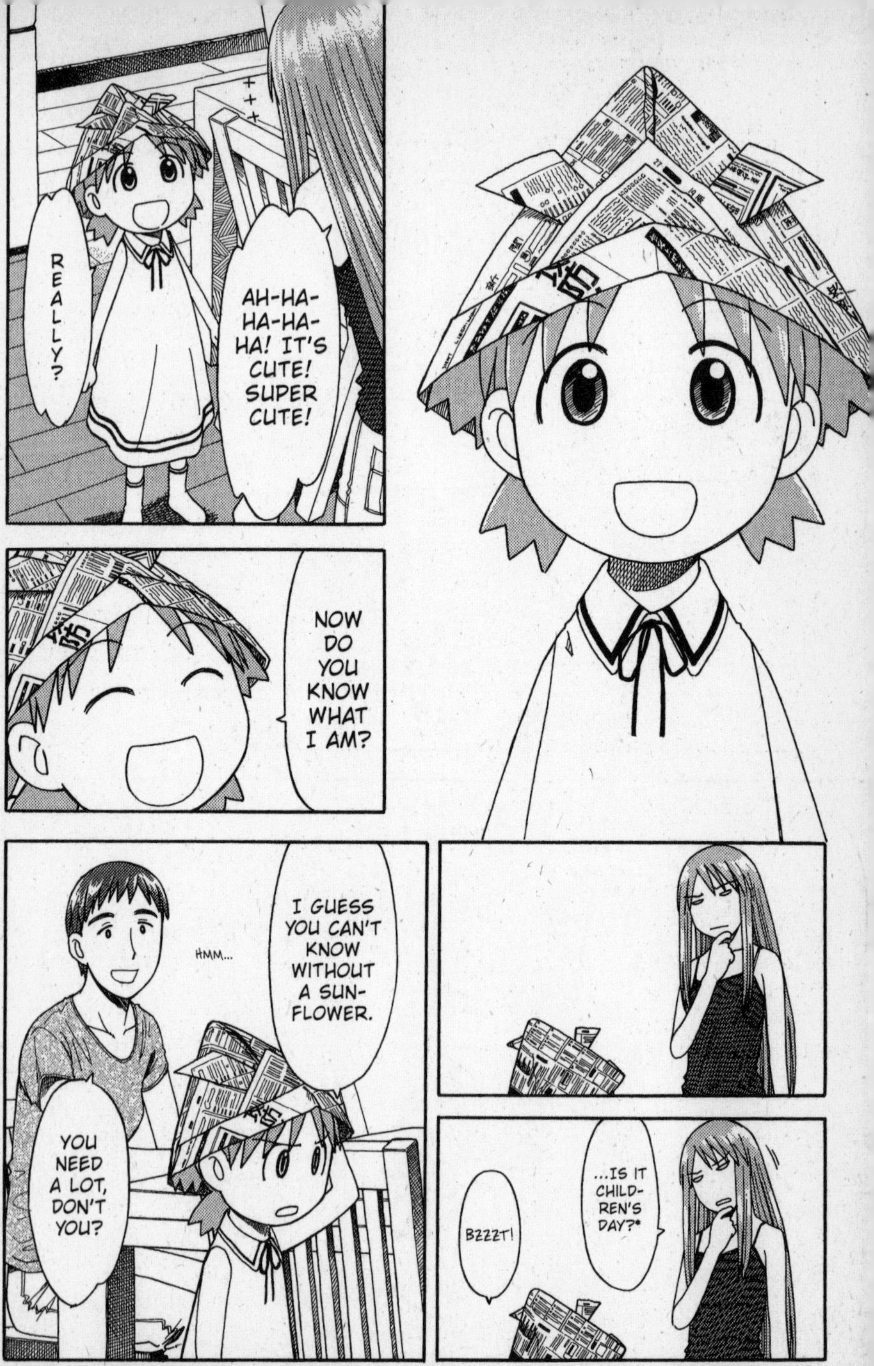
AH-HA-HA-HA-HA! IT'S CUTE! SUPER CUTE!
REALLY?
NOW DO YOU KNOW WHAT I AM?
...IS IT CHILDREN'S DAY?*
BZZZT!
I GUESS YOU CAN'T KNOW WITHOUT A SUNFLOWER.
HMM...
YOU NEED A LOT, DON'T YOU?

*CHILDREN'S DAY: A JAPANESE NATIONAL HOLIDAY, ALSO KNOWN AS THE BOYS' FESTIVAL, DURING WHICH FAMILIES DISPLAY SAMURAI DOLLS AND SAMURAI HELMETS (LIKE YOTSUBA'S HAT) IN CELEBRATION OF THEIR CHILDREN'S HAPPINESS AND PROSPERITY.

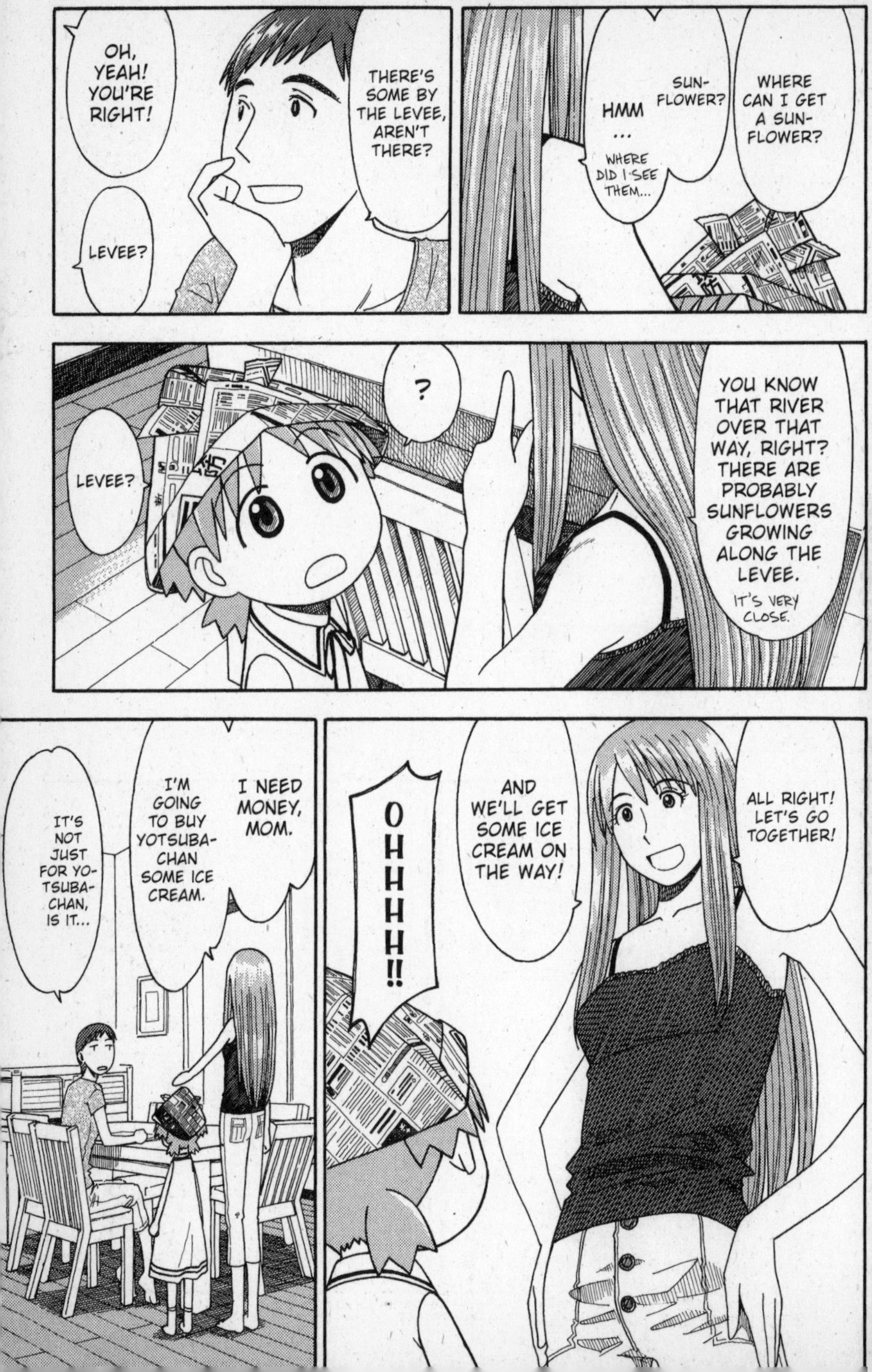
WHERE CAN I GET A SUN-FLOWER?
SUN-FLOWER?
HMM...
WHERE DID I SEE THEM...
THERE'S SOME BY THE LEVEE, AREN'T THERE?
OH, YEAH! YOU'RE RIGHT!
LEVEE?
YOU KNOW THAT RIVER OVER THAT WAY, RIGHT? THERE ARE PROBABLY SUNFLOWERS GROWING ALONG THE LEVEE.
IT'S VERY CLOSE.
?
LEVEE?
ALL RIGHT! LET'S GO TOGETHER!
AND WE'LL GET SOME ICE CREAM ON THE WAY!
OHHHH!!
I NEED MONEY, MOM.
I'M GOING TO BUY YOTSUBA-CHAN SOME ICE CREAM.
IT'S NOT JUST FOR YO-TSUBA-CHAN, IS IT...

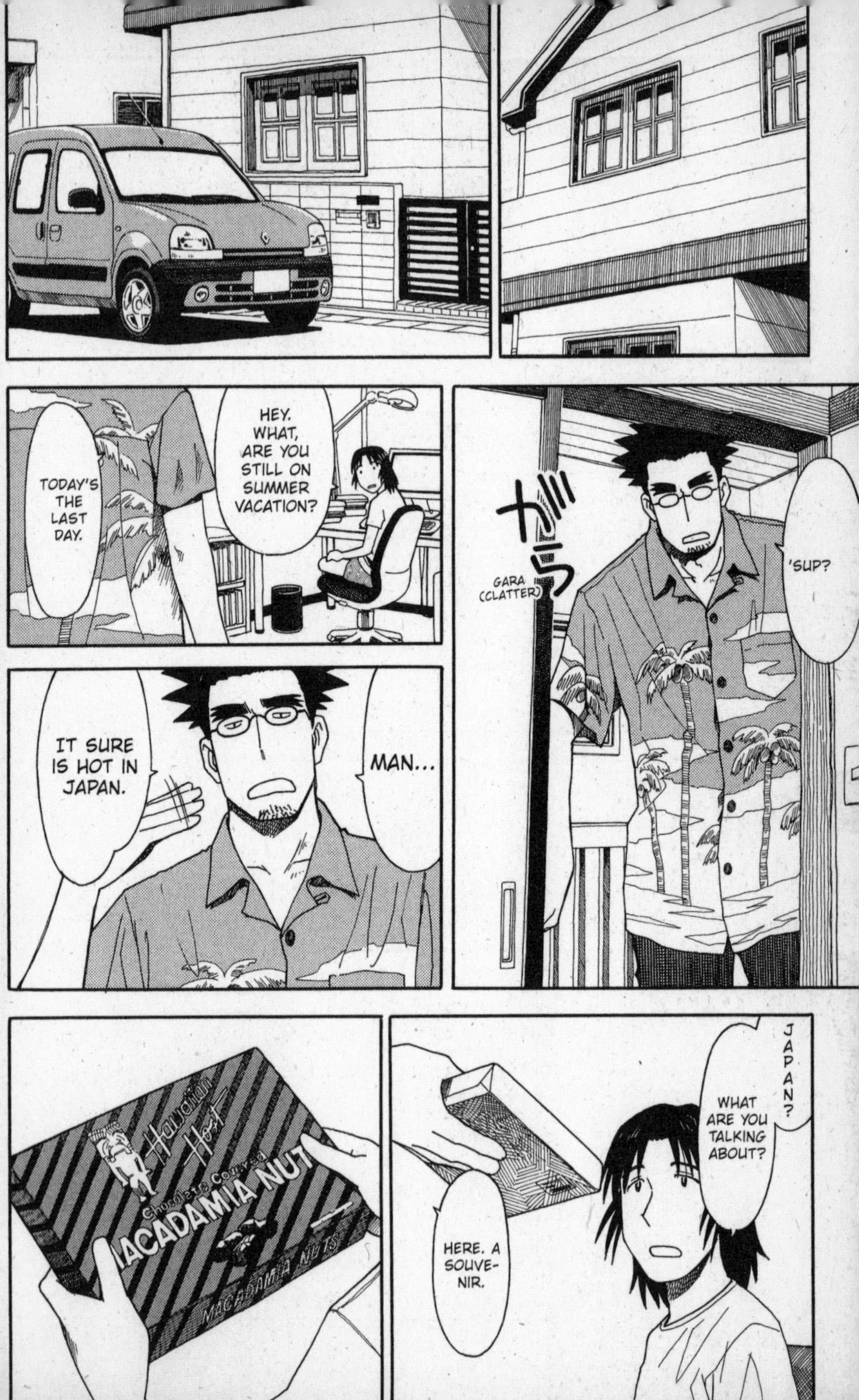
ガラ
GARA (CLATTER)
'SUP?
HEY. WHAT, ARE YOU STILL ON SUMMER VACATION?
TODAY'S THE LAST DAY.
MAN...
IT SURE IS HOT IN JAPAN.
JAPAN?
WHAT ARE YOU TALKING ABOUT?
HERE. A SOUVENIR.
Hawaiian Host
Chocolate Covered

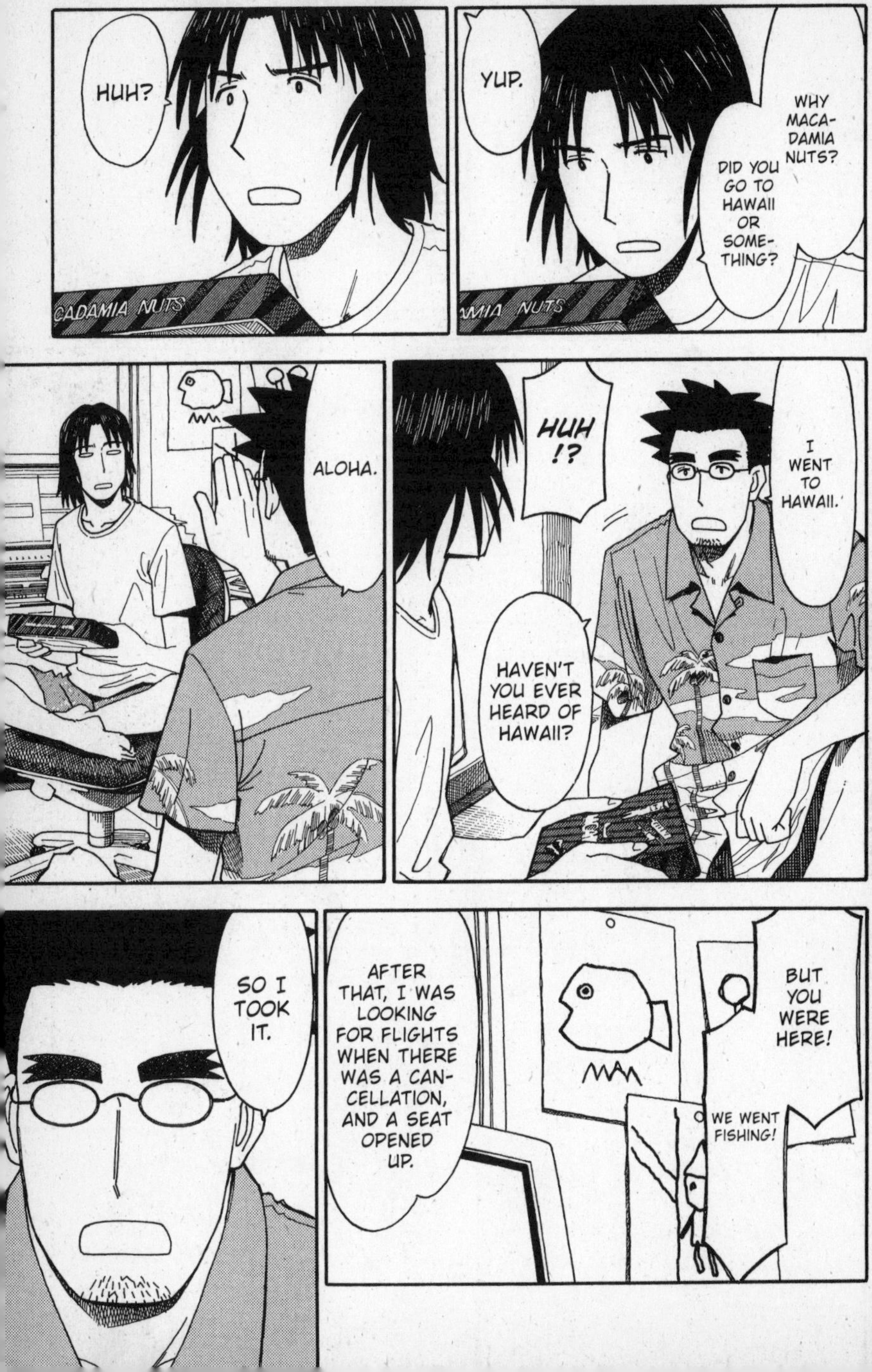
WHY MACA-DAMIA NUTS?
DID YOU GO TO HAWAII OR SOME-THING?
YUP.
AMIA NUTS
HUH?
ADAMIA NUTS
I WENT TO HAWAII.
HUH!?
HAVEN'T YOU EVER HEARD OF HAWAII?
ALOHA.
BUT YOU WERE HERE!
WE WENT FISHING!
AFTER THAT, I WAS LOOKING FOR FLIGHTS WHEN THERE WAS A CAN-CELLATION, AND A SEAT OPENED UP.
SO I TOOK IT.

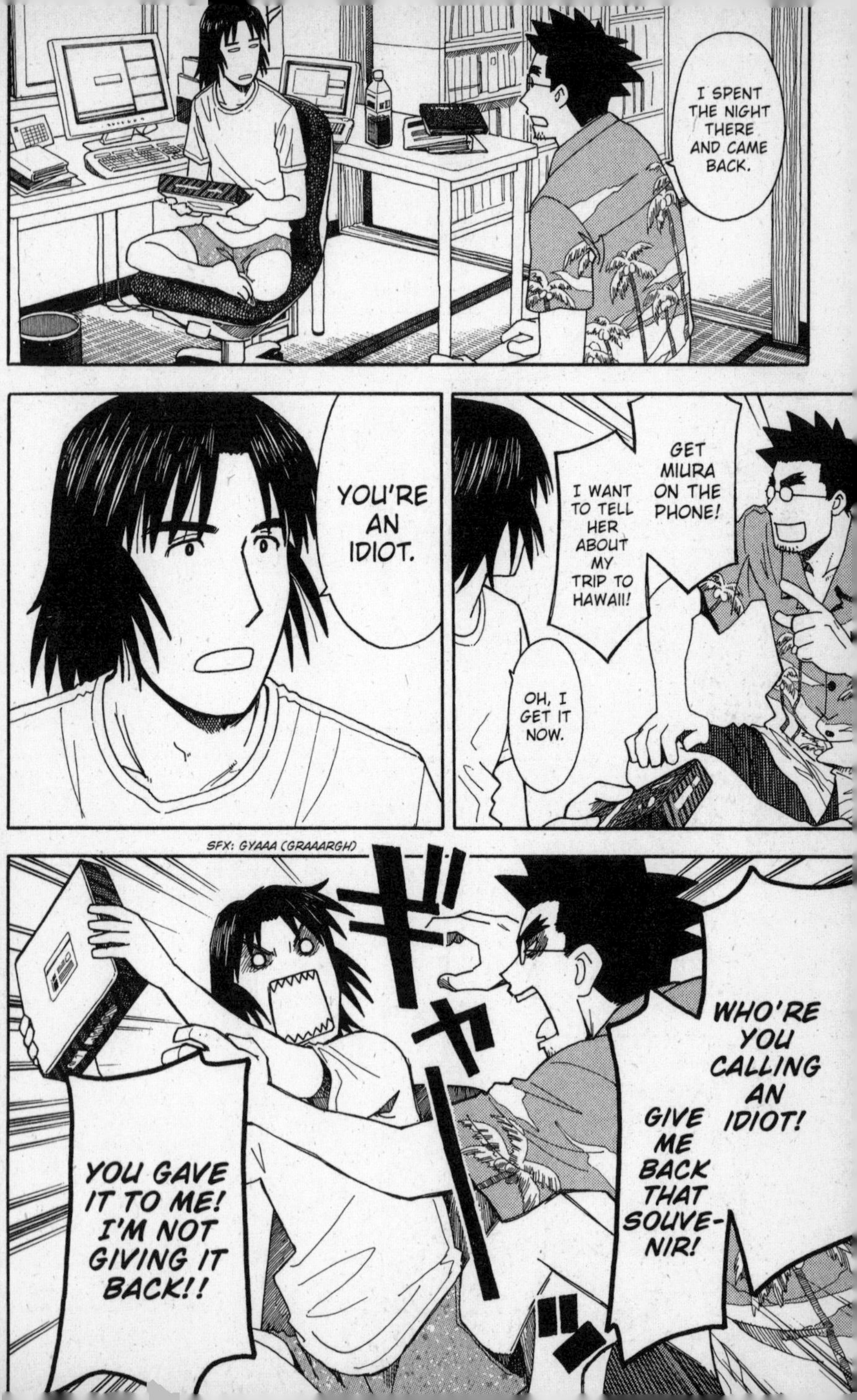
I SPENT THE NIGHT THERE AND CAME BACK.
GET MIURA ON THE PHONE!
I WANT TO TELL HER ABOUT MY TRIP TO HAWAII!
OH, I GET IT NOW.
YOU'RE AN IDIOT.
SFX: GYAAA (GRAAARGH)
ギャー
WHO'RE YOU CALLING AN IDIOT!
GIVE ME BACK THAT SOUVE-NIR!
YOU GAVE IT TO ME! I'M NOT GIVING IT BACK!!

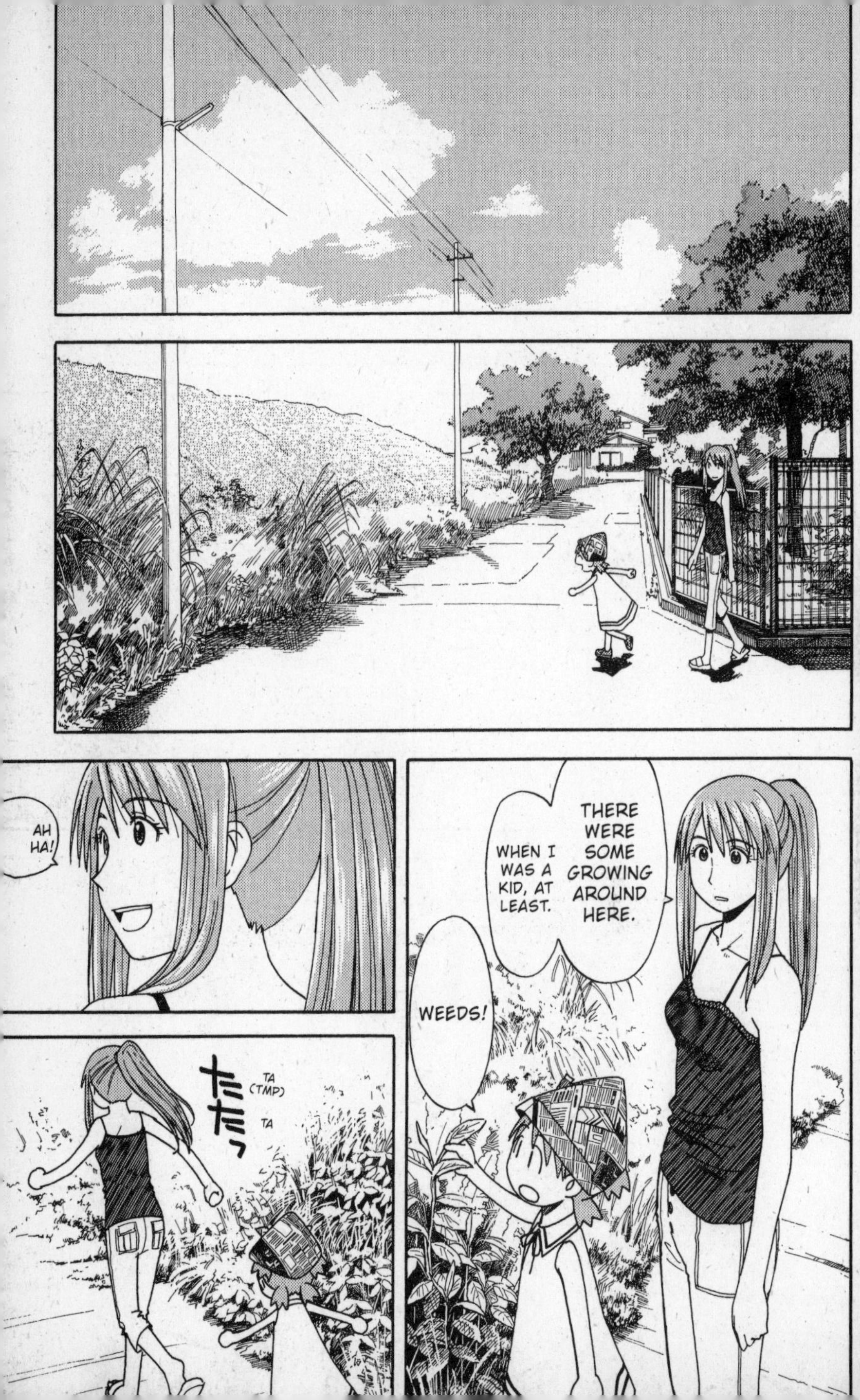
THERE WERE SOME GROWING AROUND HERE.
WHEN I WAS A KID, AT LEAST.
WEEDS!
AH HA!
たたっ
TA (TMP) TA

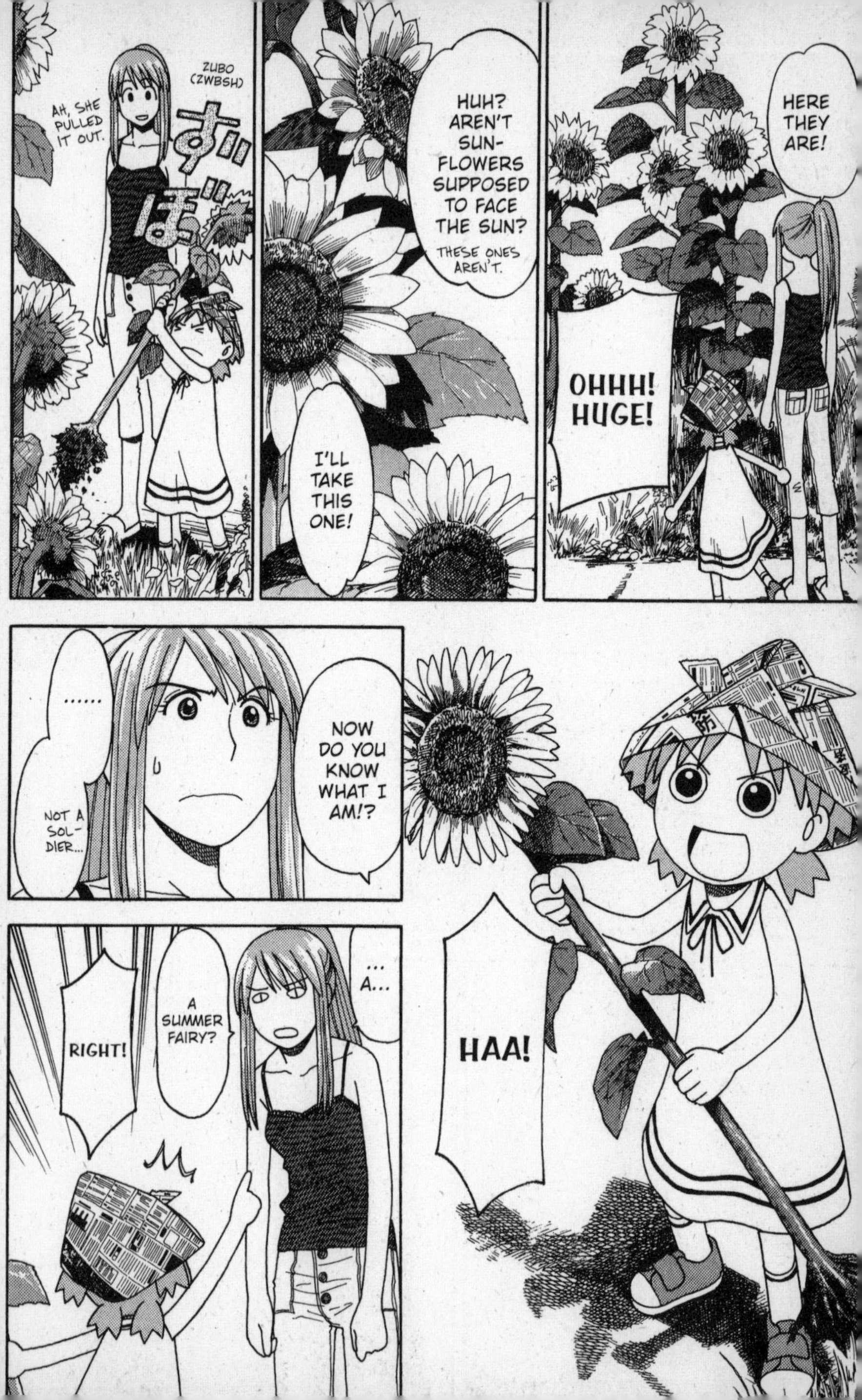
HERE THEY ARE!
OHHH! HUGE!
HUH? AREN'T SUN-FLOWERS SUPPOSED TO FACE THE SUN?
THESE ONES AREN'T.
I'LL TAKE THIS ONE!
ZUBO (ZWBSH)
AH, SHE PULLED IT OUT.
HAA!
NOW DO YOU KNOW WHAT I AM!?
......
NOT A SOL-DIER...
... A...
A SUMMER FAIRY?
RIGHT!

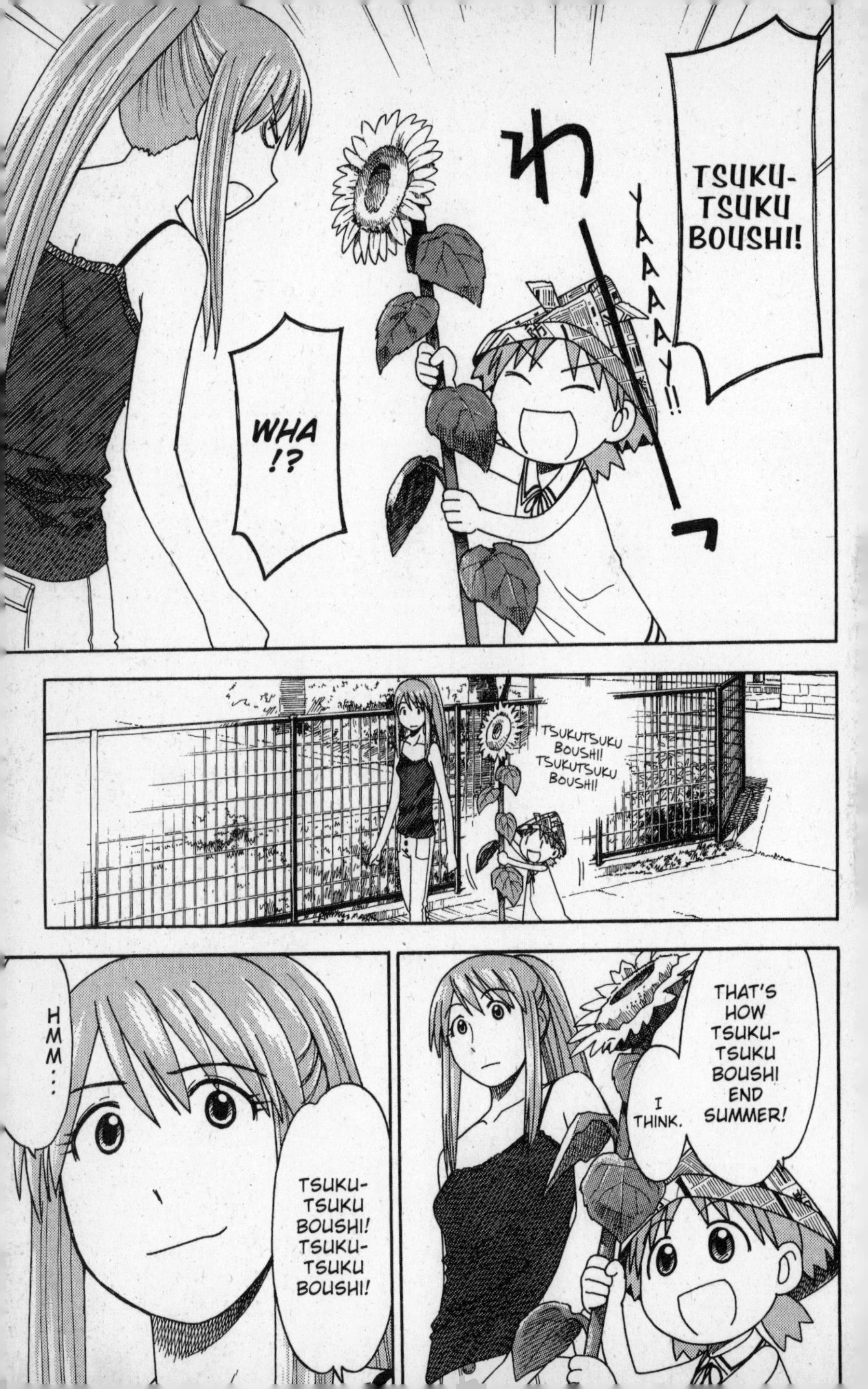
TSUKU-TSUKU BOUSHI!
わーっ
YAAAAAY!!
WHA!?
TSUKUTSUKU BOUSHI! TSUKUTSUKU BOUSHI!
THAT'S HOW TSUKU-TSUKU BOUSHI END SUMMER!
I THINK.
HMM...
TSUKU-TSUKU BOUSHI! TSUKU-TSUKU BOUSHI!

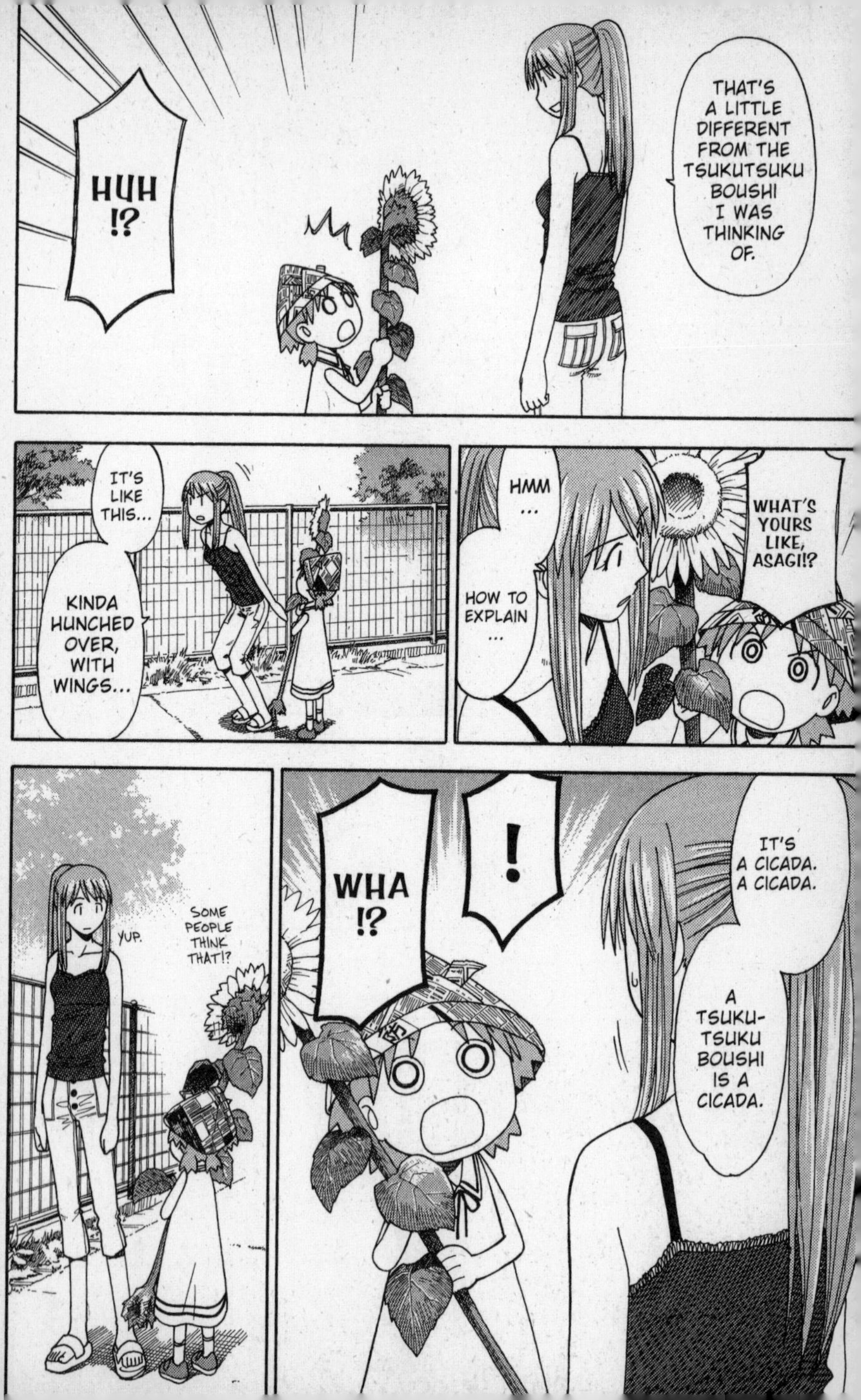
THAT'S A LITTLE DIFFERENT FROM THE TSUKUTSUKU BOUSHI I WAS THINKING OF.
HUH !?
WHAT'S YOURS LIKE, ASAGI!?
HMM ...
HOW TO EXPLAIN ...
IT'S LIKE THIS...
KINDA HUNCHED OVER, WITH WINGS...
IT'S A CICADA. A CICADA.
A TSUKU-TSUKU BOUSHI IS A CICADA.
!
WHA !?
SOME PEOPLE THINK THAT!?
YUP.

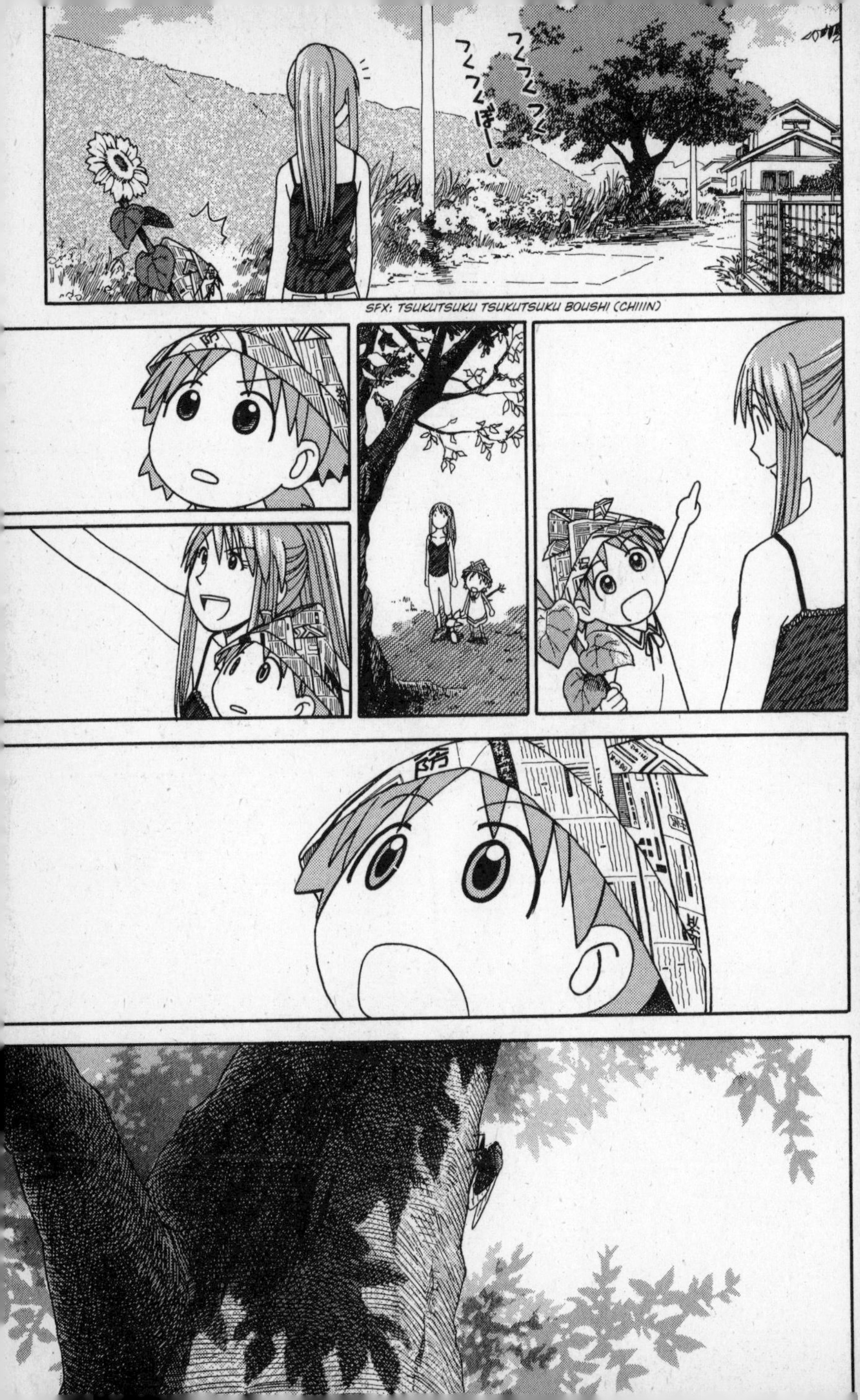
つくつくつく
つくつくぼーし
SFX: TSUKUTSUKU TSUKUTSUKU BOUSHI (CHIIIN)

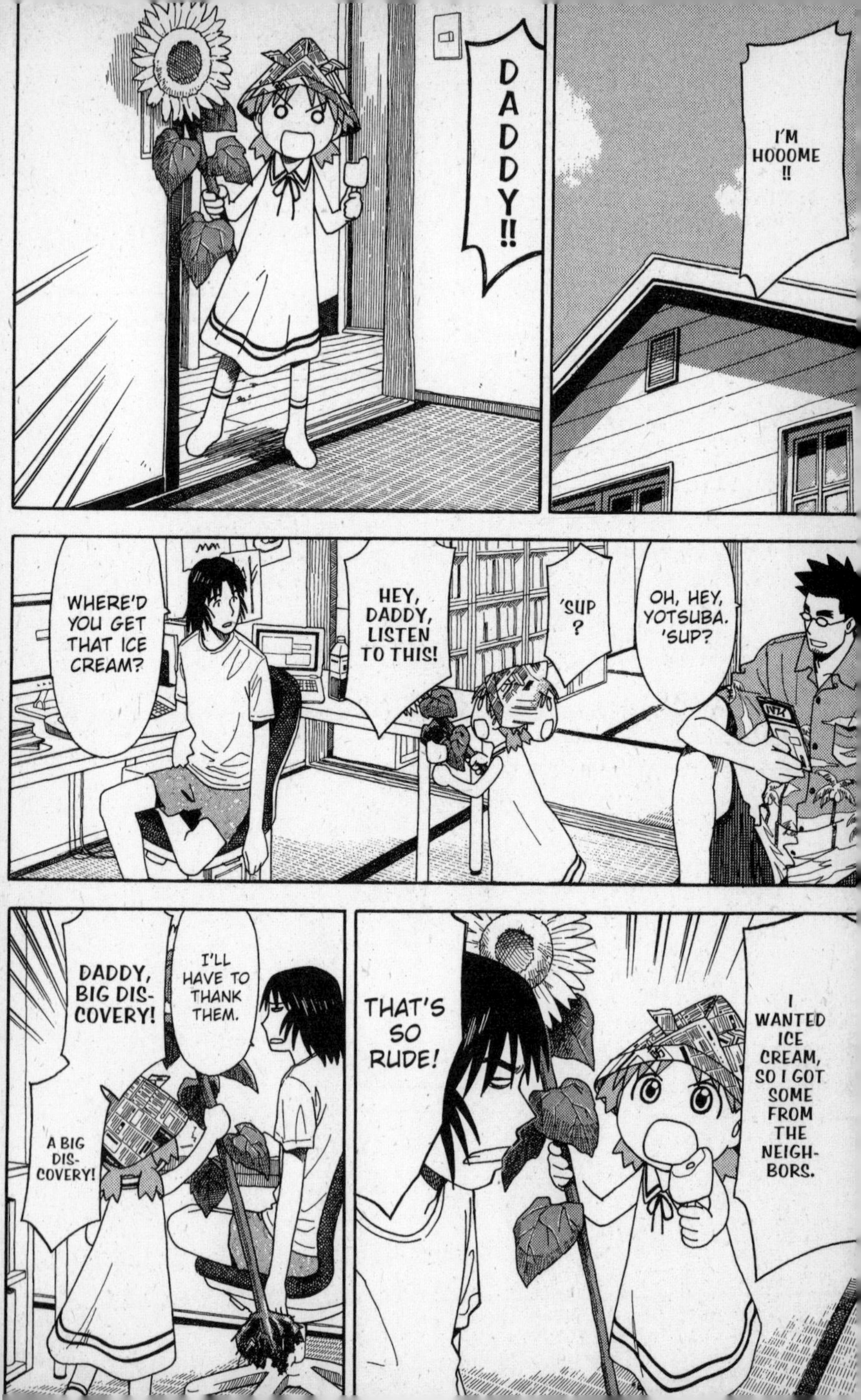
I'M HOOOME !!
DADDY!!
OH, HEY, YOTSUBA. 'SUP?
'SUP ?
HEY, DADDY, LISTEN TO THIS!
WHERE'D YOU GET THAT ICE CREAM?
I WANTED ICE CREAM, SO I GOT SOME FROM THE NEIGHBORS.
THAT'S SO RUDE!
I'LL HAVE TO THANK THEM.
DADDY, BIG DISCOVERY!
A BIG DISCOVERY!

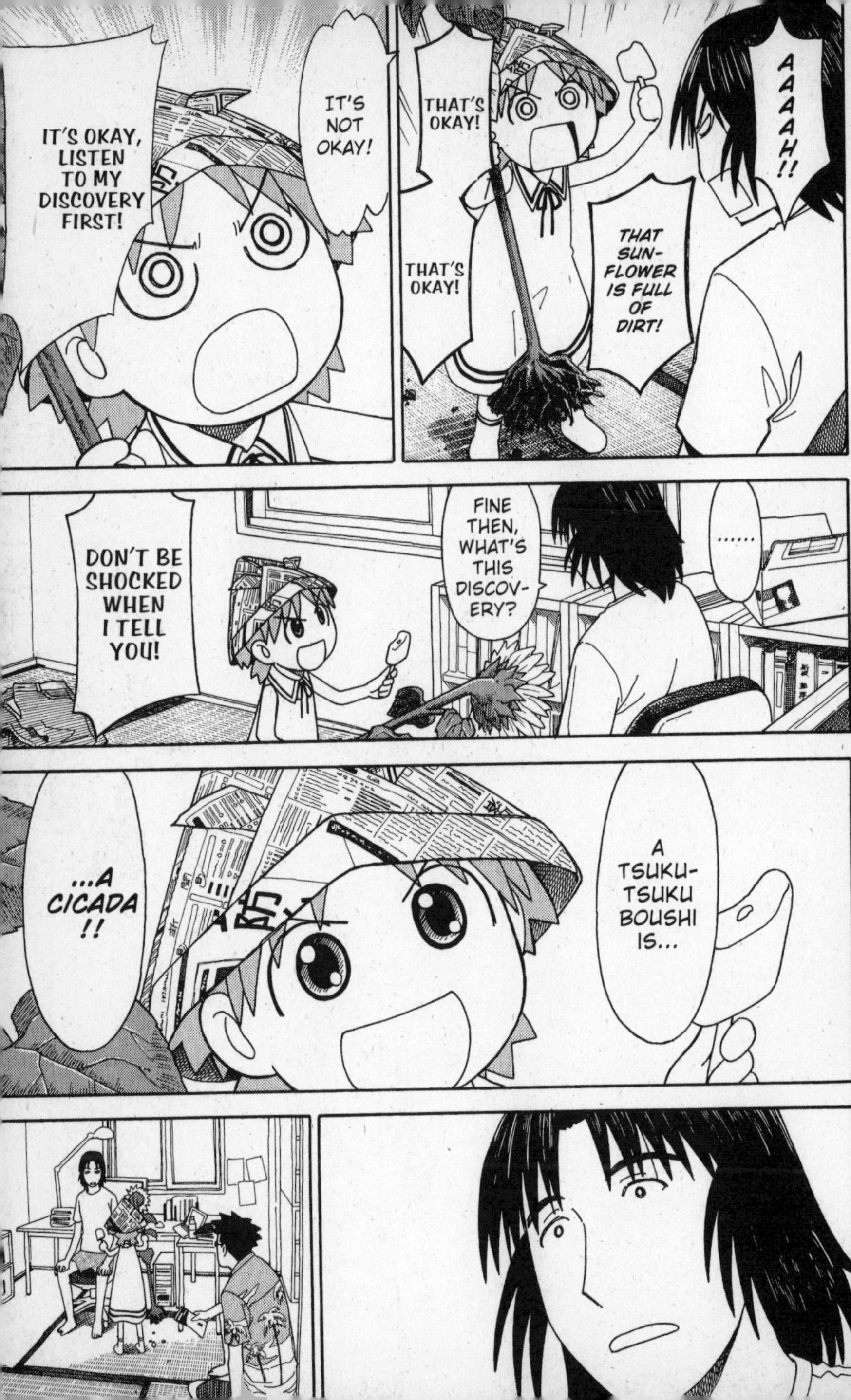
AAAAH!!
THAT'S OKAY!
THAT SUNFLOWER IS FULL OF DIRT!
THAT'S OKAY!
IT'S NOT OKAY!
IT'S OKAY, LISTEN TO MY DISCOVERY FIRST!
......
FINE THEN, WHAT'S THIS DISCOVERY?
DON'T BE SHOCKED WHEN I TELL YOU!
A TSUKU-TSUKU BOUSHI IS...
...A CICADA!!

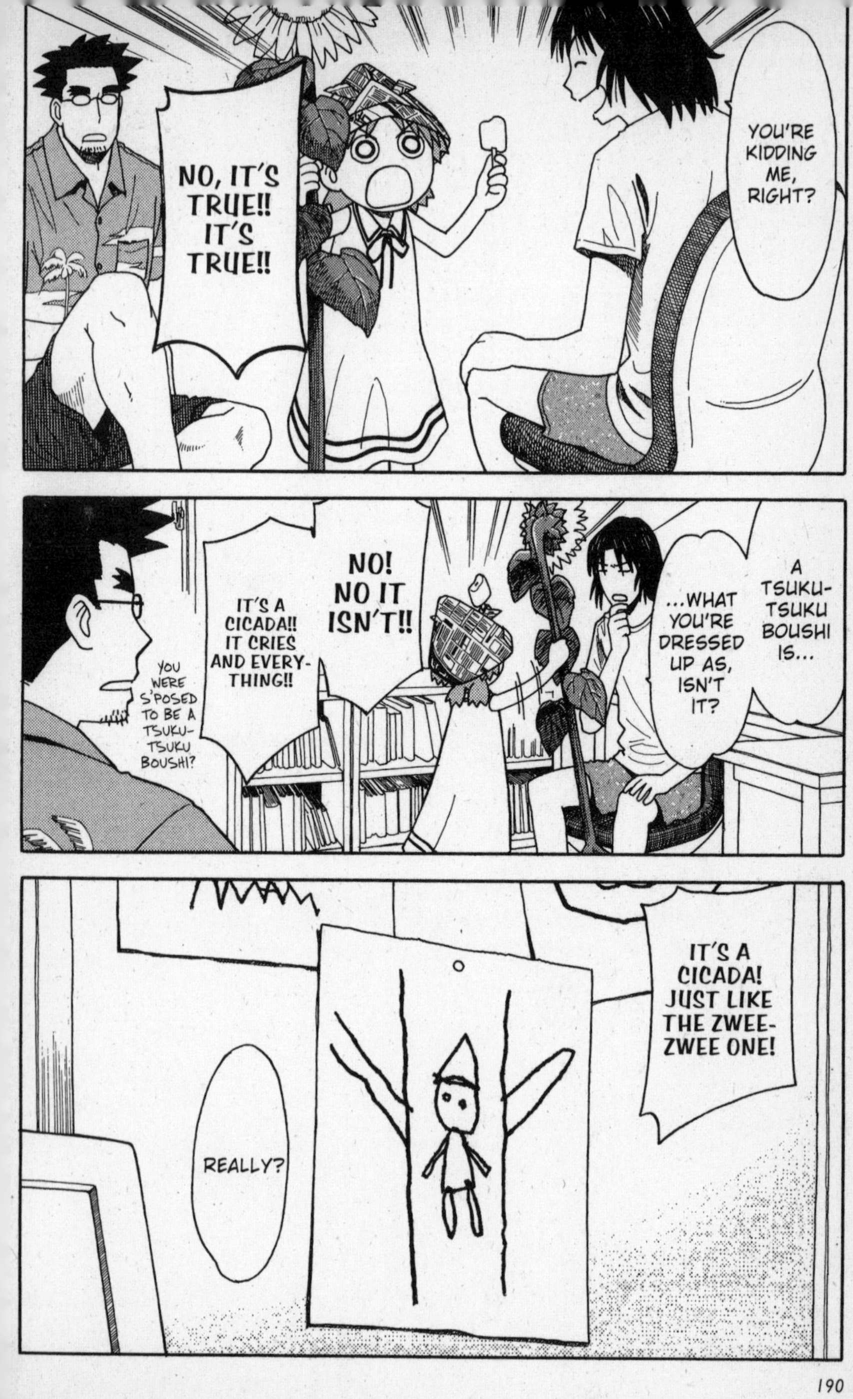
YOU'RE KIDDING ME, RIGHT?
NO, IT'S TRUE!! IT'S TRUE!!
A TSUKU-TSUKU BOUSHI IS...
...WHAT YOU'RE DRESSED UP AS, ISN'T IT?
NO! NO IT ISN'T!!
IT'S A CICADA!! IT CRIES AND EVERY-THING!!
YOU WERE S'POSED TO BE A TSUKU-TSUKU BOUSHI?
IT'S A CICADA! JUST LIKE THE ZWEE-ZWEE ONE!
REALLY?

YOTSUBA&! 4

KIYOHIKO AZUMA

Translation: Amy Forsyth
Lettering: Terri Delgado

YOTSUBA&! Vol. 4 © KIYOHIKO AZUMA / YOTUBA SUTAZIO 2005. All rights reserved. First published in Japan in 2005 by MEDIA WORKS INC., Tokyo. English translation rights in USA, Canada, and UK arranged with ASCII MEDIA WORKS INC. through Tuttle-Mori Agency, Inc., Tokyo.

English translation © 2009 by Hachette Book Group, Inc.

Yen Press
Hachette Book Group
237 Park Avenue, New York, NY 10017

Visit our websites at www.HachetteBookGroup.com and www.YenPress.com.

Yen Press is an imprint of Hachette Book Group, Inc. The Yen Press name and logo are trademarks of Hachette Book Group, Inc.

First Yen Press Edition: September 2009

ISBN: 978-0-316-07391-2

10 9 8 7 6 5 4 3

BVG

Printed in the United States of America

THERE!

YOTSUBA&!

ENJOY EVERYTHING.

OHHHHH!!

TO BE CONTINUED!